Ungentle Shakespeare

Ungentle Shakespeare

SCENES FROM HIS LIFE

Katherine Duncan-Jones

For Tom

The Arden website is at
http://www.ardenshakespeare.com

The general editors of the Arden Shakespeare have been
W. J. Craig and R. H. Case (first series 1899–1944),
Una Ellis-Fermor, Harold F. Brooks, Harold Jenkins and
Brian Morris (second series 1946–1982)

Present general editors (third series)
Richard Proudfoot, Anne Thompson and David Scott Kastan

First published 2001 by The Arden Shakespeare

Arden Shakespeare is an imprint of Thomson Learning

Picture Research by Zooid Pictures Limited

Thomson Learning
Berkshire House
168–173 High Holborn
London WC1V 7AA

Designed and typeset by Martin Bristow

Printed in Croatia by Zrinski

British Library Cataloguing in Publication Data
A catalogue record for this book is available from the British Library

Library of Congress Cataloguing in Publication Data
A catalogue record has been requested

ISBN 1-903436-26-5

NPN 9 8 7 6 5 4 3 2 1

Contents

Illustrations

PLATES *(collected between pp. 146 and 147)*

FIGURES

Illustrations

Preface

It requires some courage to defy Shakespeare's gravestone curse against any false 'friend' who presumes to 'dig the dust' that surrounds his mortal remains in Holy Trinity Church, Stratford-upon-Avon.[1] It also requires some thick-skinned doggedness. As previous biographers must have found, it is widely claimed that virtually nothing is known about Shakespeare's life. To many people, therefore, writing yet another biographical study sounds like just the sort of footling exercise in creative self-indulgence that academics are popularly thought to go in for. Nevertheless, as the labours of such great scholars as Edmond Malone, E. K. Chambers and Samuel Schoenbaum have shown, we do possess a remarkably substantial body of documents relating to Shakespeare's life, especially considering that he never enjoyed the kind of affiliation, to a college, a city company, an Inn of Court or a parish church, that would have connected him with a well-preserved set of institutional archives. Though surviving documents don't take us very far in answering the kind of questions that many post-Romantic readers may want to ask – did he love his wife? who was the 'dark lady'? what was his religious position, if any? or his overall vision of the world? – they do provide life records ranging from baptism to burial, with a good deal in between that is connected with his family, with property and with litigation. There is also a wealth of contemporary allusions to Shakespeare as player and poet, and to his writings, both in manuscript and in print. Indeed, this material is so ample that I have not even attempted to cite all of it. I have relied very heavily throughout on Samuel Schoenbaum's two great works, his *Documentary Life* (1975) and his *Records and Images* (1981), but have not attempted to replicate either his material or his approach. The existence of these books, in which most of the major documentary records are reproduced in facsimile, makes it wonderfully easy for students who wish to do so to examine images of such material as Shakespeare's will, or the depositions in the Belott–Mountjoy suit. I hope that the small samples from such documents that I quote here may inspire some students to look further.

My object has been to explore some of the areas of Shakespeare's life that I feel that Schoenbaum and others have neglected, choosing generally, for preference, the road less travelled. While Schoenbaum side-stepped certain topics because he was sensibly reluctant to speculate, I quite often risk conjecture, in the hope of putting some spectral, or speculative, flesh on those well-guarded bones. I am well aware that in so doing I am laying myself open both to challenge and, at times, to flat disbelief. In particular, I have tried to bring Shakespeare down from the lofty isolation to which he has been customarily elevated, and to show him as a man among men, a writer among writers – indeed, a writer whose manifest brilliance often made him the object of envy and malice, rather than adulation. In Oxford, as in many universities, Shakespeare is traditionally studied separately from other writers of the Renaissance, which may create the impression that, unlike other Elizabethan poets, he was writing in glorious isolation. This book is intended to break down the artificial boundary that traditionally separates Shakespeare from his contemporaries, and also to suggest some of the ways in which these contemporaries had an impact on him, sometimes painfully so.

My method is more thematic than narrative. Rather than chronicling each recorded event, play or poem in sequence, I have identified what I feel to be important topics or issues associated with particular periods, structuring each chapter as a collection of short related essays on such topics. The book offers scenes from Shakespeare's life, not a comprehensive survey. In the opening chapter, for instance, rather than starting with the words 'Shakespeare was born . . .', and then going on to reconstruct his boyhood and adolescence in laborious detail, I have placed Shakespeare's birth in the rich cultural context of the Midlands in the 1560s and 1570s, drawing attention to the large number of talented men of letters produced by the region, and to its abundance of dramatic activity. I'm conscious that this selectively thematic and contextual approach will not satisfy all readers, and that some may wish for a fuller and more straightforward narrative of life events, including some account of every single play attributed to Shakespeare. However, plenty of conventionally structured biographies are available, such as, most recently, Park Honan's *Shakespeare: A Life* (Oxford, 1998), which offers an extremely detailed and reliable chronicle.[2] My hope is, however, that I may stimulate young readers to look a good deal more widely than previous generations have done at the historical and cultural world within which Shakespeare lived and wrote, and to follow up, develop or challenge the connections that I have traced here between Shakespeare and other writers, such as Thomas Nashe, Ben Jonson, John Marston, George Wilkins and John Fletcher.[3]

In the light of this book's title, it may go without saying that I have tried not to idealize my subject. I don't believe that any Elizabethans, even Shakespeare, were what might now be called 'nice' – liberal, unprejudiced, unselfish. For most men of talent and ambition in this period, even for those who, unlike Shakespeare, enjoyed the privileges of high birth, some degree of ruthlessness was a necessary survival skill. It was also essential to be able to adapt effectively to continual change. I have tried to give some sense of the great part played in Shakespeare's life by sheer accident, such as unwanted pregnancy, sudden death, plague and fire. Three topics used to be traditionally taboo both in polite society and in Shakespearean biography: social class, sex and money. I have given a good deal of attention to all of them. In chapter 4, for instance, I have examined Shakespeare's uphill struggle to achieve, or even to purchase, 'gentle' status. In chapters 3 and 6 respectively I have suggested that Shakespeare was strongly interested in sexual relationships with well-born young men, while his sexual relations with women may, conversely, have been more functional than sentimental. In chapters 7 and 10 I show that he was reluctant to divert much, if any, of his considerable wealth towards charitable, neighbourly or altruistic ends.

It is in this last area that Shakespeare's 'ungentle' character is most clearly visible. Anyone who enters Stratford from the south will discover that the first name they encounter is not 'Shakespeare' but 'Clopton'. For modern car-drivers, some care is needed in negotiating the fine, eighteen-arched stone bridge over the River Avon which was constructed in the late fifteenth century at the expense of the philanthropic Sir Hugh Clopton, a native of Stratford who became Lord Mayor of London. Hugh Clopton was also the builder of New Place, the large mansion in Chapel Street later purchased by Shakespeare, and he paid for the restoration of the Guild Chapel, just across the road from New Place. Proceeding to the Old Town and Holy Trinity Church, the newly arrived visitor finds that the most splendid seventeenth-century monument here is not Shakespeare's, but that of Joyce, née Clopton, and her husband Baron Carew of Clopton. The Cloptons were a family of long-established wealth in Stratford, whose name continues to live on in the locality because of their commendable habits of philanthropy and their strong local pride. Shakespeare, on the other hand, though a distinctly wealthy man by the time of his death, and enjoying possession of a mansion built by Hugh Clopton, did not choose to use any of his wealth in this way. He founded no scholarships[4] or alms-rooms, he set up no charitable foundation either for the poor of Stratford or for those of any parish in London. He hoarded supplies of grain and malt during a period of shortage, he repeatedly failed to pay parish dues in London, and back in Stratford towards the end of his life he refused to challenge a local landowner's plans to 'enclose' local farmland. His token bequest of £10 to the poor of Stratford was less than the money he left to the attorney who drew up his will. Thanks to Shakespeare's name and fame, Stratford, a town in deep economic decline during his lifetime, has prospered greatly in modern times. But there is some irony in this phenomenon, for it is clear that Shakespeare himself was not interested in promoting the welfare of his native town.

In the hope of achieving clarity and freshness I have tried not to get involved in complex disputes with previous Shakespeare scholars, dead or alive. I have also avoided taking up a large amount of space in explaining either why I draw on the particular material that I do, or why other material is not discussed. Because of the constraints of my 'thematic' approach, I have not even touched on all of Shakespeare's writings. While there is a good deal here about *As You Like It*, *Hamlet*, *King Lear* and *Shakespeare's Sonnets*, for instance, there are many other plays, such as *The Taming of the Shrew*, *Much Ado about Nothing*, *The Merchant of Venice* and *Othello* that barely rate a mention. This does not mean that I believe the latter group to be less important than the former, from a literary viewpoint. It simply indicates that they did not offer material that I could connect with the biographical theme under discussion.

Scholars will be quick to notice some other absences. Four notable missing items are the 1581 will of Alexander Hoghton, with its bequest to a 'William Shakeshafte'; the Spiritual 'Testament' of John Shakespeare; Hand D in the manuscript fragment of *Sir Thomas More*; and Simon Forman's *Booke of Plaies*. In all these cases, I have yet to be convinced that these documents have anything to tell us about Shakespeare. 'Shakeshafte' was a common name in Lancashire, and the possible means by which William Shakespeare of Stratford, aged seventeen, might have been recruited into the household of Alexander Hoghton of Lancashire as a player, tutor or musician have never been explained to my satisfaction.[5] A text of Cardinal Borromeo's Spiritual Testament, inscribed with the name 'John Shakespeare', allegedly discovered in the rafters of the Henley Street house, disappeared almost as soon as it was seen. Though Malone's transcript has been shown to correspond with the text of an authentic work of Catholic spirituality, its connection with the barely literate glover John Shakespeare is, in my view, 'not proven', and it is telling that Malone himself no longer credited it by the time of his death.[6] The alleged link of this text with John Shakespeare seems to me fundamentally implausible, especially given that during his period as an alderman Shakespeare's father readily acquiesced in orders from the Reformers. The *Thomas More* manuscript is clearly of huge interest to students of Elizabethan drama. But half a dozen late signatures do not seem to me to provide an adequate sample on which to base an identification of Shakespeare's secretary hand. Nor have the circumstances in which, well on his career, he might have acted as scribe and collaborator alongside members of a rival company ever to my mind been convincingly reconstructed. Shakespearean scholars will be most startled by my omission of Forman's *Booke of Plaies*. Here, as elsewhere, I am entirely open to persuasion, should ink-dating or some other test conclusively demonstrate the authenticity of what is written on the relevant leaves in Bodleian MS Ashmole 208. But the fact that two expert seventeenth-century archivists, working independently of each other, both found here an item entitled a 'Booke of Places', and failed to note any possible bearing that this item might have on Shakespeare, requires some explanation.[7] In what we have now, the 'i' of 'Plaies' is perfectly clear. It also strikes me as strangely suspicious that Forman, who nowhere else in his copious papers reveals any interest in the theatre, should suddenly have taken to playgoing in the last year of his life, conveniently providing posterity with plonkingly moralistic comments on three plays whose public performance history is otherwise unknown.

With a few exceptions, such as the Shakespeare family epitaphs, all quotations, but not titles of books or works, have been modernized, even when they are taken from old-spelling edited texts, such as Herford and Simpson's Jonson or McKerrow's Nashe. I am not altogether happy about this procedure, but it conforms to the accepted Arden practice of presenting Shakespeare's own works in modernized form.

Except where otherwise stated, quotations from Shakespeare's works are taken from the most recent available Arden editions.

Acknowledgements

Working in the Bodleian Library in Oxford has been a constant pleasure, and I am grateful to the ever-patient and obliging staff in Duke Humfrey and the Upper Reading Room. I have also made use of Oxford's English Faculty Library (thanks for the long loan of B. Roland Lewis's vast tomes!), the Manuscripts Room of the British Library, the Stratford Records Office, the Public Record Office, the Greater London Metropolitan Archives, the Cambridge University Library, Dulwich College Archives and the College of Arms. I was also lucky enough to have a short-term Fellowship at the Folger Shakespeare Library in Washington, D.C., in the autumn of 1998, and one term of 'Carlisle Leave' from Somerville College in the summer of 2000.

Some specific debts to individuals are recorded in footnotes. Among those who have been generous with their help are Dr Robert Bearman; Mr David Cheshire; Dr James F. Day; Professor Martin Dodsworth; Professor Andrew Gurr; Ms Susan Hill; Dr Jonathan Hughes; Dr Trevor Hughes; Professor Gordon Kipling; Professor Karen Kupperman; Ms Mairi Macdonald; Professor Steve May; Professor Alan Nelson; Dr Scott Nixon; Dr J. R. Piggott; Professor Richard Proudfoot; Vicki Roth; Ms Dania Sheldon; Mr David J. H. Smith; Dr Fiona Stafford; Professor Peter Stallybrass; Sir Keith Thomas; Professor John Tobin; Professor Stanley Wells; Dr Martin Wiggins; Beatrice Wilson; Emily Wilson; Dr Laetitia Yeandle; Mr Robert Yorke. Dr Anthony James West sent me some useful extracts from his forthcoming *The Shakespeare First Folio: The*

History of the Book (vol. 1). Gordon McMullan kindly sent me proofs of the Introduction to his forthcoming Arden edition of *Henry VIII*, but unfortunately (my fault, not his!) this arrived just too late for me to make use of it.

The entire work has been commented on in detail by three discerning readers, my mother, Mrs E. E. Duncan-Jones, Professor Peter Holland and Professor Henry Woudhuysen, as well as by the excellent copy-editor Judith Ravenscroft, and is very much the better for their comments and corrections. However, I offer, with some vehemence, the usual caveats about all errors and inadequacies being my own, and as all of these individuals will know, I have in many instances stuck stubbornly to my guns, against their sage advice. I am also extremely grateful for the support and encouragement of Jessica Hodge at every stage. It was over lunch with her that this book was first conceived.

CHAPTER ONE

1564–88

Another Eden, another Arden

This song our shire of Warwick sounds,
Revives old Arden's ancient bounds.

(Michael Drayton, *Polyolbion*, 1612, proem to Song 13)

Warwickshire hath Leicester and Northamptonshire on the east, Oxford and Gloucestershires on the south, Worcester on the west, and Staffordshire on the north . . . One said, no less truly than merrily, 'It is the heart, but not the core of England'; having nothing coarse or choky therein . . . from Edgehill one may behold it another Eden.

(Thomas Fuller, *Worthies of England*, 1662)

The heart of England

There is no need to doubt whether a grammar-school boy from Stratford-upon-Avon could grow up to write great, and enduring, plays and poems. Indeed, in the late Elizabethan period the West Midlands was much the likeliest region of England to produce a major secular poet and playwright. Marcus Gheeraerts's famous 'Ditchley' portrait of Queen Elizabeth I shows her right toe pointing to Ditchley Park, in Oxfordshire, the seat of her loyal Champion (and perhaps half-brother) Sir Henry Lee, while her heel rests on the adjacent county of Warwickshire (Plate 1). This posture symbolically declares her especially proud ownership of the English Midlands. The geographical heart of England was intimately connected, as if by veins and arteries, with the Queen's own heart. She loved it in quite particular and personal ways. Not only had she spent one of her happier periods of imprisonment at Woodstock Palace; she had long been in love, probably more than with any other man, with someone whose surname and title both marked him as a Midlander, Robert Dudley, Earl of Leicester, who was in his heyday virtually King of Middle England.

Yet the substantial distance of the Midland counties from her court gave them in practice a unique creative freedom. During the twenty years of Shakespeare's childhood and adolescence the royal feet that rested on these central counties rested as yet quite lightly. Strong traditions of drama and civic pageantry, rich and generous local patrons and excellent local grammar schools all combined to make the West Midlands as a whole, and Warwickshire in particular, 'another Eden', a territory in which both learning and recreation flourished, and had robustly survived or adjusted to the religious and political storms of the mid-century, perhaps almost thriving on these difficulties. For instance, a great cycle of Corpus Christi plays continued to be performed in Coventry as late as 1579, being succeeded in 1584 by an even more expensive and spectacular pageant called *The Destruction of Jerusalem*.[1] This was not so much an Eden where people were without sin as a newly delivered, post-Reformation golden world where religious differences among those of yeoman and citizen class were for the time being accommodated with remarkably little rancour or strife, partly because the new religion was weakly enforced and poorly understood. The ancient and often repressive hierarchies of the Roman church had been removed, and new ones were not as yet effectively established. Precise distinctions between the old faith and the new forms of liturgy, doctrine and obedience were for the time being comfortably blurred. Even at the centre, doctrinal distinctions were not sharply defined in this period, and at the margins they were barely comprehended, except for a widespread bullish belief that such foreign jurisdiction as the Pope's was now to be scorned.

The reformed religion as construed by Elizabeth posed as yet no great threat to traditional vernacular culture. Most unlettered communities had only a hazy understanding of it, and they were ministered to by half-educated clergy who themselves hardly understood it. During Shakespeare's early years the great majority of Warwickshire's clergy were, according to a survey commissioned by Archbishop Whitgift in 1586, 'dumb and unlearned', jesters and tavern-haunters, barely capable either of reading or of preaching. The parson of Honiley, a village in the north of the county, is a fairly typical example:

> [being] dumb and unlearned, he can neither preach nor read well, he could not one day read the Commandments for want of his spectacles: a woolwinder and

girthmaker by his usual occupation. An old pardoner in Queen Mary's time and yet remaineth popish.[2]

And as Edgar Fripp observes, 'Until the building of the London theatres in 1576 there was no antagonism between players and preachers . . . they were in friendly co-operation, rivals in anti-Catholic propaganda'.[3]

Whatever their own private religious sympathies may have been, many patrons and schoolmasters in the Midlands in the 1560s and 1570s encouraged promising young men to develop their talents with considerably more freedom and boldness than would have been possible among the more sophisticated and tightly controlled hierarchies that surrounded the Queen's court. It was into this lively environment that Shakespeare was born in 1564, his christening being recorded as taking place on 26 April. His traditional birthday, 23 April, is a plausible guess, since children, if healthy, were generally baptized within two or three days of their birth.

The bookish Midlands

Six counties encircle Warwickshire, and during the Elizabethan period all of them bred major writers. In the order traced by Shakespeare's earliest biographer, the antiquarian clergyman Thomas Fuller (1608–61),[4] Leicestershire comes first. This produced the exceptional Burton brothers, the translator and antiquarian William, and Robert, the famous anatomist of *Melancholy* (born 1575 and 1577 respectively). Sir Robert Dallington, aphorist, traveller and translator, celebrated above all for his major translation of Francesco Colonna's *Hypnerotomachia Poliphili* (1592), was born in Geddington, Northamptonshire, in 1561. Shakespeare's future collaborator and successor John Fletcher also came from Northamptonshire (born 1579). Oxfordshire, because of its university, saw dozens of talented young writers come and go. Two such writers who had connections with Shakespeare are the poet and playwright George Peele (born about 1558), who was to figure as one of his rivals in *Greene's Groats-worth of Wit* in 1592, which will be discussed in the next chapter, and the sonneteer Richard Barnfield (born 1574) whose poems were to be mingled with Shakespeare's in *The Passionate Pilgrim* (1599). The great translator Edwin Sandys was born in Worcestershire in 1561, son of the then Bishop. Staffordshire was the birth-county of the antiquary Sampson Erdeswicke, and also of the great Oxford mathematician and magus Thomas Allen (born 1542), who cast a horoscope for Philip Sidney in 1571. One of the most celebrated theatrical performers of the period, Richard Tarlton, grew up more humbly in Condover, a few miles to the west in Shropshire, where he was talent-spotted by a servant of the Earl of

Leicester as he looked after his father's pigs. Tarlton was a 'clown' in two senses – an unlettered rustic, and also a very funny stand-up comic. It is greatly to the credit of his patrons that they saw and rewarded his natural ability. Another Shropshire man, Thomas Churchyard (born about 1520 in Shrewsbury), testified to the huge strength and popularity of secular drama and entertainment in the West Midlands. He described the performance of plays and other 'shows' each summer in a large natural amphitheatre, 'The Quarry', just outside the walls of Shrewsbury, with seating for 'ten thousand men'. As if this was not enough, there was also

> A space below, to bait both bull and bear,
> For players too, great room and place at will,
> And in the same, a cock-pit wondrous fair,
> Besides where men, may wrestle in their fill.
> A ground most apt, and they that sits above
> At once in view, all this may see for love:
> At Ashton's play, who had beheld this then,
> Might well have seen there twenty thousand men.[5]

Though it may be imagined that London's Bankside, with its great amphitheatres and bearpits, would be both novel and dazzling to a newly arrived Midlander – and no doubt in many ways it was – the Midlands of Shakespeare's boyhood offered seasonal spectacles on a comparable scale, or even larger. Still looking west towards the Welsh borders, Herefordshire produced the great collector of travel narratives Richard Hakluyt (born about 1552), the expert on heraldry John Guillim (born 1565), and a man of many talents who became a friend and admirer of both Shakespeare and Burbage, the poet and calligrapher John Davies of Hereford (born about 1565).

When we reach Warwickshire itself, 'the heart of England', it is immediately apparent that this was an even more fertile breeding ground for men of letters than its neighbouring counties. In Thomas Fuller's *History of the Worthies of England*, a county-by-county account of notable Englishmen, Shakespeare is flanked by three other Warwickshire writers, his close contemporaries, each of whom was both highly individual and exceptionally productive. Most closely analogous to Shakespeare is the man Fuller mentions first, Michael Drayton, who was born at Hartshill, near Atherstone, in 1563. Drayton's forebears, like Shakespeare's, were obscure yeoman farmers, butchers and tanners. Like Shakespeare, too, Drayton appears to have gone to grammar school for a few years, but not to university. He is thought to have spent some time at school in Coventry while he was a page in the household of Sir Henry Goodere. Also like Shakespeare, Drayton successfully raised himself to 'gentle' status and acquired a coat of arms. At the close of his life, probably because of his well-maintained relations with such patrons as Goodere, his daughter Lady Rainsford, Sir Walter Aston and Mary Curzon, Countess of Dorset, Drayton actually outstripped Shakespeare in visible public acclaim, achieving both 'laureate' status and a monument in Westminster Abbey. The second in the trio of Warwickshire writers mentioned by Fuller, Fulke Greville, is best known to posterity as Philip Sidney's closest friend and author of a memoir of him, as well as of closet dramas, a sonnet sequence and some knotty philosophical poems. For Shakespeare in boyhood, however, he was primarily notable as the son and heir of a man well known in Stratford, the hospitable Sir Fulke Greville of Beauchamps Court, who was deeply involved in Stratford's affairs and often dined, drank and slept in the town. Greville senior, and perhaps also his son, must have been quite well known to John Shakespeare during his periods as Bailiff and then Head Alderman in 1568–72. Most prolific and talented of all was the third Warwickshire man mentioned by Fuller, Philemon Holland, 'the Translator General of his age', who outdid even Shakespeare in the physical fluency of his writing: 'It was . . . Philemon Holland's proud boast that he had translated all of Plutarch's *Moralia* with only one quill, which was subsequently "garnished" in silver and kept "as a Monument"'.[6] However, Holland was not a Warwickshire man by birth. He took up residence in Coventry, where he remained for the rest of his long life, only in 1608.

Much more closely associated with Shakespeare was a man not mentioned by Fuller, the printer Richard Field, who was almost certainly with him for a while at the King's Grammar School in Stratford. Uniquely among Shakespeare's Warwickshire friends, Field achieved a friendly allusion in one of the plays, when Innogen refers to her irreplaceable master 'Richard du Champ' (*Cymbeline*, 4.2.377). Field was apprenticed to the distinguished Huguenot printer Thomas Vautrollier in 1579. After marrying Vautrollier's widow (or perhaps his daughter) Jacqueline and taking over his house and business in 1587, he rapidly rose to become one of the most versatile and up-market printers of his age. His ability to handle works in French, Italian, Spanish and Welsh, with occasional passages in Greek and Italian, is an eloquent testimony to the strong educational foundations laid down in Stratford. Vautrollier would certainly not have taken on this young man, then aged seventeen, for training as his only apprentice had he not shown literary and linguistic skills of a very high order. Nor can Richard Field's capacities be attributed to some special tuition within the Field family, for at least three other boys from Stratford were apprenticed to London stationers during the late Elizabethan period.[7] Field's printing house may have provided Shakespeare with his first lodging in London, as well as functioning as a kind of library in which he was able to carry out wide reading without having to purchase such hugely expensive volumes as (for instance) Thomas North's translation of Plutarch's *Lives of the Noble Grecians and Romans*. Another Warwickshire man who was to be closely associated with Shakespeare was the half-Italian John Marston, satirist and playwright, who grew up in Coventry. And yet another Midlander who was to be extremely important both for Shakespeare and for posterity, John Heminge,[8] came from Droitwich in nearby Worcestershire, less than twenty miles from Stratford. His early education is unknown, but it may have been at one of the many nearby grammar schools, in Worcester, Warwick, Coventry or even, just possibly, Stratford itself. Certainly there were some Heminge kindred living in the town. Sadly, Heminge and Condell's famous epistle prefaced to the First Folio in 1623 does not extend to recollections of the early years of 'the author deceased'. But it's possible that Heminge was to Shakespeare as Fulke Greville was to Philip Sidney: a lifelong companion from boyhood days, who as such felt uniquely qualified to edit and publish the literary remains of his brilliant dead friend.

Of the four post-Reformation writers listed by Fuller as Warwickshire men, only one incorporated explicit personal and local reminiscence into his writing. Perhaps Shakespeare himself might have done so had he lived a few years longer, for it was not until 1627, in his 'Epistle to Henry Reynolds', that the sixty-year-old Michael Drayton was to describe his early education in Cato and his puerile desire to be a poet:

> To my mild tutor merrily I came,
> (For I was then a proper goodly page,
> Much like a pygmy, scarce ten years of age)
> Clasping my slender arms about his thigh.
> O my dear master! cannot you (quoth I)
> Make me a poet, do it, if you can,
> And you shall see, I'll quickly be a man.

We should notice that although Drayton uses the grand word 'poet', and goes on to speak of trying childishly to gallop to the top of 'Parnassus', much of his early work was for the playing companies and written in collaboration with that group of writers now disparaged as 'Henslowe's hacks', such as Chettle, Dekker and Munday.[9] Even the most prolific professional 'poet' in this period could not hope to make a living from sonnets and pastorals alone. The playing companies offered both easy access and good financial rewards.

Fifteen years earlier, in 1612, Michael Drayton celebrated his and Shakespeare's native county in the Thirteenth Song of *Polyolbion*. There is nothing mundane or workaday about his topographical vision. England is mapped through her rivers, which are silver founts of poetic inspiration. Warwickshire, above all, is a place of poetry and swelling birdsong. That vast and ancient Forest of Arden – which perhaps never was, but supposedly once extended like a vast green girdle across England from Severn to Trent – offers liberating dreams of romance. The goddess Diana herself goes hunting there with her 'dishevelled Nymphs attired in youthful green', and beneath the forest's peaceful afternoon shade a hermit can find refuge

> From villages replete with ragg'd and sweating clowns,
> And from the loathsome airs of smoky citied towns.

Once a 'man at arms', this hermit now gathers healing flowers and herbs from Arden's rich forest floor,

> And in a little maund,* being made of osiers small,
> Which serveth him to do full many a thing withal,
> He very choicely sorts his simples got abroad.

This hermit sounds like a highly idealized portrait of Shakespeare's middle-aged son-in-law Dr John Hall, who on at least one occasion treated his neighbour Michael Drayton with 'syrup of violets' – a woodland flower, no doubt culled in the environs of Stratford. But the true Arden Forest, if it ever existed, is gone, destroyed through the long-drawn-out process of enclosure that was still continuing in Shakespeare's lifetime, and with which he was to become personally embroiled in the last two years of his life. In William Hole's illustration to Drayton's Thirteenth Song 'Arden' herself is represented allegorically as an elderly Diana with bow and arrows and a rustic hat. She gestures to the line of trees that is 'behind' her both in space and time, the first of which is already felled (Plate 2). Grief for the attrition of this ancient forest, combined with pride in its antiquity, was part of the local myth of origin that both Drayton and Shakespeare proudly imbibed with their mother's milk. Warwickshire was also a place of ancient heroism, with its very own 'English Hercules', the romance hero Guy of Warwick, who slew infidels and monsters, and gave his name to 'Guy's Cliff', just north of Warwick. For Drayton, it is clear, Warwickshire was 'fit nurse for a poetic child', and 'Arden', still more, was a name of talismanic power.

ANOTHER ARDEN

Though Shakespeare's fictitious Arden, in *As You Like It*, is supposedly in France, it does not feel like it. It is noticeable how many features this Forest of Arden shares with Michael Drayton's in *Polyolbion* – hunting, a weeping deer, a refuge from cruelty, an encounter with a wise hermit. Also, uniquely among Shakespeare's seventeen comedies, this one has a hero, Orlando, who is both

* 'maund': a small basket; and cf. *A Lover's Complaint*, 36.

loyal and courageous and a natural 'gentleman', despite his lack of education. When he and the banished Duke ritually echo the signs of their shared culture they use images that suggest a Drayton-like nostalgia for a provincial England that was both 'gentle' and hospitable:

> If ever you have look'd on better days;
> If ever been where bells have knoll'd to church;
> If ever sat at any good man's feast;
> If ever from your eyelids wip'd a tear,
> And knew what 'tis to pity and be pitied,
> Let gentleness my strong enforcement be . . .
>
> (*As You Like It*, 2.7.113–18)

For Shakespeare, the name 'Arden' had a double resonance, both external and internal, for it was his mother's maiden name. As we shall see in chapter 4, Mary Arden's connections with an ancient family of Warwickshire gentry were one day to be of pressing importance for her eldest son. Meanwhile, growing up not only with the greenwood myth of a once great Forest of Arden, but even with an inheritance of its name, gave the child a sense of enacting Englishness. If Warwickshire was the heart of England, Arden Forest and the Ardens named after it were the heart of Warwickshire. With a child's egotism he may have felt himself to be, as a little Arden of great promise, the heart of that heart.

From his mother young William inherited some pretensions to gentility, although the exact connection between the yeoman Robert Arden of Wilmcote and the gentry Ardens of Park Hall, Castle Bromwich, has never been established, and may have been quite remote. From his father he acquired a knowledge of tanning and gloving, which was to figure, for instance, in the Graveyard scene in *Hamlet*. But far more importantly, he inherited a strong interest in entertainment and mirth. A slightly muddled anecdote recorded by Thomas Plume, Archdeacon of Rochester, in the late seventeenth century suggests that John Shakespeare was, like the Nurse's husband in *Romeo and Juliet*, 'a merry man':

> He [William] was a glover's son – Sir John Mennis saw once his old father in his shop – a merry cheeked old man – that said – Will was a good honest fellow, but he durst have cracked a jest with him at any time.[10]

Sir John Mennis, born in 1599, could not possibly have remembered John Shakespeare, who died in 1601. But perhaps either Mennis's father or one of his father's friends visited Henley Street, and, as so often happens in oral reminiscence, a generation was slipped. It is entirely believable that Shakespeare's unfailing skill in turning the most solemn language into an instant quibble or bawdy repartee was a skill – or even a persistent bad habit – learned from practice during his early years at home. The younger Shakespeare, in the Stratford bust, cuts a disappointingly unpoetic, 'merry cheeked' and bourgeois figure, perhaps resembling his own father in middle age.

More solid evidence that John Shakespeare was indeed a 'merry man' is to be found in the records of Stratford Corporation. As Bailiff of Stratford in 1568–9, and Head Alderman in 1571–2, he was in a position to offer or authorize financial support to both local and visiting players, and we know that he did so. In 1569 the Queen's Men were paid 9 shillings, probably for 'the Bailiff's play' in the Guild Hall in August. This was the first, trial, performance; if it met with the approval of the Bailiff and Aldermen the players would then give a further performance for the citizenry in general. At some later date in 1569 the Earl of Worcester's Players were paid a rather modest 12 pence; perhaps this was a small contingent of performers.[11] The Bailiff may have been proud enough of his first-born son to hold him between his knees at either or both of these performances, as Robert Willis was held by his father at the Lord Mayor's play at Gloucester: 'At such a play my father took me with him, and made me stand between his legs, as he sat upon one of the benches, where we saw and heard very well.'[12] Another regular expense for the Stratford Corporation was 'for the Queen's provision', a contribution to the expenses of the Queen's large retinue as they accompanied her on her summer Progress. In 1569 this came to 3*s.* 3*d.*, but in some years it was a good deal more. The progress always involved spectacles and entertainments along the way, in addition to the glorious spectacle of the Queen herself, accompanied by noblemen and ambassadors. Locals flocked to nearby viewpoints in the hope of catching glimpses of the Queen's 'pleasures', or shows and entertainments.

Kenilworth

In 1575 these 'pleasures' took an exceptionally splendid form, when the Queen visited Warwickshire. As the high point of this well-documented Progress she spent nineteen days being entertained by her old friend – almost, in modern parlance, 'boyfriend' – the Earl of Leicester, at Kenilworth Castle, only twelve miles from Stratford. As Schoenbaum says, it is 'not implausible' that Alderman Shakespeare took his eleven-year-old son along to see as much as they could of these festivities.[13] Even those who remained in Stratford were well aware of them, for the gunfire and fireworks that greeted the Queen's arrival at the Castle were seen and heard well over twenty miles away.[14] The whole Shakespeare family, among many others, could gaze with wonder towards the brightly lit Castle from a nearby viewpoint. The father and eldest son – and perhaps nine-year-old Gilbert came too – may have made longer journeys to join the crowds who flocked to see these astonishing spectacles. As Roger Kuin has observed, there were three main types of entertainment offered to the Queen by Leicester: hunting parties, 'literary' entertainments and 'popular' entertainments.[15] The Shakespeares could have caught glimpses of all three. It is a pity that a printed account of the whole of that summer's Progress, *The pastime of the Progresse*, has vanished – its disappearance in itself a testimony to the intense popular interest in the Queen's Midland journey.[16] This book may have given an account of the exact route taken by the Progress before its arrival on Leicester's estates. We do know that the day before the Queen's arrival at Kenilworth was devoted to a hunting picnic of exceptional splendour in a specially constructed tent at Leicester's manor on Long Itchington, ten miles north-east of Stratford. Preparations both here and at the Castle occupied many weeks, requiring the labour of many Warwickshire artisans well known to John Shakespeare.

Once the Progress was on its way, it moved forward only at a slow trotting pace. There was plenty of time for news to reach surrounding villages of its approach, which in any case was signalled by festive bell-ringing. It goes without saying that boys would be let off school, for their schoolmasters were as eager as they were to glimpse the Queen, and if possible deliver learned speeches or presentations to her or to her courtiers. Again, we do not know whether the Stratford schoolmaster Simon Hunt succeeded in taking any active part in welcoming the Queen, but he may have done so.

To the south of the Castle, and outside its high walls, was a huge artificial lake modestly called 'The pool' (Fig. 1).[17] Because of its size and position this could not be shielded from public view, as most of the entertainments within the walls were. It has often been thought that Shakespeare saw what took place here, and showed his knowledge of it in one of his most courtly comedies, *A Midsummer Night's Dream*, performed for the Queen's cousin and half-brother Henry Carey, Lord Hunsdon, as part of the celebrations of his grand-daughter's wedding. Older members of the aristocratic audience in 1596 would certainly have picked up Shakespeare's allusion to the Earl of Leicester's most conspicuous display of desire for Elizabeth. Ten days into her stay, on a hot 18 July, the Queen may have imagined that the most elaborate spectacles were finished. But as she returned from a late afternoon hunting expedition, and was about to re-enter the Castle, a great water pageant began:

> Well, the game was gotten, and her highness returning, came there upon a swimming Mermaid (that from top to tail was an eighteen foot long) Triton, Neptune's blaster, who with his trumpet formed of a wrinkled whelk . . . gave sound very shrill and sonorous, in sign he had an embassy to pronounce.[18]

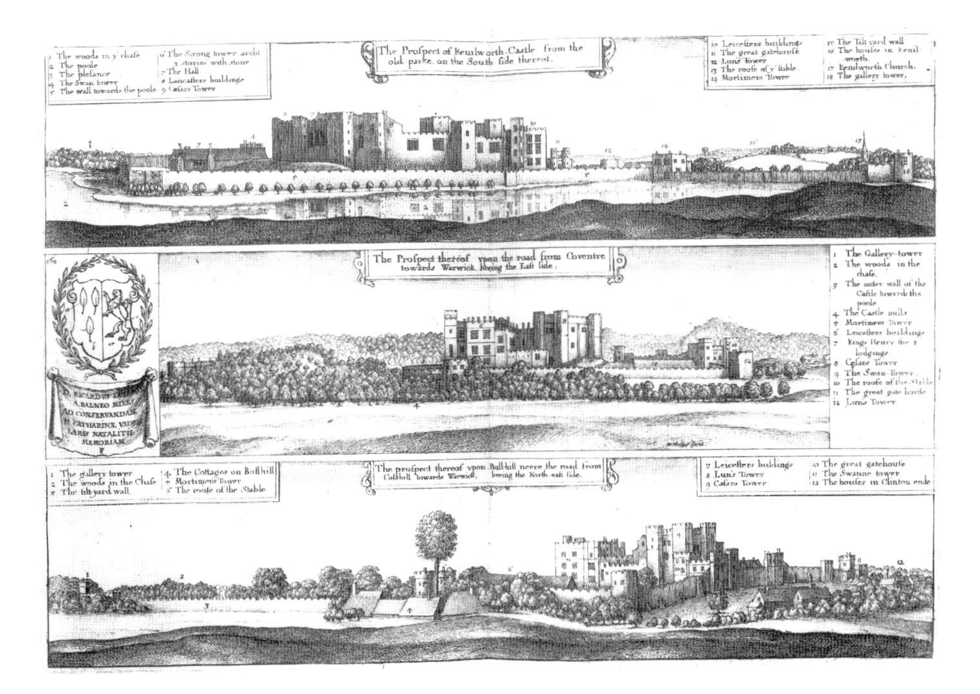

Fig. 1 Three views of Kenilworth Castle, Warwickshire, showing 'the pool', a large artificial lake on the south side, fromWilliam Dugdale, *The Antiquities of Warwickshire* (1656).

Triton's message is that 'a cruel knight, one Sir Bruce Sauns pitee', holds 'the lady of the lake' prisoner, preventing her from attending on the Queen. One full sight of the Queen's own person will shame Sir Bruce into liberating her. As the Queen lingered to watch and listen, 'it appeared straight how Sir Bruce became unseen, his bands scaled [= overcome]', and nymphs and mermaids approached on 'moveable islands'. The Queen was thanked for her gracious act of liberation by entertainment introduced by 'Arion, that excellent and famous Musician . . . riding aloft upon his old friend the Dolphin (that from head to tail was a four and twenty foot long)'. Like the rude mechanicals in *A Midsummer Night's Dream*, however, the homespun actor playing Arion was anxious to reassure the courtly spectators that this was no magic trick but an honest deception, for he cried out that 'he was not Arion, but honest Harry Goldingham'. Like many of Leicester's more 'literary' shows at Kenilworth, Arion's song and speech were written by the soldier–poet George Gascoigne, who implored the Queen to listen 'to this my floating muse', and thanked her for liberating the Lady of the Lake. All of this seems to be recalled in Oberon's speech to Puck about their shared memories of a spectacular water pageant:

Thou remembr'est,
Since once I sat upon a promontory,
And heard a mermaid on a dolphin's back
Uttering such dulcet and harmonious breath
That the rude sea grew civil at her song
And certain stars shot madly from their spheres
To hear the sea-maid's music?

(*A Midsummer Night's Dream*, 2.1.148–54)[19]

By the time the Queen listened to Arion it was 'the eving of the day', and the music composed by William Hunnis and others was heard in semi-darkness 'resounding from the calm waters'.

Yet this glorious and memorable spectacle, like the whole of the 'pleasures' of Kenilworth, was in one important sense a failure. It marked the zenith of Leicester's favour, but also the beginning of his downfall, for the 1575 progress did not lead, as many had hoped it would, to the Queen's marriage to her childhood sweetheart. Instead, Leicester soon secretly married the widowed Countess of Essex, and never fully regained the Queen's trust. A recollection of the Kenilworth water pageant as a failed courtship ploy seems to define the next part of Oberon's speech of reminiscence, in which, as King of the Fairies, he saw Cupid aiming his arrow from the heavens 'At a fair vestal, throned by the west':

But I might see young Cupid's fiery shaft
Quench'd in the chaste beams of the watery moon;
And the imperial votress passed on,
In maiden meditation, fancy-free.

(2.1.161–4)

By 1596 Elizabeth's imperial virginity could be openly celebrated as her greatest glory. Back in 1575, however, most of her subjects were still asking eagerly when and whom she would marry, not whether she would marry at all. The burning interest of this topic lent huge excitement to that summer's Progress. It would have been a wonderful thing for Midlanders, and above all for the people of Warwickshire, if the Queen had indeed married their most wealthy and lavish local magnate. She did not, but the possibility of it coloured both the events themselves and the literature that chronicled them, and helped to nourish the collective self-esteem of the shire. Even if the eleven-year-old William Shakespeare enjoyed no more than distant glimpses of the Kenilworth shows, he was surely now well advanced in literacy, and would have been able to read such associated books as *The pastime of the Progresse*, Robert Laneham's *Letter*, and George Gascoigne's *Princely Pleasures* and *Noble Arte of Venerie*, this last showing the Queen entertained by Leicester at a hunting feast (Fig. 2).

Fig. 2 Queen Elizabeth, at a hunting picnic near Kenilworth, 1575, is offered the first cut of a killed deer, from George Gascoigne, *The Noble Arte of Venerie* (1575).

Family entertainment

I shall say little more of Shakespeare's early boyhood, for little is known. He survived a severe plague outbreak in Stratford in the first summer of his life, in 1564, as he was also to survive severe plague outbreaks in London in 1592–4, 1603–4 and 1608–10. Perhaps exposure in early infancy gave him some immunity; whatever he did die of in April 1616, it was clearly not plague. Otherwise, most of what we know from the documentary record concerns the births of younger siblings, and his father's declining fortunes. William's brother Gilbert was born in October 1566; his sister Joan in April 1569; another sister, Anne, christened in September 1571, died in April 1579. Two more brothers survived to adulthood: Richard, christened in March 1574, and finally, after a six-year gap, Edmund, christened 3 May 1580, who was to become an uncle soon after his third birthday. Given John Shakespeare's declining fortune and burgeoning family, it is almost certain that William left the Grammar School precipitately, and it is altogether likely that for a while he helped his father in his craft of 'whittawing', or preparing skins for glove-making. According to Nicholas Rowe,

> [John Shakespeare] could give him no better education than his own employment. He had bred him, 'tis true, for some time at a Free School, where 'tis probable he acquired that little Latin he was master of. But the narrowness of his circumstances, and the want of his assistance at home, forced his father to withdraw him from thence.[20]

John Shakespeare's financial difficulties during the late 1570s are well documented. He lacked the funds even to hang on to all of the property he possessed, such as his wife Mary Arden's 'Asbyes' estate. Increasingly, as a short-term and desperate measure, he 'exchanged land for ready money'.[21] By the time the crypto-Catholic John Cottom arrived as Stratford's schoolmaster in 1579, replacing Thomas Jenkins, the grammar school's most famous pupil had almost certainly been gone some time. If Shakespeare was withdrawn prematurely, it was at the age of no more than twelve or thirteen, since it was normal for boys to leave grammar school at fourteen or fifteen. Two or three years' education with the obscure Midlander Simon Hunt in 1572–5, probably assisted by the curate William Gilbard, and one or two more with Thomas Jenkins, 1575–7, may have been the sum total of his grammar-school education. Indeed, he may have experienced little more than a single memorable year with Jenkins, for it was in 1576 that John Shakespeare ceased attending Council meetings, presumably a token of his decline into crippling debt. That a young man of great brilliance could make a huge amount of even a few years of study at a good Elizabethan grammar school is made clear by the analogous case of

Ben Jonson, who spent only three or four years at Westminster School before being removed to learn his stepfather's trade of brick-laying.

According to another early biographer, young Shakespeare revealed his exceptional histrionic gifts even while working with his father. The Restoration antiquary John Aubrey (1626–97) recorded that

> his father was a butcher, and I have been told heretofore by some of the neighbours, that when he was a boy he exercised his father's trade, but when he killed a calf, he would do it in a *high style*, and make a speech.[22]

Technically 'whittawers' and glovers were not butchers or slaughtermen. They were licensed only to treat animal skins provided by butchers, not to kill the animals themselves on their own premises. Yet as Douglas Hamer has suggested, Aubrey's story

> may not be a 'patently ludicrous anecdote' [23] . . . but a distorted record of a Stratford mumming play acted by boys at Christmas-time, a form of mumming play like that which was performed before the young Princess Mary at Christmas 1521: 'Item, paid to a man at Wyndesore, for killing a calfe before my ladys grace behynde a clothe'.[24]

Shakespeare later associated onstage murder with calf-killing, as in Hamlet's punning put-down to Polonius when he boasts of having acted the part of Julius Caesar at university: 'it was a brute part of him to kill so capital a calf there' (*Hamlet*, 3.2.104–5). As Hamer records, a version of the calf-killing stunt, requiring only 'a basin, carpet, horns, butcher's knives, and a butcher's blue-and-white apron', survived as late as the 1920s.[25] The actors earned a penny each. The legend of the local hero Guy of Warwick, one of whose feats, according to stories added to the medieval romance bearing his name, was to kill the Dun Cow of Dunsmore, may have made such cow- and calf-killing shows particularly popular in Warwickshire. It is entirely believable that the mirth-loving Shakespeare family regularly contributed such a show to Christmas or Shrovetide festivities in Stratford, and that young William achieved fame among neighbours for his virtuoso enactment of it. His fame may even have followed him to London, for Nashe includes in his onslaught on non-graduate playwrights in the epistle prefaced to Robert Greene's *Menaphon* (1589) 'the engrafted overflow of some killcow conceit'. A 'killcow', as a noun, was 'A swashbuckler, bully, braggadocio' (*OED*). That the word could also be associated with the mumming play is shown by one of the *Oxford Dictionary*'s quotations illustrating the adjectival use of the word. A passage in Samuel Purchas's *Pilgrimage* (1613) links the adjective 'killcow' with crude theatrical illusion: 'Like Semiramis Elephants which were but stuffed Oxe-hides, kill-cow frayes'.

The young adult Shakespeare's distinctive 'high style' in scenes of butchery is apparent in some of his earliest plays, especially in the *Henry VI* trilogy.

These include many explicit images of grandiose butchery and calf-killing. One famous scene above all, the on-stage killing of the young Prince Edward in *3 Henry VI*, 5.5, may reflect his early training in the dramatization of such sadistic spectacles. The killing of little Edward is witnessed by his mother, Margaret of Anjou, who at once sees the resemblance of her child's murder to the slaughter of a calf, and exclaims that only men who view children as 'cattle' could be brutal enough to do it:

> Butchers and villains! bloody cannibals! . . .
> You have no children, butchers! If you had,
> The thought of them would have stirr'd up remorse.
>
> (5.5.59–62)

High-style slaughter of innocents occurs in many later plays, as, for instance, when Lady Macduff and her children are murdered on-stage, or when the husband kills his own children in the probably Shakespearean *A Yorkshire Tragedy*. It is likely enough that Shakespeare as a boy did indeed frequently pretend to kill a calf 'in a high style'. This was not part of his labour in his father's workshop, however, but a regular holiday activity that was to prepare him eventually to enter a very much more lucrative craft than gloving.

1582: marriage

While Michael Drayton enjoyed the patronage of the Warwickshire Gooderes throughout his teens, it is not clear whether or when the very much more brilliant Shakespeare attracted the notice of any local patrons. The visible decline of the once prosperous Shakespeares of Henley Street may have been discouraging. No longer attending either Council meetings or his parish church because of his mounting debts, the former Bailiff John Shakespeare was unable to live at a level that enabled him to drink and dine with the Grevilles or the Lucys. In an ideal world, young William would surely have gone to Oxford or Cambridge, either as a 'sizar', or student companion, to some local nobleman's son, or as holder of one of the local scholarships set up by the philanthropic Sir Hugh Clopton. But he may have been too little in the eye of potential patrons in 1576–82 for his talents ever to have been much noticed in such quarters. In any case, a momentous episode in the summer of 1582 ensured that from then on the universities would be for ever closed to him, as would the possibility of apprenticeship to a master craftsman.[26] Undergraduates and apprentices alike were required to be bachelors.

It is just conceivable that, as Edgar Fripp claimed,[27] the eighteen-year-old William was formally betrothed to the twenty-six-year-old Anne Hathaway of

Shottery, who had inherited a small amount of property after the death of her father Richard in September 1581. Fripp and others have seen the sexual relations between William and Anne as more or less legitimated by a pre-contract. Yet if there had been such a formal betrothal, it is odd that the marriage itself, at the end of November 1582, had to be arranged in a hurry by Anne's kinsmen because of her pregnancy. To me it seems a good deal more likely that her father's death left the unmarried Agnes or Anne (the names were interchangeable) without much parental care or control, and as a mature and spirited country girl she exploited her freedom to consort with the local youth. A combination of boredom with the sexual curiosity natural to his years led to Shakespeare's dalliance with her, and to what was probably his first experience of sex. In the early modern period puberty occurred, on average, four or five years later than it does today. Some boys of eighteen or nineteen were still able to sing treble.[28] In the stickily hot August of 1582 Shakespeare was probably changing from boy into man, and experiencing the uncontrollable surges of testosterone accompanying that stage of development. The Shakespeare and Hathaway families, living only a couple of miles apart, had always known each other. Anne was unlike many young women of her age not only in being unmarried, but also in being to some extent free and independent. Once the heaviest labour of July and August was over there was a brief lull in the cycle of agriculture until the time of the apple harvest and cider-making. All hands, including women's hands, had been required for the hay and grain harvest, but the major work of late August and early September – putting dung on the fields, ploughing, sowing rye – was for men alone. Sometime during this agricultural lull sexual relations began between the orphaned husbandman's daughter and the glover's eldest son. The birthdate of Susanna Shakespeare, christened 26 May 1583, places her likely conception within the last two weeks of September 1582. Older men in the environs of Stratford were sowing rye and corn, as recommended by Thomas Tusser:

> Give winter corn leave, for to have full his lust:
> Sow wheat as thou mayst, but some rye in the dust.
> Be careful for seed, for such seed as thou sow,
> As true as thou livest, look justly to mow.[29]

But meanwhile Stratford's most talented son was sowing wild oats, with little or no thought to the lifelong problems he would reap. For there is no way that his marriage to Anne Hathaway, and responsibility for yet more young children, could help the Shakespeare family, already in severe financial difficulty, except in the very short term. Anne had inherited only a modest dowry of 10 marks, the equivalent of £6 14*s*. 4*d*.

It could be argued, therefore, that the union was a lovematch, and so in a sense perhaps it was. A young man of extraordinary talent and imagination, stuck in uncongenial employment with no prospects except the possibility of one day managing the family business better than his father was doing, found, as other men of genius have done, an outlet in sex. Initially, in the weeks of their first dalliance, the boy was grateful to Anne for her compliance, and persuaded himself that he loved her. This is suggested by an odd, and oddly simplistic, sonnet that eventually found a place in the 'dark lady' section of the 1609 *Sonnets* as 145:

> Those lips that love's own hand did make
> Breathed forth the sound that said 'I hate',
> To me, that languished for her sake;
> But when she saw my woeful state,
> Straight in her heart did mercy come,
> Chiding that tongue that, ever sweet,
> Was used in giving gentle doom,
> And taught it thus anew to greet:
> 'I hate' she altered with an end
> That followed it as gentle day
> Doth follow night, who like a fiend
> From heaven to hell is flown away.
> 'I hate' from 'hate' away she threw,
> And saved my life, saying 'not you'.

As Andrew Gurr has pointed out, the phrase 'hate away' in the penultimate line seems to pun on 'Hathaway' or 'Hattaway' – the names were interchangeable. If we read the sonnet in isolation, as a literal celebration of young William's courtship of Anne in late summer 1582, the picture, though naive, is conventional and pleasant. The sweet-tongued Anne is courted by the desperately languishing William, and in substituting one bit of blunt language – 'I hate you' – for another – 'I hate not you' – she 'saves his life', or rather liberates him from sexual frustration. However, in the context in which it reached print in 1609 the sonnet cannot possibly read so straightforwardly, but has to be taken as a piece of sardonic and affected simplicity. The sonnet that immediately precedes it, also written relatively early, since it appeared in *The Passionate Pilgrim* in 1599, is both horribly complex and unambiguously misogynistic. In this more famous sonnet 'a woman coloured ill', a promiscuous and venereally infected mistress, tries to lure away the speaker's 'better angel', a 'man right fair'. Here, as in other sonnets in the 'dark lady' group (127–154), lust is associated exclusively with heterosexual desire, and the speaker, in the grip of this desire, is driven mad with rage, jealousy and self-hatred. Yet he is unable 'to shun the heaven that leads men to this hell'. While his friendship with the fair youth is often a source of intensely obsessive pain or anxiety, it never provokes the dark, sarcastic rage that accompanies his heterosexual passion. It may well be true that sonnet 145 goes right back to 1582, being, as Gurr has said, 'Shakespeare's first poem'.[30] And as Gurr also suggested, the appearance of Thomas Watson's *Hekatompathia* earlier in the summer of 1582 could have stimulated him to make preliminary experiments with the sonnet form. The apprentice printer Richard Field could have shown or lent him a copy of this epoch-making book, the first published sonnet sequence in English.

Shakespeare's sonnet is illuminating not so much in what it tells us about the nature of the boy William's wooing of Anne as in what it tells us about his true vocation. If the early dating is correct, he was already versifying, perhaps as yet with a rather facile chop-logic wit over-influenced by his father's merry jest-cracking. He could never serve a formal apprenticeship to a master craftsman, as his friend Richard Field was doing. His dalliance with Anne, and the compelled marriage that followed it, had put paid to that for ever. But like Michael Drayton he could hope one day to enter a more loosely regulated profession, as a 'poet' attached to a playing company.

The marriage between William and Anne appears to have taken place in a tiny village called Temple Grafton. A clerk employed by the Bishop of Worcester described the bride, in the transcript of the marriage licence in the Bishop's Register, as 'Anne Whately de Temple Grafton'. The clerk's record of her surname as 'Whately' has excited much speculation, including Anthony Burgess's fantasy about two Annes, Anne Whately, with whom Shakespeare was truly in love, and Anne Hathaway, whom he was reluctantly compelled to marry. However, there is very little doubt that the reference in the Bishop's Register is to the same woman also known as 'Hathaway'. The clerk may have made an error either of mishearing or mistranscription. Anne's father's friends, Fulke Sandells and John Richardson, who secured the marriage bond on 18 November, were Shottery farmers of little or no book-learning. In any case, they probably had no chance to see the precise form in which the licence was recorded in the Bishop's Register.

Why Anne was in the parish of Temple Grafton, rather than in her native Shottery three and a half miles away, has never been satisfactorily explained. Possibly she was already living there at the time she became pregnant, and Shakespeare wooed her there. However, I think it is more likely that Anne's family and friends, on learning of her pregnancy, decided that she should be immediately removed to a more distant parish, and away from gossiping neighbours in Stratford, until she was safely married. Temple Grafton was just about far enough away from Shottery to achieve this. The conditions of evident haste in which the marriage was arranged support such a scenario. Speedy measures were adopted to get the marriage legalized by a licence from the Bishop of Worcester, perhaps immediately after lodging Anne with friends at Temple Grafton. Once the licence was procured, only a single reading of the banns would be needed before the marriage could be solemnized. The banns were probably read on Friday, 30 November, followed by marriage the following day, 1 December. In a sleepy backwater like Temple Grafton this could be accomplished with little stir.

Richard Hathaway's 'trusty friend and neighbour' Fulke Sandells was probably the moving spirit behind the whole business of making an honest woman of Anne. William Shakespeare, as a minor, needed his father's consent to his marriage. Both father and son may have been severely rebuked by Sandells for the boy's lack of control. But unless the Shakespeares could deny or somehow disprove William's paternity of Anne's child, there was little that either of them could do except acquiesce in the unwanted marriage. John Shakespeare's last attendance at a Stratford Council meeting had been on 5 September 1582. Although the chief reason for his non-attendance both at the Council and at his parish church was no doubt the fear of pursuit by his creditors, William's seduction of Anne may also have been a major consideration, delivering the final death-blow to his social standing.

William himself, fully aware of the block to his future advancement that this marriage would constitute, was very probably sulky and reluctant from the outset. Some of his deep resentment at this premature yoking may fuel Adonis's remonstrances against premature fruition in what was to be Shakespeare's first published poem:

> 'Who wears a garment shapeless and unfinish'd?
> Who plucks the bud before one leaf put forth?
> If springing things be any jot diminish'd,
> They wither in their prime, prove nothing worth;
> The colt that's back'd and burden'd being young,
> Loseth his pride, and never waxeth strong . . .'
>
> (*Venus and Adonis*, 415–20)

Nevertheless, the Temple Grafton location of the marriage ceremony offered a few short-term consolations. Not only was it well away from the bridegroom's mocking male friends in Stratford, it was a place of unusually rich associations. It is a pretty spot, offering a fine view west to the Cotswolds. It also stands by the ancient meeting place for the Court Leet of Barlichway Hundred, the same area of Warwickshire that contains Stratford. According to Dugdale, no habitation actually called 'Barlichway' survived, 'other than a little plot of ground, about eight yards square, now enclosed with a hedge, and situate upon the top of a hill in the middle way between Haseler and Brinton . . . and about half a mile from Temple Grafton'.[31] For a young man of a poetic and imaginative temperament, this location had the attraction of mysterious

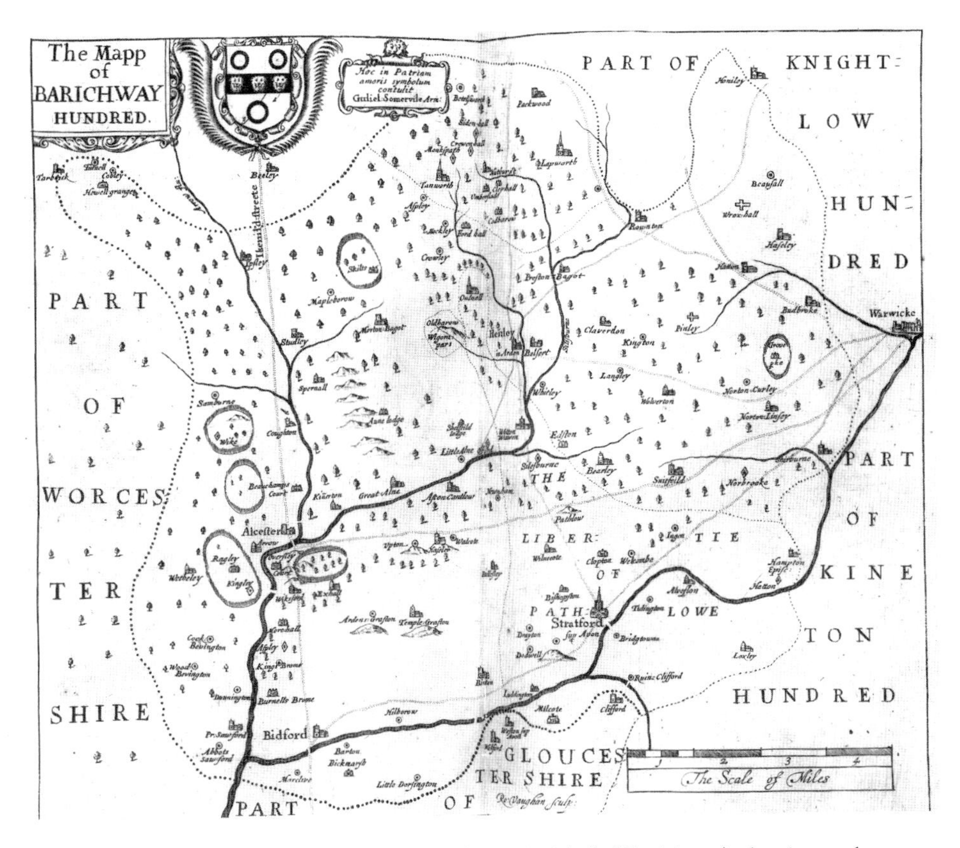

Fig. 3 Barlichway Hundred in Warwickshire (wrongly labelled Barichway), showing to the west of Stratford, Temple Grafton and Ardens Grafton, from William Dugdale, *The Antiquities of Warwickshire* (1656).

antiquity. Its name suggested a link with the Knights Templar, and its proximity to the 'Barlichway' enclosure denoted its equally ancient secular importance. Still better, shown on Dugdale's map as an adjacent hill, it was only a mile to the east of 'Ardens-Grafton', an even tinier hamlet, but one whose name linked it with Shakespeare's maternal ancestors and the mythic forest (Fig. 3). This was cider-apple country, and one of the few physical remains of any great antiquity is, at Ardens Grafton, 'an ancient CIDER MILL with apparently intact machinery'.[32] Arden/Eden in this period was particularly rich in orchards,[33] and young William, like his ancestor Adam, had tasted one apple too many.

The officiating clergyman was almost as picturesquely antiquated and rustic as the place itself. According to Whitgift's 1586 'Survey' of the ministry in Warwickshire, the clergyman at Temple Grafton was 'John Frith, vicar, an old priest and unsound in religion, he can neither preach nor read well, his chiefest trade is to cure hawks that are hurt or diseased, for which purpose many do usually repair to him'. Though not quite a 'hedge priest', Parson Frith was a bucolic character, much more interested in folk medicine than in religion, and evidently far too old to change his ways or to get his head round the Act of Uniformity. Many years later Shakespeare could make a joke out of a bad marriage solemnized by a 'dumb and unlearned' minister, and could even argue paradoxically for its practical advantages. The court jester Touchstone chooses Sir Oliver Martext to yoke him to Audrey:

> I am not in the mind but I were better to be married of him than of another, for he is not like to marry me well; and not being well married, it will be a good excuse for me hereafter to leave my wife.
>
> (*As You Like It*, 3.3.81–5)

Back in 1582, however, William is likely to have felt trapped. He and Anne went to live in the Henley Street house where the flock of young children expanded with alarming speed, for only nineteen months after the birth of Susanna in May 1583 came the boy and girl twins Hamnet and Judith in February 1585. Edmund, the youngest of Shakespeare's brothers, was still only five, and may in practice have blended with his nieces and nephew, so that the young father, who came of age only a couple of months after the birth of the twins, was responsible in all for four very young children. The fact that Edmund, like William, became a player, suggests a particularly close bond between the eldest and youngest brother.

LOST YEARS

If we think about the noise, bustle and grinding poverty of the Henley Street house during these years, in which the whole family of four adults and seven children lurched from crisis to crisis, we should not be at all surprised that the earliest part of Shakespeare's adult life is 'lost' from the documentary record. One of the very few things we know about Anne Shakespeare, née Hathaway, is that she fed her children herself. Indeed, in the epitaph written on her in 1623, probably by her distinguished son-in-law Dr John Hall, it is for this achievement alone that she is praised. But the reason was almost certainly not principle or maternal devotion, but the family's dire poverty. A family with some aspirations to gentility would in this period hope to employ a wet-nurse, but this seems to have been a luxury far beyond the young couple's means. Though some childish maidservant probably helped with the care of the babies and their laundry, Anne was obliged to feed them herself. She may even have attempted for a while to feed all three children, having maintained her lactation during the whole of her second pregnancy. In so doing, as we now know, she will have given them a considerable advantage in health terms, and it is striking that both Susanna and Judith were to be notably long-lived. But at the time, Anne's heroic labours appeared to be among the family's shameful makeshifts.

Perhaps William no longer helped his father prepare skins for gloving, but sought out some more financially rewarding activity. We may, if we believe Aubrey, imagine that 'he had been in his younger years a schoolmaster in the country'.[34] He could have worked as 'usher', or assistant master, in one of the many schools in the neighbourhood, or he could have been employed as a tutor in a private household. Either of these, had it amounted to much, would probably have left a trace in the records. At least one of his pupils would surely have boasted in later life that he had once been taught by the famous poet. But given the brevity of his own schooling, he would probably have been restricted to teaching 'petties', or children of pre-grammar-school age, educational work of rather low status. Perhaps he escaped from all those tiny children at home only to work with yet more in the schoolroom.

Malone's suggestion, strongly seconded by Fripp, that Shakespeare worked as a lawyer's clerk in Stratford, is also attractive. Such work was plentiful, and Shakespeare's undoubted skill in rapid reading and writing, at least in English, fully equipped him for it.[35] According to Fripp,

> There is little doubt that the poet on leaving school entered an attorney's office. It is not merely that, as has been often pointed out, his legal terms are legion, sometimes highly technical, frequently metaphorical, and often wrought into the very fibre of his writing, but, and this is much more convincing, *they flow from him unconsciously to the injury of his work.*

Fripp offers many examples of Shakespeare's use of legal terminology at moments of high tragedy or emotion, such as Romeo's description of his dying kiss of Juliet as the seal to 'A dateless bargain to engrossing death'.

Even more appealing is Fripp's specific suggestion that Shakespeare was working in the Town Clerk's office when the drowned body of the spinster Katherine Hamlett was disinterred, and an inquest held, on 11 February 1580. The coroner's conclusion was that her death by drowning in the Avon at Tiddington (about a mile from Stratford) on 17 December 1579, was '*per infortunium* [by accident] and not a case of *felo de se* [suicide] whereby she was entitled to Christian burial'.[36] Yet Shakespeare hardly needed to be in the Town Clerk's office in order to be fully aware of the sad story of Katherine Hamlett, for it must have been the talk of the town. And as Robert Bell Wheler pointed out, if Shakespeare had worked as an attorney's clerk he would quite often have been called upon to witness deeds or wills, yet much diligent search in the abundant local records has uncovered no such signatures.[37]

Fig. 4 *As You Like It*, 5.1: Touchstone (Anthony O'Dowell) interrogates William (Nick Holder), Royal Shakespeare Company (1992).

Shakespeare's deep familiarity with legal terminology may derive, rather, from his own practical determination to master this subject, which in this period was of vital importance for anyone who wished to make his way in the world.

Above all, I suspect, the years 1583–9 were domestic ones, dominated by the day-to-day needs and problems of parents, siblings, wife and children. So domestic were they that, once liberated from them, Shakespeare chose always to live independently in bachelor lodgings. Though he was in many ways faithful to Stratford, as we shall see, accumulating substantial property and business interests there over many years, he never again chose to live in the town for extended and continuous periods. The six months or so that he spent there when he was dying were of necessity rather than choice.

Warwickshire had been an excellent nursery for a player and a poet, but for a man of Shakespeare's abundant talents yet lowly fortunes it was also a dead-end. It is manifestly risky to treat plays as sources of personal information or reflection. Nevertheless, I think a backward gaze at Shakespeare's Stratford years may be discerned in a play already mentioned. *As You Like It* is one of the plays for which we have no performance history. However, we know that it was written by spring 1600.[38] It is generally assumed, partly because of the date, and partly because of Jaques's 'All the world's a stage' speech, that it was written for the newly opened Globe Theatre in the autumn of 1599. Alternatively or additionally, the play may have been performed for some disgruntled nobleman who presided over a lively and festive household well away from the court of the ageing and increasingly capricious Elizabeth. Essex, close friend of Shakespeare's known patron the Earl of Southampton, was in effect imprisoned in his own house, Essex House, during the early months of 1600. He certainly did commission a performance of another play by Shakespeare, *Richard II*, later that year. Another possibility is the affable Sir Fulke Greville of Beauchamps Court, who would certainly equate the ostensibly French 'Arden' with the mythic green place in Warwickshire.

But whatever the occasion of its earliest performance, this free-wheeling and relaxed comedy strikes me as Shakespeare's most explicitly personal play, with its celebration of the mythic Forest of Arden, its allusion to the (alleged) motto of the new Globe Theatre ('All the world's a stage'), and its two apparent references to the 'dead shepherd' Christopher Marlowe, whose violent death had been 'a great reckoning in a little room' (*As You Like It*, 3.3.11–12). Above all, I think, 5.1.17–59 can be read as a dialogue between Shakespeare's older and younger selves:

> Touchstone . . . How old are you friend?
> William Five and twenty sir.
> Touchstone A ripe age. Is thy name William?
> William William, sir.
> Touchstone A fair name. Was't born i'th' forest here?
> William Ay, sir, I thank God.
> Touchstone 'Thank God.' A good answer. Art rich?
> William Faith sir, so so.
> Touchstone 'So so' is good, very good, very excellent good. And yet it is not, it is but so so. Art thou wise?
> William Ay sir, I have a pretty wit.

The triumphant court comedian and companion to aristocrats that the playwright has now become interrogates, and patronizingly dismisses, the provincial clown that he once was, and might still have remained had he not transcended his 'so, so' fortunes by means of his 'pretty wit'. Each character possesses one of his names, the jester his surname, the yokel his Christian name, and both names have bawdy connotations. The name Touchstone closely mimics the name Shakespeare, for while the historical name suggests 'one who flashes a phallus', the fictional name in a bawdy sense suggests 'one who handles a testicle'. Both names, in true folk-humour style, evoke the gross bladders and clubs flaunted by mummers and maypole dancers. Shakespeare often used the word 'touch' (as a verb) with sexual connotations. The jester's rustic rival has no name but William, condescendingly praised by Touchstone as 'a fair name'. But in its diminutive Will it alludes popularly to sexual desire and/or sexual organs. Both characters are unlucky enough to be attached to the dim-witted but compliant Audrey, though William is perfectly willing to relinquish his claim on her, and Touchstone has no intention of staying with her long. Their dialogue can be read as an exchange between the wealthy and quick-witted playwright and the provincial youth he has left behind him in the Forest of Arden.

Even William's age, twenty-five, is plausible as a personal allusion. If taken literally it points to the likely year when the young Shakespeare left the Forest of Arden behind, and took his first steps towards metamorphosis into court comedian and entrepreneur, as 1589. Having served his unwanted seven-year apprenticeship to domesticity, he was more than ready to spread his wings. However, as I shall suggest in the next chapter, it's also possible that his career as a player had its origins a couple of years earlier.

CHAPTER TWO

1589–92

The Queen's Man

Yes trust them not: for there is an upstart Crow, beautified with our feathers, that with his *Tiger's heart wrapped in a Player's hide*, supposes he is as well able to bombast out a blank verse as the best of you: and being an absolute *Iohannes fac totum*, is in his own conceit the only Shake-scene in a country.

('Robert Greene', *Groats-worth of witte, bought with a million of Repentance*, 1592, sig. A3^v^)

Shakespeare's share

AFTER his re-written version of *The Murder of Gonzago* has been successful in 'outing' the guilty Claudius, Hamlet, in a state of high excitement, congratulates himself for his theatrical gifts. He playfully imagines himself no longer a Prince but making a good living as a paid sharer in a 'cry of players'. In place of his 'customary suit of solemn black', he sees himself sporting an elaborately feathery hat or helmet and flamboyantly adorned shoes:

HAMLET . . . Would not this, sir, and a forest of feathers, if the rest of my fortunes turn Turk with me, with Provincial roses on my razed shoes, get me a fellowship in a cry of players?
HORATIO Half a share.
HAMLET A whole one, I.

(*Hamlet*, 3.2.269–74)

I shall return later to the significance of feathers as one of the distinguishing accessories of the stage player. At this point I want to draw attention, rather, to what Hamlet's fantasy may tell us about the mixture of talents and skills that might qualify a young man to become a 'sharer' in an acting company. Hamlet has shown sophisticated expertise in theatrical directing, in his lengthy advice to the First Player. He has also revealed confident literary ability in dramatic writing, in his adaptation and expansion of *The Murder of Gonzago*, an old blank-verse tragedy, to make it more perfectly apt for its special court performance at Elsinore. However, despite being a discerning patron, writer and director, he has not as yet shown any particular talent for performing. Indeed, his chagrin at discovering that the First Player can express and communicate the anguish of the aged and long-dead Hecuba, while he cannot adequately mourn the death of his own father, underlines this point. Although, in truth, the role of Hamlet must always be given to a star performer, such as Burbage, the character within the play's fiction has not shown such obvious skill in professional acting as would qualify him for 'a fellowship in a cry of players' on those grounds. The possible means by which Shakespeare himself may have gained a share – or more probably, as in Horatio's put-down to Hamlet, a half-share – in a fellowship of players, and what ensued from that, is the subject of this chapter.

As Shakespeare's own English history plays were to show, one man's sudden death is very often the occasion of another man's sudden promotion. So it may perhaps have been for Shakespeare himself in the summer of 1587, which Mark Eccles described as 'The best year for plays at Stratford during Elizabeth's reign'.[1] Between December 1586 and December 1587 at least five companies of players visited the town, of which one, the Queen's Men, was especially handsomely rewarded. The Bailiff, Thomas Barber, gave them 20 shillings, 'the largest reward players had ever received at Stratford', says Eccles. Their performances must have been rumbustiously 'physical', for the town council also had to pay a carpenter 16 pence 'for mending of a form that was broken by the Queen's players'. This was presumably at 'the Bailiff's play', in the Guild Hall, which was the official preview before the Council gave their consent to more public inn-yard performances at the players' regular lodging, believed at this date to have been the Bear.[2] Perhaps they were performing one of their most celebrated pieces, *The Famous Victories of Henry V*, which would have helped to keep people's spirits up in anticipation of Spanish invasion. The entry in the Council *Minutes* makes it clear that it was the actors, and not the audience, who broke the 'form', or long bench. King Henry may have stood on it with 'his Lords' when he received the French Herald and declared war:

> Why then, with one voice and like true English hearts,
> With me throw up your caps, and for England
> Cry Saint *George*! and God and Saint *George* help us!
> *Strike Drums. Exeunt Omnes.*

This scene calls for a collective surge of martial excitement in anticipation of 'The Battle' – the Battle of Agincourt, no less. The prefatory apologies of the Chorus in the Folio version of Shakespeare's play –

> we shall much disgrace
> With four or five most vile and ragged foils
> Right ill-disposed, in brawl ridiculous
> The name of Agincourt

– suggests that the representation of that great victory of English archers over French cavalry must in all its versions have required some vigorous shouting, stamping, shaking of weapons and pre-battle pugnacity, in which a small number of players tried to compensate in noise and vigour for what they lacked in numbers. But young men whose aggression has been deliberately roused for entertainment may very easily break the artificial and invisible boundaries that separate performed violence from the real thing. In the absence of genuine Frenchmen, Turks or Spaniards, the players were apt all too often to turn either on bystanders or on each other. The well-known example of Ben Jonson's killing of a fellow actor, Gabriel Spencer, in a brawl in the summer of 1598 [3] should be seen in this context. From the start, the Queen's Men were particularly notorious for getting involved in violent affrays. This reputation may be one of the major reasons why in some towns they were paid handsomely 'not to play'.[4] In June 1583, in Norwich, two of the players pursued a member of the audience who had failed to pay, and someone, possibly the comic actor John Singer, struck the man a fatal blow on the head.[5] Warm summer weather, plentiful local beer, the gratification of audience applause and the excitement of being in a new environment – as Shakespeare's Hal was to say, 'Men are merriest when they are from home' – all contributed elements of explosiveness to the situation.

All these components were probably in place in Thame, in Oxfordshire, on the evening of 13 June 1587, when two of the Queen's Men's leading players fell to blows. William Knell pursued a fellow actor John Towne, threatening him with his sword, 'into a close called the White Hound'. Trapped on a mound, John Towne allegedly drew his own sword in self-defence and thrust it into William Knell's throat, wounding him fatally. For the next two months, therefore, the Queen's Men were seriously depleted, with Knell dead and Towne under arrest. Knell was so talented as to be still remembered and celebrated by

Fig. 5 The clown Richard Tarlton.

Thomas Nashe five years later, and by Heywood a quarter of a century later.[6] He is known to have played Henry in *The Famous Victories,* alongside Tarlton as Derrick, the Clown (Fig. 5). Towne was to be pardoned by the Queen on 15 August, when the coroner's jury accepted his plea of self-defence, but he was presumably not allowed to perform again until the inquest had sat.[7] Yet it is clear that the group of the Queen's Men that visited Thame continued to tour throughout 1587. A plausible route would be from Thame to Abingdon, then by way of Stratford to Leicester (after 16 July), reaching Coventry, where they played twice, in September. Eccles suggested that it was in Stratford itself that they recruited young William Shakespeare. This is an attractive notion. But the normal practice of the Queen's Men, according to Edmund Howes's account in the 1615 edition of Stowe's *Annales*, was to recruit the best players from existing companies under the patronage of 'divers great lords'. By so doing, they acquired players of well-established ability and experience. Companies sponsored by her leading courtiers provided the Queen with performers who had already shown their mettle, and who had gained experience in the variety of acting skills and quick changes of role that were required for the 'medley' style of play in which the company excelled.[8] When the Queen's Men were first created in 1583 three of its twelve members, Laneham, Wilson and Johnson, had been taken from among Leicester's Men. So perhaps it was from among Leicester's Men, again, that two promising new players, both Midlanders, were drafted in June or July 1587: John Heminge and William Shakespeare.

For John Heminge's eventual connection with the Queen's Men, and specifically with the late William Knell, there is powerful external evidence. He married Rebecca Knell, the young widow of the slaughtered actor, which either gave him a claim on Knell's share in the company, or consolidated his existing membership of it. The second possibility seems more probable, since it seems likely that he gained access to the young widow because he was already one of her late husband's fellows, or even his direct successor and recipient of his 'share'. Though it may have been initially a 'career' marriage, it appears to have been a happy one, producing thirteen children. Shakespeare's membership of the Queen's Men is suggested, rather, by the abundant evidence of his close and intimate knowledge of their plays, many of which he adapted or radically re-wrote in later years, most famously *King Leir*. There are other Queen's Men plays that he knew extremely well, adapting lines and catchphrases from them. There is also some reason, as we shall see, to think that he was actively involved in preparing and improving their texts.

Leicester's jesting player?

If Heminge and Shakespeare were for a time among Leicester's Men, their service may have been fairly brief. An exciting possibility is that they could have been part of that large group of Leicester's performers – musicians and acrobats, as well as actors – who went to the Netherlands in his train, and performed at Utrecht on St George's Day 1586. Neither name appears in the surviving billeting lists, but we know that these are incomplete, and in any case they relate only to 'gentlemen'. As will be discussed in chapter 4, neither man was a gentleman, though both, some years later, sought armigerous status. Alternatively, they may have been recruited to a new group of Leicester's Men pulled together after the Earl's inglorious and unhappy return from the Netherlands in November 1586. This was a deeply unhappy winter. In the Queen's eyes, at least, Leicester's expensive campaign had achieved nothing. The political and military failure of his mission was both exacerbated and symbolized in one distinguished casualty, Sir Philip Sidney, who had died of an infected leg wound at Arnhem on 17 October. Not only had Sidney been Leicester's heir and the most promising of Elizabeth's younger courtiers, he had also established himself as a generous and discerning literary patron. Though best known for his fostering of non-dramatic poets, such as Edmund Spenser and Abraham Fraunce, given time and means he would most probably have developed and expanded his uncle's interest in players.

One document may conceivably link Shakespeare both with Sidney and with Leicester's Men. This is Sidney's autograph letter to his father-in-law, Sir Francis Walsingham, written from Utrecht on 24 March 1586. By this date both Sidney and his uncle the Earl of Leicester had fallen into deep disgrace with the Queen because of Leicester's acceptance of the title of Governor-General of the rebel States in mid-January. His adoption of this semi-autonomous style was directly contrary to Elizabeth's instructions, according to which the word 'Deputy' should always be used. Sidney was acutely aware of the need to avoid aggravating the Queen's wrath further, 'considering how apt the Queen is to interpret every thing to my disadvantage', and was becoming anxiously paranoid about his own reputation at court – 'I understand I am called very ambitious and proud at home'. A few weeks earlier he had employed one of Leicester's players as a messenger, carrying some important and delicate letters over to London:

> I wrote to you a letter by William my Lord of Leicester's jesting player, enclosed in a letter to my wife, and I never had answer thereof. It contained something to* my Lord of Leicester, and counsel that some way might be taken to stay my Lady there. I since divers times have writ to know whether you had received them, but you never answered me that point. I since find that the knave delivered the letters to my Lady of Leicester, but whether she sent them you or no I know not, but earnestly desire to do, because I doubt** there is more interpreted thereof.[9]

When under stress, as he very often was, Sidney was apt to fly into a rage with servants, secretaries and letter-bearers. The most celebrated instance of this is

* 'to': probably in the sense of 'concerning'.
** 'doubt': fear.

his terse letter to one of his father's secretaries, Edmund Molyneux, in 1578, concluding with the sharp words:

> I assure you before God, that if ever I know you do so much as read any letter I write to my father, without his commandment, or my consent, I will thrust my dagger into you. And trust to it, for I speak it in earnest.[10]

In this later instance, he blames 'William my Lord of Leicester's jesting player' for failing to deliver a packet of letters to his wife, Frances, née Walsingham, as instructed, but handing them over instead to Sidney's aunt, Lady Leicester, the former Lettice Knollys.[11] This was, indeed, something of a disaster, for one of the letters concerned Lettice herself, who had been threatening to come over to the Netherlands with a splendid train of court ladies to participate in her husband's incessant round of banquets and junketings. As Sidney well realized, such a display of expensive courtierly triumph would have provoked Elizabeth's extremest displeasure. Instead of directing an economically restricted sequence of defensive military manoeuvres, the Earl and Countess of Leicester would have been seen to flaunt themselves as virtually King and Queen of the anti-Hapsburg states. If that letter-bearing 'knave' ever returned to the Netherlands, he could expect to face the full and violent force of Sidney's wrath. But who was the unfortunate 'William'? The prevailing verdict in the later twentieth century has been that he was William Kempe, the celebrated clown, dancer and stunt-man, who was undoubtedly to become a seasoned foot-traveller in later years, dancing his way from London to Norwich in only nine days (Fig. 6).[12] Certainly 'Mr. Kemp, called Don Gulihelmo', was in Dunkirk in November 1585, perhaps as part of Leicester's retinue.[13] But Kempe would surely have been one of the company's star performers. Since Leicester was planning to make St George's Day, 23 April 1586, a time when he would try to match his Dutch hosts in competitive feasting, Kempe might not have been readily spared for a journey to England in February or March, for fear that his return might be delayed. Also, he seems normally to have been referred to as 'Kempe' or 'Will Kempe', not as 'William'. A more junior recruit to Leicester's Men, highly literate and notably quick-witted, might seem a good choice for a letter-bearing errand – good partly because of his disposability. As Mark Antony says of Lepidus, 'This is a slight unmeritable man, / Meet to be sent on errands' (*Julius Caesar*, 4.1.12–13). Of course, Sidney's phrase 'jesting player' suggests 'jester', and Shakespeare was to be a 'straight' actor, not a comic or clown. Yet early references, such as Chettle's praise of his 'facetious* grace in writing',[14] single out Shakespeare's playful and spontaneous wit. Also, the word

*facetious: joking.

Fig. 6 The clown and dancer Will Kempe, from *Kemps nine daies wonder* (1600).

'comedian' is often used at this period as a synonym for 'a player in general, a stage-player' (*OED* 1a). In his bitter and angry mood, Sidney could have viewed many of his uncle's expensive and frivolous troupe as comedians or 'jesting players', this one's blunder being a joke too far. If Shakespeare was among the contingent of Leicester's Men who went over to the Netherlands, he may have impressed his masters as an intelligent and useful all-rounder, rather than as someone whose specialized talents, like Kempe's, made him indispensable to the company's performances.

Definite proof that Sidney's blundering messenger was William Shakespeare is lacking. Possibly the messenger was, after all, William Kempe, especially since jesters and tumblers seem to have been thought of as suitable letter-bearers. Shakespeare himself alludes to this practice in making the clown Peter, once referred to in a speech prefix in the second Quarto (Q2) of *Romeo and Juliet* as 'Kempe', deliver invitations to the Capulet ball. And Sidney's brother Robert employed the Queen's Men's celebrated tumbler, John Symons, to carry love gifts to a lady of the Privy Chamber in 1595.[15] Or he may have been some third William, neither Shakespeare nor Kempe, and otherwise unknown.

Sidney can at least be firmly connected with another celebrated 'jesting player' among the Queen's Men, Richard Tarlton, to whose infant son he stood godfather in 1582. For little Philip Tarlton, as for so many others, Sidney's death was an unmitigated disaster, depriving him of much needed support and protection. On the point of death, in August 1588, Tarlton wrote desperately to Sir Francis Walsingham of his anxiety about his six-year-old son, 'a godson of Sir Philip Sidney, whose name he carries',[16] fearful that his interests will not be protected by his guardian, 'a sly fellow, Master Adams, fuller of law than of virtue'. Like Heminge and Shakespeare, Tarlton was a West Midlander. As mentioned in chapter 1, he had apparently been talent-spotted by a servant of the Earl of Leicester while keeping swine and delighted him with his 'happy unhappy answers'. If this is right, he, too, served a short apprenticeship with Leicester's Men in 1582–3 before being creamed off for the Queen's. It may have been because of his employment by his uncle that Sidney knew him. His posthumous fame, powerful throughout the 1590s, is probably alluded to in 'Yorick', the dead royal jester so much loved by Hamlet. Shakespeare may have played alongside Tarlton as 'Dericke' in *The Famous Victories*.

Sir Fulke Greville's man?

John Heminge and William Shakespeare, versatile young men with a modicum of education, required a somewhat different route to preferment from Tarlton's witty swine-herding. My conjecture is that the earliest patron of both men may have been the affable and generous Sir Fulke Greville of Beauchamps Court, father of Sidney's close friend of the same name. Beauchamps Court was a couple of miles north of Alcester, and a dozen miles west of Stratford. The elder Greville had little direct contact with London or the court, but lived in considerable style in the Midlands, enjoying hawking, hunting and bear-baiting. According to a seventeenth-century history of the family he always maintained 'a brave company of gentlemen'.[17] A major landowner in Worcestershire and Warwickshire, whose ambition to become master of Warwick Castle was eventually realized by his poetical son, the elder Greville was deeply involved in local affairs. From 1591 to 1606, for instance, he was the Recorder of Stratford-upon-Avon. For many years previously he had been a regular visitor to the town. One visit that could have included an encounter with the young married man William Shakespeare took place in April 1583, when he and Sir George Digby of Coleshill[18] were entertained with sack and claret at the Bear.[19] Though not a university man himself, Greville took a keen interest in the education of younger men, sending his own son to be educated with Philip Sidney at Shrewsbury School. A distinctive feature of Thomas Ashton's curriculum at Shrewsbury was that every Thursday was a half-day, and boys in the top class had to 'declaim and play one act of a comedy' before dispersing for the afternoon.[20] By the time Shakespeare got to grammar school a decade later, Greville may have encouraged other Midland grammar schools to imitate Ashton's highly praised method. As little boys at grammar school, both Shakespeare and Heminge could have watched older boys perform, joining with them in preparations for the great public performances that took place at Whitsuntide. As they moved a little way up the school they, too, got a chance to act and declaim. Perhaps it was as performers in Christmas or Whitsuntide plays that both were spotted by Greville. For a while, these young men may have been fortunate enough to wear the 'yellow worsted in fashion in Warwickshire, and worn by Sir Fulke Greville's retainers'.[21]

The first steps of Shakespeare's route towards 'a fellowship in a cry of players' may have been taken during his training in declamatory and acting skills at Stratford Grammar School. He would have had opportunities to display those skills to large audiences in Whitsuntide plays in Stratford in the early 1580s. As a result of such seasonal performances, he perhaps came to the notice of Sir Fulke Greville of Beauchamps Court, and for a couple of years served him in some capacity, probably as a player, possibly also as a clerk or secretary. Greville was very closely allied to the Dudleys,[22] and his large retinue would be a natural source of recruitment for his powerful friend Robert Dudley, Earl of Leicester. As a member of Leicester's Men for some time between 1584 and 1586, Shakespeare would have quickly showed his versatility both in writing and in performing. He would be a natural choice to supply one of the gaps left in the Queen's Men by Knell's death in June 1587. Both he and Heminge acquired part-shares only, as must have been the case with many of the Queen's Men. McMillin and Maclean have shown in *The Queen's Men* that virtually all their plays required fourteen performers, and that for most of the year the company was divided into two groups travelling in different areas. Yet the recorded members of the Queen's payroll number only twelve. There must in practice have been more than twice as many players as the bare twelve who are listed as receiving the Queen's subsidy, with many holding part-shares only. The rest of this chapter will be based on the supposition that from about 1588 Shakespeare was indeed a Queen's Man.

THE QUEEN'S MAN

The late 1580s was the Queen's Men's most flourishing period, in terms of performance and income. Most of their plays that survive reached print between 1590 and 1595. 1594 alone saw the publication or registration of five out

Fig. 7 Londoners fleeing the plague, 1630.

of the small repertoire of nine plays accepted by McMillin and Maclean as definitely theirs, and a further five out of the thirteen attributed to the Queen's Men by other scholars. There may be good reasons why it was in the year 1594 that so many of their plays reached print. The Queen's Men's plays were relatively unfamiliar in London, since their main activity was touring. The extremely severe plague outbreak of 1593, followed by a moderately severe one in the spring of 1594, caused repeated closure of the public theatres in London. This in turn created an excellent marketing opportunity for owners of play-texts. Among the large number of Londoners who flocked to the public theatres when they were open the more monied and literate could be expected to turn, as consolation when the theatres were closed, to the purchase of printed plays, and especially of plays that they had never had a chance to see, and which had perhaps reached the end of their performing life. More will be said in the next chapter about printed literature during the plague years 1593–4. Here, however, I would like to look in some detail at the Queen's Men themselves, and at Shakespeare's contact with them.

Above all, the Queen's was a touring company, or rather, a group whose nucleus of a dozen royal servants generated two, or even three, touring companies. Even if he was with the group only for a couple of years, Shakespeare would have gained a greatly enlarged experience of English country towns and of great men's houses. It used to be thought that touring was a sign of weakness, and that playing companies toured the provinces only when times were hard, whether because of plague in London, strong competition or the lack of a permanent theatre. This notion derived partly from a misreading of a passage in Thomas Nashe's preface to Robert Greene's *Menaphon* (1589):

> Sundry other sweet gentlemen I do know, that have vaunted their pens in private devices, and tricked up a company of taffeta fools with their feathers, whose beauty if our poets had not pieced with the supply of their periwigs, they might have anticked it until this time up and down the country with the King of Fairies, and dined every day at the pease pottage ordinary with Delfrigus.[23]

This has often been taken as evidence that university dramatists, such as Greene – 'Delfrigus' is believed to figure in a lost Greene play – delivered playing companies from the hazards of touring 'up and down the country'. However, in context, I believe that Nashe (a Cambridge graduate, born in Lowestoft in 1567) is distinguishing profitable touring from unprofitable: companies such as the Queen's Men, with some very old-fashioned plays in their repertoire, have recently enjoyed great success and rich financial reward – splendid feathers in their hats, to use Nashe's headgear image – because of the excellent new plays written for them by 'sweet gentlemen'. Nashe probably has Greene, Peele, Marlowe and himself in mind.[24] The players have been in danger of thin pickings, of eating daily at 'the pease pottage ordinary' – the humblest artisan's hostelry. Instead, university-educated gentlemen – analogous to Hamlet, that witty alumnus of the University of Wittenberg – have provided them with original and inventive material. Thanks to these sweet gentlemen, they have been well paid and well fed, like the players at Elsinore, on Hamlet's orders: 'Good my lord, will you see the players well bestowed? Do you hear, let them be well used, for they are the abstract and brief chronicles of the time' (*Hamlet*, 2.2.518–20). Fine feathers have made them fine birds. As McMillin and Maclean show,[25] the Queen's Men, in particular, enjoyed very handsome rewards both from civic authorities and local noblemen, and from entry fees. Far from being a desperate measure adopted as an alternative to performance in a theatre in London, for the Queen's Men, touring 'up and down the country' was their normal mode of operation, and often an extremely lucrative one.

There was a deeper purpose in these long journeys. The Queen's players could reach parts of her realm that the monarch herself would never visit. Their mobility was remarkable. In 1589, the year after the dispersal of the Spanish Armada, one contingent played in Dublin, and another in Edinburgh. Their arrival in red royal liveries connected provincial communities with the Queen and her court, strengthening popular loyalty by offering festive entertainment in her name. Clowning was always prominent in their performances, and the combination of comic anarchy with local officialdom sometimes caused problems. In *Pierce Pennilesse* (1592) Nashe describes the pomposity of a provincial magistrate who was stupid enough to think that the Queen's servants should not be laughed at:

> he was one, that having a play presented before him and his township by Tarlton and the rest of his fellows, her Majesty's servants, and they were now entering into their first merriment (as they call it), the people began exceedingly to laugh, when Tarlton first peeped out his head. Whereat the Justice, not a little moved, and seeing with his becks and nods he could not make them cease, he went with his staff, and beat them round about unmercifully on the bare pates, in that they, being but farmers and poor country hinds, would presume to laugh at the Queen's Men, and make no more account of her cloth in his presence.[26]

Nashe's phrase 'their first merriment (as they call it)' draws attention to the deliberately variegated, 'medley' style of the Queen's Men's plays, in which the pill of patriotism was generously sugared with the sweetmeats of mirth, music and foolery. Yet another passage in Nashe suggests the way in which the Queen's players could communicate, through mirth, with men who were left cold by her preachers. In *Summer's Last Will and Testament*, written for Archbishop Whitgift in 1592, the jester Will Summers appeals for laughter rather than explicit moralizing, and cites the example of a linguistically challenged Welshman:

> Hur come to Powl* (as the Welshman sayes) and hur pay an halfepenny for hur seat, and hur heare the Preacher talge, and a talge very well, by gis; but yet a cannot make hur laugh: goe æ Theater, and heare a Queenes Fice,** and he make hur laugh, and laugh hur belly-full.[27]

Audience members felt their halfpennies well spent for the comic scenes in the Queen's Men's plays. Sometimes political elements were incorporated in the comic scenes themselves, as in their mockery of 'Martin Marprelate', which was itself a response to the Marprelate authors' use of 'Tarltonizing' techniques of ridicule in their satirical tracts against Elizabeth's bishops. But the company's involvement in ecclesiastical controversy seems to have been the beginning of its decline. In pushing mirth too far in the direction of contemporary satire they were over-playing their hand. Richard Dutton has suggested that the Privy Council were anxious about the company's adoption of such targets without the explicit authority of the Master of the Revels.[28] In their surviving plays as printed, however, the political message is characteristically simple, insular and jingoistic. Patriotic chronicles like *The Famous Victories* and *The*

* 'Powl': St Paul's Cathedral.
** 'Fice': Vice; very probably Tarlton once more.

Troublesome Raigne of John King of England were designed to fire up loyal hearts, preparing provincial yeomen to be willing recruits when troops were being mustered. Though King John was unquestionably, as in *1066 and All That*, a Bad Thing, his defiance of the authority of the Pope shows him to be a proto-Anglican and enemy of the corrupt religious orders:

> I'll rouse the lazy lubbers from their cells,
> And in despite I'll send them to the Pope.

John's reign, like that of Richard III, is a crooked path that leads to England's greater glory under the Tudors, as is shown in the Bastard's speech at the coronation of young Henry:

> Let England live but true within it self,
> And all the world can never wrong her state . . .
> If England's peers and people join in one,
> Nor Pope, nor France, nor Spain can do them wrong.

With the shining exception of Henry V, most of the kings who figure in the Queen's Men's plays are thoroughly Bad Things, whether they are scheming Machiavels from England's recent past, like Richard III, self-gratifying monarchs from legendary British antiquity, like Locrine or Leir, or savage Oriental tyrants like Selimus. The plays offer simple messages of either 'it couldn't happen here', or 'it couldn't happen now'. In contrast to such highly coloured spectacles of civil war, treachery and gratuitous cruelty in high places Elizabeth's reign can be celebrated as supremely peaceful, and she as supremely merciful. Just in case the more dim-witted among the audience fail to grasp this message, a final speech or epilogue, as in *The Troublesome Raigne*, spelt it out. What McMillin and Maclean call the 'overdetermined literalism' of Queen's Men plays was part and parcel of their propaganda function. *The True Tragedy of Richard the third*, on which Shakespeare's play is closely modelled, ends with a quick history lesson, in prose, which is quite unashamedly 'an abstract or brief chronicle of the time'. On reaching 'Worthy Elizabeth' the speech rises into rhapsodic verse in praise of her blessed and peaceful reign and her divinely appointed mission to 'put proud Antichrist to flight'. The audience is told exactly what to think and exactly what to do:

> Then England kneel upon thy hairy knee,
> And thank that God that still provides for thee.

All their hopes, all their welfare, are in Elizabeth's hands:

> For if her Grace's days be brought to end,
> Your hope is gone, on whom did peace depend.

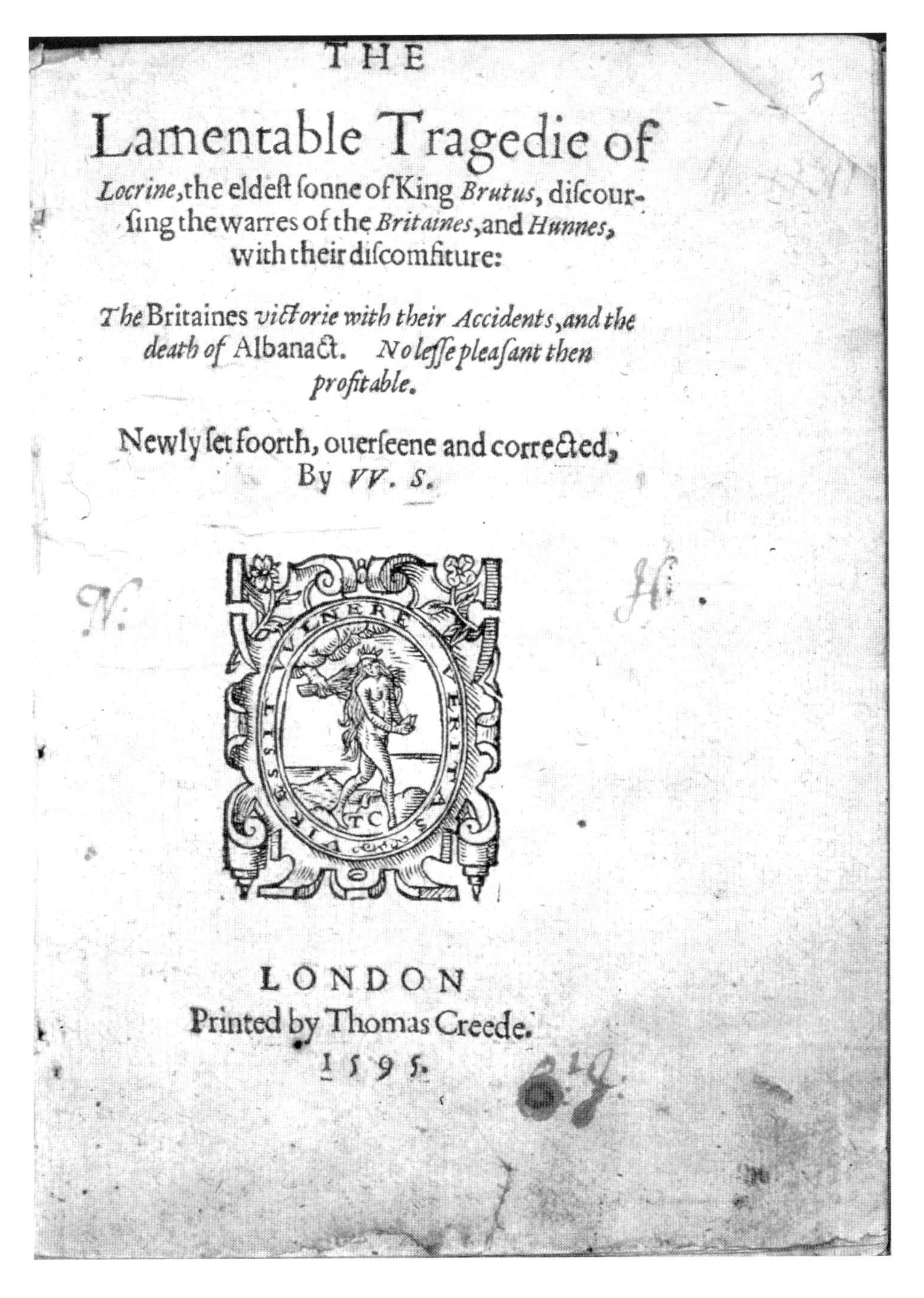

THE

Lamentable Tragedie of

Locrine, the eldeſt ſonne of King *Brutus*, diſcourſing the warres of the *Britaines*, and *Hunnes*, with their diſcomfiture:

The Britaines *victorie with their Accidents, and the death of* Albanact. *No leſſe pleaſant then profitable.*

Newly ſet foorth, ouerſeene and corrected, By *VV. S.*

LONDON
Printed by Thomas Creede.
1595.

Fig. 8 Title-page of the play *Locrine* (1595).

The arresting image of England's 'hairy knee' alludes to the prevailing maleness and rusticity of the audience.[29] The play's rhetoric is designed to fire up the courage of potential soldiers, who when required to do so will fight valiantly against Elizabeth's enemies. And provincial England's knees are 'hairy' also because they are cased in good woollen breeches, not in the impractical, and imported, silk worn by courtiers.

An even more laboured speech closes *Locrine*, in which Ate, the god of strife, paradoxically eulogizes peace:

> So let us pray for that renowned maid,
> That eight and thirty years the sceptre swayed,
> In quiet peace and sweet felicity;
> And every wight that seeks her grace's smart,
> Would that this sword were pierced in his heart.

W. S. THE OVERSEER

It is *Locrine*, printed by Thomas Creede in 1595, that gives us the best indication of the nature of Shakespeare's work with the Queen's Men, for it is described on the title-page as 'Newly set foorth, overseene and corrected, By *W. S.*' (Fig. 8). Though the Third Folio's inclusion of it among Shakespeare's own plays must be erroneous, there is no good reason to doubt that he was indeed the 'overseer' of the text. The many eager readers who were buying *Venus and Adonis* (1593), already in its second or third edition, and *Lucrece* (1594), will readily have guessed 'W. S.' to be that same 'William Shakespeare' who signed the confidently worded dedications of those poems to the young Earl of Southampton. Such a link would be a good selling point for what is, in truth, a fairly undistinguished 'medley' play. None of the other printed Queen's Men plays mentions 'overseers', which points either to something special about this one, or else to some extra effort to market it. It has been plausibly suggested that a man called Charles Tilney was the author or part-author of *Locrine*. A couple of years after his death, the Queen's Men may have decided to include it among the clutch of their plays that were sold to the printer Thomas Creede in the plague years 1594–5,[30] with Creede's payment shared between the declining company and their former fellow and text-improver W. S. The play was entered in the Stationers' Register on 20 July 1594, so W. S.'s editorial task was finished by that date. The work of tidying the text and copying it out for the press may have taken no more than a week or two of his 'idle hours', in contrast to his concentrated labours over the grave and weighty *Lucrece*, entered in the Register two months earlier. As printed, the play reads as if the man who wrote it had read a good deal more deeply in the ancients than had the man who prepared it for the press. Such spellings as 'Atey', for 'Ate', 'Polyphlemus', 'Anthropomphagie', 'Puriflegiton', suggest copy prepared by a man with little or no Greek.

If *Locrine* was a Queen's Men play, and Shakespeare the man who bombasted up its blank verse for the press, we can to some extent reconstruct the nature of his work while he was a full-time member of the company in the late 1580s. As a young man of exceptional quickness whose 'hand and brain', as Heminge and Condell were to testify, went together with great 'easiness', he perhaps fulfilled the offices of book-keeper and stage-keeper. His book-keeping job was to prepare the master copy of each play to be performed, and also to pen the 'parts', with cues, to be conned by individual actors. His stage-keeping job was to direct performances to ensure that performers were ready on cue, that all physical action, including dumb shows, was correctly performed, and perhaps to act as prompter. On occasion he also played major roles, such as those once played by William Knell. His superb verbal memory enabled him to understudy anyone. And in addition to all this he was, like Prince Hamlet, adept in mending, altering and radically re-modelling old plays. He transformed the Queen's Men's *King John* and their *Richard III*, and probably their *Felix and Felismena*,[31] so fully that they became brilliant new works, triumphantly liberated from that 'overdetermined literalism' that had made them suitable only for rustic out-of-town audiences. No wonder he was soon to be attacked as Mr Do-it-all.

The upstart Crow

Schoenbaum entitled the tenth chapter of his *Documentary Life* 'The Upstart Crow'. The phrase figured in the dying Greene's (supposed) attack on Shakespeare in 1592, whch Schoenbaum described as 'the first unmistakable reference to Shakespeare in London'.[32] I shall work back from this passage in *Greene's Groats-worth of Wit*, quoted at the head of this chapter, and explore circumstantial evidence that Shakespeare, while a Queen's Man, may have excited envious excitement among rival playwrights in London as early as 1589.

Both Thomas Nashe and Henry Chettle went out of their way to deny authorship of the passage describing Shakespeare as an 'upstart Crow'. However, the one thing that can be firmly agreed on is that the prolific poet and playwright Robert Greene himself had little or nothing to do with it. Just as the dead, in law, cannot be libelled, so the dead cannot themselves be punished for uttering libel. The safety of death made it possible to libel both Greene himself, and, as if from his dying lips, others. Numerous writers in the immediate aftermath of the 'fatal banquet of Rhenish wine and pickled herring' [33] that supposedly killed Greene found it extremely convenient to elaborate the myth, initiated by the man himself when alive, of Robert Greene's prodigal life and penitent end, attributing to him remarkably voluminous and often abusive utterances to and about those who survived him. Since his death also took place during a severe plague epidemic – which indeed, rather than pickled herring, may have been the immediate cause of his death – the opportunity to make money by fictionalizing, moralizing and quarrelling about the circumstances of his death was a golden one for those who normally made a living from the public theatres, closed for most of 1592–3. Printers of Greene's writings had once been delighted to 'pay him dear' for 'the very dregs of his wit'.[34] Equivalent sums were now available to anyone quick witted and plausible enough to produce posthumous or apocryphal 'Greene' works. Several recent scholars have identified the printer-poet Henry Chettle as the chief author or re-writer of the *Groats-worth*.[35] Yet Thomas Nashe is by far the stronger suspect, at least as far as the 'upstart Crow' passage is concerned. Chettle may indeed, as he acknowledged, have acted as scribe in preparing the copy of *Groats-worth* for the printer from a rather disparate collection of papers in several hands, and he may also have written or revised or tidied up some sections of it in Greene's loose and sentimental style. And some of the poems, such as 'Lamilia's song', do read like Greene at his lyrical best. But there is good reason to think that the passage referring to Shakespeare and other writers, the epistle supposedly penned by Greene *To those Gentlemen his Quondam acquaintance that spend their wits in making plays*, is the work of Nashe. For one thing, it is a memorably brilliant piece of writing – glancing, allusive, learned, and double-edged in a manner beyond the reach of the journeyman Chettle. Nashe was already well experienced in writing satirical and controversial pamphlets carefully concealed under pseudonyms, from his work for Archbishop Whitgift in answering the (also pseudonymous) Marprelate tracts in 1588–9. He had also shown a particular bent for literary satire, for the first book that he published under his own name, *The Anatomie of Absurditie* (dedicated to Charles Blount, Lord Mountjoy, early in 1598), is largely composed of an onslaught on bad love poets among his contemporaries, along with some savage sideswipes at the frivolity of women which were perhaps ill-judged for the taste of Mountjoy, lover of Penelope Rich, 'Stella' to the dead Sidney's 'Astrophil'. Some years before the *Groats-worth*, then, Nashe had already shown his mettle as an exceptionally versatile prose satirist, and he had also learned to dodge counter-attacks by pseudonymous concealment and – if necessary – flat denial.

In an epistle prefaced to the second edition of *Pierce Pennilesse* to be published in 1592 Nashe explicitly denied having any part in the *Groats-worth*, calling it 'a scald trivial lying pamphlet'. Many modern scholars have taken this denial at face value, perhaps misled by the fact that the dying Greene is made to criticize Nashe himself as a talented 'young juvenal' who is making enemies by satirizing people too indiscriminately. Yet in the next sentence but one of the *Pierce Pennilesse* epistle Nashe seems half to confess that he did indeed have a hand, if not in *Groats-worth*, then in works very much like it: 'I am grown at length to see into the vanity of the world more than ever I did, and now I condemn myself for nothing so much, as playing the dolt in print.' Indeed, it seems as if Nashe is here adopting Greene's own posture of repentant prodigal, and is half confessing that though his present, penitent, self did not have any part in the composition of *Groats-worth*, a former self, which he now labels 'dolt', may have done. Certainly Nashe boasted, in one of his earliest attacks on the Cambridge academic Gabriel Harvey, that Greene had been his very good friend, and that he knew very much more than Harvey did about Greene's personal circumstances. Not only had he drunk deep with Greene at Cambridge, where 'in one year [Greene] pissed as much against the walls as thou and thy two brothers spent in three', he was with him in London near the end:

> I and one of my fellows, *Will. Monox* (Hast thou never heard of him and his great dagger?) were in company with him a month before he died, at that fatal banquet of Rhenish wine and pickled herring.[36]

One of the most celebrated terms of vituperation used against Shakespeare in the 'upstart Crow' passage is, I think, a giveaway. That 'upstart Crow, beautified with our feathers' is described also as 'an absolute *Iohannes fac totum*'. As the italicization indicates, this is a somewhat learned phrase, sanctified in its citation by one of Nashe's favourite writers, Erasmus. It is a term of abuse occurring in various forms, such as *Magister factotum*, or *Dominus factotum*, or, in Italian, '*fa il tutto*', meaning 'Mr Do-it-all', or 'a Jack of all trades, master of none', or, as *OED* has it, 'a would-be universal genius'. Those who used the phrase tended to be university men, such as Timothy Kendall, of Oxford and Staple Inn, who in his *Flowers of Epigrammes* (1577) applied it to a man of overweening pride:

> Thy mounting mind doth still aspire,
> thou still dost boast and crack:
> And Leonel thou wouldest be
> *Magister totum fac* . . .[37]

The learned author of the influential libel on Elizabeth's favourite, *Leicester's Commonwealth* (1584), declared that 'Throughout all England my Lord of Leicester is taken for *Dominus factotum*.' Most of those major literary figures of the period who had not been to university, such as Shakespeare himself, never used the phrase. Even Ben Jonson, that grand master of learned vituperation, used it only once, very late in his career.[38] Nashe, however, used it conspicuously on two occasions in works published under his own name. In *The Unfortunate Traveller* when Jack Wilton's mistress, the Venetian courtesan Diamante, is appointed as his gaoler, Wilton remarks, 'My courtesan is left my keeper, the keys are committed unto her, she is mistress *fac totum*.'[39] Seven years later, in *Nashes Lenten Stuffe . . . the praise of the Red Herring* (1599), he refers to the red herring, or kipper, that has made Yarmouth such a wealthy town as 'this old *Ticklecob*, or *Magister fac totum*'.[40]

There are other parallels between the epistle *To those Gentlemen his Quondam acquaintance* and Nashe's attested writing. In particular, *The Unfortunate Traveller*, written by June 1593, though not published until early 1594, displayed Nashe's skill in writing admonitions to the living placed in the mouth of the dying. The murderer and rapist Cutwolfe, on the point of execution and dismemberment, delivers an 'insulting oration' which functions like a villain's closing speech in a tragedy. Cutwolfe narrates his atrocious villainies and finally claims, with brilliant subversiveness, that

> Revenge is the glory of arms and the highest performance of valour; revenge is whatsoever we call law or justice. The further we wade in revenge, the nearer come we to the throne of the almighty . . .[41]

The device of having a dying man utter sentiments that in the mouth of the living would be held seditious, blasphemous or slanderous is common to *The Unfortunate Traveller* and the epistle in *Groats-worth*. Also, Jack Wilton's pithy conclusion, 'Unsearchable is the book of our destinies',[42] closely parallels the Biblical sentence in the epistle in *Groats-worth*, '*Quam inscrutabilia sunt Dei iudicia*'.[43] I believe that not only was it Nashe, rather than Chettle or Greene, who wrote the famous address *To those Gentlemen his Quondam acquaintance*, but that he was returning, as was his wont, to a previous target. Nashe became notorious for his tenacious and repeated onslaughts on the learned Cambridge academic Gabriel Harvey – a quarrel that took root in the dead body of Greene, for it all started with Harvey's attempts to rebut Greene's libel on Harvey and his two brothers in his *Quip for an upstart Courtier*. This later, much more prolonged and conspicuous controversy, finally brought to an end by the 'Bishops' Ban' on all the works of Nashe and Harvey in 1599, may have veiled the fact that Nashe had also baited and taunted the unlearned Midland playwright William Shakespeare. Nashe's onslaughts were, however, something of a compliment, since the provincial grammar-school dropout possessed a natural wit so brilliant and versatile that he threatened to outstrip the university-educated Marlowe, Peele, Greene and Nashe.

As for the nature of the attack itself, its chief thrust is against the over-weening pride of a provincial non-graduate who has the temerity to write plays as well as to act in them. Atheist Marlowe and satirist Nashe are Cambridge men, and their almost equally talented colleague George Peele is from Christ Church, Oxford. All three should – allegedly – learn from graduate Greene's unhappy end not to depend in future on 'so mean a stay' as the playing companies. Things now look bleak for these university-educated gentlemen, for those 'puppets' – professional players – who until recently used to speak lines written for them and to wear costumes for parts invented for them by university men are now turning to the brilliant work of that 'upstart Crow beautified with our feathers'. Feathery hats or head-dresses were a major distinguishing mark of the player. Hamlet, in the passage quoted at the beginning of this chapter, tells Horatio that he is now qualified to be an actor himself: 'Would not this, sir, and a forest of feathers . . . get me a fellowship in a cry of players?' (*Hamlet*, 3.2.269–72). The upstart Shakespeare successfully flaunts 'our' feathers – that is, he performs parts composed by Greene, Marlowe, Nashe and Peele – and yet displays a savagely ungrateful ambition. One of his own most celebrated lines, from York's rhetorical onslaught on Queen Margaret in *3 Henry VI*, 1.4.111–49, is turned against him. For Shakespeare's 'O tiger's heart wrapp'd in a woman's hide' Nashe substitutes '*Tiger's heart wrapped in a Player's hide*'. The well-known Biblical image that underlies both York's speech, addressed to the 'She-wolf of France, but worse than wolves of France', and the line in *Groats-worth*, is that of the wolf in sheep's clothing (Matthew, 7.15). D. Allen Carroll has suggested that, as used by Greene himself in *Mamillia* (1580), the image carried a covert allusion to that group of the Queen's Men led by John Laneham, whose surname suggests 'Wool Am' (from Latin *lana* or French *laine* = wool).[44] If an analogous allusion is present also in *Groats-worth*, it seems far more likely to to be the work of the ingenious Nashe than the humdrum Chettle.

A more direct allusion to the Queen's Men can be discovered in the final words of the epistle: 'yet whilst you may, seek you better masters; for it is pity men of such rare wits should be subject to the pleasure of such rude grooms'. As Chambers (*Shakespeare*) and others have pointed out, the Queen's Men from 1583 'were sworn the Queen's servants, and were all allowed wages and liveries as grooms of the chamber'. Despite being on the Queen's payroll, however, these performers were but 'rude' – unlettered, ill-educated, as well as ill-mannered. Their most famous member was the clownish and now dead Tarlton. The associates of such rude clowns should not, in a just world, be permitted to triumph over such learned gentlemen as Greene, Marlowe, Nashe and Peele.

What has been most often discussed in the passage is its implication that Shakespeare was a plagiarist, and that his literary plagiarism has killed Greene, rather as a review in the *Quarterly* allegedly killed John Keats. This implication may indeed be present. Mr Do-it-all believes he can write blank verse 'as well as . . . the best of you', and he may believe this partly because he is a re-writer or close imitator of other men's work. However, I think the primary emphasis is on 'Shake-scene', or Shakespeare, as a mere 'player', who wears borrowed robes and speaks borrowed words, and is neither a gentleman nor a graduate, but an 'upstart'. Like 'factotum', 'upstart' is a word Nashe often liked to use,[45] and the word was to be particularly associated with his kind of satire, as in the subtitle of the seventeenth-century satire *Tom Nashe his Ghost, To the three scurvy Fellowes of the upstart Family of the Scufflers, Rufflers and Shufflers.* Instead of sticking to acting, this 'upstart' has turned his untutored talent to writing, and believes himself to be already England's paramount stage-keeper–player–poet – he 'is in his own conceit the only Shake-scene in a country'.

Hamlets or handfuls

Nashe's earliest published attacks on Shakespeare may have occurred in his signed epistle 'To the Gentlemen Students of Both Universities' which was prefaced to his drinking and pissing companion Greene's romance *Menaphon*. *Menaphon* is, in truth, an absurd, second-rate and second-hand piece of writing, which mimics some superficial features of Sidney's *Arcadia* (incestuous entanglements) and some of John Lyly's *Euphues* (zoological similes), while offering, with no discernible sense of the ridiculous, a desert-island fantasy in which a disguised woman is wooed simultaneously by her father, her husband and her son. Nashe must have been perfectly well aware – given his own deep devotion to the poetry of Spenser, which set a standard that Greene could never approach – that Greene's romance was little more than popular trash. Yet as his friend and sometime drinking-companion, he felt obliged to do him what favour he could and, in any case, it gave him a chance to sound off in the forefront of what was bound to be a very popular publication. Avoiding any detailed reference to *Menaphon* – indeed, it is not clear whether he had actually read it – he decided to focus above all on the fact that the romance is the work of a university man, a Master of Arts, as if that in itself were justification enough. He praises *Menaphon* as 'University entertainment', also turning to its supposed advantage the fact that it is a piece of literary hackwork, written at great speed and with considerable nonchalance. Like most of Nashe's encomia, his praise of *Menaphon* comes close to being a mock-encomium or send-up. He displays great ingenuity in finding a rhetorical strategy which enables him to praise to the skies, and at some length, a work that both he and most of his readers must have known to be shallow and trivial. But Nashe's agenda is never uncomplicated, nor does he stay long with any particular point. Though *Menaphon* is a prose romance interspersed with songs, Nashe shifts rapidly to the topic of drama, claiming that only university men, like himself or Greene, are qualified either to use classical mythology or to write blank verse. Nashe's glancing allusion to 'the alchemists of eloquence, who (mounted on the stage of arrogance) think to out-brave better pens with the swelling bombast of bragging blank-verse' could be read as including the player–poet Shakespeare within a broad attack on the swelling tyrant plays of the late 1580s. Here as elsewhere, Nashe seems to imply that only those fully trained in the classical hexameter have the technical mastery required for English blank verse. Yet nothing at this stage seems to point more specifically to Shakespeare than to other non-university playwrights as his target. The passage that most closely parallels the epistle in *Groats-worth* occurs four pages later, when Nashe turns his attention to playwrights who, though almost wholly without learning, have the audacity to imitate Seneca. Here we find an earlier version of the 'Mr Do-it-all' insult in *Groats-worth*, this time combined with a suggestion that mere grammar-school boys should not attempt to write tragedies:

> It is a common practice nowadays mongst a sort* of shifting companions, that run through every art and thrive by none, to leave the trade of *Noverint*, whereto they were born, and busy themselves with the endeavours of art, that could scarcely Latinize their neck verse if they should have need; yet English Seneca read by candle-light yields many good sentences, as, *Blood is a beggar* and so forth; and if you intreat him fair in a frosty morning, he will afford you whole Hamlets, I should say handfuls, of tragical speeches.[46]

Traditionally this passage used to be read as an exclusive reference to the playwright and translator Thomas Kyd, especially because of the allusions soon after to 'the Kid in *Aesop*' (though really in Spenser's *Shepheardes Calender*) and to translations from Italian. But as R. B. McKerrow, Nashe's editor, pointed out, though Kyd's father was indeed a scrivener, he belonged to a considerably higher class of scribe than those dismissed by Nashe as '*Noverint* makers', being described in the registration of Kyd's birth as writer of 'a court hand'. '*Noverint* makers' were the most mechanical rank of lawyers' clerks, whose job was to copy out endless writs which began with the formula '*Noverint universi* . . .', or 'Know ye all by this present . . .'. I think that some allusion to Kyd may indeed be present in the passage from which the above is an extract, but that another member of the 'sort of shifting companions' referred to is Shakespeare – not, of course, the son of a scrivener, but, as the grammar-school-educated son of a barely literate Warwickshire yeoman, a man who should never aspire further than the rank of lawyer's clerk. Neither Shakespeare nor Kyd, Nashe may be implying, had any business to be writing

* 'sort': crew, gang.

tragedies that 'smell of the lamp' ('English Seneca read by candle-light'), since they had not been to university. The calculated slip of the pen, 'whole Hamlets, I should say handfuls', is very startling, and indicates the existence by 1589 of some early version of *Hamlet*, perhaps penned by Shakespeare, Kyd and others, that was more pretentiously Senecan than the ones we have, and much closer to the mannered rhetoric of Kyd's *Spanish Tragedy*. That such a version existed, most scholars agree; and increasingly they suspect that Shakespeare himself was among its authors or adapters. The writers of these tragedies were 'shifting companions' both in the sense that they could 'make shift' – use a variety of strategies or resources to get a living – and in the sense that they would, as travelling players, 'shift' from place to place, driven by economic necessity. This, as we have seen, was the plight of the Queen's Men at the end of the 1580s, after their too close involvement in the Marprelate controversy.

The value of the spectacle

How did it come about that, as early as 1589, Shakespeare had managed to excite the envy of Nashe, and possibly also of Greene and others? The full answer may lie buried somewhere in that early, lost, tragedy of *Hamlet*. But two plays that do survive may provide some clues. The first is Nashe's single publicly attested work of literary collaboration, *The Tragedie of Dido, Queene of Carthage*. Many twentieth-century scholars, uncomfortable with the notion of collaboration despite ample evidence that it was normal practice in this period, have minimized Nashe's part in this play. Yet there is no reason to doubt that it is, indeed, the work of both writers.[47] By the time it was printed, in 1594, Marlowe was dead, which is perhaps why his name is placed first on the title-page. Nashe was very much alive, and would have been quick to protest if either attribution were incorrect. It may have been Nashe himself who prepared and sold the text to the printers. The play's dating is problematic, but it most probably belongs to the earliest period in which both Marlowe and Nashe, fresh from Cambridge, were together in London. Marlowe had left under a cloud, Nashe desperately short of money: both were determined to make lucrative theatrical capital out of their classical learning. Virgil's *Aeneid* is the play's only literary source, and it includes many passages closely modelled on the original. However, in some places the authors take great liberties. Some of these consist of embroideries required for the purposes of theatrical presentation, such as the Jupiter–Ganymede induction, and the love interest between Anna and Iarbas. Others are gratuitously sensational. One such sensational addition occurs in the long opening scene of Act 2, otherwise closely based on *Aeneid*, 2, in which Aeneas tells Dido about the fall of Troy. In the famous passage in which Hecuba witnesses the killing of her husband Priam the Greek Pyrrhus manifests his contempt for the pleas of the old Trojan king by chopping off his hands:

> Not mov'd at all, but smiling at his tears,
> This butcher, whilst his hands were yet held up,
> Treading upon his breast, struck off his hands . . .
> (*Dido*, 2.1.239–41)

The extreme brutality of this recalls some of the more revolting passages in *The Unfortunate Traveller*. And as in *The Unfortunate Traveller*, it gets worse. The distraught Hecuba, in a surreal and impossible manoeuvre, keeps her husband alive 'in his eyelids hanging by the nails', and Priam briefly revives and tries to grapple with his murderer, 'Forgetting both his want of strength and hands' (ibid., 251). This black joke, again, seems extremely characteristic of Nashe.

If Marlowe and Nashe achieved early success with a tragedy of Rome's origins, Shakespeare, in emulation, went ten better. *Titus Andronicus*, a play set at the opposite end of Rome's history, shows its great empire collapsing into moral and political anarchy. It features spectacular scenes of amputation, both off stage and in one case, Titus's foolish offer of his own right hand to Aaron the Moor (3.2), on stage. In what is performed, rather than narrated, Nashe and Marlowe's *Dido* is a gentle tragedy of the African queen whose claim on Aeneas must be rejected in favour of the Tuscan Lavinia, the destined first Queen of Rome: Shakespeare's savage melodrama shows a Lavinia who, dismembered, raped and voiceless, provides a terrible symbol of Rome's end. *Titus* can be viewed as in several ways a counterpart or reply to *Dido*. But the way in which it most clearly answers and trumps *Dido* is in being a piece of genuinely popular entertainment. *Dido* was, as the title-page of the printed edition proclaims, performed by the Children of the Queen's Chapel. *Titus* was written for performance by a large cast of men and boys, and by the time it was printed for the second time its title-page proclaimed that it had been performed by four different companies, Pembroke's, Derby's, Sussex's and the Lord Chamberlain's. It was both popular and lucrative, and continued to be so, undergoing repeated performance and revision for up to thirty years. One of the earliest likely allusions to *Titus* occurs in what is undoubtedly a Queen's Men's play, *The Troublesome Raigne of John King of England*. On the point of death, King John chronicles his misdeeds in a speech which includes the lines:

> How, what, when, where, have I bestowed a day
> That tended not to some notorious ill . . .

Fig. 9 Drawing by Henry Peacham of a scene from *Titus Andronicus*.

If *Titus* belongs to the period 1588–9, being written immediately after Nashe and Marlowe's *Dido*, the lines must be indebted, as J. C. Maxwell has pointed out, to Aaron the Moor's analogous confession in *Titus*:

> Even now I curse the day – and yet, I think
> Few come within the compass of my curse –
> Wherein I did not some notorious ill . . .
>
> (5.1.125–7)

It is possible, though, that the influence went the other way, and that Shakespeare, now with Pembroke's Men, was recalling lines from one of the plays he had worked with for the Queen's.

Titus was celebrated both early and late. Jonson went out of his way to scoff at its continued popularity in the Induction to *Bartholomew Fair* (1614). His pairing of it with Kyd's *Spanish Tragedy* (later played under the title *Hieronimo*, or *Hieronimo's Mad Again*) may also testify to a period when Shakespeare and Kyd were known to have worked together, or in parallel, producing 'Senecan' plays that were annoyingly durable in public esteem:

> He that will swear, *Jeronimo*, or *Andronicus* are the best plays, yet, shall pass unexcepted at, here, as a man whose judgement shows it is constant, and has stood still, these five and twenty, or thirty years.

Jonson may not have known the exact year when either of these plays was originally written, but his correction of 'five and twenty' to a rounded-up 'thirty' carries them, if taken literally, into the mid-1580s – making 1588–9 very plausible, allowing for some exaggeration on Jonson's part. *Titus* was so popular as to be alluded to early on in other plays in the confidence that audiences would pick up the reference. In the very popular *A Knack to Know a Knave*, which starred Edward Alleyn as King Edgar and Will Kempe as the Clown, a character called Osrick draws a sustained analogy which only those who had recently seen *Titus* could understand:

> My gracious Lord, as welcome shall you be . . .
> As *Titus* was unto the Roman Senators,
> When he had made a conquest on the Goths . . .
> As they in *Titus*, we in your Grace still find,
> The perfect figure of a princely mind.

The first act of *Titus*, in which Titus returns to Rome as the conqueror of the Goths, seems to have made a huge impression on early audiences. A scene from it, in which Tamora pleads for the life of her two sons, inspired the only early illustration of a Shakespeare play, the well-known drawing done by Henry Peacham (Fig. 9).[48] Unusually, too, we have evidence that *Titus* was performed in aristocratic households, as we know from Sir John Harington of Exton's commissioning it for performance at Burley-on-the Hill in January 1596.[49] Jaques Petit's remark that 'the spectacle had more value than the theme' may reflect the broad reason for this play's enormous popularity – the opportunities it offered for visual spectacle and pageantry, rather than its disturbing and confusing subject matter. Though deficient in clowning, *Titus* still retains elements of the Queen's Men's 'medley' style. The stage direction governing Titus's first entrance in Q2 indicates, in its amplitude, how spectacular this should be, with plenty of music and a large cast:

> *Sound drums and trumpets, and then enter two of* Titus' Sons, *and then two men bearing a coffin covered with black, then two other* Sons, *then* Titus Andronicus, *and then* Tamora, *the Queen of Goths, and her sons,* Chiron *and* Demetrius, *with* Aaron *the Moor, and others as many as can be. Then set down the coffin and* Titus *speaks.*

A minimum of eleven actors is required for this entrance, in addition to musicians, in splendid and exotic costumes – and notice that phrase 'as many as can be', suggesting that even more extras costumed as captive Goths would improve the pageantry. It may have been this opening scene, with its ritual display of military triumph, that above all ensured the play's spectacular popularity in the years immediately following the defeat, or dispersal, of the Spanish Armada in the autumn of 1588. But it was another episode, a little later in the play, that provoked the still envious Nashe to further mockery of Shakespeare. I shall have more to say about this in the next chapter.

CHAPTER THREE

1592–4

Plague and poetry

Brightness falls from the air,
Queens have died young and fair,
Dust hath closed Helen's eye.
I am sick, I must die:
Lord, have mercy on us.

(Nashe, *Summers Last Will and Testament*, performed 1592)

Why should the private pleasure of some one
Become the public plague of many moe?

(*The Rape of Lucrece*, 1594, 1478–9)

Brightness falls from the air

Plague was a defining context for all Shakespeare's writing, but above all for his non-dramatic writing. When plague deaths rose above thirty a week in London[1] the civic authorities closed the public theatres. Those who normally made a living from them had to diversify or starve. Though curiously absent from Renaissance drama and poetry as an explicit topic,[2] plague hovers menacingly in its margins, sometimes in ways that a modern audience may scarcely notice. In *Romeo and Juliet*, for instance, it is plague that operates as the stars' controlling agent in crossing the lovers' hopes of happiness, hopes that seemed so near to fulfilment. Mercutio's dying cries of

'A plague on both your houses' are more than empty expletives. Friar Lawrence's vital letter to Romeo telling him about the device by which Juliet has taken a long-acting sleeping potion fails to arrive. The letter-bearers, Friar John and a companion, never get to Romeo in Mantua, but remain under house-arrest in Verona:

> ... the searchers of the town,
> Suspecting that we both were in a house
> Where the infectious pestilence did reign,
> Seal'd up the doors and would not let us forth ...
> (5.2.8–11)

Shutting up houses which were thought to have been 'visited' by plague was a standard procedure, both in medieval Italy and, later, in Tudor London.[3] Great cruelties were committed in the name of public health, but we do not hear much about them from poets or dramatists. The crazy soldier William Reynolds, who hung about the city streets scattering letters and petitions during the 1592–4 epidemics, bears witness to the terrible sufferings caused by this practice:

> there has been such ungodly and uncharitable severity used in the time of this your plague, that women and others has perished by your strict courses for want of relief and tendance, and a woman of mine own knowledge being sick and great with child (ready to be delivered) travailed in great anguish, and both she and her child died having no help of man or woman. O you dogs, O you devils and damned spirits, void of humanity and natural compassion ... O villainous villains that lock up the sick in outrageous manner, not regarding to visit them as their necessity requires.[4]

From 1518 [5] the front doors of infected houses in London were conspicuously marked with a poster-sized paper, which in 1592–3 was painted with a large red circle within which was written the desperate prayer 'LORD HAVE MERCY UPON US'. Nashe used this as the refrain of his best-known poem, written during the 1592–3 plague. James Joyce wanted to rationalize the line 'Brightness falls from the air' to 'Brightness falls from the hair'. But this reflects a misunderstanding of how plague was believed to strike. It was thought to descend from the air above, destroying all in its path, as a direct and immediate punishment sent down from the planets for what William Reynolds repeatedly refers to as the 'sodomitical sins' of city-dwellers. In a typically brilliant elision, Nashe's line envisages 'brightness' as struck down from above by the descending vapours, pursuing it like a host of avenging angels. The belief that infection rained down, in a literal and physical sense, 'from the air' is one that Shakespeare develops in one of his most extended images of plague. It occurs – appropriately, as we shall see – in the only play which takes the role of the courtly patron as its central focus. The embittered Timon of Athens, hating the great city that has proved so ungrateful to him, tells Alcibiades to destroy it:

> Go on.
> Be as a planetary plague, when Jove
> Will o'er some high-vic'd city hang his poison
> In the sick air.
>
> (*Timon of Athens*, 4.3.109–12) [6]

When plague descended upon the 'high-vic'd city' of London towards the end of 1592, redoubling its force in the summer of 1593, it fell as a severe blow to many ambitious young writers who had recently embarked on careers as dramatists. Losing the increasingly lucrative 'public means' (sonnets, 111.4) of support that the playing companies had provided, they looked instead towards aristocratic patrons.

There is a twofold connection between plague and literary patronage, for there were two main ways in which aristocratic patrons could protect writers from the effects of plague. On their country estates they could offer writers physical refuge from filthy lodgings in the densely populated city; and they could reward them financially for non-dramatic writing. Two among the young play-makers who sought aristocratic patronage in the plague years 1592–4 were Nashe and Shakespeare, and it is in these years that competition between them became most intense. Nashe was ever a weathercock, and seems to have oscillated between generous admiration of the Midlander's talents and intense and bitter jealousy. In *Pierce Pennilesse* he offered one of the earliest and warmest tributes to Shakespeare, whose work provides a vital supporting plank in his sustained '*defence of Playes*'. In a passage supposedly devoted to the evils of Sloth, Nashe praises plays for being neither slothful nor corrupting, but virtuous and uplifting – indeed, the best possible occupation for the leisurely afternoon hours. Above all, he praises historical plays: 'wherein our forefathers' valiant acts (that have lien long buried in rusty brass and worm-eaten books) are revived, and they themselves raised from the grave of oblivion'.[7] The key example he presents of inspired patriotic drama is taken from the play now known as Shakespeare's *1 Henry VI*:

> How would it have joyed brave Talbot (the terror of the French) to think that after he had lien two hundred years in his tomb, he should triumph again on the stage, and have his bones new embalmed with the tears of ten thousand spectators at least (at several times), who, in the tragedian that represents his person, imagine they behold him fresh bleeding.

It has been claimed that Nashe did not realize that Shakespeare was the author, or chief author, of this play, but praised it simply from his own experience as a theatregoer. More recently, however, it has been suggested that Nashe had actually collaborated with Shakespeare in writing it, and this seems to me more likely.[8] I am inclined to think that Nashe knew very well indeed that Shakespeare was the main writer, and that at the time when he wrote this passage it suited his purposes to celebrate the extraordinary and versatile gifts – his own and Shakespeare's, as well as those of Marlowe, Greene and Peele, and of such actors as Knell, Tarlton and Alleyn – that had recently combined to raise the status of popular drama, while bringing in huge crowds and rich financial rewards. For a year or so, both Nashe and Shakespeare enjoyed the intelligent and generous patronage of Ferdinando Stanley, Lord Strange, later Earl of Derby.

The earliest recorded performance of 'harey the vi' was by Strange's Men, at Philip Henslowe's Rose Theatre on 3 March 1591/2.[9] Henslowe marked the reference in his *Diary* with his mysterious 'ne', meaning that the play may have been new, or newly revised, or new to Strange's Men. Nashe's reference to 'ten thousand spectators . . . at several times' suggests a popular piece, often revived because it could always be relied upon to attract a good house. *Henslowe's Diary* records that it was performed again only four days later, bringing Henslowe an almost equally large sum, £3, as compared with £3 16*s.* 8*d.* at the earlier performance. It received ten further performances until the theatre was closed because of plague after 22 June 1592. Whether or not the play, or an earlier version of it, had been written and performed some time earlier than March 1592, it is probably to its spectacular run at the Rose that Nashe alludes, looking back on it from some distance both in time and place. While writing *Pierce Pennilesse*, published in the late summer of 1592, he was lodged with 'my Lord', being, as he says in 'A private Epistle of the Author to the Printer', 'the plague's prisoner in the country'.[10] *Pierce* is a work that has direct and obvious connections with London's plague epidemic, being a graphic though disorderly account of the gross vices that have, supposedly, brought down plague on the citizens. However, Nashe's '*defence of Playes*', an apparent digression, may be in truth the work's nucleus, designed to encourage Lord Strange, and perhaps also Archbishop Whitgift, to continue their generous support of players in private locations that were unaffected by the plague orders. The celebration of plays and players is the foremost of the 'variable delights', or agreeable digressions, promised on the title-page.

During the same summer, and also for Ferdinando Stanley, Nashe wrote his brilliant pornographic poem 'The choice of valentines', later labelled 'Nashe's dildo'. This deals with urban vice in a very different way, describing the visit of 'Thomalin' to a charming and well-dressed young prostitute, Frances, now to be found in a 'house of venery' in Upper Ground Street on the South Bank of the Thames, just by the public theatres. In this work, too, Nashe may be looking back on London life and London pleasures in the spring and summer of 1592, before plague emptied the city. Here there is no hint of disease, whether plague or syphilis. The problem is, rather, human, or male, impotence, which symbolizes the transience of all earthly delight. Like Marlowe's Doctor Faustus on the point of damnation, Nashe's persona Thomalin prays desperately, and unsuccessfully, for the prolongation of earthly and erotic pleasure:

> Stay, stay sweet joy, and leave me not forlorn,
> Why shouldst thou fade, that art but newly born?
> Stay but an hour, an hour is not so much;
> But half an hour, if that thy haste be such:
> Nay, but a quarter; I will ask no more . . .
> He hears me not, hard-hearted as he is,
> He is the son of time, and hates my bliss.[11]

The inspiration both for Nashe's passage and Marlowe's is in Ovid's *Amores*, 1.13, and had already been drawn on by them in *Dido, Queen of Carthage*. The 'right Honorable the lord S.' to whom the poem is dedicated in a preliminary sonnet is certainly Lord Strange, for he is described both as a poet,[12] and as the 'fairest bud the red rose ever bare', alluding to the red rose of Lancaster borne by the Stanley family, which also happened to be the emblem of the Rose Theatre, lately so thronged and successful.

FAIR PHOEBUS LEAD ME

While Nashe was writing pornography for Lord Strange, Shakespeare was initiating relations with a younger and even more promising 'Lord S.', Henry Wriothesley, Earl of Southampton. He may have had some preliminary contact with the young lordling in the summer of 1592, when he was eighteen, rising nineteen. Certainly the tone of his dedicatory epistle to *Venus and Adonis*, modest and deferential though it is, suggests that Southampton may have some acquaintance with the poem's author. While Nashe was sheltering from the summer plague in the north-west, in one of Lord Strange's great houses there, Knowsley or Lathom, Shakespeare may have spent some time with Southampton at Titchfield in Hampshire. The period within which *Venus and Adonis* was brought to completion is between June 1592, when the London theatres were closed because of plague, and 18 April 1593, when the poem was entered in the Stationers' Register by Shakespeare's Stratford school-fellow Richard Field. As we shall see, this was not a case of a patron being selected, or substituted, at the last minute. The poem's subject matter and treatment were carefully chosen for their suitability to the position and interests of its

VENVS
AND ADONIS

Vilia miretur vulgus: mihi flauus Apollo
Pocula Caſtalia plena miniſtret aqua.

LONDON
Imprinted by Richard Field, and are to be ſold at
the ſigne of the white Greyhound in
Paules Church-yard.
1593.

Fig. 10 Title-page of *Venus and Adonis* (1593).

dedicatee. The poet probably set his sights on his young patron soon after the closure of the theatres. Although Shakespeare's exceptional fluency in writing is witnessed both in his own early plays and in the testimony of Jonson, Heminge and Condell, there is every reason to think that *Venus and Adonis* was the product of unusually careful and studied labour. It may have taken a considerable time to perfect, perhaps between six and ten months, the end-product being the most concentrated and meticulous composition of Shakespeare's whole career. While Nashe had presented Ferdinando Stanley with two wildly exuberant products of his 'extemporal vein', *Pierce Pennilesse* and 'The choice of valentines', what Shakespeare offered to Southampton was a sophisticated poem that was both deeply pondered and carefully polished. The title-page epigraph suggests as much:

> *Vilia miretur vulgus: mihi flavus Apollo*
> *Pocula Castalia plena ministret aqua.*

It derives from Ovid's *Amores,* 1.15, translated by Marlowe as

> Let base-conceited wits admire vile things,
> Fair Phoebus lead me to the Muses' springs.

The first three words, *Vilia miretur vulgus*, could be more bluntly translated as 'Let the crowd gawp at common shows'. While Nashe looked back to the theatrical triumphs of 1592 with nostalgic admiration, Shakespeare here coolly repudiates them. His Talbot and King Henry may have lately drawn the sweaty multitude to the theatre, but his Muse is now of a higher strain. Taking a subject from classical mythology, he prays for fresh inspiration from the clear Castalian fountains presided over by golden-haired Apollo. But his own name does not appear on the title-page. It was not yet a selling point. As a playwright, Shakespeare was well used to having his works identified by title and subject matter only. Even as a 'sharer' in the Queen's and Strange's Men – and possibly Pembroke's – his name was not recorded, and yet, as we saw in chapter 2, there is little doubt of his membership. So it may have come naturally to omit his name from the title-page of *Venus and Adonis.* Nashe, too, had used an Ovidian epigraph on the title-page of *Pierce Pennilesse*, '*Barbaria grandis habet nihil*', from *Amores*, 3.74, translated by Marlowe as 'Now poverty great barbarism we hold'. Perhaps both Nashe and Shakespeare were drawn to the *Amores* by the work of their friend Marlowe, who translated the whole collection. But Nashe saw to it that his authorship was clearly displayed, the book being 'Written by *Tho. Nash*, Gent.'. Those last four letters could not as yet be placed after the name 'William Shakespeare', and this may have been an additional reason for not putting his name at the forefront of the book. Nevertheless, he trumped Nashe – and, indeed, all those of his contemporaries who pursued courtly patrons – with his epistle to Southampton, intimate in tone, and signed off 'Your honour's in all duty, / William Shakespeare'. While Nashe had concluded the sonnet in which he dedicated 'The choice of valentines' to Lord Strange with the vague promise that 'better lines ere long shall honour thee', Shakespeare's promise is far more confident and purposeful in tone:

> . . . only, if your honour seem but pleased, I account myself highly praised; and vow to take advantage of all idle hours, till I have honoured you with some graver labour.

We should pause for a moment to consider that phrase 'idle hours'. It implies both that Shakespeare had some regular business and occupation, even in time of plague, and that he expected Southampton to be aware of this. Not all his hours are 'idle' ones. He does not claim here, as his speaker was to do in sonnet 57.3–4, that

> I have no precious time at all to spend,
> Nor services to do, till you require . . .

Perhaps the allusion is just to the everyday 'business' of getting and spending, litigation and investment, keeping affairs in order both in Stratford and in London. No doubt such affairs did indeed take up a certain amount of time. But the reference may also be to the most pressing business of getting a fresh repertoire of plays written or revised in readiness for the re-opening of the theatres, whensoever that might happen, and whether under the patronage of Strange or Southampton or Pembroke. The 'idle hours' to be devoted to composing a second, 'graver', poem for Southampton had to be snatched from hours spent preparing play-texts, as reviser, scribe and poet.

The poem's central theme, like the title-page epigraph, has roots in Ovid. In that sense it was fresh and accessible to the young Southampton, for the *Metamorphoses* was one of the pleasanter texts that every schoolboy was required to study. There is no doubt that Southampton had been well tutored in Latin at Cecil House in the Strand, under the close eye of tutors hired by Lord Burghley. But Shakespeare extracts only one segment of Ovid's account of Venus and Adonis. He entirely omits Adonis's conception – the fruit of father-daughter incest – and birth – his pregnant mother is metamorphosed into a tree, causing severe obstetric problems. Shakespeare's 'Rose-cheek'd Adonis' simply rides 'to the chase' from nowhere. He materializes as suddenly in that mysterious forest as do the knights in Spenser's *Faerie Queene*, or the older romances on which Spenser drew. Somewhere off stage, as we learn seven hundred lines later, Adonis has 'friends' who are waiting for him, but they are wholly unidentified. All that Shakespeare builds on in Ovid are the accounts of Venus loving Adonis, and trying, unsuccessfully, to persuade him not to risk his life by hunting dangerous prey; Adonis being killed by the boar; Venus's grief; and Adonis's metamorphosis into a flower. He makes one highly original and radical alteration to the myth as treated by Ovid and other classical writers, an alteration that is the key to the poem's success. Whereas in the sources Adonis is a handsome young man, with whom Venus enjoys a fully consummated, though too brief, love affair, Shakespeare's Adonis is a child, perhaps not yet advanced into puberty. In a single movement Venus 'pluck[s] him from his horse' (30), and a later line refers to his 'hairless face' (487). When he finally escapes from her clutches he seems like a little boy who needs a nurse to hold his hand: 'And now 'tis dark, and going I shall fall' (719). Early readers, familiar with Ovid's account, must have pressed on and on, perhaps sexually excited by the strangely long delay of an expected consummation, for Shakespeare's treatment of Venus's wooing is both physical and titillating, only to discover that Adonis, rumpled, flustered and increasingly petulant, continues to resist Venus's 'sweating lust' (794) and 'wanton talk' (809). The poem's exceptional and well-deserved popularity derives from this strange dynamic. While the reader is increasingly enchanted and fascinated by Venus's brilliantly agile rhetoric and promise of magic tricks:

> 'Bid me discourse, I will enchant thine ear,
> Or like a fairy trip upon the green,
> Or like a nymph, with long dishevell'd hair,
> Dance on the sands, and yet no footing seen . . .'
>
> (145–8)

Adonis remains quite unmoved. If anything, he is increasingly irritated by her persistence. William Reynolds, the first recorded reader of the poem, noticed this, although he may only have leafed through the opening pages of the book, perhaps in John Harrison's shop 'at the sign of the White Greyhound':

> within these few days there is another book made of Venus and Adonis wherein the Queen represents the person of Venus, which Queen is in great love (forsooth) with Adonis, and greatly desires to kiss him, and she woos him most entirely, telling him although she be old, yet she is lusty fresh & moist, full of love and life (I believe a good ell more than a bushel full) and she can trip it as light as a fairy nymph upon the sands and her footsteps not seen, and much ado with red and white. But Adonis regarded her not, wherefore she condemns him for unkindness; those books are mingled with other stuff to dazzle the matter.[13]

For Reynolds, a born-again Puritan who had apocalyptic visions of England as the scourge of Catholic Antichrist and King Philip's *cavalieros* (he had been to the West Indies with Drake in 1585), the poem was manifestly about himself. Puritan Adonis rejects the lascivious advances of Venus–Elizabeth, just as

Reynolds in an earlier letter had rejected what he saw as the Queen's ingenious attempts to lure him into her presence: 'By God I swear, I have heard many say you are a merry wench and a very pleasant gentlewoman . . . And for love, why you are Venus herself, even a god of love.'

Probably the bookseller's patience ran out, and Reynolds was unable to read to the end and discover that Adonis dies and is metamorphosed into a flower. Reynolds was wrong in describing the poem, on 21 September, as published 'within these few days', for an elderly teller of the Exchequer, Richard Stonley, had bought a copy for 6*d*. on 12 June.[14] It was an uncharacteristic purchase. Other books he bought in 1593 include two sermons by Henry Smith, anti-Catholic works by Richard Bancroft and Thomas Bell, and Hooker's *Lawes of Ecclesiastical Polity*.[15] While Reynolds read the book, but did not buy it, Stonley bought the poem, but possibly did not read it. He was attracted to it by its dedication, for Southampton's guardian, Lord Burghley, was, as Lord Treasurer, Stonley's boss. He is unlikely to have shared Shakespeare's empathy with Venus's eloquent desire, for he was fond of such misogynistic maxims as 'Be thou not moved with the weeping words of the wife when she is angry, for a woman when she weepeth goeth about with her tears to work deceit'.[16] Nevertheless, his habit of buying brand-new books and punctiliously recording his purchases is useful. It tells us that *Venus* was on sale by 12 June, and at the price of 6*d*. Perhaps its publication day, appropriately for such a hot, midsummery poem, was 11 June, the longest day of the year, Spenser's 'Barnabe the bright'.

Adonis, Narcissus, Southampton

For Southampton, as for Reynolds, *Venus and Adonis* had evident personal connotations. It would not be difficult for him to discover some reflection of himself in Shakespeare's portrait of Adonis, 'the fairest flower of all the field' – perhaps a punning reference also to the poem's printer, Richard Field. Like Adonis, the orphaned Southampton was just on the brink of manhood. He too may have been barely into puberty, for in September 1592, when he was present at the Queen's visit to Oxford, he was described as almost smooth cheeked.[17] In the poem, Venus's appeals to the need for procreation are slightly comic, for it is clear that the last thing she really has in mind is having babies, and in any case Adonis himself is still a child:

> 'Torches are made to light, jewels to wear,
> Dainties to taste, fresh beauty for the use,
> Herbs for their smell, and sappy plants to bear:
> Things growing to themselves are growth's abuse.

> Seeds spring from seeds, and beauty breedeth beauty;
> Thou wast begot, to get it is thy duty . . .'
>
> (163–8)

Yet passages like this could well have been approved of by Southampton's advisers and guardians, as reinforcements to their own attempts to get him suitably matched. Young though he was, Southampton was already under extremely strong pressure to marry, the proposed bride being Burghley's granddaughter, Elizabeth Vere. This project began when the young Earl was only sixteen. Another poet, John Clapham, had already used Ovidian poetry to tempt or cajole him. Clapham was one of Burghley's secretaries, and was later to write both a history of Elizabeth's reign and a biography of Burghley. His Latin poem *Narcissus*, published in 1591, re-located the myth in England, and shows Narcissus being instructed in the arts of courtship by Cupid. In spite of this tuition, however, as Akrigg says,

> Narcissus . . . mounts an untamable horse called 'Lust', who bolts off with him, finally hurling him headlong into the spring Philautia (self-love). After drinking of this, Narcissus falls in love with his own image reflected in the pond, not recognizing it as his own. When night obliterates the reflection, the desperate youth falls headlong into the pond and drowns. Venus, lamenting, gives him a new life in the form of the flower Narcissus.[18]

The strong links between this poem and Shakespeare's, two years later, are obvious. In both poems a beautiful youth is instructed unsuccessfully in the arts of love – by Cupid in Clapham's, by Venus in Shakespeare's. In both the youth has a lustful horse, though Adonis dissociates himself from his. Both poems close with the youth's death and metamorphosis into a flower. But Clapham's fairly undistinguished poem scarcely veils its propaganda purpose. In its echo sequence, for instance, line 17's echo word is '*vere*' no doubt alluding to Elizabeth Vere. Shakespeare's poem can be read, as we have seen, in all sorts of ways. Perhaps, indeed, Shakespeare hoped that Burghley would read *Venus and Adonis* as a more sophisticated version of *Narcissus*, endorsing the need for a young nobleman to marry, while Southampton himself could take it as complimenting him for his resistance to forced desire. Perhaps, also, Burghley could be relied on not to read the poem through to the end, while Southampton was far more likely to do so, and to discover its extraordinary shifts of tone and register as Venus mutates from lustful woman to worried parent and finally, in glorious lift-off, to an injured and remote goddess who disappears into the empyrean in a dove-drawn chariot (Plate 3).

That the poem was a success with huge numbers of other readers, there can be no doubt. Of the first 1593 printing only a single copy survives – one that belonged to a woman book-collector, Frances Wolfreston. Only two copies survive of the 1594 printing, one of the ?1595 one and two of the 1596 one. The combination of constant reprintings with low survival rates points to a work of exceptional popularity that was not just bought, but read. It is likely that some early printings have vanished altogether. William Reynolds's allusion to the book in late September 1593 as published 'within these few days' may point to the existence of such a vanished reprint – the June print-run being already sold out. Richard Field may have regretted selling his rights in the poem to John Harrison in April 1594, though the fact that he did so indicates that Harrison knew he was on to a winner, and offered Field a handsome price for the transfer. The poem soon became Shakespeare's most quoted and most popular work, passionately loved by what Gabriel Harvey was to call 'the younger sort'. For many early readers it seems to have functioned as a sort of wooing manual or rhetorical handbook. Whole stanzas were adapted as models of courtship, with a surprisingly easy transfer of language and conceits used by a woman, or goddess, to a boy, to ploys to be used by male wooers of young women.

Yet the poem can be read quite differently. By focusing on Venus's desire for the boy Adonis, and portraying him as wholly indifferent, Shakespeare also opens up the classical myth to a homoerotic reading. The whole emotional thrust of the poem depends on endorsing the intense desirability of a fair youth. Humiliatingly, Venus has to enumerate the feminine charms of her own body, for Adonis is unmoved, even repelled, by them. This, too, may have been congenial to Southampton, for as we shall see there is some reason to believe that both he and the young Earl of Essex, also under Burghley's tutelage, were strongly inclined towards same-sex relationships, both in their teens and later. Though there is little contemporary evidence that the poem was read homoerotically, an account by a later reader, John Addington Symonds, suggests the availability of such a reading to a young man to whom it was congenial:

> the first English poem which affected me deeply – as it has, no doubt, impressed thousands of boys – was Shakespeare's 'Venus and Adonis'. I read it . . . before I was ten years old . . . In some confused way I identified myself with Adonis; but at the same time I yearned after him as an adorable object of passionate love . . . I took 'Venus and Adonis' in the way Shakespeare undoubtedly meant it to be taken. And in doing so, it stimulated while it etherealized my inborn cravings after persons of my own sex.[19]

Whether or not Symonds's response was indeed how Shakespeare consciously 'meant' the poem to be read, there is little doubt that in practice it is open to such an interpretation.

Whatever the exact nature of Southampton's reading, *Venus* must have been accepted by him with pleasure and approval, for every subsequent printing includes Shakespeare's dedicatory epistle. It can be safely assumed that Southampton both gave Shakespeare some financial reward, perhaps between £5 and £10, and encouraged him to persevere with that 'graver labour' mentioned in the epistle. In the context of Southampton's own position vis-à-vis marriage, the final sentence of Shakespeare's epistle was a masterly piece of ambivalence: 'I leave it [the poem] to your Honourable survey, and your Honour to your heart's content, which I wish may always answer your own wish, and the world's hopeful expectation.' By Burghley, this could be construed as 'may you soon realize that "your heart's content" must be reconciled with "the world's hopeful expectation" through marriage to Elizabeth Vere'. But Southampton himself could read the sentence quite differently, as a more intimate and sympathetic endorsement of the need to accommodate 'your own wish' and 'your own heart's content' to 'the world's hopeful expectation'. According to this interpretation, Shakespeare is saying 'I wish you to have what you *really* desire, and to be made happy by it, and for the world's expectation of you to be fulfilled in a way that reflects this'. Such slippery language, in which a speech could be quite differently received by different individuals, showed how well advanced Shakespeare already was in writing for the theatre, the medium which most requires that texts permit such fluidity of response.

THE RIVALS

Hard on Shakespeare's heels trod, first, Barnabe Barnes, then Thomas Nashe. Barnes's inventive and occasionally obscene sonnet sequence *Parthenophil and Parthenophe* was entered in the Stationers' Register on 10 May 1593, only three weeks after *Venus and Adonis*. While Shakespeare's poem promises, but denies, sexual congress, Barnes's sequence concludes, outrageously, with consummation. In a final double sestina, amid magic spells and in an enchanted wood, Parthenophil enjoys Parthenophe's body. At a late stage in printing, and inconsistently, given the preliminary verses on the work as a 'bastard orphan' lacking a patron, Barnes appended six sonnets commending the sequence to six young aristocrats, three men, three women. Southampton is third among the men, coming after Henry Percy, Earl of Northumberland, and Robert Devereux, Earl of Essex. Barnes seems to have studied Shakespeare's epistle, mimicking the metaphor of husbandry in the phrase 'never after ear so barren a land, for fear it yield me still so bad a harvest', in lines 3–4:

> These worthless leaves, which I to thee present
> Sprung from a rude and unmanured land . . .[20]

There is no evidence of any further connection between Barnes and Southampton, but he may have been well rewarded both by the printer – probably his friend and landlord John Wolfe – and by his courtly patrons. Of *Parthenophil and Parthenophe*, as of the first edition of *Venus*, only a single copy survives, but in this case there seem to have been no further printings.

Unlike Barnes, Nashe had some personal acquaintance with Southampton. As Akrigg points out, they overlapped at St John's, Cambridge.[21] His suggestion that Nashe seized a chance to 'drop around at Titchfield' on his way back from the Isle of Wight early in 1593 sounds a little over casual, but is nevertheless a strong possibility, if Nashe travelled back to London with some of Sir George Carey's retainers in January or February 1593. However, all we know for sure about Nashe's dealings with Southampton is that he dedicated the first printing of *The Unfortunate Traveller* to him. Though not published until the autumn of 1594, the first edition bears at the end the date 'June 27. 1593', thus locating it within the same month in which *Venus* was printed, which was also the month following the shocking murder of Christopher Marlowe. It was probably the tearaway success of Shakespeare's poem that emboldened Nashe to identify Southampton as a promising patron for what is still his most celebrated work, one which some have seen as the first English novel. A further link between Nashe and Southampton may be also suggested by the fact that the printer of *The Unfortunate Traveller*, Thomas Scarlet, had printed Clapham's *Narcissus*. The first two-thirds of Nashe's dedicatory epistle is quite unlike Shakespeare's. Nashe adopts the risky strategy of challenging the custom of dedicating printed works 'to one great man or other', and yet makes it quite clear – albeit by denial – that he is hoping for a cash reward: 'Prize them as high or as low as you list: if you set any price on them, I hold my labour well satisfied.' Perhaps alluding to their shared years at St John's, he claims that he has long desired to do service to Southampton:

> Long have I desired to approve* my wit unto you. My reverent dutiful thoughts (even from their infancy) have been retainers to your glory. Now at last I have enforced an opportunity to plead my devoted mind.

Given that Nashe's two previous works were dedicated to the Careys, *Christs Teares* to Lady Carey, *The Terrors of the Night* to her daughter and namesake, this claim was either tactless, as an implicit rejection of the Careys who had treated Nashe so generously, or, more probably, a piece of obsequious fiction. Nashe had seen Shakespeare – and perhaps Barnes – winning lavish rewards from Southampton, and hoped to cash in too. It is in this spirit that we should read the sentence 'A dear lover and cherisher you are, as well of the lovers of

* 'approve': demonstrate.

poets, as of poets themselves'. In the final passage, it becomes clear that Nashe is amplifying Shakespeare's epistle, probably in the hope of winning even more ample reward. Shakespeare had implicitly identified his poem with a burgeoning plant, saying, 'I know not . . . how the world will censure me for choosing so strong a prop to support so weak a burden'. Nashe floridly elaborates this images, with 'leaves' of his book identified with leaves on a tree:

> except these unpolished leaves of mine have some branch of nobility whereon to depend and cleave, and with the vigorous nutriment of whose authorized commendation they may be continually fostered and refreshed, never will they grow to the world's good liking, but forthwith fade and die on the first hour of their birth.

With the final phrase, compare Shakespeare's 'the first heir of my invention'. Both Shakespeare and Nashe appealed to Southampton to sponsor and reward new and original writing, and in analogous terms. But less is more. Shakespeare's terse but richly rhythmical epistle is not only more likely to have been closely read by its addressee than Nashe's longer one, it is also carefully correct in its obsequious deference. Nashe first rashly questions the whole patronage system, and then lays on his adulation with a shovel. Southampton was a highly intelligent young man, and probably found Nashe's tone quite irritating. If he remembered him from Cambridge days, it may have been as a louche young man who got drunk in taverns with Marlowe and Greene.

As for the work itself, Nashe himself calls it a 'fantastical treatise', promising his readers only 'some reasonable conveyance of history, and variety of mirth'. Of 'history' in the sense of 'narrative', it certainly has plenty, though such 'history' as it offers in the modern sense of 'chronicle of past events' is, like the whole book, a deliberate travesty, conflating events that were more than twenty years apart. The treatment of place is equally arbitrary. The antihero, the page Jack Wilton, moves between countries and cities in the twinkling of an eye, or the flicker of a quill. Unlike *Venus and Adonis*, *The Unfortunate Traveller* twice alludes to plague, the defining context of both works. Nashe's first plague narrative concerns the 1517 'sweating sickness', which he treats as a rhetorical challenge, producing a succession of sick jokes and surreal 'special effects':

> I have seen an old woman at that season, having three chins, wipe them all away one after another, as they melted to water, and left her self nothing of a mouth but an upper chap . . . Masons paid nothing for hair to mix their lime, nor glovers to stuff their balls with, for then they had it for nothing; it dropped off men's heads and beards faster than any barber could shave it . . . It was as much as a man's life was worth, once to name a frieze jerkin; it was high treason for a fat gross man to come within five miles of the Court.[22]

Readers in 1594 found this passage to be rather too close for comfort. Although the Henrician 'sweating sickness' was a different disease from the Elizabethan 'pestilence', many felt it to be no laughing matter. A later passage on plague in Rome offers even more explicit analogies with London's 1593–4 epidemic:

> it being a vehement hot summer . . . there entered such a hotspurred plague as hath not been heard of: why, it was but a word and a blow, Lord have mercy upon us, and he was gone . . . All day and all night long car-men did nothing but go up and down the streets with their carts and cry, 'Have you any dead bodies to bury?' – and had many times out of one house their whole loading: one grave was the sepulchre of seven score, one bed was the altar whereon whole families were offered . . . I saw at the house where I was hosted, a maid bring her master warm broth for to comfort him, and she sink down dead herself ere he had half eat it up.[23]

Even assuming that such passages came under the heading of 'history' rather than 'mirth', they made grim reading for Londoners in 1594. It was perhaps with good reason that most Elizabethan writers did not make much, or any, explicit allusion to those plague epidemics which were the context for their non-dramatic writings.

Yet Nashe's book appears to have been popular, being printed a second time, later in 1594. There is only one major change: the dedication to Southampton is omitted. McKerrow offers a rather strained hypothesis that by the time of the second edition 'Nashe had a patron who was not on good terms with Southampton'. The more obvious inference, however, is that Southampton himself was not pleased either with Nashe's work or with his attempt to associate it with him, and refused to have anything more to do with it. Perhaps, indeed, it was at Southampton's insistence, rather than because of good sales, that *The Unfortunate Traveller* was so promptly reprinted without its dedicatory epistle. Apart from Nashe's clumsily overdone epistle, there are two other passages that might have given offence, the first to Southampton himself, the second to his protégé Shakespeare. A large part of the first half of the book is devoted to Jack Wilton's service to Henry Howard, Earl of Surrey, and was far more likely to amuse the book's secondary patrons, 'the dapper monsieur pages of the Court', than the ambitious young Earl. The page repeatedly outwits his noble master, mocking his adoration of the fair Geraldine, and getting both of them into trouble with his knavish tricks. They exchange clothes, and Jack takes outrageous sexual liberties with his earl-like disguise. But perhaps most offensive to the young Earl to whom the story was dedicated was Nashe/Jack's account of a great tournament in Florence, which brilliantly burlesques chivalry in general, and more specifically, an account of a court tournament in Sidney's *Arcadia*.[24] Surrey in his tilting armour is made to appear utterly ridiculous, wearing a 'helmet round proportioned like a gardener's water-pot', which seems to sprinkle 'small threads of water' on the lilies and roses with which his armour is decorated. Surrey's horse is decked out and plumed like an 'Estrich' (ostrich), with huge artificial wings that turn the horse into a 'Pegasus'. As the wings flap up and down in the air they 'make a flickering sound, such as eagles do'. Though Surrey is shown as victor of the tournament, the whole account is grotesque and comic, functioning as subversive send-up both of courtly chivalry and of the high style of a lately dead courtier, Sir Philip Sidney.

It was most unwise of Nashe to assume that a young nobleman would enjoy seeing court pageantry and poetry satirized. That Southampton was both struck by this passage, and displeased by it, is suggested by the way in which his protégé Shakespeare later drew on it. Transforming a comic passage into a heroic one is a difficult feat, yet Shakespeare managed it. He incorporated bits of Nashe's account of Surrey into a famous speech in *1 Henry IV* that itself marks a crucial change of register. Hearing that the King and his followers are marching towards Shrewsbury, the rebel Hotspur prepares to mock at 'his son / The nimble-footed madcap Prince of Wales', and expects to be told that he is roistering in the tavern with his cronies. Instead, unfolding the first shaft of Hal / Henry's sun-like brightness, Vernon reports on his battle-readiness in a speech closely based on Nashe's description of the Earl of Surrey:

> All furnish'd, all in arms;
> All plum'd like estridges that with the wind
> Bated, like eagles having lately bath'd,
> Glittering in golden coats like images...
> I saw young Harry with his beaver on,
> His cushes on his thighs, gallantly arm'd,
> Rise from the ground like feather'd Mercury,
> And vaulted with such ease into his seat
> As if an angel dropp'd down from the clouds
> To turn and wind a fiery Pegasus . . .
> (*1 Henry IV*, 4.1.97–109)

While Nashe made the mounting of elaborately armed knights on elaborately adorned horses sound clumsy and farcical, Shakespeare, while adopting Nashe's 'estridges', 'eagles' and 'Pegasus', gives Vernon's description of Prince Hal in armour a miraculous lightness. By adding the comparison of Hal to 'an angel' he also prepares the way for Hal's eventual metamorphosis into the divinely blessed victor of Agincourt. Southampton himself, another young Hal growing into a noble Henry, was a young man with strong military and chivalric ambitions. He may already have shown his mettle in court tournaments. Certainly he had already been mentioned as a possible Knight of the Garter, in May 1593.[25] He took part in the 1595 Accession Day Tilt, and was praised as 'gentle and debonair' by George Peele in *Anglorum Feriae*.[26] Nashe's notion of entertaining him with an over-the-top send-up of a court tournament was clearly misguided. By alluding to Nashe's account, yet using it to support an unironic celebration of military splendour, Shakespeare in *1 Henry IV* showed himself to be the kind of writer that Southampton, and other ambitious young noblemen, could be proud to sponsor. Among other things, Vernon's speech may have been designed to redress Nashe's offensive sauciness. An audience which picked up the Nashe allusion in the phrase 'plum'd like estridges' would, like Hotspur, expect a comic treatment of an armed knight. Instead, like Hotspur, they discover with amazement that Hal is now transformed into a godly warrior who seems to have dropped from heaven.

Shakespeare also had his own bone to pick with Nashe over *The Unfortunate Traveller*. An even more sensational passage than the account of the Florentine tournament is the rape scene. The hired assassin Esdras of Granado breaks into a plague-stricken mansion in Rome and locks up Jack and his courtesan, who have taken refuge there. He then sets out to rape the mature mistress of the house, Heraclide, having first killed her 'zany', or fool. Heraclide pleads vehemently with him – 'art thou ordained to be a worse plague to me than the plague itself?' – and threatens God's vengeance, in the form of plague, if Esdras persists. She has buried a hundred plague victims from her house, including her own thirteen children, and believes she has the power to infect him. But Esdras, a seasoned villain who has survived imprisonment and the galleys, defies her, and proceeds to attack her with a violence that is deeply disturbing: 'he traileth her up and down the chamber by those tender untwisted braids [of silver hair], and setting his barbarous foot on her bare snowy breast, bade her yield or have her wind stamped out'. Despite her repeated appeals, 'On the hard boards he threw her and used his knee as an iron ram to beat ope the two-leaved gate of her chastity. Her husband's dead body he made a pillow to his abomination.' [27] It is this last detail that shows that Nashe had Shakespeare in mind, for it recalls the rape of Lavinia in *Titus Andronicus*, in which Tamora's sons first kill her husband and then decide to 'make his dead trunk pillow to our lust' (*Titus*, 2.2.130).[28] Blending the rape scene in *Titus* with the account of Hecuba and Pyrrhus in his own and Marlowe's *Dido*, Nashe inflates the motif of a tragic beldame to a climax of absurdity. Heraclide's suicide cannot be taken as anything but burlesque:

> Point, pierce, edge, enwiden, I patiently afford thee a sheath: spur forth my soul to mount post to heaven . . . So (thoroughly stabbed) fell she down, and knocked her head against her husband's body: wherewith he, not having been aired his full four and twenty hours, start as out of a dream: whiles I, through a cranny of my upper chamber unsealed, had beheld all this sad spectacle.[29]

However hard we may struggle to read this episode as tragic, Nashe will not allow us to do so. The astonishing revelations, first that Heraclide's husband wasn't really dead, and then that Jack has been watching everything through a peephole, reduce the whole affair to a dirty farce. As far as Shakespeare is concerned, Nashe was dealing out a right and a left: mocking both the rape scene in his popular *Titus*, and the suicide of Lucretia, theme of the second of his poetic offerings to Southampton. The second allusion raises some problems of dating, for by 27 June 1593 – the date at the end of the first edition of *The Unfortunate Traveller* – *Lucrece* was not yet written. But this date may be one of Nashe's many historical fictions, veiling the fact that by the time it was printed, in the first half of 1594, it had been heavily revised. Indeed, it could have been the *Lucrece* dedication that prompted Nashe, too, to try his luck with Southampton, if, as was normal, the dedication was added at the end of the printing of the main text.

Whatever the exact order of events, it seems that both Shakespeare and Southampton had reason to be displeased with Nashe's *Unfortunate Traveller*: Southampton because of Nashe's mockery of a youthful Earl called Henry who was in love with chivalry, Shakespeare because of the travesty of the rape scene in *Titus*. But in terms of Nashe's and Shakespeare's competing bids for Southampton's favour, the summer of 1594 saw game, set and match won by Shakespeare. Nashe's envious railing had harmed only himself.

Some graver labour

Lucrece was both a sequel to *Venus* and, in numerous ways, a counterpart to it. Like *Venus,* the poem is based on a well-known classical source, and like *Venus*, it focuses for much of its length on the consciousness of a woman. This was something Shakespeare could not easily do when writing for the theatre, though in the major and complex role of Queen Margaret in the *Henry VI* trilogy he had tested the stamina of the boy player to its limit. External circumstances were also similar. The early months of 1594 saw a recurrence of plague in London, though this outbreak turned out to be much less prolonged than that of 1592–3. In the event, the theatres were to be closed only for the months of February and March.[30] But for a while Shakespeare may have envisaged a continued career as a non-dramatic poet, which would be sustainable only if he could acquire some sort of office or stipend to compensate for the substantial income that he had briefly enjoyed as a leading player and sharer in Lord Strange's Men.[31]

After a short season at the Rose after Christmas 1593, playing was forbidden because of plague with effect from 7 February 1594. The players, or their managers, were quick to seek some compensation for their losses. *Titus Andronicus*, which had been revived very successfully by Sussex's Men at the Rose, was sold to Nashe's friend and landlord, the printer John Danter, only three days after the restraining order. Shakespeare may have been already some way on with the writing of *Lucrece*. The successful revival of *Titus*, followed so quickly by its appearance in print, probably had an impact on his handling of the story. *Titus* showed a silenced rape victim. Lavinia has her hands cut off and her tongue cut out, so that she cannot reveal the identity of her attackers. She stands on stage as a mute and pitiful symbol of reduced and dismembered Rome, her name being that of Aeneas's destined bride, Rome's founding mother. Her maimed silence figures the unspeakable horror that has descended on Rome's once great Empire. In another work by Ovid, the *Fasti*, printed by Richard Field's master Thomas Vautrollier in 1574, Shakespeare had encountered a story at the opposite end of Rome's history that chronicled the birth of Rome's greatness. Like the rape of Lavinia, the rape of Lucretia had both political causes and political consequences. A virtuous young wife is raped by the eldest son of the ruling family, the Tarquins, and as a direct result of this single act of violence 'the Tarquins were all exiled, and the state government changed from kings to consuls'. Lucretia is an archetype of *Romanitas* – Roman courage, steadfastness and dedication to family honour. Apart from the bare fact of undergoing rape, she could scarcely be more different from the pathetic, voiceless and child-like Lavinia (Fig. 11).

From Shakespeare's point of view, the Lucretia story offered scope for doing some of the things he had not done in *Titus*. Unconstrained by the limits of a boy player's capacity to memorize speeches and perform them, he was able to endow his heroine with what F. T. Prince was to call 'remorseless eloquence'. The leisure enforced on him by the latest plague outbreak influenced both the poem's length – at 1855 lines, it is as long as a short play – and the manner in which the topic is handled. Lucrece's complaints and meditations occupy the night after Tarquin's departure and before the early morning arrival of Collatine and the Roman lords, and are leisurely and expansive. At well over 800 lines, they exceed what could be readily be memorized even by an experienced adult actor, let alone a boy. Shakespeare himself may have found the poem hard to complete. It was entered in the Stationers' Register three weeks later in the year than *Venus* – 9 May, as against 18 April – despite the fact that the earlier poem's epistle to Southampton suggests that he already had a 'graver labour' in mind, and perhaps in hand. Although in some respects liberated by the form of non-dramatic poem, he had imposed testing limitations on himself. One was a determination never to deviate from 'gravity'. *Lucrece* is perhaps the only joke-free zone in the whole of Shakespeare's works, lacking, for the most part, even his habitual plays on words and shifts of tone. The rime royal verse form is also a good deal more exacting than the six-line stanzas of *Venus*. The poem's great length is part of its raison d'être, as a piece of grandly reflective rhetorical amplification, but it may also be a symptom of laborious composition by a deeply dispirited poet. Shakespeare

Fig. 11 Lucretia killing herself, painting by Ambrosius Benson (1495–1550); the background scene shows Tarquin entering her chamber and climbing into her bed.

found himself with an unwelcome excess of 'idle hours', because of the renewed suppression of the playing companies, which might, for all he knew, be permanent.

But in contrast to the poem itself, the dedicatory epistle, presumably written at the end and therefore in a period when playing had resumed, is a masterpiece of terseness (Fig. 12). It opens: 'The love I dedicate to your Lordship is without end; whereof this pamphlet without beginning is but a superfluous moiety.' While the 1593 epistle spoke of 'honour' and deference, this one's simple affirmation of 'love' betokens an advance in his relationship. The poem's brilliantly swift opening –

> From the besieged Ardea all in post,
> Borne by the trustless wings of false desire,
> Lust-breathed Tarquin leaves the Roman host . . .

– is alluded to as if it were careless – 'without beginning' – rather than a piece of poetic finesse. In calling it a 'pamphlet' he stresses the fact that it is of less than book length – whatever book length would be. The word 'moiety', probably used here simply for 'small portion', rather than 'half', also implies that the super-long poem is nevertheless incomplete. Carefully varying the earlier epistle, which described the smoothly rhetorical *Venus* as 'unpolished lines', Shakespeare refers now to 'untutored lines', alluding both to his own lack of university education and to his bold choice of a theme from Roman history. Yet his tone is assured, setting against his own poor qualifications 'The warrant I have of your honourable disposition'. The fourth sentence of the epistle, beginning 'Were my worth greater', will be discussed in the next chapter.

Although *Lucrece* is conventionally bracketed with *Venus and Adonis* as a 'narrative poem', it is, in truth, deficient in narrative. Actions, ranging from Tarquin's journey to Collatium, by way of the rape itself, to the banishment of all the Tarquins in the final line, are indicated with such economy that they may easily be missed or misread. Many young male readers, seeing the word '*Rape*' in the poem's running title, must have hoped for titillation comparable to what they found in *Venus*. They were to be sadly disappointed. Most of the poem's length is occupied with speech and moral reflection, and physical action, when it occurs, tends to be suggested figuratively. For instance, when Tarquin first strides 'wickedly' into Lucrece's bedchamber his eyes are betrayed by the 'high treason' of his heart:

> Which gives the watch-word to his hand full soon,
> To draw the cloud that hides the silver moon.
>
> (370–1)

That is, he pulls back the curtain of Lucrece's bed to gaze on her. For a poem whose defining event is the violation of a body, *Lucrece* is astonishingly unfleshly. While the earlier poem, to the distaste of many twentieth-century readers, gives a powerful sense of Venus's sweating, panting, blushing, weeping body – we can almost feel its warmth and wetness – Lucrece's body is fragmented into metaphor and conceit. Even when stabbed, her body behaves allegorically, as the blood pours out:

> And bubbling from her breast, it doth divide
> In two slow rivers, that the crimson blood
> Circles her body in on every side,
> Who like a late-sack'd island vastly stood
> Bare and unpeopled in this fearful flood.
> Some of her blood still pure and red remain'd,
> And some look'd black, and that false Tarquin stain'd.
>
> (1737–43)

Both in his choice of subject and in his treatment of it Shakespeare may have been inspired by Sidney's account of 'the right poet' in the *Defence of Poesy*. While literal-minded artists record only what they see, the true artist, like the 'right poet', deals in moral absolutes:

> the more excellent . . . bestow that in colours upon you which is fittest for the eye to see: as the constant though lamenting look of Lucretia, when she punished in herself another's fault, wherein he painteth not Lucretia, whom he never saw, but painteth the outward beauty of such a virtue.[32]

That the poem has its roots in the analogous art of painting is suggested by its most successful passage of complaint and meditation, that in which Lucrece seeks solace in gazing on 'a piece / Of skilful painting, made for Priam's Troy' (1366–7). If it is to be associated with any actual painting, it suggests a Florentine *cassone* panel. The Troy story was a popular theme for such paintings, and either Southampton or Burghley may have possessed one (Plate 5). Initially, Lucrece is entranced by the painting's concentration and technical skill, which recalls some of the work of Mantegna, and especially the use of visual synecdoche, in which a single detail stands for a larger whole:

> The very eyes of men through loop-holes thrust
>
> (1383)

or (describing crowds of Greeks)

> The scalps of many almost hid behind,
> To jump up higher seem'd, to mock the mind
>
> (1413–4)

TO THE RIGHT
HONOVRABLE, HENRY
VVriotheſley, Earle of Southhampton,
and Baron of Titchfield.

HE loue I dedicate to your Lordſhip is without end: wherof this Pamphlet without beginning is but a ſuperfluous Moity. The warrant I haue of your Honourable diſpoſition, not the worth of my vntutord Lines makes it aſſured of acceptance. VVhat I haue done is yours, what I haue to doe is yours, being part in all I haue, deuoted yours. VVere my worth greater, my duety would ſhew greater, meane time, as it is, it is bound to your Lordſhip; To whom I wiſh long life ſtill lengthned with all happineſſe.

Your Lordſhips in all duety.

William Shakeſpeare.

A 2

Fig. 12 Dedicatory epistle of Shakespeare's *Lucrece* (1594).

or

> . . . for Achilles' image stood his spear
> Gripp'd in an armed hand; himself behind
> Was left unseen, save to the eye of mind . . .
>
> (1424–6)

But her eyes soon close in on one figure in particular, 'despairing Hecuba', in whom she finds consoling counterpart to her own sufferings. On Hecuba's behalf – for she is only a painted Hecuba, and cannot speak – Lucrece rails at Pyrrhus, and at Paris and Helen whose unrestrained lust has caused such anguish:

> '. . . here in Troy, for trespass of thine eye,
> The sire, the son, the dame and daughter die.
>
> 'Why should the private pleasure of some one
> Become the public plague of many moe? . . .'
>
> (1476–9)

This passage forms a bridge between Marlowe and Nashe's account of Hecuba in *Dido* and Shakespeare's own later one in the Player scene in *Hamlet.* Nor is this the only link with *Hamlet.* One of the most concentrated and dynamic stanzas in this often diffuse poem shows Lucrece gazing on the traitor Sinon and discovering, as Hamlet does, that 'one may smile and smile and be a villain':

> 'It cannot be,' quoth she, 'that so much guile' –
> She would have said, – 'can lurk in such a look.'
> But Tarquin's shape came in her mind the while,
> And from her tongue 'can lurk' from 'cannot' took:
> 'It cannot be' she in that sense forsook,
> And turn'd it thus: 'It cannot be, I find,
> But such a face should bear a wicked mind.
>
> (1534–40)[33]

Considered as an offering to Southampton, *Lucrece* is at once flattering and admonitory. It compliments him in assuming his interest both in early Roman history and in the newly fashionable poetic genre of 'complaint', initiated by Samuel Daniel's *Complaint of Rosamond* in 1592. But in so far as its villain hero is a young man of great eminence whose single evil act brings ruin on his family and conflict in the state, it is also a warning to Southampton of the dangers of losing self-control. From this point of view, the poem was well tuned to the views of Southampton's elderly guardian Lord Burghley during the final months of his ward's minority. If *Lucrece*, unlike *Venus*, was written with Burghley's approval prominently in view, some of the features already mentioned are accounted for – Shakespeare's struggle to complete it, the poem's extreme length, its unremitting gravity. Though it is a brilliant piece of writing, few have found it genuinely enjoyable. It is notable that, compared with *Venus*, large numbers of clean copies survive of the early printings. It was bought, but not read.

CLIPPING AND HUGGING

In writing such a solemnly didactic poem for public presentation to his twenty-year-old patron Shakespeare may have been drawing a deliberately sombre veil over the true nature of their relationship. For what kind of 'love', exactly, was it that Shakespeare so boldly proclaimed in his epistle? Rhetorically, the devotion of client to patron was often eroticized. Gabriel Harvey declared (though in Latin) that he was 'all liver' – the liver being supposedly the seat of libido – when he gazed on Philip Sidney. Nashe predictably taunted him for courting such a distinguished young man 'as he were another Cyparissus or Ganimede'.[34] Despite Nashe's envy, however, Sidney fostered and favoured Harvey, and may have relished such eroticized praise. After all, in his own *Arcadia* the two young princely heroes frequently kiss each other, and when the younger one is disguised as an Amazon the elder is instantly attracted to him. There is no doubt, either, that players were seen as both sexually promiscuous and sexually predatory. In that very streetwise play *Poetaster*, Ovid Senior is appalled to hear that his expensively educated son is writing a play: 'What? shall I have my son a stager now? an ingle for players? a gull? a rook? a shot-clog*? to make suppers and be laughed at?'[35] Stage-struck young gentlemen would invite players to supper after the show, and the players, Jonson's passage implies, would introduce these young gentlemen to same-sex practices. In another Jonson play, *The Case is Alterd*, the cobbler Juniper greets the hack playwright Antonio Balladino (modelled on Anthony Munday) as his 'sweet ingle'.

That Southampton himself was viewed as receptive to same-sex amours is suggested by the Midlander William Burton's dedication to him of his translation of the Hellenistic romance *Clitophon and Leucippe* (by Achilles Tatius) in the summer of 1597. Burton's dedicatory epistle has verbal echoes of both of Shakespeare's, but includes also a defensive appeal to Southampton's protective power: 'if the gracious beams of your favour shine therein, no carping Momus can shadow it'. There was a good deal here that could be challenged by a 'Momus', or severely moral critic, for in addition to sensational scenes of rape

* 'shot-clog': a wealthy fool who pays the 'shot', or bill.

and torture the romance includes an extended debate over the respective merits of the love of women and the love of boys, with the last word being delivered on behalf of the latter. A young Egyptian, Menelaus, claims that 'boys are more perfect than women, and their beauty is of more force to delight the senses with pleasure'. The most desirable beauty, he claims, is that which is most transient, and that of pre-pubertal boys lasts less long that that of young women. This is why Ganymede, unlike any of his female loves, was carried up to Olympus by Jove. Though Clitophon, in reply, praises the kisses and embraces of women, it is with Menelaus's rebuttal that the debate is concluded. Women, he says, are sly and deceitful:

> truly you will think them barer than a jay ... when all his stolen feathers are plucked from his back: but the beauty of boys is not besmeared with the counterfeit of painting, neither sponged up with borrowed perfumes: the very sweat of the brows of a boy, doth excel all the sweet savours of musk and civet about a woman: and a man may openly talk and play with them and never be ashamed ... the very image and picture of their kisses are so sweet and pleasant, that you might very well think, that heavenly nectar to be between your lips.

There is no reason to think that Southampton repudiated or scorned Burton's dedication of *Clitophon and Leucippe*, as he seems to have done Nashe's of *The Unfortunate Traveller*.

It might be thought that the social distance between the young nobleman and the yeoman playwright was far too wide to permit of physical intimacy. Yet later examples, such as those of Oscar Wilde and E. M. Forster, suggest that wide social difference can in itself act as an aphrodisiac. There is in addition some testimony, once more from the soldier William Reynolds, that both Southampton and his close friend Essex were in the habit of engaging in physical intimacies with male subordinates. Reynolds provides eye-witness testimony, for he served in Essex's ill-fated Irish campaign in 1599. Here he writes to Robert Cecil in the aftermath of Essex's revolt:

> I do marvel also what became of Piers Edmonds,[36] called Captain Piers, or Captain Edmonds, the Earl of Essex's man, born in Strand near me, and which has had many rewards and preferments by the Earl of Essex. His villainy I have often complained of, he dwells in London, he was corporal general of the horse in Ireland under the Earl of Southampton. He ate and drank at his table and lay in his tent, the Earl of Southampton gave him a horse, which Edmonds refused a hundred marks for him. The Earl Southampton would clip and hug him in his arms and play wantonly with him. This Piers began to fawn and flatter me in Ireland offering me great courtesy, telling me what pay, graces and favours the Earls bestowed upon him, seeming to move and animate me to desire and look for the like favour.[37]

Even more remarkable than what Reynolds reports of the sexual predilections of both Essex and Southampton is his claim that 'rewards and preferments', including very lavish gifts, were bestowed by Southampton on his male favourites. The possibility that Shakespeare enjoyed comparable reward to that of Piers Edmonds, and for comparable reasons, should be borne in mind in the next chapter. Perhaps Shakespeare's 'love' for his young patron was distant and formal, and such as even Lord Burghley himself could not fault. Perhaps, on the other hand, it was not. Puritans like Reynolds may have been on to something when they associated plague outbreaks with 'sodomitical sins'. Though such 'sins' were not, as Puritans claimed, the direct cause of plague, they were an almost equally pervasive feature of Elizabethan urban culture.

CHAPTER FOUR

1595–8

Spear-shaking Shakespeare

> . . . if it be a sin to covet honour
> I am the most offending soul alive.
> (*Henry V*, 4.3.28–9)

> he's a mad yeoman that sees his son a gentleman before him
> (*King Lear*, 3.6.13–14)

A purchase he had a mind to

Ben Jonson gloried in his own singularity. He took no steps to change his name or title, except to introduce a grandly simple modification of his surname ('Jonson' rather than 'Johnson') that made it more plausible in its Latin form, 'Ionsonus'. He sought peers and role models only among the ancients, figures such as Horace and Ovid, ancients whom he viewed in self-gratifyingly 'humorous', or quirky, terms. The unknown man who caused the words 'O RARE BEN JONSON' to be inscribed on his gravestone in Westminster Abbey understood this. Jonson was, and desired to be, a *rara avis*, the only one of his kind, beyond any of his contemporaries either in talent or in rank. Also, as the stepson of a bricklayer and, from October 1598, a branded and convicted felon, he was well aware that he had no chance whatsoever of being granted armigerous status. Even his schoolmaster and friend William Camden, Clarencieux King of Arms from 1594, could not fix this for him. Jonson decided, instead, to develop for all it was worth his 'rare' status, as a creative genius who was also an exceptional scholar.

Shakespeare, conversely, sought worldly recognition on the world's terms. It was important to him to be accepted and respected not only as what Shylock calls 'a good man' – a man of financial credit and substance – but also as a 'gentleman'. Unfortunately he came of stolidly yeoman stock on his father's side, and had not improved his position by marrying an even less 'gentle' Hathaway. Nor, as the attack on him in *Groats-worth* had stingingly reminded him, had he been able to elevate his standing by going to university. If he had graduated, this would have enabled him to use the title 'Dominus' or 'sir'.[1] Even better would have been a spell at an Inn of Court. Sir John Ferne grudgingly acknowledged that 'the student of the common laws . . . hath the best assurance of his bare title of Gentleman'.[2] But Shakespeare lacked such an 'assurance'. Ferne also conceded the possibility of gentle status to some courtly poets and devisers of pageantry, but explicitly excluded those who write for the public theatres: 'If they be played for the cause of gain, to move laughter and sport to the people, such plays be reprobate.'[3]

As he reached the mid-1590s Shakespeare's position was extremely frustrating. His work had enjoyed spectacular acclaim in the public theatres, as is shown by Nashe's allusion to the large audiences at *1 Henry VI*,[4] and probably also with some command performances of his plays to aristocratic and court audiences. Even more notably, he had achieved – as none of his other clients had – sustained and visible support from the Earl of Southampton. Each reprinting of *Venus and Adonis*, complete with its dedicatory epistle, proclaimed Shakespeare's success in securing this exceptionally desirable patronage.[5] But meanwhile, back in Stratford, his father's health was declining, and his own little son Hamnet was growing up. What did his father have to leave him except debts and unfinished business? And what did he, in turn, have to leave to his own son except empty fame and an empty name? After nearly three years of severe plague, not to mention the sudden deaths of Greene, Marlowe and Ferdinando Stanley, fear of death was pressing and inescapable. Robert Greene had become a figure of pathos and ridicule almost before his body was interred at Shoreditch. How could Shakespeare ensure that, if plague took him, this would not be his fate also? Not to die a debtor and a prodigal, like Greene, would certainly help. Iago's advice 'put money in thy purse' was evidently one of his own favourite maxims. But almost equally important was to use his money to good and durable ends, to secure both his own dignity and that of his descendants. It was mortifying to be able to articulate the innermost thoughts of kings and noblemen, both in writing and acting, and yet have no 'name' or status in private life. Still worse was to enjoy some glorious acquaintance with a young earl of spectacularly splendid inheritance, and yet be, in the eyes of arrogant university graduates, no more than a 'rude groom'.

I believe that it may have been Southampton himself who encouraged Shakespeare to improve his social position. But the steps Shakespeare took to do so backfired badly, leading both to the cessation of his friendship with Southampton, and to painful humiliations which were to recur for many years to come. It was most probably in the summer of 1594, rewarded handsomely by Southampton for *Lucrece*, that Shakespeare first began to lay down plans for his future. With Hamnet approaching his tenth year, it was time to set the Shakespeares of Henley Street on a better footing, one that reflected the fame and financial success he had earned in London. The transmission of inheritance and family honour had been a major theme in *Lucrece*. It is the need to prevent any possible stain on her family, should she give birth to a child of uncertain parentage, that is Lucrece's most compelling motive for suicide. Tarquin's action has polluted not only her body, but potentially her family's whole posterity. The rapist Tarquin is equally conscious of the threat posed to his own family honour by his moral turpitude, and shows a preoccupation with the symbols of such honour:

> 'Yea, though I die the scandal will survive
> And be an eye-sore in my golden coat;
> Some loathsome dash the herald will contrive,
> To cipher me how fondly I did dote:
> That my posterity sham'd with the note,
> Shall curse my bones, and hold it for no sin
> To wish that I their father had not been . . .'
>
> (*Lucrece*, 204–10)

It was particularly appropriate that this poem should pave the way for the poet's own negotiations with the Heralds, and from several points of view its dedicatee Southampton was just the man to help him. Not only was the youth still in a mood to be expansive and generous, having not yet discovered the limits of his purse and power,[6] he had special and intimate connections with the Heralds. His great-uncle Sir Thomas Wriothesley had been Garter King of Arms for nearly thirty years, from 1505 until his death in 1534. He built a house for himself in Cripplegate called 'Garter House'. It was he who, after some experiment, evolved the elaborate spelling of the family name, once plain 'Writh', as 'Wriothesley', pronounced 'Risely',[7] which was to be adopted both by his own descendants and those of his brother. Even while writing *Lucrece*, or at least by the time of its completion, Shakespeare may have had it in mind to solicit Southampton's help in acquiring armigerous status. Some words in the dedicatory epistle support this possibility: 'Were my worth greater, my duty would show greater; meantime, as it is, it is bound to your Lordship . . .' The implications of that 'meantime' should be examined. If Shakespeare was already considering acquiring a coat of arms, and if Southampton was aware of this, the suggestion is: 'This (poem) is the best I can do for you while I am a mere yeoman; but once I am a gentleman, imagine how much more I shall be able to do.' Nicholas Rowe's *Account of the Life, &c, of Mr. William Shakespeare*, though often unreliable, may nevertheless have something to tell us here. Rowe clearly had no notion that Shakespeare applied for a grant of arms, for he asserts that 'His family, as appears by the register and public writings relating to that town [Stratford] . . . are mentioned as gentlemen'.[8] He therefore made no connection between Shakespeare's rising social position and the favour he received from Southampton. Nevertheless, he reluctantly transmitted an anecdote that may be relevant:

> There is one instance so singular in the magnificence of this patron . . . that if I had not been assured that the story was handed down by Sir William Davenant, who was probably very well acquainted with his affairs, I should not have ventured to have inserted: that my Lord Southampton, at one time, gave him a thousand pounds, to enable him to go through with a purchase which he heard he had a mind to.

It should be stressed at the outset that the sum reportedly named really is incredible, and had probably been multiplied by a drunken Davenant. £100 is just possible; £1,000 not. Nevertheless, Davenant may have had access to a genuine tradition that Shakespeare was very handsomely rewarded by Southampton, and that this was not the reward conventionally given in response to a dedication, which was a cash gift for the writer to use as he wished, but was a special one-off benefaction connected with some specific 'purchase' that Shakespeare had in mind. Most biographers have repeated Chambers's suggestion that the gift related to Shakespeare's acquisition of a share in the Chamberlain's Men. However, according to Andrew Gurr,[9] it was probably his play-manuscripts, carried with him from previous companies, that paid for this. A few have connected it with the purchase of New Place in 1597. This purchase did indeed form part of Shakespeare's larger plan to turn himself into a gentleman. But the specific 'purchase' with which Shakespeare sought Southampton's aid may have been one that required not just financial munificence, but powerful connections and influence. I believe that the 'purchase' Shakespeare had set his heart on was that of a coat of arms, together with all concomitant expenses. These included, in the near future, a suitable residence on and in which that coat and crest could be displayed. Acquiring a coat of arms was always an expensive business, and seems to have been particularly so when the Heralds were being asked to legitimate a claim that was distinctly fragile. There was probably an inverse relationship between the strength of a claim and the fee charged for granting it. In the early 1590s the notoriously quarrelsome and self-willed Sir William Dethick, Garter King of Arms, awarded dozens of patents to dubious claimants, and in some cases extracted extremely high fees. For instance, he charged £10 for providing a pedigree and an absurdly elaborate coat and crest to 'Parr the Embroiderer, whose father was a pedlar by occupation, and not able to prove his surname to be Parr' (Plate 7).[10] One 'Robert Wythens of London vintner' was also charged £10.[11] Twice that sum, £20, was charged to a lawyer, 'Sergeant Warberton', for a coat that really belonged to another family of the name.[12] Jonson may not have been exaggerating much when he depicted the 'essential clown', Sogliardo, 'so enamoured of the name of a gentleman, that he will have it, though he buys it', paying £30 for his patent of gentility.[13]

The actual patent, however, was only part of the expense. By definition, any man who wanted a coat of arms was also going to want to display it conspicuously. This meant having it painted, embroidered, gilded or carved on his moveables and immoveables, such as trunks, furniture, bed canopies, book-bindings, glass windows, seal-rings, as well as carved and painted above the entrance to his gentleman's residence.[14] He would also want new suits of clothes made of silk, to which he was now entitled, for 'A gentleman is honoured also in the attire and apparelling of his body: for to them it is lawful to wear silks and purple colour'.[15] A sum of £100 might well be required by Shakespeare for first securing a patent and then meeting all the ensuing expenses. In selecting – as we shall see – a coat covered almost entirely with gold and silver he also committed himself to large expenditure on gold and silver leaf. Ordinary colours would have been much cheaper. If we take it that the purchase of a patent for a coat of arms, combined with the purchase of New Place, constituted the 'purchase' that Shakespeare 'had a mind to', a sum of £100 seems entirely plausible. The fee paid to the King of Arms could be as high as £20, as we have seen, and painting and carving the coat on possessions, combined with the purchase of new clothes, could easily add up to as much again. New Place was recorded as costing 'sixty pounds in silver', and though Schoenbaum calls the sum named in the deed 'a legal fiction', it has some plausibility as a valuation.

GAMES IN COURT

A possible order of events is as follows: Southampton gave Shakespeare a good reward for *Lucrece* – probably between £5 and £10 – in April or May 1594. Not only was Shakespeare more handsomely rewarded for *Lucrece* than for *Venus*, the poem also reflected closer relations between the poet and the stylish young nobleman – perhaps, as suggested at the end of the last chapter, including sexual relations. It may have been in 1594–5, and for Southampton, a reluctant bridegroom who eventually had to pay a large fine for refusing to marry

Burghley's grand-daughter Elizabeth Vere, that early versions of sonnets 1–17 were written, of which Burghley would thoroughly approve. On 6 October 1594, as Burghley noted, Southampton came of age. Freed at last from his guardian's heavy control, he was able to use his money as he wished. He proceeded almost at once to raise a large amount of cash by letting off much of Southampton House. He was already living lavishly, with a large retinue, and deploying both his wealth and his status with rash generosity for the support of his friends, such as the Danvers brothers, to whom he gave shelter after they committed a murder. Some time during the winter or spring 1594–5 Shakespeare was bold enough to mention to Southampton his strong desire to improve his family's position by acquiring a coat of arms. Flush with the new freedom of his adult status, Southampton made the one-off lavish gift that was to make this possible. Shakespeare was keeping excellent company at this period, for we have documentary evidence that, along with Burbage and Will Kempe, he was now a leading member of the Lord Chamberlain's Men, who performed before the Queen that Christmas. As Schoenbaum says, 'This record is the first to connect Shakespeare with an acting company, and the only official notice of his name with respect to a theatrical performance'.[16] The company also performed *The Comedy of Errors* at Gray's Inn on 28 December 1594 before a crowded and tumultuous assembly. This unusually learned farce was the only play that Shakespeare modelled entirely, though probably with the help of a translation, on a classical original, Plautus's *Menaechmi*. It may have been prepared during the lean, partly plague-ridden summer of 1594, soon after the appearance in print of John Lyly's play *Mother Bombie*, which also includes a character called 'Dromio'.

In terms of aristocratic patronage, 1595 could be called Shakespeare's *annus mirabilis*. To that year belong, almost certainly, *Romeo and Juliet* and *Richard II*, the latter being offered by Sir Edward Hoby as entertainment for Sir Robert Cecil in early December 1595. Above all, Shakespeare was giving superb service to his immediate master, Henry Carey, Lord Hunsdon, Lord Chamberlain, who was the Queen's first cousin, and probably also half-brother. He was an old man, almost seventy, and in practice his retinue of players was increasingly under the direction of his eldest son Sir George Carey, a generous, affable and discerning man, who lived in high style and rewarded his servants lavishly. But Sir George – who, like his father, was autocratic and irascible – was enraged, in the autumn of 1595, by the collapse of a long-laid scheme for his much loved only child Elizabeth to marry young William Herbert, heir to the Earldom of Pembroke. After the young people were introduced to each other the match had to be abandoned, because of the young man's 'not liking'. A rapid about-turn led to Bess Carey's betrothal, instead, to the Carey family's second choice, Sir Thomas Berkeley, heir to the Earldom of Berkeley. At some time during the Christmas season the Chamberlain's Men, and their leading poet,

Shakespeare, were commanded to prepare a festive play for the Carey–Berkeley marriage. The ceremony was scheduled for 19 February, to allow for a week of revelry before the period of pre-Lent fasting began. It also coincided with a new moon, highly auspicious for marriage.[17]

For this occasion, Shakespeare returned to the theme of autocratic parents and star-crossed lovers that he had so recently handled in *Romeo and Juliet*, but turned it all round. He doubled the young lovers – multiplication always favours comic effect, as with the fourfold love affairs of *Love's Labour's Lost* – and showed all four young people as touchingly vulnerable in their innocence. Boldly, he aired the theme of paternal authority, yet showed how with Hymen's blessing family ambition and youthful desire could be reconciled, and the effects of bad luck or malice (Puck's antics, Titania and Oberon's quarrel) could be cancelled and forgotten. When Juliet compares her new love to a flash of lightning the audience is painfully aware of her prophetic insight:

> I have no joy of this contract tonight:
> It is too rash, too unadvis'd, too sudden,
> Too like the lightning which doth cease to be
> Ere one can say 'It lightens'.
>
> (2.2.117–20)

In *A Midsummer Night's Dream* Lysander's much more sustained reflections on 'the course of true love' serve to remind the Lord Chamberlain's guests of the earlier play, yet, somehow, the lightning image now leaves them less chilled:

> Swift as a shadow, short as any dream,
> Brief as the lightning in the collied night,
> That, in a spleen, unfolds both heaven and earth,
> And, ere a man hath power to say 'Behold!',
> The jaws of darkness do devour it up.
> So quick bright things come to confusion.
>
> (1.1.144–9)

Here, the brilliant swiftness of young love betokens the almost painful swiftness of the play itself, its speed, lightness and delicacy, as a prelude to the consummation of the marriages both of Theseus and Hippolyta and of Thomas and Elizabeth. The bride, Bess Carey, took an interest in dreams. Her father had written to her in 1593 about such 'games in court' as 'dreams and the interpretations of them', as well as of 'going to the wood with letters', and 'awakings at their mistress' name, and showing the causes why, or sleeping, and likewise showing cause wherefore'.[18] All these 'games' seem to pave the way for *A Midsummer Night's Dream*, and there is every reason to think the play made a great impression on the Carey family. Only a few months after Sir George

Carey's letter describing 'games in court' Nashe dedicated a treatise on dreams, *The Terrors of the Night*, to Elizabeth Carey. But just as Shakespeare had upstaged Nashe in the favour of Southampton, his *Lucrece* trumping Nashe's *Unfortunate Traveller*, so he may have done with the Careys. Though Nashe had enjoyed favour in 1593–4, when Sir George Carey bailed him out of Newgate and carried him off to spend Christmas on the Isle of Wight, this favour seems to have declined by 1595–6. Shakespeare's play, meanwhile, had something for everyone. Theseus's praise of hunting will have gratified the bridegroom and his parents, for whom hunting was a consuming passion. Sir George Carey enjoyed rough and rustic merriment, and will have liked Bottom and his companions. He was to mark his departure from the Isle of Wight in August 1596 with a lavish outdoor feast in Parkhurst Forest, with dances, plays and other high jinks performed by clownish islanders. Some have doubted whether 'mechanicals' ever, in practice, performed plays for aristocrats, but Sir John Oglander's account of Carey's farewell feast makes it quite clear that on this occasion they did.[19] *A Midsummer Night's Dream*, performed at or near Carey Court in Blackfriars, marked a dazzling high point both in Shakespeare's career and that of the Lord Chamberlain's Men.

O insupportable and touching loss

Just when everything was going so well, two blows fell, one on Shakespeare's professional life in London, the second on his family life in Stratford. The first blow was severe, but turned out to be temporary. From the second no recovery was possible.

On 23 July 1596 the old Lord Hunsdon died at Somerset House, aged seventy, leaving the office of Lord Chamberlain vacant and his company of players without a protector. That this was a wretched summer for the former Lord Chamberlain's Men is witnessed by Thomas Nashe in his only surviving letter, written to William Cotton, a protégé and employee of the new Lord Hunsdon, in September 1596. Nashe himself was among those hard hit by the old Lord Hunsdon's death:

> In town I stayed (being earnestly invited elsewhere) upon 'had I wist' hopes,* and an after harvest I expected by writing for the stage and for the press, when now the players, as if they had writ another *Christs Teares*, are piteously persecuted by the Lord Mayor and the aldermen, and however in their old Lord's time they thought their state settled, it is now so uncertain they cannot build upon it.[20]

*'"had I wist" hopes': vain, mistaken hopes.

The comparison is grim, for the Lord Mayor had sent Nashe to Newgate for writing *Christs Teares*. The Lord Chamberlain's Men 'thought their state settled' because they had assumed that the generous Sir George Carey would immediately succeed his father in the office of Lord Chamberlain. But Sir George Carey, though the Queen's cousin, had not been assiduous in his attendance at court, preferring to lord it over his own little realm of Wight – of which he called himself 'Governor', though he was strictly speaking only 'Captain' – and he and the players were to suffer for it. The new Lord Hunsdon's supporters Essex and Southampton were away on the 'Islands Voyage', a botched raid on the Spanish treasure fleet in the Azores, and not able to plead his case. In August the office was given to William Cobham, Lord Brooke, who was already nearly seventy, and no great friend to players. However, he had been assiduous in his attendance on the Queen, to judge by the New Year's Gift lists. Whether Cobham really hoped to see the theatres entirely suppressed, as some have speculated, or whether he simply took little or no interest in fostering and protecting players, is not clear. All that is certain is that the period of Cobham's Chamberlainship was a bleak one, and his death on 6 March 1597 nothing but a relief to the players, since it led immediately to the appointment they had originally counted on, thinking 'their state settled'. Only ten days after Cobham's death Sir George Carey was appointed to his late father's office of Chamberlain. As Richard Dutton points out, 'the Howards and the Hunsdons shared [the post of Lord Chamberlain] throughout Elizabeth's reign – saving only Cobham's tenure'.[21] Carey's appointment led to an immediate explosion of dramatic activity and creativity, along with an outbreak of vigorous satirical digs at the late Lord Cobham and his forebears: Shakespeare's 'Oldcastle', later emended to 'Falstaff' in response to protests from Cobham's family; his jealous 'Brooke', emended to 'Broome', in *Merry Wives*; Jonson's 'Cob' in *Every Man In his Humour* (1598); and Nashe's last work, the splendid *Lenten Stuffe* (1599), with its elaborate mock-encomium of the 'cob', or herring. More will be said in the next chapter about the glorious post-Cobham renaissance enjoyed by the Chamberlain's Men.

Only two or three weeks after old Lord Hunsdon's death came a far more 'insupportable and touching loss' (*Julius Caesar*, 4.3.148). Little Hamnet Shakespeare, aged eleven and a half, was buried at Holy Trinity on 11 August. It is generally assumed that his father was present in Stratford at least for the funeral, and possibly already at the time of his death. This may well be so, especially since late summer seems to have been a time Shakespeare often spent in Stratford, and in any case the death of Lord Hunsdon probably led to a swift dispersal of his players. It is not uncommon for one of a pair of twins to be markedly smaller and frailer than the other, having received less nourishment from the placenta before birth. Perhaps the little boy always had been rather frail. The disparity between his life-span and that of his twin sister Judith, who lived to the great age of seventy, is striking. Of the father's grief we know nothing. When Ben Jonson lost his first son, and namesake, to plague, aged seven, in 1603, he had a divining dream of the child 'with the mark of a bloody cross on his forehead as if it had been cutted with a sword'. Next morning he received a letter telling him of the boy's death.[22] He gave his grief public and permanent shape in the epigram 'ON MY FIRST SONNE', published in the 1616 *Workes*:

> . . . Rest in soft peace, and asked, say here doth lie
> BEN. JONSON his best piece of poetry.[23]

However, Jonson's second son survived, and lived almost as long as his father. An awareness that Shakespeare left no physical son may colour Jonson's comment on the First Folio plays, 'Look how the father's face / Lives in his issue'. Shakespeare's 'lines' were to be his true and only sons: he left lines of verse, but no blood-line.

We might imagine that an Elizabethan father in Shakespeare's position would try to beget another son. It is a strange sequence of events, that he should procure a coat of arms and a gentleman's residence just after the death of the only child who could carry on his name. Yet these projects were probably under way, or at least decided on in principle, while Hamnet still lived. We cannot be sure that Shakespeare made no further attempts to father a child, whether after the birth of the twins in 1585, or after the death of Hamnet in 1596, though I am inclined to doubt it. My own suspicion is that conjugal relations between William and Anne ceased some time in the 1580s, and by the time of Hamnet's death were quite extinct. Yet while there's death there's hope. Fairly naturally, given the discrepancy in their ages, Shakespeare may have dreamed that he would eventually outlive Anne and that he might one day be able, as a gentleman of substance, to make a better marriage, and beget another son. A parallel would be Edward Alleyn's second marriage, aged fifty-seven, to Constance Donne, aged about eighteen. With such distant prospects in view, he visited the College of Arms in Upper Thames Street in October 1596.

Not without right

When Shakespeare approached the Heralds he probably had a clear idea of the design of his coat of arms. Perhaps he had already paid a painter to do a mock-up to his own specifications, which was one of the 'abuses' of which William Smith was to complain in about 1605–6.[24] The final sketch may have been made by his colleague Richard Burbage, who was to paint an *impresa* for the

Earl of Rutland, to Shakespeare's design, in 1613. The concept of a spear on a bend may have been already in place when, or if, his father attempted to acquire a patent some twenty years before, for which the then Clarencieux Herald, Robert Cooke, had allegedly drawn a 'pattern'. But the note, at the end of the second of the drafts that survive, suggests an assertion rather than reference to a solid piece of documented evidence.[25] According to one authority, 'any man is allowed to enter a large proportion of facts concerning his own pedigree from his grandfather on his own solemn affirmation, without the formality of the production of actual documentary proofs'.[26] Probably Shakespeare affirmed various 'facts', relating to his father's status, wealth and ancestry, and alluded to a previous application, without documentation. Many of the erasures and inconsistencies in the drafts – especially in Draft 1 – suggest oral reports and instructions beset with some vagueness and inconsistency. Essentially, I believe, both the initiative and the shaping ideas came from the younger Shakespeare. By securing armigerous status for his father John, who was not in good health, and might well die quite soon, he ensured that he could himself enjoy gentle status – indeed, more securely gentle than that of his father. Rather as the crown descended to Henry V 'with an easier grace' than to his usurper father, the younger Shakespeare could hope to enjoy gentle status more comfortably through the natural process of inheritance than could his father, as the technical recipient of the patent. Also, by securing a grant for his father rather than for himself, he might hope to avoid being the target of mockery such as that of Nashe, who satirized upstart swineherds' sons who spend their patrimony on self-promotion, 'bestowing more at one time on the Herald for arms, than his father all his life time gave in alms'.[27]

Like many Elizabethan 'new men', the Shakespeares were attracted to 'canting', or punning, heraldry – a coat of arms that closely resembled a quite different form of symbolism, the chivalric *impresa* borne in tournaments. Heraldic imagery is intended to be permanent, and in the early Middle Ages was often purely geometric. It does not generally convey any specific meaning beyond the determination to distinguish a particular family, in war or peace. Even if the family dies out, its own particular coat belongs to that family only, and does not become available for re-allocation to another. The *impresa*, on the other hand, is a transient, but richly expressive, device, which reflects the bearer's situation, outlook or aspirations within a particular context and at a particular period of his or her life. It generally consists of an image and a short motto whose meaning can only be discerned in combination. Philip Sidney showed characteristic brilliance in combining word and image when taking part in a court tournament soon after the birth of a son to his uncle, the Earl of Leicester, in the spring of 1583. To show that he had now lost all the hopes of inheritance that he had once enjoyed, he displayed the word SPERAVI ('I have hoped'), but with a line drawn through it, SPERAVI, 'to show that his hopes therein were dashed'. Both the audience and the occasion were precisely specific to that stage of Sidney's career. Shakespeare's notion for his family's coat of arms was more confident, and set off daringly bold chivalric associations. In so far as it was punning, symbolic and expressive of the holder's outlook and aspirations, it was far more like an *impresa* than a coat of arms. Yet its *impresa*-like symbolism also pointed all too aptly to what proved to be its vulnerability.

In a period 'when heraldry was becoming increasingly elaborate, and many shields were overloaded and fussy in detail', the 'simple beauty and dignity' of the Shakespeare coat has been praised.[28] Its simplicity, however, derives from a coat first awarded in the early thirteenth century. As we shall see, its simplicity of design also makes its symbolic message particularly clear. Yet coats of arms were not really meant to convey a specific message, beyond that of defining the distinctive genealogy and status of the holder. There are two metals in the Shakespeare coat, gold and silver. The single colour, black, serves simply to divide them and to provide a foil, so that the 'bright metal', sunbright gold, gleams brightly 'on a sullen ground'. Laid on a 'bend sable', or black band, is a golden tilting spear. In the first of the two surviving drafts of the grant of arms Sir William Dethick's clerk has twice hesitated over whether the point of the spear should be 'argent' – silver – or 'proper' – the same colour as the rest of the spear. However, the second draft makes it clear that the spear is to be 'of the first', that is, the colour first mentioned, gold, but 'steeled argent', that is, with a silver tip. It seems that there was also some discussion about the colouring of the spear, and whether its point should be differentiated from its shaft. It was no doubt Shakespeare himself who insisted on the differentiation of the spear's tip, which was symbolic rather than naturalistic. In both drawings the form of the spear is that of a tilting staff, and in genuine tournaments tilting staffs had fragile wooden tips that could readily splinter or break against an opponent's shield or armour. But the grand simplicity of a golden tilting staff laid on a golden field evokes both wealth and chivalric achievement. According to Gerard Legh, a combination of gold with silver signifies the holder 'To be a victor over all infidels, Turks and Sarazins'.[29] These precious metals serve to imply that the Shakespeares of Henley Street are the kind of men who formerly participated in court jousts and ceremonies, and in the distant past had been Crusaders.

Combined with the allusion to John Shakespeare's 'great grandfather' (probably in truth, in so far as truth comes into it, William's great-grandfather, John's grandfather) and his 'faithful and approved service to the late most prudent prince King Henry VII of famous memory', the boldly simple tilting staff suggests that previous generations of Shakespeares were court servants or even courtiers. Suggestions have been made that a forebear fought under Richmond – later Henry VII – at the Battle of Bosworth. Yet this is rather unlikely, both because Richmond's soldiers are known to have been for the most part Bretons, not Midland yeomen, and because such service would surely have rated an explicit mention. Indeed, if a Shakespeare had served notably at Bosworth, it would probably not have been necessary for his great-grandson to be applying for gentle status. Four soldiers called Shakespeare who were archers have been identified half a century later.[30] But though skilled and often heroic, as at Agincourt, the archer was only a lowly foot-soldier. This golden tilting staff, with its silver tip, not only alluded to the 'spear' of the family name, it presented that spear in a grandly courtly and ceremonial form.

Laid on the coat of arms, sloping up at an angle of 45°, the golden spear or staff could also be read in other ways. With its silver tip, it could resemble a silver-tipped pen. Some modern representations of the coat, such as that drawn by C. W. Scott-Giles (Plate 4),[31] bring out this resemblance, adding a central line for shading on the spear's point which has the effect of making it look very like a modern silver pen-nib. To Elizabethans, for whom the feather-quill pen was the standard tool, the resemblance of the spear to a pen poised for writing would not be quite so obvious, though it might remind them of the gold or silver pens awarded as prizes to outstandingly skilled penmen. Such a golden pen, worth £20, was awarded to Peter Bales in a writing competition on Michaelmas Day 1595.[32] Others will have followed up the punning implications of the name 'Shakespeare', which could be 'a nickname for a belligerent person or perhaps a bawdy name for an exhibitionist'.[33] According to this popular reading, the courtly looking tilting staff could be viewed as figuring, or flashing, a rather less courtly erect phallus.

The Shakespeare crest was if possible even more courtly than the coat. It comprised a silver falcon, 'his wings displayed', 'standing on a wreath of his colours'. That courtly bird the falcon, or falcon gentle, presented a confident assertion of rank. It is a falcon gentle who is the bird of highest status in Chaucer's *Parlement of Foules*. When Thomas Nashe poured scorn on the Danes for making their young courtiers perpetual schoolboys, permitting them no scope for advancement, he used the falcon gentle to symbolize their crushed aspirations: 'to clip the wings of a high towering falcon . . . now she sits sadly on the ground, picking of worms'.[34]

It seems beyond coincidence that Shakespeare's recent patron the Earl of Southampton had four silver falcons in his own coat of arms, 'Azure, a gold cross between four silver falcons'. The Wriothesley coat was both especially splendid and especially well known to anyone interested in heraldry, for a version of it, with silver doves in place of silver falcons, became the coat of the College of Arms.[35] It derived from Southampton's great-uncle, Sir Thomas Wriothesley, who had a nearly thirty-year reign as Garter King. Coming from such a family, Shakespeare's young patron must have been, even by Elizabethan

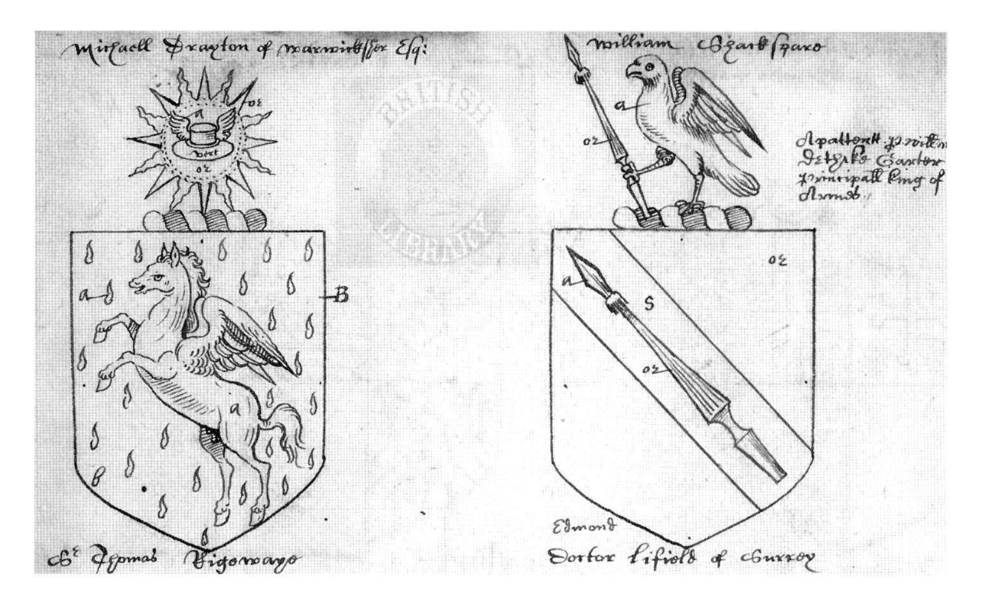

Fig. 13 Shakespeare's coat of arms beside Michael Drayton's.

standards, acutely aware of the visual ceremony and symbolism that expressed a family's honour and rank.

Michael Drayton had used his coat of arms to allude to an institution, the Inner Temple, with which he was strongly associated, and to which he owed support and patronage. Drayton's coat was almost identical to that of the Inner Temple, except for the addition of water drops to the azure ground on which a winged horse – 'Pegasus salient' – prances.[36] His crest was odd and distinctive, being a green 'cap of Mercury' against a golden sun, alluding presumably to his own literary gifts, Mercury being the god of language. Analogously, whether on Southampton's suggestion or otherwise, Shakespeare assumed a silver falcon which linked him visibly with his munificent patron. It would be pleasant to think that, in giving him a handsome sum of money for 'a purchase which he heard he had a mind to', Southampton also said airily 'do use a falcon to show your connection with me', rather as if he were permitting his protégé to adopt his livery. However, I suspect, rather, that while Shakespeare was indeed inspired by the example of the Wriothesley arms to choose a falcon for his crest, in so doing he was over-bold, as befitted his belligerent name. Possibly his presumption in selecting a silver falcon for his crest contributed to the withdrawal of Southampton's patronage.

While the four silver falcons on the Wriothesley coat are shown in profile, the silver falcon on the Shakespeare crest has 'his wings displayed'. The intention is to suggest the moment called 'shaking', which in falconry was the bird's action immediately before taking flight. Rather than shaking the spear that it holds, bolt upright, in its right claw, the bird is itself enacting the 'shake' part of the bearer's name. There may also be an allusion to the idiom 'shake the feather', meaning 'to make a display of one's honours'.[37] The self-assertive message is doubled and reinforced. Not only does the Shakespeare crest show an aristocratic object, a golden tilting staff, held upright by a bird that has chivalric and aristocratic associations, the falcon itself exemplifies the bearer's exhibitionistic, swaggering pride in his inheritance. This gentleman, it is implied, is more than ready to take on all comers. The visual imagery seems to say 'we Shakespeares are courtly warriors, of gentle rank'. And lest anyone should raise a doubt, the motto NON SANZ DROICT ('not without right'), also chivalric in its use of medieval French, should quash all uncertainty: 'We are of ancient military lineage, with legitimate claim to bear arms.'

NOT WITHOUT MUSTARD

As well as giving some problems to Dethick's clerk, who made three attempts to write it out, Shakespeare's motto led to his being mocked by Jonson. Jonson's depiction of Sogliardo in *Every Man Out*, acted by the Lord Chamberlain's Men in 1599, has already been mentioned. Sogliardo, a country bumpkin of manifest stupidity, could not possibly be construed as a portrait of Shakespeare. Jonson's general target here is the current craze for procuring arms in an extravagant and ignorant manner. Sogliardo has sold four or five acres of land to pay for smart clothes, declaring that 'I'll be once a little prodigal in a humour, i'faith, and have a most prodigious coat.' The wildly extravagant, over-coloured, over-detailed coat that he procures is not in the least like Shakespeare's, though it does resemble that of 'Parr the Embroiderer' (see above, p. 86, Plate 7). But in a play conspicuously peppered with allusions to Shakespeare's recent work, especially *Henry IV* and *Julius Caesar*, it is impossible not to find a Shakespearean reference also in the 'word' that Puntarvolo suggests to round off Sogliardo's absurd coat and crest with its dissected boar, '*Not without mustard*' (3.4). Immediately, this is a quotation from Nashe's *Pierce Pennilesse*, where it is the saving condition of a shipwrecked man's promise never again to eat 'haberdine' if he escapes drowning. But for the Lord Chamberlain's Men an allusion to their fellow player's war-cry 'NON SANZ DROICT' would be unmissable, especially since he had played a major role with them in *Every Man In* the previous year. Also, the bright yellow colour of mustard surely alludes to the lavish gold / yellow of the Shakespeare coat.[38] Jonson continued to mock Shakespeare for his 'gentle' status even after his death. While praising the way in which 'he seems to shake a lance' in every line he writes, he makes it seem grotesquely as if the spear-shaking crest, his boldly assumed trademark, is stamped into every detail of his writing.

Spurts of rough banter from Jonson were to be the least of Shakespeare's immediate problems with his coat of arms. His hard-won and dear-bought honour was to be jeopardized and compromised to such an extent that it was never absolutely clear whether his inheritance of the title 'gentleman', after his father's death in 1601, was indeed sound in the view of experts on such matters. Twelve years after the grant of arms, when Shakespeare prepared his long-awaited *Sonnets* for publication, he did not use the title *Sonnets. By W. Shake-speare, Gent.*, but resorted instead to a Jonson-like display of singularity and self-promotion: *SHAKE-SPEARES SONNETS.*

Yet for a short time, in 1596–7, all seemed well. The acquisition of a coat of arms for his father in the autumn of 1596 was succeeded in the spring of 1597 by the purchase of New Place, at the corner of Chapel Lane and Chapel Street in Stratford. As a house built originally by Sir Hugh Clopton, this was undoubtedly a residence for a man of dignity and substance, although in much need of repair. Its vendor in 1597 was a slightly shady young man, William Underhill, whose father was Clerk of Assizes at Warwick. As so often, the epithet 'New' paradoxically betokened some antiquity, and it was clearly a house for a gentleman. Over the central door of this five-gabled frontage, with its extensive gardens and outbuildings behind, the Shakespeare arms could soon be carved and painted.

A play which can be dated with unusual precision, *The Merry Wives of Windsor*, marks this phase of triumph and expectation. It belongs to the spring of 1597, being associated with the forthcoming installation of the new Lord Chamberlain, Sir George Carey, Lord Hunsdon, to the Order of the Garter. It has been convincingly argued that he commissioned Shakespeare to write it for performance before the Queen at the Garter Feast at Whitehall Palace on St George's Day, 23 April. The comedy may have been shown after supper, as Carey's special contribution to the festivities.[39] This is entirely compatible with Rowe's claim that the Queen herself asked Shakespeare to continue the character of Falstaff 'for one play more, and to show him in love'.[40] Carey was both Elizabeth's first cousin and, probably, her nephew, his father Henry being the fruit of Henry VIII's affair with Mary Boleyn. Now that he was fully under her eye at court, the Queen was able to express her extremely intimate and familial affection for him. It makes perfect sense that she should tell him what kind of play she wanted, a command he quickly conveyed to his players. Mistress Quickly's closing speech, as 'Queen of Fairies', makes the Garter Feast context fully explicit. She bids the fairies form themselves into a ring 'Like to the Garter's compass', and to clean and adorn Windsor Castle with appropriate flowers:

> And *Honi soit qui mal y pense* write
> In em'rald tufts, flowers purple, blue, and white,
> Like sapphire, pearl and rich embroidery,
> Buckled below fair knighthood's bending knee . . .
>
> (5.5.69–72)

Although the play was performed at Whitehall, its own internal setting is of course Windsor. It looks forward to the formal installation of the new Garter knights – at which the Queen would not be present – at the Castle on 24 May. *The Merry Wives* also celebrates Shakespeare's own new glory as a court poet.

Yet the play is surprisingly bourgeois. Not only is it Shakespeare's only comedy with an English setting, it is also almost the only one which lacks kings or noblemen. There are no dukes or earls, except, off-stage, the comic-sounding 'Duke de Jarmany', alluding to the Duke of Würtemberg, who was to be installed as a Garter knight *in absentia*. The character of highest rank, Sir John Falstaff, undergoes a succession of humiliations at the hands of the merry and witty wives, including a brief disguise as a fat old woman. Perhaps, by contraries, the defeat of a phoney and ignoble knight points to the dignity of true knightly values. Deliberate send-up of Elizabethan chivalry is also suggested by Falstaff's grotesquely inappropriate adaptation of a line written by a true knight, Sir Philip Sidney, whom many present at the feast would remember, the courtly exclamation 'Have I caught my heavenly jewel?'[41] Though the play was primarily designed to please and compliment its merry patron Sir George Carey and his mistress the Queen, it can also be read as a celebration of the lives of citizens. The Pages and the Fords are gentry, but city gentry, the kind who live in substantial houses on a street, not in country manors. They have maintained and consolidated their 'gentle' status through holding such local government offices as Bailiff or Justice of the Peace. They are, in short, on just the same social level as that new-made gentleman Master John Shakespeare of Henley Street. The opening scene has Masters Shallow, Silence and Evans talking entirely of matters of status. 'Robert Shallow, Esquire' will not take any nonsense from Sir John Falstaff, for he is a chief Justice of the Peace and 'a gentleman born . . . who writes himself *Armigero*, in any bill, warrant, quittance, or obligation – *Armigero*' (1.1.7–9). As Leslie Hotson discovered, Shallow is probably a parody of the litigious Justice of the Peace William Gardiner, whose arms when quartered with those of his wife, Frances Luce, included 'three luces Argent' – compare the 'dozen white luces' of Shallow's 'old coat'.[42] Shallow and Silence are indeed old gentry, but they are also tedious old fools. The future, it seems, belongs to families such as the prosperous Pages and Fords, who live comfortably and secure good prospects for their children. In the schoolboy William Page, whose elder sister Anne is just at marriageable age, we may find a reincarnation of Hamnet Shakespeare. As the first and only son of a father called 'William', the child may even have been familiarly known as 'young William'. His sister Susanna's fourteenth birthday was coming up just two days after Carey's installation as a Garter Knight on 24 May. The cameo portrait of little William Page, the promising schoolboy who impresses both the unlettered Mistress Quickly and his own mother with what his tutor Evans calls his 'good sprag memory', may be the nearest Shakespeare came to a public memorial to his own son. While Jonson called his dead son 'his best piece of poetry', Shakespeare seems to have assimilated his into what he happened to be writing in the spring after his death. But though other comedies accommodate moments of intense pathos, the context of this one meant that it had to be a festive farce, with no scope for any expression of private grief.

Dethick's abuses

The Merry Wives openly celebrated the Lord Chamberlain's new honour, and more covertly, for his fellow players, Shakespeare's. But while Sir George Carey was secure in his splendour, Shakespeare was deeply vulnerable. Many would argue that only honourable men could bestow honours, and the allocation of honours by Sir William Dethick, Garter King of Arms, was increasingly the target of professional criticism. Dethick had been introduced to the College of Arms at an early age by his father Sir Gilbert Dethick, also Garter King. Both men were violent and quarrelsome to a degree remarkable even in the Elizabethan period. Their own family origins were extremely questionable. Though they claimed to descend from the Derbyshire Dethicks, they seem, in fact, to have been a Dutch family whose name was originally 'Dericke'. A single example indicates the younger man's psychopathic violence. Back in May 1573, when he was York Herald, not yet Garter, William Dethick made a brutal attack on the wife of the then Chester Herald, with whom he had some obscure quarrel. Chester Herald's wife, Mary Hart, wrote a complaint to Lord Burghley from which this is an extract:

> I being alone in my chamber, he put me in fear of my life ... he spurned me with his foot so oft my head was very near the fire, and my hair like to be burned, as it may appear by my cap which I had next my hair. He put a deep coal basket lined with leather on my head with some coals and dust in it, and kept it so long about my head and shoulders that my breath was almost gone ... my chamber pot of urine he poured on my bare head and thereafter rubbed hot ashes into my hair and dipped a basin into a stand of new drink and flashed so much full on my face, that

> I could not see for a time . . . he said before Richmond and Somerset Heralds that I lied like a pocky drab (or a quean) and would have runned on me again with his foot, but his mother held him back.[43]

Over the years William Dethick became notorious for his violence, attacking clergy at funerals, wounding his own brother with a dagger and striking his father. He beat the minister at Sir Henry Sidney's funeral at Penshurst in 1586. For calling a clergyman 'a bald rascally priest' and striking him he was at one time sentenced by the spiritual court to imprisonment and a fine of £100.[44] Yet, as Dethick himself was to observe when, on the Queen's orders, he declared Essex a traitor on 8 February 1601, 'an herald, though a wicked man, is nevertheless an herald'. This is the same mode of thinking as the Article in the Elizabethan Book of Common Prayer that declares that 'the unworthiness of the minister hindereth not the effect of the sacrament'. However, by 1601 Dethick's brutal ways had given the whole College of Arms a very bad name. It was no doubt with Dethick above all in mind that Essex – who as Earl Marshal presided over the Heralds – cried out on that fateful 8 February that 'a herald would proclaim anything for two shillings'. Early in James's reign Dethick was first temporarily replaced as Garter King by William Segar, and then, after yet more outrageous behaviour at the investiture of a later Duke of Würtemberg, he was persuaded to surrender his office, in return for a handsome payoff of £200 a year and exemption from all taxes.

It is not clear where Dethick's removal from office left all those 'gentlemen' to whom he had issued patents for coats of arms. Henry Howard, Earl of Northampton, who presided over the hearing of Brooke's challenge to Dethick at the Earl Marshal's Court in May 1602, suggested that 'a general *feu de joie*', or bonfire, should be made of all the patents issued by him during the previous thirty years.[45]

Attempts to remove Dethick from office began in the mid-1590s. Ralph Brooke or Brokesmouth, York Herald from 1593, undertook a painstakingly hostile scrutiny of the recent activities of his fellow Kings of Arms. His work was first made public in 1596 in a book dedicated to Essex, in which he challenged many of the genealogies in Camden's *Britannia*.[46] According to Brooke, the respected Camden, Clarencieux King of Arms, derived much of his supposed learning from notes left by the late Robert Glover, but 'I would his gloves might have fitted your hands in such sort, as you might have smoothly carried them away: his notes (I mean) I wish you had neither misunderstood, nor misreported.'[47] There is a strong play of sardonic humour throughout Brooke's treatise, for instance on the unnatural and incestuous unions created by Camden's alleged blunders:

> In this title of Berkeley, you make Maurice the son of Robert Fitz-harding to be son to his own wife, and the said Robert to marry his son's wife: which unnatural marriages, though well liked of by yourself, yet never known or allowed of by any others.[48]

Apparently Camden got wind of Brooke's critique while it was in the press, and tried unsuccessfully to persuade his 'friends the Stationers' to suppress it.[49] Meanwhile Brooke was also scrutinizing the many grants of arms made by Dethick. This was a far larger, more complex and more evidently scandalous story, involving 'abuses' extending over several decades. Numerous documents testify to Brooke's challenge to Dethick, and Dethick's defence, which are no doubt only a small proportion of what originally existed. Of most interest to us is the debate between Brooke and Dethick over his grants of arms. Brooke listed twenty-three individuals to whom Dethick had wrongly granted armigerous status, the name 'Shakespeare' coming fourth.[50] Evidently Brooke delivered his challenge to Dethick by displaying a 'scroll' showing the twenty-three wrongly awarded arms, with the arms from which they were derived, where applicable. The scroll itself does not survive, but from the responses to it of Dethick and Camden we can deduce much about the nature of Brooke's allegations. Many awards, Brooke claimed, had been made to 'mean persons', such as graziers and ironmongers, and also many coats rightly belonging to ancient families had been bestowed on these 'mean persons'. The Shakespeare coat was challenged on both grounds. The vindication of it concerns both its similarity to the arms of Lord Mauley (Plate 5), and the status of John Shakespeare. Piers de Mauley had been a favourite of King John, and was reputed by some chroniclers to have been the murderer of Prince Arthur of Brittany. Though the Barony de Mauley died out in 1415, when the eighth Piers de Mauley died, this did not render the coat available to others. The vindication of the coat awarded to Shakespeare attempts to answer both points. It is claimed that the coat is clearly distinguished from Lord Mauley's by 'the spear on the bend', and John's armigerous credentials are defended as being, in effect, those of Justice Shallow, Esquire: 'the man was a magistrate of Stratford upon Avon: a Justice of peace. He married the daughter and heir of Arden, and was of a good substance and ability.' As we saw in chapter 1, though John Shakespeare had indeed been a Justice of the Peace, his period of active involvement in the peaceable government of Stratford was extremely brief. The Arden whom he married was only the youngest daughter of a junior and obscure branch of the family, yeomen not gentry. He was also in considerable financial difficulty. The word 'ability' here refers to 'pecuniary power, wealth, estate'.[51] But it was the son, not the father, who could now lay claim to considerable 'substance and ability', as a Lord Chamberlain's Man and master of New Place.

It was contrary to all principles of honour that the son should bestow gentility on the father, rather than the other way round. As the Fool was to say in *Lear*, 'he's a mad yeoman that sees his son a gentleman before him'. Yet this in effect was what happened in the Shakespeare family.

My name receives a brand

Schoenbaum dismissed the debate between Brooke and Dethick as 'a heraldic tempest in a teacup'. Yet it was, as we have seen, very much more than that. It is true that the Heralds were a quarrelsome lot, especially during the period of what Anthony Wagner called 'The Elizabethan Troubles'. But the long and disgraceful reign of William Dethick as Garter King of Arms was no trivial matter. Nor was Brooke's challenge to him a private and inconspicuous affair. Heralds, after all, were professionally concerned with controlling the public display of the visual symbols of honour. Ralph Brooke no doubt made sure that his scroll of wrongly awarded arms, showing the incorrect arms alongside the ones they usurped, was publicly visible. The fact that Shakespeare attempted in 1599 to have the Arden coat quartered with that of Shakespeare – an attempt which seems to have been unsuccessful, since the quartering was not shown on his funeral monument – reflects his painful awareness that the patent he acquired so expensively in 1596 was highly questionable, and well known to be so. Establishing gentility with reference to the Ardens, if it could have been done, might have helped, although strict theorists did not accept female descent. John Ferne, for instance, said that 'if a gentlewoman . . . shall marry with a yeoman . . . his state and condition is nothing at all advanced by this act of matrimony, no, not so much as in the participating of the nude and bare title of gentle'.[52] Dethick's public shaming brought with it a slur on the names and status of all those to whom he had issued dubious patents. On the day of his attempted coup Essex said, when told to obey the Herald, 'I see no herald here but that branded fellow, whom I took not for a herald.' The view of Essex as Earl Marshal, supreme judge of the whole College of Arms, should not be lightly dismissed. If Dethick, Garter King of Arms, was notoriously a 'branded fellow', where did that leave Shakespeare? He too, surely, had been 'branded'. As a mere 'player', he should never have sought arms, in the view of many authorities. But worse than that, he was unlucky enough to acquire his patent from a herald who himself was disgraced. By the time the *Sonnets* were being put into final shape for publication Dethick had been deprived of office: and 'Thence comes it that my name receives a brand', says the speaker in sonnet 111. The three sonnets 110–12, all dealing with the speaker's poor reputation and the 'brand' 'Which vulgar scandal stamped upon my brow' (112.2) make good sense as agonized commentaries on Shakespeare's misery in finding that all his efforts to improve his social status have resulted, instead, in shame and disgrace because of the shame and disgrace of Dethick.

A passage in John Davies of Hereford's *Microcosmos* (1603), a poem in which he introduces the little world of England to the newly acceded Scottish King, shows that these troubles were well known. Addressing Shakespeare and Burbage, as a marginal note indicates, Davies exempts them from his attack on proud and overweening players because of their undoubted talent:

> Players, I love ye and your quality,
> As ye are men that pass time not abused:
> And some I love for painting, poesy,
> And say fell Fortune cannot be excused,
> That hath for better uses you refused:
> Wit, courage, good shape, good parts, and all good,
> As long as all these goods are no worse used,
> And though the stage doth stain pure gentle blood,
> Yet generous ye are in mind and mood.[53]

Davies's epithet 'generous' alludes to the Latin '*generosus*', the normal term for a 'gentleman'. His fourth and fifth lines strongly parallel Shakespeare's sonnet 111.1–4:

> O, for my sake do you with Fortune chide,
> The guilty goddess of my harmful deeds,
> That did not better for my life provide
> Than public means, which public manners breeds.

Both Burbage and Shakespeare, though players, had attempted formally to become gentlemen. Neither, in the world's eyes, could ever really be so, because of the 'stain' of the 'stage'. Yet Davies, from his own secure position as a protégé of the Earl of Pembroke and his mother, comfortingly if patronizingly says that for his part he greatly admires their additional talents – Burbage's for painting, Shakespeare's for writing – and regards them as essentially gentlemen. For Shakespeare, this was cold comfort. He might have done better to cultivate singularity, like Jonson.

CHAPTER FIVE

1599

Our bending author

Thus far, with rough and all-unable pen,
Our bending author hath pursued the story,
In little room confining mighty men,
Mangling by starts the full course of their glory.

(*Henry V*, Epilogue, 1–4)

Precious time

ART imitates life – imitates art – imitates life. In the mid-1590s Shakespeare had written three plays about a young Henry who publicly rejects a former companion, and he also anticipated and personally experienced a version of this exclusion inflicted on him by his own young Henry. At the end of *2 Henry IV,* [1] the prodigal jesting knight Sir John Falstaff had been crushingly repudiated by his 'sweet boy', newly crowned King, who now embraces a calling far higher than fooling around with his social inferiors. Yet Shakespeare was not so much rejected as forgotten or marginalized. His young patron was caught up in great affairs at home and abroad to such an extent that he may never again have had much 'precious time to spend' in private with the poet he had rewarded and befriended in 1593–4. Southampton joined his friend Essex in his madcap raid on the Spanish port of Cádiz in 1596, and also in the 'Islands Voyage' the following year. In 1598 he went with Sir Robert Cecil on an embassy to Paris. In 1599 he was to make two separate trips to the war zones in Ireland. At court, between whiles, he was carrying on a love affair with Elizabeth Vernon, a cousin of his friend Essex, whom he made

Fig. 14 Portrait of the Earl of Southampton showing his long lock of hair.

pregnant and hastily married just before his departure for France.[2] He also found time to get into violent rows with other courtiers. One such scuffle took place in 1598, after Ambrose Willoughby, an Esquire of the Body, ordered Southampton to abandon a game of cards with Sir Walter Ralegh in the presence chamber at Whitehall as the Queen was about to pass through on her way to bed. Southampton was furious, and threatened to get his own back on Willoughby; they fell to blows in the palace garden, and in the fray, Willoughby pulled off some of the young nobleman's 'lock'.[3] Portraits of this period show Southampton sporting very long hair, which hangs to the front on his right shoulder, perhaps in emulation of native American chiefs encountered and described by the colonists of Virginia in 1582–5 (Fig. 14). Travel and adventure were his consuming passion. Gervase Markham's sonnet commending his poem on the brave death of Sir Richard Grenville near the Azores may have given far more pleasurable stimulus to Southampton's 'courageous thoughts' than the long-drawn-out musings of *Lucrece*.[4] To more sober courtiers at home, his prodigality and narcissistic self-display were no doubt extremely annoying. Though he still often behaved like a madcap Hal, Henry Wriothesley was, since his twenty-first birthday in October 1594, every inch an earl, and all too eager to pull rank and to claim his place near the throne. After the death of his former guardian Lord Burghley in August 1598 there was no older person who was able effectively to exercise control over him.[5]

It is doubtful whether Shakespeare could ever have addressed the young nobleman as 'Hal'. Yet the temptation to commit a terrible *faux pas* like Falstaff's, in speaking publicly to the newly crowned King in terms of private endearment, was something he knew all about:

> God save thy Grace, King Hal, my royal Hal! . . .
> God save thee, my sweet boy! . . .
> My King! My Jove! I speak to thee, my heart!
>
> (*2 Henry IV*, 5.5.41–6)

We should notice that the third line echoes Daniel's *Rosamond*, in which Rosamond Clifford appeals to King Henry II, her former lover. As social inferiors to the young men they love, both Falstaff and Shakespeare's speaker in the *Sonnets* readily fall into 'the woman's part', viewing themselves as neglected royal minions:

> Nor dare I chide the world-without-end hour
> Whilst I, my sovereign, watch the clock for you . . .
>
> (57.5–6)

When he wrote *2 Henry IV* in 1597/8 Shakespeare was already fully aware of the dangers of invoking a past, private, relationship in a public arena. In the years after the play was finished he continually re-lived Falstaff's rejection – not so much because he was publicly scorned, as because, like the fair young nobleman of sonnet 57 to whom the speaker is 'slave', Southampton simply had no time for him. Instinctively, Shakespeare had mapped out his humiliation in advance. He had made amends for the deliberate offence given to the historical Oldcastle descendants, the Brooke family, with the character's original name, 'Sir John Oldcastle', by giving the fat knight a self-disabling version of his own name. 'Falstaff' is the flip side of 'Shakespeare', denoting, not a spear that shakes with threat and brave assertion, but a staff – and remember that the 'spear' in the coat of arms is in truth a tilting-staff – that bends and falls in desertion or defeat. Detumescence and cowardice were already faintly hinted at in 'Shakespeare', for a spear may shake with fear rather than with menace. But defeat is written boldly and inescapably into the fat knight's name. As his name leads us to expect, far from becoming a great man when his Hal becomes King, Falstaff is humiliatingly banished, and is allowed no place within ten miles of the young man's person. With Southampton now so often either abroad or at court, Shakespeare too, though not technically banished, felt himself to be so. *Lucrece* was reprinted in 1598, and *Venus*, twice, in 1599. But their dedicatory epistles now mocked him with reminders of more intimate times. In a year or so, as we shall see in the next chapter, Southampton found it useful to re-invoke his connection with Shakespeare. But this summons would bring near disaster, not advancement, to Shakespeare and his colleagues. It certainly did not lead to a resumption of personal friendship.

Waiting for the end

Yet professionally, the year 1599 was another *annus mirabilis*, one in which Shakespeare rose by bending. His ability to adapt himself and his writing to a constantly changing social and cultural environment was the secret of his rise and rise. While many other writers encountered extreme difficulties in 1598–9, Shakespeare had become unassailably prominent as a writer both of poems and of plays. Francis Meres had publicly praised the narrative poems and 'his sugared sonnets among his private friends, etc.' (of which more in chapter 8), as well as six comedies and six tragedies.[6] Not only did the turn of the century see an explosion of citations and quotations, with Falstaff, in particular, becoming a household name, it also saw Shakespeare receiving the irritating compliment of piracy, in the form of the printer William Jaggard's little unlicensed volume *The Passionate Pilgrim*, which contains only two definitely authentic Shakespeare sonnets, its title brazenly followed by the phrase 'By W. Shakespeare'. We know that Shakespeare was enraged by this piracy, which gave the impression to anyone who bought Jaggard's volume that Meres had wildly over-praised his 'sugared sonnets', but he was so busy that he took no immediate steps to deal with it.

For Shakespeare and his fellow members of the Lord Chamberlain's Men the year was dominated by the construction of the new Globe Theatre on Bankside. The players' excitement, in common with that of their contemporaries, was tinged with some apprehension as the end of the sixteenth century came into view. With it must surely come some great change in the state. Publicly, many poets resorted to fantastical denial, claiming that the divine Elizabeth would outlive all her subjects. Thomas Dekker made this claim in a play performed before the Queen at Christmas 1599. In the Prologue to

Dekker's *Old Fortunatus* two old men arrive at 'the temple of Elisa', and declare that a whole year of adoration of her seems like no more than a single day. In the Epilogue the old men pray for her to live and live for hundreds of years, 'Till these young boys change their curled locks to white'.[7] Privately most of the Queen's subjects knew perfectly well that, at sixty-seven, she must in truth be approaching the end of her mortal life. In different ways the unmentionable, undiscussible 'succession question' coloured all of Shakespeare's writings in 1599. Three brilliantly diverse plays belong to that year. The first, an English history with a happy ending, was, like Dekker's *Old Fortunatus*, a powerful re-write of a popular old play. As the glorious new Globe playhouse was constructed in part with timbers from the old Theatre, so *Henry V* was a glorious new play constructed in part from the once popular, but now stale, *Famous Victories*. The second was a Roman history with a partly tragic ending, and the third a free-wheeling comedy based on a best-selling romance. For a populace increasingly weary of being ruled by a slow and cautious old woman *Henry V* re-enacted the greatness England had once achieved under a young king who was full of energy and military zeal. Henry's triumph at Agincourt also figured the triumph that many hoped would soon be achieved by Elizabeth's young favourite, Essex, in crushing the rebellion of Tyrone O'Neill in Ireland. *Julius Caesar* showed the assassination of a self-willed and childless autocrat by a younger faction, yet it in no way endorsed their conspiracy. The 'spirit of Caesar' is too powerful for Brutus and Cassius, who are destroyed by their own treachery. The power vacuum is filled, instead, by the one man still loyal to Caesar, Mark Antony, a man who, like Prince Hal, has been underestimated politically because of his love of revelry. *As You Like It* celebrates an 'alternative' court in the Forest of Arden, a court that is almost explicitly an image of the theatre. Its hero is a younger son whose natural good-heartedness and courage make him more truly 'gentle' than those who have enjoyed the wealth and education that he has been denied.

All three of these plays had things in them to please Southampton. It is possible that he saw all of them, watching from the 'lords' room' at the back of the stage of the new Globe, while being watched, in turn, by the rest of the audience. By the autumn he was neglecting his career as a courtier, having become impatient of its formality and restraint, and in deep sympathy with his friend Essex, under house arrest after his unlicensed return from Ireland. According to Rowland Whyte, writing to Robert Sidney on 11 October 1599, 'My Lord Southampton and Lord Rutland come not to the court; the one doth but very seldom; they pass away the time in London merely in going to plays every day.'[8] These young aristocrats probably saw all three of Shakespeare's 1599 plays, and perhaps also *Every Man Out of his Humour*, which marked Jonson's bold comeback after his troubles in 1598.

While the trajectory of Shakespeare's success, in 1597–9, was up and up, both Nashe and Jonson were in deep disgrace after their collaboration on the satirical comedy *The Isle of Dogs*, which the Privy Council found to be 'seditious'. Jonson, additionally, needed to recover money and social standing after being branded and deprived of his goods as a convicted felon for his murder of his fellow actor Gabriel Spencer. He had also converted to Catholicism. Yet, despite having even more difficulties to overcome than had his collaborator Nashe, Jonson made a stronger and fuller recovery. As the century neared its end his public prominence increased. Indeed, as the 'humorous' poet publicly attacked by Dekker[9] he was to become the leading exponent of the period's buzz words 'humours' and 'humorous'. Nashe, on the other hand, valiantly attempted a comeback, but with pitifully little success. He had to avoid London for some months, having escaped imprisonment for the 'seditious' *Isle of Dogs* by fleeing to Great Yarmouth, probably by sea. When he published what was to be his last newly written work, *Nashes Lenten Stuffe*, early in 1599, he could find only a joke patron to whom to present it. The diminutive Humphrey King, a 'tobacconist', or tobacco smoker, and zealous tavern haunter, had little to offer Nashe as reward except a jester's goodwill. As a man known – if at all – mainly as a consumer of ale and tobacco, King brought the right sort of associations to Nashe's eulogy of Yarmouth's plentiful smoked herring. But King is unlikely to have been able to give Nashe much in the way of reward except the odd meal and round of drinks. Slightly desperately, and misleadingly, Nashe included in his elaborate title the words 'With a new Play never played before, of the praise of the RED HERRING'. For readers who hoped for a glimpse of *The Isle of Dogs* – since there is nothing like censorship for stimulating interest – this may have been an appealing label. But the work is actually a prose pamphlet, which among many ingenious fancies includes a re-writing of the story of Hero and Leander, the tragic lovers celebrated in verse by Nashe's dead friend 'Kit Marlowe'. In Nashe's burlesque version the drowned Leander is metamorphosed into 'ling' and Hero into herring. Both 'ling' and herring were the food of fasting and poverty, associated with writers down on their luck like Robert Greene in 1593–4, and Nashe himself in 1599.

OUR BENDING AUTHOR

Shakespeare's position in 1599, on the other hand, was increasingly comfortable. At a time when many of the poorer townspeople of Stratford were starving after a succession of bad harvests, he had been listed as possessing (or rather hoarding) ten quarters of corn and malt. There was no need for him to subsist on the tavern diet of pickled herrings. On 25 October

1598 his friend and neighbour Richard Quiney, staying in London at the Bell Inn in Carter Lane to deal with law business, had written a letter to his 'loving good friend and countryman' Shakespeare to ask for a loan of £30, possibly to enable another Stratford man, Abraham Sturley, to pay his own debts to the Corporation.[10] It is not clear whether a copy of Quiney's letter was delivered, or whether, if so, Shakespeare made the loan. But the fact that Quiney and Sturley had decided to approach Shakespeare with a request for such a large sum indicates that his prosperity was well known to his old friends.

One of the reasons why Shakespeare was now a rich man was that he knew how to give audiences exactly what they wanted. Any private agendas or personal 'humours' in his plays were extremely well veiled. The year 1599 shows this particularly clearly. In the light of what we know from external evidence about Shakespeare's continued efforts towards self-gentrification we may feel that certain elements in *Henry V* have a bearing on the author's changing status. The Archbishop of Canterbury's inordinately long 'Salic law' speech, surprisingly, appears in full even in the 1600 'bad' Quarto text. Its defence of the legitimacy of descent through the female line can be seen as reflecting Shakespeare's own preoccupations in the year in which he attempted, unsuccessfully, to have the new Shakespeare arms quartered with those of his mother's forebears the Ardens. Yet the last thing that any uninformed spectator or reader would guess is that this extended piece of royal genealogy might have a personal application, by analogy, to the play's author. Likewise, in the even more celebrated 'Crispin Day' speech of 4.3 the young king makes some promises that would have been of intense personal interest to Shakespeare and his fellows:

> . . . he today that sheds his blood with me
> Shall be my brother; be he ne'er so vile,
> This day shall gentle his condition.
>
> (4.3.61–3)

As we saw in the last chapter, the battlefield was hallowed by tradition as by far the best place to win honour. In October 1596 Shakespeare's ancestors' faithful service to King Henry VII – in battle, it was implied – had been cited as part of the case for a grant of arms. After the battle, it's true, Henry V conveniently forgets the rhetorical promise made in his 'Crispin Day' speech. There is no mention of any common soldier being elevated to gentle status, and the specific promise made to the common soldier Williams to 'meet' him (in a duel) is handed over to Fluellen. Yet even this discrepancy could suit Shakespeare's personal agenda. If the common soldiers who contributed to such famous victories as Agincourt or Bosworth merited 'gentling', but in practice often got overlooked, that lent further plausibility to the claim that though a Shakespeare

Fig. 15 Laurence Olivier as Henry V in his 1944 film.

forebear did good and faithful service to the first Tudor monarch his descendants remained – until the Heralds put this right – mere yeomen.

If we take life records as our starting point, these analogies can readily be teased out of Shakespeare's play. But none of them would occur to anyone who didn't happen to know that the playwright had just been in search of honours for himself. Shakespeare's fellow players may have picked them up, especially since many of them were also in pursuit of honour and 'gentle' status. King Henry's lines 'if it be a sin to covet honour / I am the most offending soul alive' (4.3.28) could be spoken in a particularly heartfelt way by the actor who played him, Richard Burbage, who seems to have constructed the signs of gentle status for himself without recourse to the Heralds. Yet Shakespeare has covered his tracks beautifully. While Jonson made it abundantly, even irritatingly, clear in his 1599 *Every Man Out* that he had personal battles to fight and scores to settle, on issues such as the correct definition of comedy, or the distinction between corrective satires and mere 'railing', Shakespeare has rendered his own preoccupations virtually invisible. Indeed, his very invisibility is as it were made visible in the opening lines of the final sonnet-Chorus, which – like the other Choruses – I think of as spoken and performed by Shakespeare himself:

> Thus far, with rough and all-unable pen,
> Our bending author hath pursued the story,
> In little room confining mighty men,
> Mangling by starts the full course of their glory.

So vivid are the play's events as dramatized in *Henry V*, a play unrecognizably improved on its forebear, the old Queen's Men's *Famous Victories*, that the audience may well have forgotten, or never have had time to consider, that the words they have just heard have been devised by a 'bending author' – an author who bent over his writing desk to compose the play, and who now bends front-stage at the Globe to bow to the honourable assembled company and receive their applause. A further point made quietly but firmly in the phrase 'Our bending author' is that this immediately successful play is the work of a single writer only. While Jonson notoriously quarrelled with collaborators, and did all he could to expunge their contribution from his texts, for instance in the printed text of his tragedy *Sejanus*,[11] Shakespeare draws attention to his sole authorship so unobtrusively and tactfully that modern readers, quite accustomed to single authorship, may not even notice that anything unusual is being claimed. By combining this assertion of sole authorship with profuse apologies for the inadequacy of what he has written he invites sympathy and reassurance on the part of the audience.

Shakespeare, indeed, 'bent' beautifully to the desires and preoccupations of his contemporaries in 1599. As refreshment to people weary of the regime of a cautious and capricious old woman he offered them a re-enactment of a time when England's prince was young, male and decisive. Yet he did it in such a way that neither Elizabeth nor her advisers could possibly find any harm in it. Young Henry's overseas campaign in waterlogged northern France could be seen as prefiguring Essex's eagerly expected victory over the Earl of Tyrone in boggy Ireland – a victory not just over an Irish rebel, but, it was believed, over his Spanish confederates. Famously, the analogy between Henry and Essex is made explicit in the Chorus which opens Act 5. The joyous return of Henry V from France, greeted by the Lord Mayor and huge crowds of citizens, is compared to the longed-for return of 'the General of our gracious Empress'. It is interesting that the Chorus twice suggests that victory over Tyrone will be a lesser triumph than was Henry V's conquest of France, calling it a 'lower . . . likelihood', and saying that the Londoners who turned out in such numbers to greet King Harry did so with 'much more cause'. But even this ranking was brilliantly tactful. To have made the two campaigns exactly equivalent would have been to suggest that the whole of Ireland was in rebellion against the Queen, rather than that her troops were merely sorting out a little local difficulty. Ireland didn't need to be entirely re-conquered in 1599 – as France did in 1415 – only to be locally pacified.

The conquering Caesar

The Act 5 Choruses contextualize *Henry V* in several ways. Not only are Henry's victories compared with the expected triumph of Essex, they are also located within the body of the author's own increasingly victorious dramatic achievements. Shakespeare looks forward to his next play in the initial comparison of the return of Henry from Agincourt with that of Caesar from his triumph over the sons of Pompey:

> The Mayor and all his brethren in best sort,
> Like to the senators of th'antique Rome,
> With the plebeians swarming at their heels,
> Go forth and fetch the conquering Caesar in . . .
>
> (5.0.25–8)

He thus neatly provides the Globe audience with some of 'the story so far' as background to *Julius Caesar*, which opens with the Roman commoners being rebuked for making holiday at a time when Caesar has *not* returned in triumph. The emphasis on the assembly of large crowds that both ends *Henry V* and opens *Julius Caesar* comments implicitly on the Globe Theatre's own 'full house', a mixed and wavering mob moved this way and that by powerful speeches. The Epilogue also reminds the audience of Shakespeare's early work, the *Henry VI* cycle, 'Which oft our stage hath shown'. Though Shakespeare has often been viewed as careless about personal fame or personal control of his own texts, these allusions show him effectively 'puffing' his own history plays,

English and Roman, old and new, but doing so in such an affable and relaxed way that we scarcely notice that it is being done.

It could be said – and, as we shall see, Jonson went out of his way to say it – that for a grammar-school dropout from Stratford to undertake to write tragedies based on Roman history was foolishly audacious. Until 1599, the Elizabethan writers who wrote or translated classical Roman tragedies had been either university graduates, or aristocrats, or both. The Countess of Pembroke, no less, had translated Robert Garnier's tragedy *Marc-Antoine*, as *Antonie*, dating her version 1590. Her protégé the Oxford-educated Samuel Daniel complemented this with his own *Cleopatra*, first published in 1594. As Polonius's recollections of stardom at university suggest – 'I did enact Julius Caesar. I was killed i'th' Capitol' (*Hamlet*, 3.2.102) – the rise and fall of Julius Caesar was an excellent topic for students. Richard Eedes wrote a Latin play *Caesar Interfectus*, of which only the epilogue survives, for performance at Christ Church, Oxford, in the early 1580s.[12] But two positive factors emboldened Shakespeare to take on the challenge. The first was the extraordinary success of his two great cycles of English history plays, now complete, all eight of them based on Raphael Holinshed's *Chronicles*. He had served a full seven-year apprenticeship in exercising his theatrical imagination on historical sources, and had become quite accustomed to composing his plays with a fat folio at his elbow, 'in little room confining mighty men'. He had learned how to compress and expand, how to embroider and embellish, and how to weave in non-historical material or characters in order to bring past worlds to theatrical life. However, there is considerably less embroidery and embellishment in the Roman histories than there is in the English ones. There are no equivalents of those leisurely scenes in Justice Shallow's orchard in *2 Henry IV*, let alone of such major invented characters as Falstaff. When it came to Roman history Shakespeare knew that he would be unwise to deviate too far from his sources. Notoriously, he often retains not just the plot outlines he found in Sir Thomas North's translation of Plutarch's *Lives*, but very often whole speeches, similes and all, delicately honed into blank verse.

The second positive factor relates to Shakespeare's easy access to his new source materials through his old friend, the printer and publisher Richard Field. Like Shakespeare, Field was now doing extraordinarily well in his London career. He succeeded his master Thomas Vautrollier in 1590, when he also married a Jacqueline Vautrollier who was either his dead master's widow or daughter. Like Shakespeare's, Field's career had led him to the fringes of the court. He printed Puttenham's *Arte of English Poesie*, dedicated to the Queen, in 1589, and Sir John Harington's translation of Ariosto's *Orlando Furioso* in 1591. This great epic was dedicated to Elizabeth, for Harington was the Queen's favourite godson, and working for him (Harington took a close and controlling interest in this publication) gave Field a professional link with the inner circle of courtiers. In 1595 he reprinted North's Plutarch, yet another work dedicated to the Queen, originally printed by Vautrollier in 1579. It is not the only book printed by Field to be drawn on by Shakespeare at this time. As Andrew Gurr has shown, in *Henry V* he also drew on Richard Crompton's *The mansion of magnanimitie*, printed by Field for the upmarket publisher William Ponsonby.[13] Perhaps either the Lord Chamberlain's Men or Shakespeare himself purchased these books for his use (the Plutarch folio of nearly 1200 pages would probably have sold for two or three pounds). But another possibility, or even likelihood, is that Shakespeare regularly used Field's printing house in Blackfriars, near Ludgate, as a working library, and even did his writing there. This gave him unlimited access to the historical sources he needed.

Field's printing house was conveniently close to the Lord Chamberlain's residence, Carey Court, in Blackfriars, though some way away from Shakespeare's own lodgings in Bishopsgate, where he was cited as a tax defaulter in November 1597 and in October 1598.[14] As the century approached its close, and the new Globe Theatre was opened, Shakespeare appears to have moved south of the river, for in October 1599 and 1600 he was yet again cited as owing tax, this time in 'Sussex', that is, on the Surrey side of the Thames.[15] It is plausibly claimed that from 1599 Shakespeare lived in the Clink parish, that of St Saviour's, Southwark. Yet he appears not to have made Easter payments there, though these were technically compulsory, or any other parish dues. As befitted a man who had once been a travelling player, Shakespeare's life was highly peripatetic. While investing large amounts of capital in the house and lands in Stratford that supported his claims to 'gentle' status, he economized, as professional men have often done, on his living arrangements in London. Some of his working hours in 1599 needed to be spent in the Globe itself, rehearsing and directing. While Burbage, a painter and carpenter's son, supervised the physical construction of the theatre Shakespeare functioned above all as what would now be called the company's 'artistic director'. But for the composition of those single-authored plays on which he was now working so actively he needed somewhere well away from the hurly-burly of the theatre in which they were to be performed. The journey between Southwark and Blackfriars would take no more than half an hour, tide permitting, and Lord Hunsdon may have made one of his barges available to his players' leading writer. Sometimes, perhaps, Shakespeare worked late and spent the night either with the Fields, in Wood Street, or with their friends the Huguenot Mountjoys in Silver Street, where he was to lodge formally from about 1604. The likeliest explanations for his repeated tax defaulting are that he spent so little time in his supposed residences that he was never at home when the tax collectors arrived, and also that he viewed himself as not really owing dues in a parish where he only occasionally laid his head or took his meals. He may also have known that the parish officers would not dare to come down hard on a favoured servant of the powerful and generous Lord Hunsdon.

In many ways, then, Shakespeare's professional life in 1599 was a privileged one. Jealousy of this privilege was one of the reasons why Jonson repeatedly sniped at him in his own 1599 play.

No offence i'th' world

Shakespeare's second play in 1599 was much less obviously, or at least much less pleasingly, apt for its time than the triumphalist *Henry V*. Certainly it didn't offer hopeful images either of warfare or of monarchy, and in so far as it dealt with the problems of an ageing ruler and uncertain succession its topicality was potentially dangerous. The huge civic junketings surrounding the Roman Feast of Lupercal in Act 1 could be readily seen as analogous to England's popular, and sometimes riotous, Accession Day celebrations. As the frailly human Caesar was increasingly asking to be viewed as a god, so too was the ageing Elizabeth. Cassius's brilliantly insidious account of the swimming match between him and Caesar implies that physical ageing and weakness in themselves disqualify a leader from continuing to exercise monarchical power. His resentment at having to 'bend his body' to a man who is a mere mortal like himself can be sharply contrasted with the confident appeal for applause of 'our bending author' at the end of *Henry V*:

> this man
> Is now become a god, and Cassius is
> A wretched creature, and must bend his body
> If Caesar carelessly but nod on him.
>
> (1.2.115–18)

Yet even in these opening scenes we are left in no doubt that Cassius is envious and deeply untrustworthy. He exploits the idealism of the foolishly honourable and trusting Brutus with forged petitions and specious arguments. We may worry, indeed, about Brutus's malleability – but still more about that of the Roman people, who can be swayed by rhetoric far more easily than can the intellectual Brutus, and whose ebb and flow is explicitly compared with that of a theatre audience: 'If the tag-rag people did not clap him and hiss him, according as he pleased and displeased them, as they use to do the players in the theatre, I am no true man' (*Julius Caesar*, 1.2.257–60). Like an over-excited theatre audience, the Roman mob can quickly turn dangerous, as they do after Mark Antony inflames them to revenge Caesar's murder. Yet in Antony's reading of Caesar's will theatre-going Londoners in 1599 could, conversely, find pacification. Even the increasingly remote Elizabeth of 1599 remained adept at enacting her love for her people in public or semi-public appearances, and Londoners may have hoped that, like Caesar, she would one day remember them all in her will. On 24 June 1599 she graciously attended the wedding of the obscure Mary Hennington, and throughout that summer she continued to be greeted by loyal peals of bells as she travelled from place to place.[16] If any of her younger courtiers were plotting to overthrow her they would find no comfort or encouragement in Shakespeare's play, which ends with the two chief conspirators, Cassius and Brutus, falling on their swords. Though Brutus had argued speciously to his fellow conspirators that

> We all stand up against the spirit of Caesar,
> And in the spirit of men there is no blood
>
> (2.1.166–7)

it is precisely his spirit that the conspirators have failed to quench with their public blood-letting. The two admonitory appearances of Caesar's ghost to Brutus serve also to affirm his semi-divine status. In its first, 1599, context *Julius Caesar* could be viewed by civil authority as an awful warning to any hot-blooded young courtiers who might be wearying of Elizabeth's long reign. Like Julius Caesar, she was uniquely valuable and irreplaceable:

> ANTONY ... Here was a Caesar: when comes such another?
> 1 PLEBEIAN Never, never.
>
> (3.2.243–4)

And like Caesar, Elizabeth appeared to be more than half-way to being divine, and would surely return to haunt any audacious traitor who spilled her blood. Shakespeare had succeeded in writing a play about conspiracy and assassination that could be happily admired, in the summer of 1599, as an admonitory image of something that 'couldn't happen here'. Its 'lofty scene' was 'acted o'er ... in sport', and contained 'No offence i'th' world', as Hamlet was falsely to reassure Claudius about his re-written tragedy *The Mousetrap* (*Hamlet*, 3.2.229–30).

Certainly it was thoroughly enjoyed as a harmlessly diverting spectacle by a young Swiss student, Thomas Platter. He watched it at the Globe on the afternoon of 21 September – just a week before Essex's fateful return from Ireland, which was to change the complexion of everything. Platter was particularly impressed by the splendid costumes worn by English actors, purchased cheaply from the wardrobes of lately dead noblemen, and by the afterpiece at the end of the show: 'at the end of the play they danced together admirably and exceedingly gracefully, according to their custom, two in each group dressed in men's and two in women's apparel'.[17] Perhaps Caesar sported a velvet doublet once worn by the great Lord Burghley. The actor playing Caesar was seen by the audience reappearing first, within the play proper, as a sheeted Ghost, and then, after its conclusion, as a merry old man (or middle-aged player) treading a stately measure with the boy who had played Calpurnia. These reappearances contributed to the play's inoffensiveness. Within the play, the autocratic Caesar gets his revenge on his assassins; and beyond its frame, the audience are firmly reminded that what they have just seen was only 'sport', harmless entertainment. For the time being, Shakespeare was steadily raising both his own profile and that of the Lord Chamberlain's Men.

Every Man Out

Jonson had a more uphill struggle. His first response to his difficulties was, in an almost literal sense, to rebuild his social standing by becoming a member of the Worshipful Company of Tilers and Bricklayers. Some patron or patrons must have furnished the 3 shillings and 4 pence (a quarter of a mark) that bought him citizen status. This was a much cheaper purchase than Shakespeare's acquisition of a coat of arms from the College of Heralds in October 1596. Nevertheless, since Jonson had been deprived of his goods, he was presumably dependent on credit. Perhaps his friends and admirers at the Inns of Court clubbed together to get him afloat. His compulsion to steer near the wind was not much abated by his recent troubles. The 'Bishops' Ban' on published satires, issued on 1 June 1599, might have driven him to experiment with less controversial genres, ones that could not be accused either of sedition or of personal railing. Yet it did not do so. Some time after Shakespeare's *Julius Caesar*, probably in the second half of 1599, Jonson wrote his second 'Humours' comedy, *Every Man Out of his Humour*, a far more savage and abusive work than its predecessor, full of satirical digs and gibes that invite personal construction. The connection of one character, Carlo Buffone, with the well-travelled clown Charles Chester, is well established,[18] and must have been immediately obvious to audiences in 1599.

There are two ways in which *Every Man Out* sheds light on Jonson's relationship with Shakespeare. The first is an argument from eloquent silence. From the 1616 folio of Jonson's works we learn that Shakespeare, his name listed top left, took the leading position among the 'principal comedians' in the original 1598 performance of *Every Man In*. Probably he played the poetical Ed Knowell, opposite Burbage as the versatile Brainworme. In *Every Man Out* the top-left position is occupied, instead, by Burbage, and Shakespeare's name does not appear. The fact that the leading player in Jonson's first 'Humour' play took no part in his second is rather striking. There are several possible explanations.

The traditional view would be that Shakespeare was so busy writing plays that he no longer had much time for acting in them. My own belief, however, is that the prominence and continuity of Shakespeare's career as a player have been consistently under-estimated. After all, he did once again, in 1603, play a leading part in a Jonson play, *Sejanus his Fall*. There are other possible explanations for his absence from *Every Man Out*. Shakespeare, the new-made gentleman's son and master of New Place, may have shrunk from further collaboration with the newly stigmatized Jonson. Perhaps the murdered player Gabriel Spencer was a friend of his, and he was shocked that Jonson had got off so lightly. He may also have felt sufficiently insecure in his own newly acquired status to worry about contamination through public and visible contact with a man so recently branded on the thumb with 'T' for Tyburn – next time, the gallows. Yet a further possibility is that he read through the manuscript of Jonson's play, saw that he was himself one of the targets of Jonson's satire and had no wish to perform in a work in which he found himself to be mocked. While 'in' jokes about Shakespeare's recent life and work might well contribute to the comedy's success both with the Chamberlain's Men and with the Globe's audience, they were scarcely likely to endear the play to Shakespeare himself. Collectively, the ways in which *Every Man Out* builds on Shakespeare's burgeoning success are sniping rather than complimentary.

There are four verbal allusions to Shakespeare's recent work in *Every Man Out*, two to *Julius Caesar*, two to *Henry IV*. There is also one major satirical theme which alludes pointedly to Shakespeare's personal advancement, and another that paints a savage picture of a practice of which Shakespeare, among others, was guilty. All of these allusions suggest Jonson's determination to prick the bubble of his colleague's success.

(1) In 3.4 the foppish young men about town, Clove and Orange, decide to 'talk fustian . . . and make 'em believe we are great scholars'. Clove does this with remarkable skill, coming out with grand words and concepts strung together to make pretentious nonsense: 'Then coming to the pretty Animal, as *Reason long since is fled to animals*, you know, or indeed for the more model-lizing, or enamelling, or rather diamondizing of your subject'. The phrase '*Reason . . . animals* ', based on a misunderstanding of a pseudo-Aristotelian account of the transmigration of souls, picks up Antony's exclamation over the murdered Caesar:

> O Judgement, thou art fled to brutish beasts
> And men have lost their reason.
>
> (*Julius Caesar*, 3.2.105–6)

His re-assignation of this memorably theatrical line to one of a pair of 'tame parrots' is perhaps the earliest example of Jonson's critical view of Shakespeare

Fig. 16 The assassination of Julius Caesar (Lewis Calhern) in Joseph L. Mankiewicz's 1953 film.

as being apt, in his haste, to write gibberish. It is probably significant also that this citation occurs near the beginning of the scene that offers the most explicit critique of Shakespeare's rise and rise.

(2) In 5.6, the scene in which the flamboyant travelling knight Puntarvolo shuts up Carlo Buffone's mouth, Carlo's last words, apparently addressed to

Macilente, who holds up a lamp while Puntarvolo applies hot wax, are '*Et tu Brute*'. The effect of placing Caesar's dying words to his former friend (*Julius Caesar*, 3.1.77) in the mouth of a buffoon is clearly satirical. Jonson invites the audience to connect the scene of Carlo's silencing with that of Caesar's assassination, and to ridicule it in retrospect.

(3) The two allusions to *Henry IV* are more easy-going, less barbed. They suggest mainly that leading characters in these plays have now become household names. In 5.2 Fastidious Briske tells the court lady Saviolina that the would-be young gentleman Fungoso, newly dressed up in silks, 'is a kinsman to Justice Silence' – that is, he will not speak. However, the effect of this citation is not merely to provide a more elaborate way of saying 'don't expect Fungoso to speak', but to hint – although Saviolina fails to pick up this implication – that he is, like Master Silence, a rustic and tedious fool.

(4) The play's final line is spoken by the emaciated and envious Macilente: 'you may (in time) make lean Macilente as fat as Sir John Falstaff'. The effect of this is to suggest, not just that the audience's applause will mellow the bitter railing of Macilente, but that the playwright Jonson – financially and socially diminished, whatever his physical girth – aspires to the ample popular success, and consequent wealth, now enjoyed by Falstaff/Shakespeare. By giving enthusiastic applause to Jonson's play the theatre audience have the power to 'fatten' him.

(5) The clearest attack on Shakespeare occurs in 3.4, and was discussed in chapter 4 (pp. 96–7). This is, of course, not an allusion to Shakespeare's recent writings, but a sharp dig at his social aspirations, and in particular his recent acquisition of a coat of arms. As such, it may have given even greater pain. In the immediate context of the play performed by Shakespeare's fellows at the Globe, the similarity of '*Not without mustard*' to Shakespeare's pretentiously defensive motto 'NON SANZ DROICT' was all too obvious. Though many of the audience may have been unaware of Shakespeare's recent acquisition of a coat of arms – unless, which is possible, it was displayed conspicuously in the theatre itself – his fellow players, many of them also in pursuit of gentility, will clearly have picked it up straight away.

(6) The upwardly mobile Sogliardo has an even more contemptible brother, the 'hob-nailed chuff' Sordido, a miserly farmer. The years 1596, 1597 and 1598 had all seen wet summers with poor harvests. In this precisely topical play Sordido hopes for yet another bad summer so that he can extort money from the starving. When he discovers that the almanac predicts some spells of good weather he tries to hang himself. During these years the hoarding, 'rebating' or 'engrossing' of foodstuffs had become a very widespread practice, and one that the civic authorities repeatedly tried to punish and prevent. We know, and Jonson probably also knew, that William Shakespeare had been listed in

February 1598 as hoarding ten quarters of malt in New Place. He was by no means alone, but it is noticeable that among the numerous miserly householders of Stratford's Chapel Street ward Shakespeare's hoard was the second largest. Jonson's depiction of the 'hob-nailed chuff' Sordido is of course no more a portrait of Shakespeare than is that of his brother the 'essential clown' Sogliardo. Nevertheless, the fact that Sordido is characterized as engaging in a miserly practice of which he, too, was guilty may have stung Jonson's fellow playwright deeply, especially given the play's association of grain-hoarding with lumpish rusticity, something the rising Shakespeare was trying strenuously to transcend. The Porter's speech in *Macbeth*, in which the first villain summoned into hell is 'a farmer, that hang'd himself on th' expectation of plenty' (*Macbeth*, 2.3.4–5), suggests both that Shakespeare remembered Sordido some years later, and that he now wanted publicly to signal his disapproval of grain hoarders.

THE REPLY CHURLISH

The earliest testimony to some sort of literary or theatrical quarrel between Jonson and Shakespeare occurs in a scene late on in *The Second Return to Parnassus*, performed at St John's College, Cambridge, in the Christmas holidays of 1601–2. In a dialogue between Burbage and Kempe the latter expresses contempt for plays written by 'the university men', whose works are too full of classical and mythological allusions, as Kempe says:

> Why here's our fellow Shakespeare puts them all down, aye, and Ben Jonson too. O that Ben Jonson is a pestilent fellow, he brought up Horace giving the poets a pill, but our fellow Shakespeare hath given him a purge that made him beray his credit.

BURBAGE It's a shrewd fellow indeed.[19]

It is not quite clear whether Burbage's response refers to Jonson or to Shakespeare – whether he is saying 'but sharp-witted Shakespeare gave as good as he got', or 'yes, Jonson was indeed pestilent, and thoroughly deserved what Shakespeare did to him'. But for the purposes of this discussion, I shall work with the second interpretation: Burbage is aligning himself with Kempe and Shakespeare against their common enemy Jonson, who no longer writes plays for the Lord Chamberlain's Men. This much discussed passage is made particularly confusing by its specific allusion to *Poetaster* (1601), in which the verbose Crispinus, a caricature of Marston, is given an emetic to make him vomit up his empty rhetoric. Though a memorable piece of literary quarrelling, this anecdote seems to have nothing to do with Shakespeare. I should like to suggest that Kempe's speech elides the complex interactions of Jonson and Shakespeare in 1599–1601, while confusingly citing an example of Jonson's 'pestilent' nature taken from a play that probably does not form part of his attack on Shakespeare.[20] Shakespeare's 'purge' to Jonson, I suggest, was delivered promptly, and probably within the year 1599. *As You Like It*, as Jonson's editors Herford and Simpson observe,

> contains in the character of Jaques the only attempt made by Shakespeare to portray a Jonsonian 'humour'. Jaques's speeches in Act 2, scene 7, lines 9–87, repeat, in a changed setting, in a milder tone, and with a romantic touch alien to Jonson, the language of Asper:
>
> Give me leave
> To speake my minde, and I will through and through
> Cleanse the foule bodie of th'infected world,
> If they will patiently receive my medicine.[21]

I would like to develop their observation further. As is well known, Shakespeare added two important new characters to his source in Thomas Lodge's *Rosalynde* (1590): the court jester Touchstone, and the banished malcontent Jaques. Touchstone is a triumphantly successful courtier who moves on easy and companionable terms with the Duke's daughter Rosalind, and is able to run rings round all the clownish rustics he meets in the Forest of Arden. He is a man whom everyone, even Jaques, likes and is amused by. His cynical courtship of the goat-herd Audrey does not disqualify him from joyful participation in the festive wedding dance at the end of the play. His amiability and quick wit make him a universal favourite. He has, in short, a great deal in common with that popular and sweet-tongued Shakespeare who was riding so high in 1599. Yet Jaques, too, has his admirers. Duke Senior is constantly looking for him and asking about him, and his witty satirical melancholy is widely appreciated – so much so that its barbs never stick very deep. We first hear of Jaques as mourning over a hunted deer, a motif that may recall Puntarvolo's grief for his dead dog – 'O, my dog, born to disastrous fortune!' – in *Every Man Out*, given the plays' close proximity in time. But Jaques is self-willed, sullen and envious, loath to give any credit to others, even to his generous patron the Duke: 'He is too disputable for my company, I think of as many matters as he, but I give heaven thanks and make no boast of them' (*As You Like It*, 2.5.31–4).

The way in which Jaques denies pride or ambition, yet affirms his own pride even in the manner of his denial, is extraordinarily Jonsonian. Like Jonson in 1599, Jaques is a satirist with a murky past, who believes himself nevertheless perfectly entitled to anatomize the follies and vices of others. The verse he adds to Amiens's song 'Who doth ambition shun' (2.5.35–42) mocks both patrons and their clients in a highly Jonsonian manner, the clients being 'Gross fools', and the patron exhibiting 'A stubborn will'. That much discussed line 'Ducdame, ducdame, ducdame' may have quite a simple meaning – so simple as to baffle the courtly Amiens. From the Latin *da me*, 'give me', and 'Duke', Jaques has constructed a catchphrase that can be glossed as dog Latin (it should be *da mihi*) for 'Duke, gimme, gimme, gimme'. The famous setpiece on the seven ages of man reduces human life to a series of 'humorous' caricatures. But his bitter portrayal of the last two ages is immediately corrected by the arrival of old Adam, whose very name (it had been 'Adam Spencer' in Lodge) affirms his symbolic importance as humanity's forefather. He is by no means 'sans everything', but an embodiment of the human capacity to 'pity and be pitied' whose entitlement to participate in the feast is far more evident than that of the malevolent Jaques.

Like Jonson, Jaques stakes out a claim for unique individualism. He refuses to accept for himself the labelling that he is so ready to apply to others. This is made clear in 4.1, when he expounds his own special brand of melancholy, 'compounded of many simples', which leaves him 'in a most humorous sadness'. Nevertheless, despite all his protestations of non-conformity, Jaques does find a group of fellow spirits, off-stage, at the end of the play. Hearing of Duke Frederick's rapid conversion by 'an old religious man' he makes an instant decision to join 'these convertites'. Opposition is what suits Jaques, not the centre. Now that Duke Senior is to be reinstated, Jaques chooses a new and perhaps even more congenial form of oppositional exile in religious life. The rapidity of his conversion strongly recalls that of Jonson in 1598. He went into prison in late September an Anglican, and emerged only two weeks later, having talked with an elderly imprisoned priest, a Catholic.

However, the point which most strongly convinces me that Jaques is Shakespeare's satirical portrait of Jonson, revenging Jonson's double assault on him in Sordido and Sogliardo, does not concern his conversion. One of Jaques's satirical quips closely parallels one which Jonson claimed as his own. When Orlando arrives at the outlaws' feast with drawn sword and crying out 'Forebear, and eat no more!', Jaques, quick as a flash, comes back with the 'Reply Churlish' 'Why, I have eat none yet' (*As You Like It*, 2.7.87–8). Nearly twenty years later Jonson boasted to Drummond that 'he never esteemed of a man for the name of a Lord', and described his own conduct at a great man's table:

> being at the end of my Lord Salisbury's table with Inigo Jones and demanded by my Lord why he was not glad, 'My Lord,' said he, 'you promised I should dine with you, but I do not'; for he had none of his meat. He esteemed only that his meat which was of his own dish.[22]

Though the dinner referred to here is of later date, it suggests that Jonson habitually protested at his own lowly position in the pecking order at great men's tables. The privilege of attending a noble feast while remaining 'below the salt' was one that he vociferously resented. The older Jonson was a visibly conspicuous consumer, who drew attention to his 'mountain belly', and liked to measure his writings in terms of the number of barrels of sack or claret needed to fuel their production, and of the eminence of the patrons who provided him with liquid inspiration.[23] Jonson's self-assertive materialist quip about 'eating' at a feast – rather than merely attending it – was one that he devised early on, and often repeated. Shakespeare, I suggest, had heard it, and included it as part of his revenge on Jonson, showing him as a malevolent outsider/insider at the 'good man's feast' in *As You Like It*. While Shakespeare and his fellows danced and feasted together under the generous patronage of the Lord Chamberlain Sir George Carey, Lord Hunsdon, Jonson, like Jaques, would no longer dance or feast with them, but must seek his theatrical fortune with the Children of the Chapel. Despite his recent troubles, he had been given an opportunity to write for them, and perhaps, in time, to join their fellowship. He had spoilt this by his niggardly malice against their leading playwright. Shakespeare showed that for once he, too, could write a play which had a strong vein of 'railing', and which made it abundantly clear that Jonson was not going to get fat at his expense.

Crabbed age and youth

As I have already mentioned, we have neither an early printing of *As You Like It*, nor any reference to early performance, unless, just possibly, an allusion by Sir John Harington in 1605 suggests that it had recently been performed in Cambridge. However, it is the first-named of four plays listed in a preliminary leaf in the Stationers' Register as 'to be stayed' on 4 August 1600. The other three plays all soon reached print; *As You Like It* did not. The play's latest editor, Alan Brissenden suggests that the 'staying order' may be connected with the 'Bishops' Ban' on printed satires.[24] This play which has seemed to so many modern critics one of the gentlest and most relaxed of Shakespeare's comedies may have been perceived by Elizabethan censors as doubly vexatious. Not only did the play celebrate the pleasures of an 'alternative' court, not unlike that of Essex House during the months leading up to the violent 'rising' of February 1601, it also reflected a vehement quarrel between two leading playwrights.

Even before it was overtaken by the public events of 1600–1 *As You Like It* had been a play whose loose-knit playfulness lightly veiled its political and personal satire. The confident mock modesty of the Choruses of *Henry V* is replaced by a much deeper anxiety about being misconstrued when Touchstone–Shakespeare exclaims to the insensible Audrey, 'When a man's verses cannot be understood, nor a man's good wit seconded with the forward child, understanding, it strikes a man more dead than a great reckoning in a little room' (3.3.9–12). The final phrase has often been taken to allude to the 'great reckoning' paid by Christopher Marlowe in a 'little room' in Deptford when he was stabbed in the eye by Ingram Frizer on 30 May 1593. Perhaps in part it does, especially since Marlowe is both alluded to and quoted a few scenes later:

> Dead shepherd, now I find thy saw of might,
> 'Who ever loved that loved not at first sight?'

But Marlowe had recently been 'killed' once again by the civic authorities, for 'Davies's Epigrams, with Marlowe's Elegies' was among the books called in by the Bishops on 1 June 1599. Touchstone's speech functions as a claim that for a writer to stay alive, but be misunderstood, is even more crushing than the physical extinction suffered by Marlowe. As he rose to the summit of his creative powers Shakespeare was becoming anxious on his own behalf both about whether his writings were properly understood and appreciated and about whether they would last. A flurry of publications was to mark the turn of the century, the 1600 Quarto of *2 Henry IV* offering Jonsonian-sounding diversions in 'the humours of sir John Fal-staffe, and swaggering Pistoll'; also printed in 1600 were *Henry V* (minus its Choruses), *The Merchant of Venice*, *A Midsummer Night's Dream* and *Much Ado*. However, the absence from this list of two of his most recent plays, *Julius Caesar* and *As You Like It*, is telling. Initially inoffensive, both began to look dangerously topical at the turn of the century. A poem attributed to Shakespeare, wrongly but publicly, in Jaggard's piratical bibelot *The Passionate Pilgrim* also turned out to be horribly prophetic:

> Crabbed age and youth cannot live together
> Youth is full of pleasance, age is full of care;
> Youth like summer morn, age like winter weather;
> Youth like summer brave, age like winter bare.

For in a most literal sense, the ageing Elizabeth could no longer live with, or control, the youthful energies of her younger courtiers. Essex's unlicensed return from Ireland on 28 September 1599 changed everything.

Initially, the Queen was taken completely by surprise, and may even have been flattered and sexually excited by the astonishing liberties taken by Essex with her body (remember that 'neck' means 'breasts'):

> Upon Michaelmas Eve, about ten o'clock in the morning, my Lord of Essex alighted at Court Gate in post, and made all haste up to the presence, and so to the Privy Chamber, and stayed not till he came to the Queen's bed chamber, where he

> found the Queen newly up, the hair about her face; he kneeled unto her, kissed her hands, and her fair neck, and had some private speech with her, which seemed to give him great contentment; for coming from her Majesty to go shift himself in his chamber, he was very pleasant, and thanked God though he had suffered much trouble and storms abroad he found a sweet calm at home. 'Tis much wondered at here, that he went so boldly to her Majesty's presence, she not being ready* and he so full of dirt and mire that his very face was full of it.[25]

Instead of coming home in triumph at the head of a conquering army, to be acclaimed by the citizens of London, as Shakespeare had foreseen in *Henry V*, Essex returned alone, still sweaty and dirty with Irish mud when he arrived at Nonsuch Palace. Though Essex had great sexual charisma, as his portraits show (Plate 9), he was deluded in believing that he had 'found a sweet calm at home'. As soon as the Queen had had time to talk with her advisers, in particular Robert Cecil, Essex was ordered to 'keep his chamber'. Robert Sidney's agent Rowland Whyte remarked, 'It is a world to be here, to see the humours of the time. Blessed are they that can be away and live contented.'[26] That long period of impasse began during which Elizabeth tried to contain and control Essex and his faction, and finally failed to do so. This prolonged period of stand-off culminated in Essex's abortive coup and subsequent execution in February 1601.

In the early weeks of 1601 the Lord Chamberlain's Men became dangerously connected with that 'alternative' and increasingly fortress-like court at Essex House. Essex's close friend and former steward Sir Gilly Meyrick offered the company forty pieces of silver to perform *Richard II* on 6 February, only two days before Essex's abortive 'rising' in the City of London. Their spokesman Augustine Phillips – perhaps pushed forward to save the skins of the more senior and surely more culpable Burbage and Shakespeare – claimed that they had been deeply reluctant to put on a play that was 'so old and so long out of use', because 'they should have small or no company at it'.[27] But it was presumably Shakespeare's long-standing connection with Essex's close friend and confederate Southampton that constituted the first and most compromising link between the players and the two malcontent Earls. Only seven years earlier Shakespeare had publicly promised to Southampton that 'what I have to do is yours, being part in all I have devoted yours'. Now was the time for Shakespeare to demonstrate the sincerity of this extravagant promise. Though the players, through their spokesman Phillips, claimed that their reluctant performance of *Richard II* had been a simple case of bribery, they must have been perfectly well aware that the Earls' request for this particular

* 'ready': dressed.

play, out of their now very large repertoire, was by no means a harmless whim. After all, Sir John Hayward had recently got into serious trouble for publishing a prose account of Richard's abdication and dedicating it to Essex, and he was to remain in prison for the rest of Elizabeth's reign. Shakespeare's play, like Hayward's treatise, showed the anointed king publicly handing over his crown to a popular nobleman (Bolingbroke), as many were hoping Elizabeth would do to the popular nobleman Essex. Some of the players may have believed that this really would happen, and that under the rule of the theatre-loving Essex and his friends they would soon enjoy great wealth and protection. The 'bending author' who was their leading playwright was to be put into jeopardy by that very versatility and capacity to please that made his plays so successful.

Elizabeth, famously, was well aware of the historical parallels studied by Essex and his followers, and is alleged to have remarked to the antiquary William Lambard, 'I am Richard II, know ye not that? . . . He that will forget God, will also forget his benefactors; this tragedy was played forty times in open streets and houses.' There may indeed have been numerous performances of the play before the one recorded on 6 February 1601. If there had been, Augustine Phillips, fighting for his freedom and for that of his fellow players, would scarcely have said so. Schoenbaum and others have remarked on the players' narrow escape from severe punishment at this time; perhaps they were protected only by being servants of the Queen's close kinsman Lord Hunsdon. Like Richard, Elizabeth saw herself as a divinely ordained monarch. To rebel against her was to commit sacrilege. Neither Elizabeth nor the Lord Chamberlain's Men are likely to have overlooked a further historical parallel to the timing of Essex's defection: the year in which Richard II abdicated had been 1399.

CHAPTER SIX

1600–3

Sweet Master Shakespeare!

O sweet Master Shakespeare, I'll have his picture in my study at the court!

(*The First Part of the Return from Parnassus*,
performed at St John's, Cambridge, 1599/1600)

William the Conqueror

As the sixteenth century turned, Shakespeare enjoyed huge fame and popularity among new, young, readers and audiences. Flatteringly, most of them were, as he was not, university men. But he also underwent renewed onslaughts from jealous rivals. For instance, in an elegy on Queen Elizabeth in the spring of 1603, his old enemy Henry Chettle took occasion to rebuke him for failing to pay any tribute to his royal patroness, implying that he was guilty of the vice of ingratitude. Shakespeare's poetical 'sweetness', repeatedly invoked by his admirers, is alluded to by Chettle both in the name 'Melicert' [1] and in the phrase 'honeyed muse', but is rejected by Chettle as insincere and false:

> Nor doth the silver tongued Melicert,
> Drop from his honeyed muse one sable tear
> To mourn her death that graced his desert,
> And to his lays opened her royal ear:
>   Shepherd, remember our Elizabeth,
>   And sing her rape, done by that Tarquin, death.[2]

Perhaps, like some other creative geniuses, Shakespeare preferred always to move forwards, not to waste his energy in backward glances. But in any case, his churlish failure to elegize 'that bright occidental star' Queen Elizabeth is only the most conspicuous testimony to a consistent and distinctive characteristic. Other ambitious writers in this period cultivated and sought to please, not only the Queen, but also courtly patronesses, the wives, widows and daughters of noblemen. Such ladies often had considerable wealth and influence, as well as leisure in which to read and respond to literary works which would perhaps be given little more than a cursory glance by their menfolk. Even the bullishly macho Jonson, a man's man if ever there was one, found that it suited his purposes to cultivate court ladies, such as Lady Mary Wroth, to whom he dedicated *The Alchemist*, and whose sonnets he praised in a rare sonnet of his own. Yet there is not one single instance of Shakespeare addressing a work to a well-born woman, whether royal, noble or gentle. From the Earl of Southampton to Sir John Salusbury to 'Mr. W. H.' to Francis Manners, Earl of Rutland, Shakespeare's visible patrons were all male. Even his most explicitly 'Elizabethan' play, *The Merry Wives*, though reputedly written to feed the Queen's appetite for the fat knight Sir John Falstaff, is far more conspicuously associated with the new Lord Chamberlain Sir George Carey than it is with his cousin and Queen (see above, pp. 97–9). Chettle's allegation that while the Queen had 'graced his desert', Shakespeare failed to commemorate her, was a palpable hit.[3] Nor had Shakespeare attempted, as Nashe had done, to consolidate his favour with his patron the Lord Chamberlain by dedicating works to his wife and daughter.

A half-acknowledged awareness of the consistent maleness of Shakespeare's friends and patrons may be one of the driving forces behind the post-Romantic quest for the 'dark lady', the supposed provoker or inspirer of the *Sonnets*. Nowhere else in Shakespeare's work is there any evidence whatsoever for his associating his personal or artistic achievements with a woman. The *Sonnets* were the only texts that could conceivably be wrenched to provide some testimony to Shakespeare, grotesquely inappropriate though this was, as an adoring, and heterosexual, lover and love poet. The dedication to Mr. W. H. had to be sidelined as entirely the quirk of Thomas Thorpe; the great majority of the sonnets themselves had to be ignored or re-assigned; and the closing sonnets had to be read as if they were sonnets of romantic love, not anatomies of sexual obsession and disgust. Nevertheless, this was the approach taken by many scholars and critics during the nineteenth and twentieth centuries, to such powerful effect that the historical evidence for the maleness of all Shakespeare's major patrons has not been discussed, even by Schoenbaum.

The period to be discussed in this chapter provides a rare anecdote about Shakespeare's sex life. If this is to be believed, it indicates that Shakespeare had a 'normal' sex drive. It also testifies to Shakespeare's quickness of wit and resourcefulness. But it hardly suggests respect either for women or for female intelligence. Indeed, it matches the portrayal of the speaker in sonnets 127–52 as compulsively requiring sexual release – being almost what would now be called a 'sex addict' – without any demand for reciprocal tenderness or companionship. On 13 March 1601 the law student John Manningham, who loved to collect jests and saucy anecdotes, recorded one that he had just heard from a friend at the Inner Temple, William Towse:

> Upon a time when Burbage played Richard the Third there was a citizen grew so far in liking with him, that before she went from the play she appointed him to come that night unto her by the name of 'Richard the Third'. Shakespeare, overhearing their conclusion, went before, was entertained and at his game ere Burbage came. Then message being brought that Richard the Third was at the door, Shakespeare caused return to be made that William the Conqueror was before Richard the Third. Shakespeare's name William.[4]

Several points should be noticed about this passage. First, the social status of the stage-struck woman: she was a 'citizen', not a gentlewoman. Her husband was presumably a member of a city company or guild, and may have had some trade, craft or 'mystery', such as tailoring or printing, that kept him safely at his workplace until the evening. He was not a gentleman, still less a gentleman of leisure. Secondly, the story suggests that there was a strong physical similarity between Shakespeare and Burbage. Though the charismatic Burbage no doubt looked different in his Richard III costume, the substitution could not have been attempted unless the two men were of similar height, build, colouring and, perhaps above all, voice. The portrait of Burbage among material bequeathed to Dulwich College by 'Mr Cartwright' suggests that the two men were indeed alike: slightly thickset, slightly balding, with dark eyes and mid-brown hair (Fig. 17). Even if the story is not true, it would surely not have passed current among the theatre-going students of the Inns of Court without such resemblance, since they were perfectly familiar with the appearance of both men. Thirdly, the story also provides its own evidence of Shakespeare's acting skills. On this occasion he successfully impersonated Burbage, and a Burbage who had come freshly from one of his most powerful (and sexy) performances. But most of all, I believe, this anecdote offers us a glimpse of Shakespeare as a well-loved 'fellow' in the Lord Chamberlain's company, a merry man among merry men, who demonstrated his strong affection for his colleagues through jocular banter and sexual competition. The point of his speedy visit to the citizeness was not only to win the sexual prize but also to outwit a close male friend in the sexual arena, and in so doing, paradoxically, to strengthen his intimate bond with him. One further point should be added.

Fig. 17 Richard Burbage.

Players who were living in London away from their families may often have paid for the services of prostitutes. Here was a woman offering her services free, and the ever-resourceful Shakespeare was quick to outwit his friend in the consumption of this commodity.

Though Manningham's story sounds in some ways too good to be true, its basic components conform remarkably well to the poetic analysis of the lustful 'Will' of sonnets 127–52. While courtly love poets have traditionally devoted their creative energies to the service of well-born and unattainable ladies, this cynical 'Will' glories shamelessly in his transactions with a promiscuous woman of little beauty and no breeding. He is artistically competitive, claiming in the famous sonnet 130 that 'I think my love as rare / As any she belied with false compare', the satire here being partly against himself, for thinking a plain woman 'rare' or exceptional, but chiefly against the many other male poets who have lied about their mistresses. More tellingly, what he is most troubled by is the woman's sexual enticement of his male 'friend' (133–4). In 144, a sonnet that we know was written before 1599, since it appeared in *The Passionate Pilgrim*, the speaker identifies 'a woman coloured ill' with his evil angel, and 'a man right fair' with his 'better angel'. Though eagerly promiscuous women like the citizeness of Manningham's anecdote might be a regular sexual convenience for him, they did not provoke any deep emotions beyond feelings of resentment and dislike. 'Will' passionately resents the power that the woman has to draw him into the morally polluting 'hell' of lust (129.14), and of her possibly infected body. Even more intensely he resents her capacity to foul up his relationship with a male friend, for it is in upwardly mobile male friendship that his deepest emotions are invested. And as for court ladies: it may be that, for all his verbal and actorly skill on the stage, Shakespeare was ill at ease with them, and also resented the power they exercised over the handsome young noblemen who were his preferred patrons.

O, sweet Master Shakespeare!

In the period 1600–3 Shakespeare can be connected with many men, patrons, colleagues, friends, admirers and enemies, but with no women, except that nameless 'citizen'. For instance, as Manningham's anecdote suggests, the years immediately following the opening of the Globe in 1599 were ones in which Shakespeare's professional and personal relationship with Richard Burbage grew stronger, warmer and deeper. The knowledge that the central performer in his plays, his 'fellow' and close friend, was versatile, charismatic and master of an extraordinarily wide register of moods, gave him huge creative scope. Without Burbage, we might have no *Hamlet*. It was probably during this period, also, that Shakespeare consolidated his relationship with a generous, lively, highly literate young nobleman who was eventually to be even more important to him than Southampton: William Herbert, Philip Sidney's nephew, who succeeded to the earldom of Pembroke in January 1601. Some rapid shift of allegiance was required at just this time, after the execution of Essex on 25 February. Southampton, Essex's close friend and fellow conspirator, was lucky to escape with his life. Imprisoned in the Tower, where he was picturesquely portrayed with a handsome (but perhaps largely symbolic) black-and-white cat for companion (Fig. 18), he was no longer in a position to offer any kind of patronage. Continued association with him would be extremely unwise, especially for the company of players who had been bribed by him to put on *Richard II*.

Shakespeare must have been aware of young William Herbert as early as the autumn of 1595, during the unsuccessful attempt to betroth him to Sir George Carey's daughter Elizabeth (see above, pp. 87–8). At what point he first saw and properly met him is more questionable. Some scholars – most notably J. Dover Wilson[5] – have connected sonnets 1–17 with renewed attempts to persuade Herbert to marry at the time of his seventeenth birthday, on 8 April 1597. Certainly this hypothesis has the merit of suggesting a reason why there are just seventeen sonnets devoted to persuasions to marriage, no more, no less. It gains some additional support from the allusion to 'April' (the month of Herbert's birthday) in sonnet 3, and images derived from his uncle Sidney in several sonnets in this group, most notably 5 and 6, whose identification of marriage with distilled rosewater can hardly be understood without reference to their source in the *Arcadia*, which had been splendidly re-published under the care of Herbert's mother in 1598.

There is no doubt that young William Herbert was strongly drawn to London in the late 1590s, and eager to immerse himself in the culture of both court and city, well away from his aged and ailing father, and to some extent also from his pious, learned and 'controlling' mother. Like Southampton, Herbert had been cultivated by Lord Burghley, who tried to marry him to his younger grand-daughter Bridget Vere. Like Southampton, too, he enjoyed access to considerable money and property even before he came of age. At the time of his father's death he was still three months short of his twenty-first birthday. If anything, Herbert was even more generous to poets and writers than Southampton had been at the same age, and he was also considerably warmer and more extrovert in personality. Though we do not know for sure whether he frequented the public theatres at this time, as Southampton and Rutland did, it is very likely. His sustained 'favour' towards Shakespeare, which Heminge and Condell were to celebrate in the First Folio, may have begun as early as 1598 or 1599. Also like Southampton, though in a rather more trivial matter, Herbert soon got into trouble with the ageing Queen. Early in 1601 he was briefly imprisoned, and then banished from court, after impregnating the Maid of Honour Mary Fitton the previous summer. However, this banishment turned out to be politically advantageous for him, since it kept him away from London during the period of Essex's 'rising' and execution – like most of the younger courtiers, he, too, was a friend of Essex.

For Shakespeare, therefore, the two years from February 1601 until Elizabeth's death in March 1603 were ones in which aristocratic patronage was at an all-time low. Southampton was imprisoned in the Tower, and young Pembroke banished to faraway Wiltshire. Meanwhile the generous Lord Chamberlain Sir George Carey was ageing and in failing health – he was to die within a few months of the Queen. And yet it was in just these two years that

Fig. 18 The Earl of Southampton imprisoned in the Tower in 1601,
with a cat which also dislikes confinement.

Shakespeare produced what could be claimed as his greatest, most fertile, most astonishingly original and diverse writings: *Hamlet*, *Twelfth Night*, *Troilus and Cressida* (see below, chapter 8), many of the sonnets, *A Lover's Complaint* and that extraordinary lyric known as 'The Phoenix and the Turtle'.[6] If nothing had survived except these, it is likely that Shakespeare would still be judged one of the greatest writers of all time. There may be a connection. If all great art is born of difficulty and limitation, then Shakespeare's struggle, in these years, was to please newer, larger, younger audiences, both in London and elsewhere, and the struggle was stimulating and fruitful. As a playwright, he now took his cue not so much from the need to gratify individual aristocratic patrons, as from the pressing need to draw large audiences to the Globe, and above all to capture the lively 'Inns of Court' market, from which others would follow. He was also determined to make the best possible use both of the still-new playhouse and of the maturing strength and collective talent of the Lord Chamberlain's Men. He was engaged in increasingly fierce and hostile competition with Jonson, now writing for the Children of the Chapel Royal, and in much more friendly competition with a newly fledged graduate playwright, John Marston. Three of Shakespeare's writings in this period can be closely connected with Marston, who was a fervent admirer as well as a friendly rival.

As the Cambridge academic Gabriel Harvey, among others, bears witness, Shakespeare had become a 'cult' writer among bright young men in Oxford, Cambridge and the Inns of Court. In or around 1601 Harvey observed that 'the younger sort' delighted in *Venus and Adonis*, the 'wiser sort' in *Lucrece* and *Hamlet*. Fresh out of Cambridge, the diminutive John Weever included a passionately enthusiastic sonnet *Ad Gulielmum Shakespear* in his 1599 *Epigrammes*, in which he praised the two narrative poems, and '*Romea Richard*; more whose names I know not'.[7] Presumably Weever had heard about other works by Shakespeare, but had not as yet managed to procure printed copies, even though Meres's *Palladis Tamia*, published the previous year, had mentioned fourteen or fifteen works in all. Both as poet and playwright Shakespeare was flavour of the century with students. The title-page of the first Quarto *Hamlet* records that by 1603 the play had been performed in both universities, 'and elsewhere'. In 1598 an Oxford graduate, Richard Barnfield, in a sonnet called 'A remembrance of some English poets', gave pride of place to Shakespeare both for *Venus* and *Lucrece*. Barnfield's own poems soon became tangled up with Shakespeare's, two of them being included in the piratical *Passionate Pilgrim* in 1599. A possible explanation for this is that Jaggard got hold of a manuscript that contained the twenty poems in his collection, reflecting the taste and / or personal associations of its compiler which accommodated both Shakespeare and Barnfield. It is notable that Barnfield – a Midlander, who came from south Staffordshire – also uniquely shares with Shakespeare the distinction of having written a male-on-male sonnet sequence. And like *Shakespeare's Sonnets* in 1609, Barnfield's *Cynthia. With Certaine Sonnets* (1595) (the 'Sonnets' being addressed to 'Ganymede') was printed with an extravagant commendation by an exuberant admirer signing himself T[homas?].T[horpe?].

Little has been made of Barnfield's curious links with Shakespeare, perhaps because he has been seen as a trivial and lightweight poet, as well as because of the homoeroticism of his verse. Yet we cannot safely assume that Shakespeare consorted only with his intellectual equals. Indeed, the evidence is that he did not. Of those with whom we know he worked closely, Burbage alone can be seen to be comparable in talent. Young Midlanders who, unlike himself, had been to university, may have been among his preferred companions, with whom he enjoyed a somewhat Falstaffian comradeship. While leading them in merry wit-combats, he also picked up and mimicked some of their learned phrases and concepts.

By the turn of the century Shakespeare was beginning to undergo the mockery that is the usual consequence of huge popularity. In *The First Return from Parnassus*, performed at St John's College, Cambridge in the Christmas holidays of 1599–1600, the foolishly love-sick young gentleman Gullio is teased for his uncritical devotion to 'pure Shakespeare and shreds of poetry that he hath gathered at the theatres'. It seems that the amorous young men who adored Shakespeare's 'sugared' writings also adored his person. Later in the same play Gullio exclaims, 'O sweet Master Shakespeare, I'll have his picture in my study at the court!' Sadly, no authentic portrait of Shakespeare can be identified so early – but Gullio's remark, in this very 'knowing' piece, strongly suggests that it was not merely Shakespeare's published and performed writings, but even his image, that had become the subject of a 'cult' by the century's end. While modern students may plaster their study walls with posters of pop singers or film stars, the stage-struck young students and gallants of the last years of Elizabeth's reign worshipped that actor–poet–playwright who had not himself had the benefit of a university education. Such icons constituted a deliberately youthful statement. Though their tutors might prefer students to gaze on images of Homer or Cicero, they felt far more passionate about a contemporary English writer whose works were to be enjoyed at the public theatres, and who could himself be seen both on the stage and in the tavern, and occasionally around the Inns of Court.

O, 'twas a moving Epicedium!

Richard Barnfield had overlapped at Brasenose College, Oxford, with John Marston. Marston, too, though half-Italian, was a Midlander. His father's family came from Shropshire, and he had grown up in Coventry, a rich centre for theatrical activity, as we saw in chapter 1. He took up residence in the Middle Temple towards the end of 1595, and together with his father acted as a guarantor for another newly admitted Middle Templar, Shakespeare's cousin Thomas Greene,[8] later to become both Stratford's Town Clerk and the Middle Temple's Treasurer. This was not Shakespeare's only link with the Middle Temple. Numerous other Warwickshire gentry, such as William Catesby, the poet Fulke Greville and Drayton's patron Henry Goodere, were Middle Templars, as was Shakespeare's close friend Thomas Russell.[9] But Greene is of particular interest, being not only a family connection of Shakespeare's, and on such close and friendly terms with him that for a while he lodged in New Place, but also a close associate of a man whose earlier writings run closely parallel to Shakespeare's in 1600–3. It was probably through Thomas Greene that Shakespeare first encountered young John Marston, and perhaps also, through Marston, Barnfield. Though Greene went on to a distinguished career as a lawyer, both in Stratford and in London, he was, like most law students, a lively and fun-loving young man. Manningham records one of his sayings: 'There is best sport always, when you put a woman in the case.'[10]

Not only did the Inns of Court offer young men fresh from university 'a convenient solution to London's severe housing shortage',[11] they constituted a major centre of literary and thespian activity. The reading and writing of poetry and drama had for some decades been the chief diversion of law students. Jasper Heywood celebrated Inns of Court poetry in his preface to his translation of Seneca's *Thyestes* as early as 1560:

> In Lincoln's Inn and Temples twain
> Gray's Inn and other moe,
> Thou shalt them find whose painful pen
> thy verse shall flourish so,
> That Melpomen thou wouldst well ween
> had taught them for to write,
> And all their works with stately style,
> And goodly grace t'endite.[12]

Highly elaborate Christmas holiday revels, in which the four Inns competed with each other, provided a regular public showcase for their talents. But with such a high proportion of Templars writing poetry, it was inevitable that many would be versifiers of little talent. Two such were a Welsh gentleman, John Salusbury of Lleweni, and his side-kick (later chaplain) Robert Chester. Salusbury was a man of distinguished lineage, as a direct, though illegitimate, descendant of Henry VII.[13] His status as a courtier was established by his appointment as an Esquire of the Body to the Queen at the same time as his admission to the Middle Temple. However, despite its Tudor blood, the family included some troublesome individuals. John Salusbury's elder brother Thomas had been executed in 1586 for his complicity in the Babington Plot.

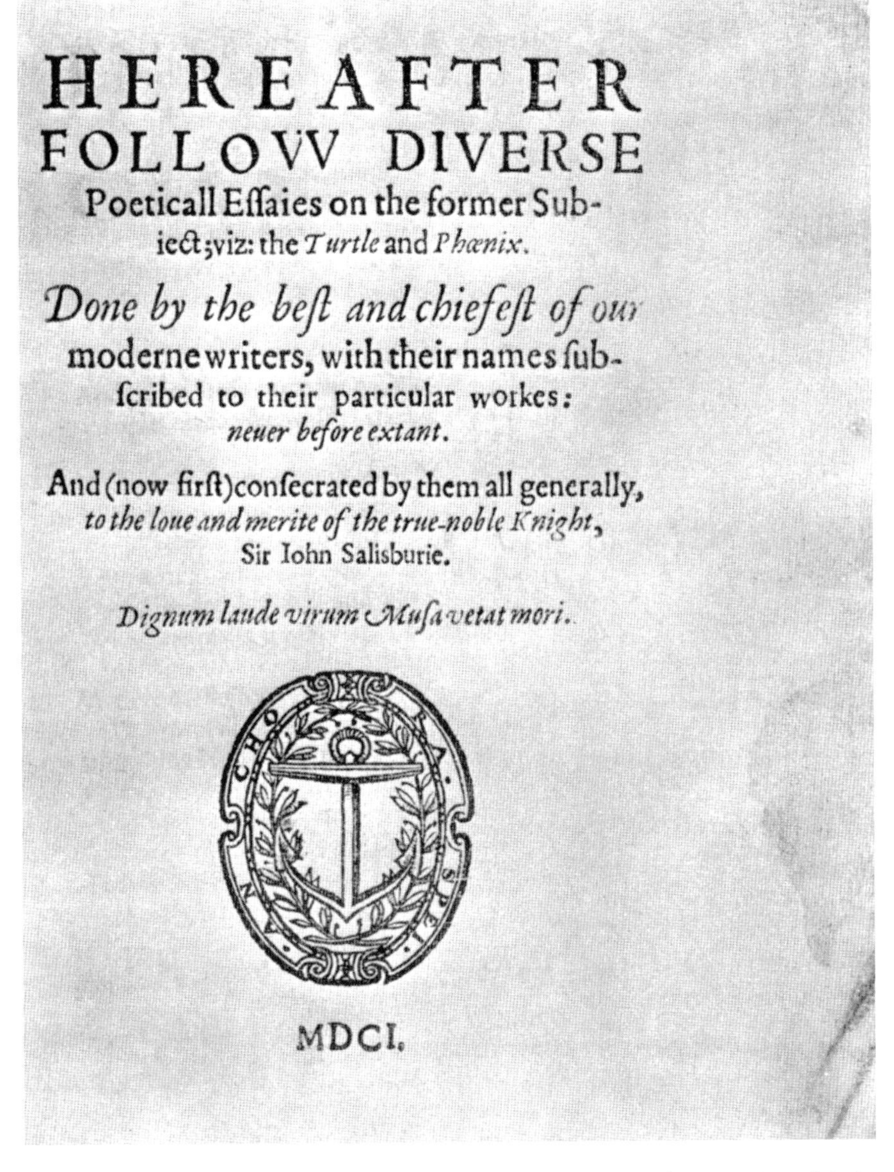

HEREAFTER
FOLLOVV DIVERSE
Poeticall Essaies on the former Sub-
iect; viz: the *Turtle* and *Phœnix*.

Done by the best and chiefest of our
moderne writers, with their names sub-
scribed to their particular workes:
neuer before extant.

And (now first) consecrated by them all generally,
to the loue and merite of the true-noble Knight,
Sir Iohn Salisburie.

Dignum laude virum Musa vetat mori.

MDCI.

Fig. 19 Title-page of the *Poeticall Essaies* appended to Robert Chester's *Loves Martyr* (1601).

Fifteen years later his cousin, Captain Owen Salusbury, was fatally shot through a window of Essex House while it was under siege on the day of the rising; his brother Thomas also fought for Essex. John Salusbury, too, was a contentious and arrogant man, who had many enemies in Denbighshire.

In 1593 he had been involved in a violent sword fight with his cousin Owen, whom he wounded quite severely. He was congratulated on this victory by his brother-in-law Henry Stanley, fifth Earl of Derby. Like many well-born young men, he was married rather young, in 1586, to Ursula Stanley, an illegitimate, but fully acknowledged, daughter of the fourth Earl of Derby. By the time Salusbury arrived at the Middle Temple his wife had already given birth seven times[14] – a point worth mentioning, for it makes it extremely unlikely that the phrase in Shakespeare's poem appended to Chester's *Loves Martyr*, 'Leaving no posterity', has any literal bearing on John Salusbury's marriage. Even if Shakespeare didn't know Salusbury very well he could hardly fail to be aware that his marriage had been fruitful. By the time of the publication of *Loves Martyr*, in 1601, three more children had been born, one, Ferdinando, named after Shakespeare's old patron Lord Strange.

The *Poeticall Essaies* appended to *Loves Martyr* – and above all Shakespeare's contribution – compose one of the most dense literary riddles of the period. It is not just Shakespeare's poem that is cryptic; so, in almost equal measure, are those of Marston, Chapman and Jonson. However, it may reasonably be assumed that, as the title-page claims (Fig. 19), these submissions are all indeed devoted 'to the love and merit of the true-noble knight, Sir John Salisburie', who had been knighted on 1 June 1601 for his part in suppressing the Essex rising. It is also fairly safe to assume that this public tribute was connected with Salusbury's vigorous attempt to raise his profile at court in 1601, and to triumph over his rivals and enemies in Denbighshire. Whatever is going on in the *Loves Martyr* volume is evidently shaped by what Puttenham called 'the courtly figure *Allegoria*, which is when we speak one thing and think another, and that our words and our meanings meet not'.[15] But since it was vital for Salusbury to continue to dissociate himself emphatically from his pro-Essex kinsmen, I do not think the recent theory that Shakespeare's poem celebrates Elizabeth's relationship with Essex can be right. These were dangerous times. Not only had Essex just been executed as a traitor; as we saw in chapter 5 it was also becoming increasingly unwise for writers to anticipate the death of the Queen, however evident it might be that she was now a frail old woman,[16] and however elaborately their images of her death might be wrapped up in allegory. The ashes alluded to in the final lines of the 'Threnos' surely cannot be those of Elizabeth:

> To this urn let those repair
> That are either true or fair;
> For these dead birds sigh a prayer.

The difficulties of understanding the *Poeticall Essaies* are also compounded by the fact that their allegorical frame of reference had been set in place by the

Fig. 20 Salusbury family tomb in St Marcella's, Whitchurch, Denbigh; Shakespeare's patron's grandparents are shown above, their children below.

poetaster Robert Chester, perhaps some years earlier. *Loves Martyr* proper is old-fashioned, cumbersome and rambling. Much of it consists of a dialogue between Dame Nature and the (female) Phoenix, who is given an aerial view of Britain, including an encyclopaedic catalogue of its plants, trees, minerals and birds, the last-named leading rather awkwardly to an introduction to the Turtle-dove who is to be her mate. But while Chester's poems are mundane and pedestrian, stuffed with catalogues of material objects, the ensuing *Poeticall Essaies* are notably abstract and rarefied. Shakespeare's lyric has been admired by William Empson and others for its 'metaphysical' qualities, and it is certainly unusual among his writings in its deployment of such philosophical concepts as 'Number', 'Property' and 'Reason'. Yet a few lines can also be construed more literally. For instance,

> Hearts remote, yet not asunder;
> Distance and no space was seen,
> 'Twixt this Turtle and his Queen

could be read as alluding to the close loyalty to Elizabeth of the older John Salusbury despite his physical distance from court in faraway north Wales.

Elizabethan Welshmen were notoriously obsessed with genealogy. According to Thomas Fuller, 'every Welshman is born a herald'. One possibility is that the female 'Phoenix', as developed by the writers of the *Poeticall Essaies*, does not represent any single woman, but rather symbolizes the female Tudor line, alluding occasionally to Elizabeth, but more often to Salusbury's mother and daughter. As applied to Elizabeth, the 'Phoenix' is a fairly common image – Shakespeare was to call the infant Elizabeth a 'maiden phoenix' in *Henry VIII*. But it is striking that it had also been applied to Sir John Salusbury's mother, Catherine of Berain, Henry VII's great-grand-daughter.[17] She became a legend in her own lifetime in Wales, being styled 'Mam Cymru', or 'Mother of Wales' (Fig. 20).[18] When she died in 1591 one Welsh poet writing in Latin celebrated her both as '*Catherina Tudir*' and as '*britannica Phoenix*'.[19] In 1601 the eldest Salusbury child, Jane, was approaching the marriageable age of fourteen. A decade after one great Tudor lady had died, another, her grand-daughter, was ready to carry on the line. The Phoenix myth, in which the unique bird dies and is eventually re-born from its own funeral pyre, lends itself very readily to the idea of royal or aristocratic succession: 'la reine est morte; vive la reine'. It may have seemed that the most effective way in which Sir John Salusbury could raise his status in 1601 was by emphasizing his own descent, through a female line, from the first Tudor monarch, while also identifying both his father and himself with an undeviatingly loyal 'Turtle-dove', who presented no possible threat or challenge to the sovereignty of the Phoenix. Like the 'Phoenix', the 'Turtle' may be a composite figure representing both the newly knighted Sir John Salusbury and his father and namesake, Catherine of Berain's first husband. The fact that the son was born close in time to the death of his father may also feed in to the poems' many images of birth-in-death. The choice of the inoffensive 'Turtle' image, rather than the heraldic one of the Salusbury white lion that figures in some of Salusbury's own poems,[20] indicates that, despite his Tudor inheritance, Salusbury had no intention of making any claim to royal succession, being committed only to the role of faithful court servant.

It has often been suggested that Shakespeare didn't fully understand what was required of him in connection with *Loves Martyr*, since his poem is a funeral elegy, while the other poets celebrate the mysterious re-birth and continuance of the Phoenix. However, since this myth entails a ritual of fiery death preceding re-birth, it may be that the senior poet was specifically given the delicate assignment of writing an elegy, while the other, younger, writers had the task of celebrating the re-born Phoenix. While Shakespeare's poem lamented two 'dead birds' who in some sense corresponded with Salusbury's parents, the other poets brought much ingenuity to the mystical elevation of Tudor womanhood embodied in Jane Salusbury. Their extraordinary collective effort may be compared with that which another Inns of Court poet, John

Fig. 21 The Great Hall of the Middle Temple, London.

Donne, was to bring to commemorating a girl whom he had never met, but whose father, Sir Robert Drury, he wished to cultivate as a patron, in his *Anatomy of the World* in 1611. But for the purposes of this study, I wish to draw attention above all to the rather theatrical way in which, immediately following Shakespeare's 'Threnody', Marston comments on it, as if it has just been recited or performed: 'O, 'twas a moving Epicedium!' It was probably Marston who recruited three older and better-known poets, described on the title-page as 'the best and chiefest of our moderne writers', to offer their individual tributes, in conditions of some haste,[21] to his fellow Templar the newly knighted Sir John Salusbury. In this line he makes it clear that he sees Shakespeare's contribution as pre-eminent. Marston also proclaims his own leading membership of that fan club of bright young men who idolise 'sweet Master Shakespeare', paying tribute to him, as T. S. Eliot did to Ezra Pound, as *il miglior fabbro*, the greater artist, the young man's model and unmatchable example. In so doing, Marston also offers a glimpse of the parallel, yet connected, lives led by the two writers during these turn-of-the-century years.

For by the time Marston praised Shakespeare's 'moving Epicedium' he had become very familiar with the man and his work. During this period both

Marston and Shakespeare wrote comedies called *What You Will*. Shakespeare's was performed as the climax of the Candlemas 'feast' at the Middle Temple, while Marston composed his as an active member of that same community (Fig. 21). Even the shared title has an 'Inns of Court' feel, suggesting the 'quodlibets', or playful, free-ranging debates in which the students learned to sharpen their wits through disputation. In the very same period each man also wrote a revenge tragedy in which a highly-strung son is required to avenge the death of his father, who appears as a ghost, and whose mother is wooed by her husband's murderer. In the case of the tragedies, there are extraordinarily close links in imagery, style and dramatic structure that suggest that the plays were written simultaneously, with each man regularly looking over the other's shoulder. While the older man wrote a complex full-blown tragedy for performance by the Chamberlain's Men, the younger wrote a poignant pastiche – sometimes verging on black farce – for Paul's Boys. None of the four plays can be dated really precisely, but I shall proceed on the presumption that *Hamlet* and *Antonio's Revenge* were written during 1600–1, and *What You Will* and *Twelfth Night* during 1601–2. It is possible, however, that there was some degree of overlap in the composition of all four plays, with Shakespeare and Marston setting out in friendly emulation each to write a comedy and a tragedy whose initial situation entailed a recent death, or supposed death, since this is a feature common to all four. The first impetus towards this subject matter may have come from Marston, preparing to write the sequel to his tragicomedy *Antonio and Mellida*, which had established the situation of Antonio's doomed love for the daughter of the tyrant Piero.

At one stage life, as so often, overtook art. Shakespeare's father John was buried at Holy Trinity, Stratford, on 8 September 1601. He does not appear to have made a will. He may have lacked the assistance of Stratford's amateur lawyer the curate William Gilbard, of whom more below. Nevertheless, his eldest son William could now style himself 'gentleman', and also inherited his father's large house in Henley Street, although it continued to be occupied both by his widowed mother and by his sister Joan Hart and her family. He soon consolidated his 'gentle' status further by extending his property holdings around Stratford. On 1 May 1602 he expended the very large sum of £320 on a substantial plot of farmland in Old Stratford, purchased from William Combe. He was presumably in London at the time of this transaction, for his brother Gilbert stood proxy for him.[22] A few months later he also extended the curtilage of New Place by purchasing an adjacent cottage and quarter-acre of garden from the Dowager Countess of Warwick.[23] Had Shakespeare been at all inclined to cultivate noble ladies, Anne Dudley, née Russell, would have been a good choice. She had certainly been an active patroness in her youth, attracting over twenty dedications.[24] But she may have been too old and frail to take any direct interest in this minor transaction with the local poet–playwright, for she died only five months later, on 9 February 1603.

Perhaps a sense that his father's death was not far off had some bearing on Shakespeare's interest, in these plays, in questions of social advancement and inheritance. But rather as what he happened to be writing in the aftermath of his son's death happened to be a comedy – *The Merry Wives* – so it proved in the aftermath of his father's death in 1601. The work in hand at the time of his own bereavement happened to be a festive comedy, in which it is established early on that 'Care's an enemy to life', and that anyone who grieves for more than a few moments for a dead family member is a fool.

Do the boys carry it away?

In his excellent edition of *Antonio's Revenge*[25] Reavley Gair identified three theories about the relationship of the play to Shakespeare's *Hamlet*. Either it precedes *Hamlet*; or it follows *Hamlet*, and 'reeks of theft'; or – and this is the view Gair himself favours – 'Shakespeare and Marston were working at the same time and in competition.' However, Gair precludes the possibility of any direct collusion between the two playwrights, suggesting, rather, that many of the plays' common features derive from the lost early version of *Hamlet*. Yet the presence at the Middle Temple of Shakespeare's cousin Thomas Greene, sponsored by Marston and his father, provides solid evidence for Shakespeare's personal connections both with the Middle Temple and with Marston. Taken in conjunction with Marston's public tribute to Shakespeare in the 1601 *Poeticall Essaies*, it supports the likelihood of Marston's being not just one of the many young men who admired and imitated Shakespeare's writings – as evidenced, for instance, in echoes of *Venus and Adonis* in his *Metamorphosis of Pigmalions Image* (1598)[26] – but his personal friend. Gair himself provides further material that strengthens the likelihood that *Hamlet* and *Antonio's Revenge* were written in close collusion. Gair's painstaking analysis of Marston's idiosyncratic vocabulary, vocabulary for which he was soon to be savagely ridiculed by Jonson in *Poetaster*, shows that out of 327 words in *Antonio's Revenge* that require glossing an astonishing 62 per cent are shared with Shakespeare. Using Spenser and Jonson as 'controls', Gair finds only 38 per cent of Marston's rare words to be shared with the former, 26 per cent with the latter.

The implications of Gair's work can be pursued a good deal further. In several of the instances where distinctive words or phrases are shared by Marston and Shakespeare they occur in the equivalent position in their tragedies. For instance, the Ghost of Andrugio, Antonio's dead father, opens the grim fifth act of Marston's play with a prophecy of vengeance soon to fall on his murderer Piero:

> now is his fate grown mellow,
> Instant to fall into the rotten jaws
> Of chap-fall'n death.
>
> (*Antonio's Revenge*, 5.1.8–10)

The fifth act of *Hamlet* opens in a graveyard, in which, famously, Hamlet gazes at the skull of a dead jester, perhaps setting off recollections of the Queen's Man Richard Tarlton, and asks:

> Where be your gibes now, your gambols, your songs, your flashes of merriment, that were wont to set the table on a roar? Not one now to mock your own grinning? Quite chop-fallen?
>
> (*Hamlet*, 5.1.183–6)

That odd phrase 'chap-fall'n' or 'chop-fallen', alluding to the collapsed lower jaw of a skull, caught the sharp eye of Ben Jonson, who used it – again in the final act – in *Poetaster*. Captain Tucca refers to Crispinus and Demetrius as 'a couple of chap-fall'n curs', perhaps intending an insult to Shakespeare as well as to Marston. But even closer parallels can be found in Act 3 of the two plays. In both of these revenge tragedies in which a newly dug grave provides occasion for a further death and a further 'opening' of the earth for burial there is a pervasive preoccupation with open graves as open mouths. Gair notes the parallel use of 'yawns', applied to open-mouthed, yawning, graves, in *Antonio's Revenge*, 3.3 and *Hamlet*, 3.3, but does not point out the broader analogies between the speeches in which the word occurs. In both plays the passage marks the escalation of the hero's revenge, as he begins to appropriate the very savagery he seeks to punish. Each speech is punctuated by an emphatically iterated 'now' that prepares the audience for fresh spectacles of horror. First, Antonio, who has just brutally killed Piero's young son Julio:

> Now barks the wolf against the full-cheeked moon,
> Now lions' half-clammed entrails roar for food,
> Now croaks the toad and night-crows screech aloud,
> Fluttering 'bout casements of departing souls;
> Now gapes the graves, and through their yawns let loose
> Imprisoned spirits to revisit earth.
> And now swart night, to swell thy hour out,
> Behold I spurt warm blood in thy black eyes.
>
> (*Antonio's Revenge*, 3.3.43–50)

Plate 1 The 'Ditchley' portrait of Queen Elizabeth I standing on a map of England, by Marcus Gheeraerts the Younger, *c.* 1592.

Above: Plate 2 William Hole's illustration to the Thirteenth Song in Drayton's *Polyolbion* (1612), showing Warwickshire and the Forest of Arden, from a coloured copy once in the possession of Elizabeth of Bohemia.

Below: Plate 3 Venus carried heavenward in a dove-drawn chariot, engraving by Bernieri after Raphael, 1786.

The Armorial Bearings of
WILLIAM SHAKESPEARE
of Stratford-upon-Avon.

College of Arms,
London.

Chester Herald
and Registrar.

Right: Plate 4 Shakespeare's coat of arms, from C. W. Scott-Giles, *Shakespeare's Heraldry* (London, 1950).

Below: Plate 5 Shakespeare's disputed coat of arms, on the left, with the arms of Mauley, Harley and Ferrers for comparison on the right.

Hall

Clark

Shakespere

Peake

Hall

Lo. Mauley

Harley

Ferrers

Plate 6 Panel painting of the siege of Troy, by Biagio di Antonio, Florence, *c.* 1490.

These be the Armes and Crest of Parr
Marquis of Northampton the Last Male
of his house.

These 3 Crests wᵗʰ the Armes of Parr and the other 4
forged coats were geven to Parr the Embroderer
whose father was a Pedler by occupacion and not
abbe to proue his surname to be Parr, for wᶜʰ Armes and
a forged Pedigree to mayntayne yᵉ same Garter had £ 10.

p William Detheck Garter
principall kinge of Armes

Plate 7 On the right, 'forged' coat of arms awarded by William Dethick to 'Parr the Embroiderer', with the authentic Parr family arms shown on the left.

Plate 8 Effigy of the poet John Gower in Southwark Cathedral, formerly St Saviour's.

Plate 9 Portrait of Robert Devereux, second Earl of Essex, by Nicholas Hilliard.

Plate 10 Queen Elizabeth being carried in procession, painting by Robert Peake, *c.* 1600; the grey-haired man in the foreground, wearing the Garter below his knee may be Shakespeare's patron, the second Lord Hunsdon, the Lord Chamberlain.

Plate 11 Funeral procession of Queen Elizabeth, possibly drawn by William Camden.

Plate 12 (*Overleaf*) Title-page of Drayton's *Polyolbion* (1612), showing an allegorical figure of Great Britain seen through a triumphal arch; from a coloured copy once in the possession of Elizabeth of Bohemia.

POLY-OLBION
GREAT BRITAINE
By
Michaell Drayton
Esqr:
London printed for M Lownes. I Browne.
I Helme. I Busbie.
Ingraued by W Hole

Next, Hamlet, who has just uncovered Claudius's guilt by means of the play, and is about to visit his mother, in wild and murderous mood:

> 'Tis now the very witching time of night,
> When churchyards yawn and hell itself breathes out
> Contagion to this world. Now could I drink hot blood,
> And do such bitter business as the day
> Would quake to look on.
>
> (*Hamlet*, 3.2.379–83)

Both speeches conjure up Gothic images of nocturnal horror, and are calculated to scare the audience, who see the play's previously sympathetic and pitiable hero suddenly transformed into a murderous monster who will 'spurt warm blood' (Antonio) or 'drink hot blood' (Hamlet). Audiences who watched both Marston's miniaturized tragedy at St Paul's and Shakespeare's very large-scale one at the Globe or 'else-where' could admire the ingenuity with which the younger and older writer had deployed many such verbal parallels and variations on a theme. Both plays were powerful in their own terms, offering studies of tyranny and vengeance in full-size – or even outsize, *Hamlet* being Shakespeare's longest play, notoriously too long to perform without cutting – and in miniature. Indeed, the little-and-large image is one that Shakespeare himself uses, when Hamlet compares the success of the boys' companies with the popular value placed on pictures 'in little' of the new king Claudius, for which people are willing to pay 'twenty, forty, fifty, a hundred ducats apiece'. This famous scene, in which Rosencrantz tells Hamlet of the huge success of the theatrical 'eyrie of little children', explicitly connects Shakespeare's play with Marston's. Rosencrantz and Guildenstern describe the current rivalry between boy players and men, in which the boys triumph:

> HAMLET Do the boys carry it away?
> ROSENCRANTZ Ay, that they do, my lord, Hercules and his load too.
>
> (*Hamlet*, 2.2.357–8)

In its original context this passage had the effect of extravagant compliment to Paul's Boys and Marston's *Antonio* plays, suggesting whimsically to the massed Globe audience that these choice productions were actually superior to the superb performance that they were currently watching. While the new Globe Theatre's sign showed Hercules shouldering the world, or 'globe' (Fig. 22), it seems that the child actors in their tiny performance space are being praised as even more successful than the Lord Chamberlain's Men: it is not the men, but the boys, who carry away the whole world on their young shoulders.

Fig. 22 Hercules bearing the world on his shoulders.

The Hercules image can be explored a little further. Hamlet explicitly disclaims any resemblance to Hercules, alluding to Claudius as 'no more like my father / Than I to Hercules'. Marston's Antonio, on the other hand, in one of several passages of near comic pathos, throws himself down in grief with the mawkish exclamation

> Behold a prostrate wretch laid on his tomb;
> His epitaph thus: *Ne plus ultra*.* Ho!
> Let none out-woe me, mine's Herculean woe.
>
> (*Antonio's Revenge*, 2.3.131–3)

* '*Ne plus ultra*': [There is] nothing more beyond [these]': alluding to the Pillars of Hercules, the supposed limit of the civilized world.

While Hamlet struggles both to feel appropriate grief and to find adequate expression for that grief, envying the First Player's capacity for both, Antonio has no doubt of his own sincerity:

> I will not swell like a tragedian
> In forced passion of affected strains.
> (*Antonio's Revenge*, 2.3.104–5)

Hamlet, a mature and complex character performed by the mature and complex Burbage, is well aware that he is no Hercules, no muscle-man superhero, while Marston's childish Antonio is naively certain of his own heroic, Herculean status. Each play explicitly gestures towards the other. From its position of manifest superiority in scale and sophistication Shakespeare's *Hamlet* pays *Antonio's Revenge* an extravagant compliment that should not be taken too seriously. Rather as a grown man may pretend to be fatally hurt by a child with a toy gun, Shakespeare playfully pretends that the boys' companies in general, and the Paul's Boys in particular, offer a severe threat to the Lord Chamberlain's Men and their leading playwright. The fiction that audiences will be drawn away by the boys' companies is, in truth, an expression of Shakespeare's assured confidence that he was writing at the top of his form. He could hardly have known that *Hamlet* would fall just half-way through his writing career, yet he was clearly well aware that this, his longest play, was also his best to date. As measured by allusions and quotations it soon overtook both the narrative poems and *Romeo and Juliet* in popularity.

Money matters

Though the Paul's Boys may indeed have been doing rather well, the scale of their operations, contained within a theatre that seated barely a hundred spectators,[27] meant that they could hardly pose a very serious economic threat to the Lord Chamberlain's Men and their vast playhouse that accommodated 3,000. As holder of a share in the Globe amounting to one-fifth of a moiety, that is, 10 per cent of the theatre's takings, from 1599, Shakespeare now enjoyed a regular annual income of several hundred pounds.[28] Rewards for special performances at court, in noblemen's houses and at Inns of Court, together with incomings from property and commodities in Stratford, further increased this sum. Yet there is some reason to believe that, despite his financial prosperity during these years, Shakespeare did not always provide adequately for his wife and family. In March 1601 an old husbandman, Thomas Whittington, who had worked with Anne Hathaway's father as his shepherd, made a will in which as the very first item he bequeathed to 'the poor people of Stratford' a sum of

40 shillings 'that is in the hand of Anne Shakespeare wife unto Master William Shakespeare and is due debt unto me being paid to mine executor by the said William Shakespeare or his assigns according to the true meaning of this my will'. He went on to make three further bequests to the poor, leaving £3 to the poor of Stratford, *6s. 8d.* to the poor of Old Stratford and *30s.* to the poor of Henley in Arden. A supplementary list of debts due indicates that Whittington had lent money to half a dozen of the Hathaways, including two of Anne's brothers, sums ranging from 3 to 55 shillings. In the case of the other Hathaway debts, however, Whittington's intention seems to have been simply to indicate to his executor, his 'kinsman' William Whittington, that these sums as itemized were owed to his estate, and should be recovered. The allusion to Anne Shakespeare is quite different, in that the requirement here is that her husband pays the debt to the executor for the benefit of the poor. It carries two implications, both rather damaging to the playwright. First, at some time Anne had been left short of money by her husband, and had turned, as so many of her family evidently did, to her father's old friend – apparently a bachelor – for help. Secondly, Whittington felt that the poor of Stratford were not receiving sufficient benefit from their celebrated townsman's prosperity. If we compare Shakespeare's position at this point of his career with that of another man who was making good money from the theatre, the actor–manager Edward Alleyn, we can see the force of this. Alleyn was already preparing to set up some of the many charitable foundations for which he was to become celebrated, and which ensure that his name is widely commemorated in Dulwich to this day. He was a pillar of his parish church, St Saviour's, Southwark, and was active in collecting the parish dues that provided alms for the poor.[29] Shakespeare did nothing of the kind – indeed, as we saw in chapter 5, he repeatedly avoided paying parish dues. Whittington's bequest delivers a double reproach: the new-made gentleman's son had neglected the needs both of his own family and of the poor of his native town.

The passage also points to antagonism between the Shakespeares and the Hathaways that may go right back to the time of his reluctant marriage. In this antagonism, the Hathaways and their associates were probably supported by the 'scriptor' or writer of the will, William Gilbard alias Higges, Stratford's faithful curate and assistant schoolmaster. The pious formulas that open Whittington's will are virtually identical to those which had opened Richard Hathaway's, drawn up by Gilbard twenty years earlier. Drafting wills for the illiterate was one of the many services Gilbard regularly performed for the parishioners of Stratford, along with teaching their young and maintaining the town's clocks.[30] A determination to find a portrait of Gilbard in the fictional curate Nathaniel in *Love's Labour's Lost* has led to his being characterized as 'inoffensive' and 'mild and obliging'.[31] However, though there could well be some generic connection between the fictional Nathaniel and the historical curate Gilbard, such a portrait should not be accepted too literally. It was almost certainly from Gilbard that Shakespeare received his own earliest tuition, and the relationship between them in later life may not have been comfortable – especially if Gilbard detected a caricature of himself in the unheroic Sir Nathaniel with his comical lack of acting skill. Such a committed and public-spirited denizen of Stratford may have viewed his pupil's rise and rise with considerable disapproval. Stratford, and in particular the town's grammar school, had performed crucial services for young William, preparing him in those skills of speedy reading and writing and confident oral declamation which had carried him to fame and fortune. Living in a house that abutted on the Guild Hall and school, Gilbard and his large family witnessed much that his former pupil in faraway London preferred not to see: the steady decline of the former alderman John Shakespeare, and the relative poverty of the neglected Anne and her daughters. In the eyes of Gilbard, a good family man and an upright citizen, the fashionable poet was far from 'sweet'. Perhaps he hoped to use the clause in Whittington's will to prick Shakespeare's conscience. But whether Shakespeare was stung by this – or even whether he paid over the 40 shillings promptly as required – we don't know.

'Drown'd? O, where?'

In his excellent account of the many 'incidental similarities' between *Hamlet* and *Antonio's Revenge* Harold Jenkins does not explicitly discuss the drowning of Ophelia, saying only that in both plays 'the beloved dies broken-hearted off stage'.[32] This omission is quite natural, for it is not immediately apparent that there is any special connection between this episode and the reported drowning of Antonio in Marston's play. Nevertheless, as so often, there is a positional parallel: both deaths by water are reported late on in the fourth act of their respective plays. But in *Antonio's Revenge* Antonio is actually present on stage, disguised as a bubble-blowing fool, as a witness to his friend Alberto's fictitious narrative:

> PIERO Antonio drowned? How? How? Antonio drown'd!
> ALBERTO Distraught and raving, from a turret's top
> He threw his body in the high-swollen sea,
> And as he headlong topsy-turvy dinged down
> He still cried 'Mellida'.
>
> (*Antonio's Revenge*, 4.3.80–4)

If we bear in mind the likelihood that audience members had impressions of one revenge play freshly in mind when they saw the other, we can see that it was particularly important for Shakespeare to establish clearly that the report of Ophelia's death by drowning is not just a melodramatic fiction, but something that they are invited to believe in as a narrative event. Gertrude's famous eye-witness report beginning,

> There is a willow grows askant the brook
> That shows his hoary leaves in the glassy stream.
> Therewith fantastic garlands did she make
> Of crow-flowers, nettles, daisies, and long purples
> That liberal shepherds give a grosser name,
> But our cold maids do dead men's fingers call them.
> (*Hamlet*, 4.7.165–70)

is a lyrical tour de force, a piece of rich poetic scene-painting that provides the audience with some much-needed emotional release in the simplicity of its pathos. Those 'long purples', both phallic and deathly,[33] suggest the feminine fragility of both women amid a throng of men who either seduce them, or die, or both. By using Gertrude as the reporter of Ophelia's drowning Shakespeare both reveals the underlying kinship between the two women and enforces audience belief. There are many characters in this play, from the Ghost downwards, who seem quite capable of elaborate story-telling or feigning, but the too acquiescent Gertrude is not one of them. By having the circumstances of Ophelia's death recounted in such vivid detail that Millais, for one, felt able to paint it (Fig. 23), Shakespeare ensures that the audience feel that they, too, have witnessed it. In the following scene the audience will guess, long before Hamlet does, that the body for which a grave is being dug must be that of Ophelia.[34] In general, it is a risky literalism that seeks originals or analogues in 'real life', so-called, for exceptionally powerful passages of Shakespeare's writing. Yet in the case of Gertrude's account of Ophelia's death there is one that cannot be ignored. Indeed, a possible reply to Laertes's stunned question, which prompts Gertrude's speech, 'Drown'd? O, where?', is 'in Warwickshire, just outside Stratford'. As mentioned in chapter 1, on 17 December 1579 an unmarried girl called, extraordinarily, Katherine Hamlett, drowned in the river Avon at Tiddington while trying to fill a pail with water. An inquest had to be held to determine the exact cause of her death, so that she might have lawful burial:

> the aforesaid Katherine, standing on the bank of the same river, suddenly and by accident slipped and fell into the river aforesaid, and there, in the water of the same river . . . was drowned, and not otherwise nor in other fashion came by her death.[35]

Fig. 23 *Ophelia* by John Everett Millais.

A combination of theatrical instinct and local memory made Shakespeare especially determined to give this episode a rich visual immediacy. His own new landholdings in and around Stratford re-connected him with his native 'country', and its riverside vegetation, and rather as a bald sentence in Holinshed could be the germ of a richly inventive passage in an English history play, we can see the bare event of Katherine Hamlett's death richly embroidered with flowers. From this passage, in turn, another, far more extended account of a forsaken maiden seems to have germinated: that strange one-off, *A Lover's Complaint*. This poem's unnamed 'fickle maid' is encountered beside the 'weeping margent' of a river, into which she is throwing, not herself, but the jewels, rings and love letters received from her high-born and devilishly charming seducer.

Reports of drowning play a crucial part in the plots of all four plays written by Shakespeare and Marston in 1600–2. Antonio's feigned drowning allows him to remain safely in disguise at Piero's court while he prepares his revenge. Ophelia's accidental drowning triggers off a second revenge plot, that of Laertes against Hamlet, which carries events to their long-awaited bloody conclusion. The opening situation in Marston's *What You Will* is that the lady Celia, who believes her husband Albano to be drowned, is being pursued by eager suitors. Finally, in the second scene of *Twelfth Night, or What You Will* Viola has just escaped drowning in a shipwreck, and fears that her brother Sebastian is indeed drowned. However, in this most self-consciously theatrical or metatheatrical scene, Viola begs to be reassured – 'perchance he is not drown'd?' – and with comic eagerness immediately accepts the Captain's equally fictional-seeming account of seeing him clinging to the wreckage among the waves – 'For saying so, there's gold.' In contrast to Olivia, initially pledged to seven years' mourning for *her* dead brother, Viola shows no further anxiety about Sebastian until she is re-united with him in the final scene, by which time she appears to have reverted to belief in his drowning:

> Such a Sebastian was my brother too:
> So went he suited to his watery tomb.
>
> (*Twelfth Night*, 5.1.231–2)

In this most delightfully stagey of comedies, it seems that Shakespeare has elaborated the running motif of reported drowning and turned it into an in-joke. Fresh from *What You Will*, audiences came to the other comedy which bore almost the same name quite as ready as Viola is to be told that someone who was apparently drowned is not so really. Further devices hint that everything is happening in a playhouse, transiently labelled 'Illyria'. There is, for instance, an obsessive preoccupation with costume – Viola must collect her 'maiden weeds' from the Captain, but we know perfectly well, this being the closing scene, that what is meant is simply 'from the tiring-house'. The brother and sister affirm their recognition of each other not by the most obvious method, looking at each others' faces, but by means of yet another ridiculously elaborate romance motif:

> VIOLA My father had a mole upon his brow.
> SEBASTIAN And so had mine.
>
> (5.1.240–1)

While the two off-stage drownings in Marston are similar, each being an elaborate fiction that essentially supports the plot, Shakespeare's two are at opposite poles. The drowning of Ophelia is at once resonantly poetic and wholly credible. Of all the many reported events in *Hamlet* this is the one that most tends to lodge in our minds as something we feel we have witnessed. On the other hand, the shipwreck in *Twelfth Night* is such a transparent plot device that an audience immediately forgets it. Its function is simply to transport both Viola and Sebastian to Illyria, and to provide Viola with a reason, albeit a flimsy one, for her disguise as 'an eunuch'.

CROSS-GARTERING

Marston wrote *What You Will* primarily for performance by Paul's Boys in their playhouse, but possibly also for performance in his own residence, the Middle Temple. That Shakespeare's analogous comedy was performed in the

Middle Temple there is no doubt at all, for John Manningham saw it there on Candlemas (2 February) 1602:

> At our feast we had a play called 'Twelve night, or what you will', much like the *Comedy of Errors*, or *Menaechmi* in Plautus, but most like and near to that in Italian called *Inganni*. A good practice in it to make the steward believe his Lady widow was in love with him, by counterfeiting a letter, as from his Lady, in general terms, telling him what she liked best in him, and prescribing his gesture in smiling, his apparel, etc. and then when he came to practice, making him believe they took him to be mad.[36]

In referring to Olivia as a 'Lady widow' Manningham may betray a confusion with Marston's play of near identical title, in which the heroine believes herself to be a widow until the return of her supposedly drowned husband in the final scene. He seems to have recognized the play as Shakespeare's, connecting it with his early *Comedy of Errors*, another play featuring twins separated by shipwreck, and one also performed, though some years earlier, at an Inn of Court – at Gray's Inn, 1594. Manningham's identification of the comedy's chief source as 'that in Italian called *Inganni*' (translatable as 'Errors'), has not been taken as seriously as it should,[37] perhaps because of the difficulty of working out quite how Shakespeare could have gained access to an untranslated Italian play. It is true that Shakespeare seems also to have drawn on Barnabe Riche's prose tale of 'Apolonius and Silla', contained in his *Riche his Farewell to Militarie Profession* (1581). But with the half-Italian Marston as his friend and almost his collaborator, neither access to a recent Italian book, nor a good grasp of its narrative contents, seems at all problematic. Manningham's source attribution may reflect the talk going round the Middle Temple that night: Shakespeare had drawn on the more recent of the two Italian plays entitled *Gl'Inganni*, that by Curzio Gonzaga, published in Venice in 1592. In this one, uniquely, the cross-dressed heroine calls herself 'Cesare', resembling Viola's transformation into 'Cesario'.

There are other practices shared by Shakespeare and Marston in their writing during these years. Both incorporated surprisingly intimate personal details in their plays, details which suggest that they were addressing audiences some of whose members would be able to pick up such allusions. In *Antonio and Mellida*, the play with which the newly revived Paul's Boys' company seem to have opened their season in 1599–1600,[38] Marston includes a whimsical allusion to his own age, possibly accompanying a portrait of himself. The self-important and dim-witted Sir Jeffrey Balurdo looks at two pictures, one labelled 'Anno Domini 1599', the other 'Aetatis suae 24'. John Marston, christened on 7 October 1576, was in his twenty-fourth year in 1599–1600. He was almost certainly drawing attention to this fact, a significant one, since that was the age at which it was possible to be ordained deacon.[39] In *What You Will* Marston carried personal allusion a good deal further, at least if we accept, as I do, Philip Finkelpearl's argument that Lampatho Doria, the cynical law student turned satirist, is Marston's self-portrait.[40] At one point he is addressed as 'Kinsayder', one of Marston's satirical aliases, carrying a pun on 'Mar-stone'.* As for Shakespeare: we may clearly view the scenes with the players in *Hamlet* as broadly personal. It also seems quite reasonable to see Hamlet's extended advice to the Player, which opens 3.2, as an expression of his own views on acting technique. Whether or not a personal onslaught on the huffing style of Edward Alleyn is intended, there is clearly a broad critique of old-fashioned, crude, noisy performances, which may by implication still be encountered at Alleyn's Rose:

> O, it offends me to the soul to hear a robustious periwig-pated fellow tear a passion to tatters, to very rags, to split the ears of the groundlings, who for the most part are capable of nothing but inexplicable dumb-shows and noise. I would have such a fellow whipped for o'erdoing Termagant. It out-Herods Herod. Pray you avoid it.
>
> (*Hamlet*, 3.2.8–14)

As delivered by Burbage, this speech encouraged the audience to appreciate the radical difference between his own sophisticated acting style and the sort of thing the young playgoers might have witnessed at the other large playhouse south of the Thames, or that older men and women might recall from mystery plays seen in childhood.

The 'Player' scenes in *Hamlet* had personal resonances shared by Shakespeare with his colleagues the Lord Chamberlain's Men, for all of whom such topics as play-revision, rehearsal and the effective delivery of theatrical speeches were by definition consuming interests. But in *Twelfth Night* there are some elements that are personal above all to the playwright. Shakespeare was drawing on a tradition of ironic self-presentation that had a long history. Chaucer, for instance, makes a joke of his own unimpressive role as 'Chaucer the pilgrim'. The poet who is in truth the author of all the *Canterbury Tales* makes himself the teller of a story (*The Tale of Sir Topas*) so old-fashioned and tedious that the other pilgrims don't want to hear it out: 'Thy drasty rymyng is nat worth a toord', says the Host. Likewise, the brilliantly sophisticated Thomas More presents himself, in the preliminaries to *Utopia*, as the naive and gullible 'Morus', who has listened uncritically to Hythlodaeus's traveller's tale. The polished and articulate Sidney creates as his alter ego the supposedly inarticulate and tunnel-visioned 'Astrophil', and also makes a joke of the

* The job of a 'kinsayder' was to geld animals; testicles were called 'stones', so a 'kinsayder' was someone who 'marred stones'.

Sidney coat of arms, a gold arrowhead on a blue ground, and its ironic connection with Cupid's arrows. But Shakespeare's self-ridicule in *Twelfth Night* was even closer to his own bone, as it were, than any of these. In just the period during which he was – or wasn't – coming into his own as an armigerous gentleman, he made a joke of his own aspirations.

As discussed in chapter 4, the grant of arms to John Shakespeare entitled the older man, and from September 1601 his son and heir, to make many highly visible displays of his 'coat'. Its essential component is a gold background, generally represented in paint by yellow, diagonally scored across with a black band. At just the period when *Twelfth Night* was first performed the Herald who awarded the patent, Sir William Dethick, was in the process of being called to trial by his fellow heralds in the Earl Marshal's Court. Not only were dozens of grants of arms, including, conspicuously, the one made to Shakespeare, now called into question, so was Dethick's very capacity to hold office as Garter King of Arms. It is impossible that Shakespeare could have been unaware of all this. It was particularly humiliating that during the very period of his life when his wealth, his landholdings and the death of his father all combined to support his entitlement to call himself 'Gentleman' the legal means he had taken to acquire his patent should be called in question. Characteristically, his way of dealing with it was to turn the whole thing into a self-mocking joke.

The killjoy steward Malvolio, whose name marks him as a man of 'ill will', is tricked by Sir Toby and Maria into revealing his overweening social ambition. The feigned letter that encourages him to press his suit with his employer, the lady Olivia, offers him glorious visions of self-advancement and metamorphosis:

> *Some are born great, some achieve greatness, and some have greatness thrust upon 'em. Thy fates open their hands, let thy blood and spirit embrace them, and to inure thyself to what thou art like to be, cast thy humble slough, and appear fresh.*
>
> (*Twelfth Night*, 2.5.145–9)

The particular manner in which Malvolio is to 'appear fresh' – 'Remember who commended thy yellow stockings, and wish'd to see thee ever cross-garter'd' – must have been immediately obvious to Shakespeare's fellow players as a personal allusion, for yellow stockings cross-gartered visibly mimicked that now disputed coat of arms. The reason that the resemblance of Malvolio's cross-gartered yellow hose to Shakespeare's coat of arms has not been noticed in modern times may be because later stage tradition has had Malvolio grotesquely arrayed with garters that criss-cross the whole of his lower legs, lattice-wise. Even by the time of the Restoration the particular associations that made cross-gartering comic were largely forgotten. Correctly, however, cross-garters encircled the leg only twice, once, slant-wise, below the knee, and once, slantwise, above, where they were tied in a bow at the side. By 1600, cross-garters 'were worn chiefly by old men, Puritans, pedants, footmen, and rustic bridegrooms'.[41] The correct cross-gartering structure ensured that a version of Shakespeare's coat of arms would be seen on Malvolio's legs twice, with a 'bend sinister' below the right knee, and again, in mirror-image with 'bend dexter', below the left (Fig. 24). For Shakespeare's fellow players, fully aware both of Shakespeare's pursuit of gentility and of Jonson's mockery of it in a play in which they themselves had performed (*Every Man Out*), the effect must have been exquisitely ridiculous – all the more so because garters, *per se*, could signify the utmost grandeur. The humble device for keeping up stockings was associated with that most noble order of chivalry, the Order of the Garter, of which their benevolent patron, the Lord Chamberlain, was a Knight. The players must often have gazed at silk-clad noblemen wearing the blue silk token tied elegantly below the right knee over a white silk stocking (see the foreground figure in Plate 10). But Malvolio's cross-garters over old-fashioned yellow hose were, conversely, a fashion reminiscent, says Maria, of 'a pedant that keeps a school i' th' church' (*Twelfth Night*, 3.2.72–3) – in fact, just the sort of dowdy rig likely to be worn by a man like the Stratford curate and schoolmaster William Gilbard.

While *Twelfth Night*'s love intrigue involving twins and cross-dressing derived from *Gl'Inganni*, what most tickled John Manningham – and has delighted audiences ever since – was Shakespeare's addition to it, the Malvolio plot. His cross-gartered entrance in 3.4 clearly brought the house down with the raucous young students assembled in the Great Hall of the Middle Temple in 1602. If Shakespeare himself took the role, the analogies between the self-display and subsequent humiliation of Malvolio and recent developments in the playwright's own life, of which some of the young men were aware, would be irresistible. While the Lord Chamberlain Hunsdon wore the true Garter, his leading 'man', in authentic Misrule fashion, sported a grotesquely inept caricature of it, one that both re-enacted and ridiculed his own overweening dreams of social advancement.

In the taunting of the 'mad' Malvolio by Feste disguised as 'Sir Topas the curate' there is a clear literary allusion, and possibly also a covert personal one. For auditors who were even moderately well read, the name 'Sir Topas' immediately recalled Chaucer's 'drasty rymyng', and signalled the presence of some authorial self-mockery, in the Chaucerian manner, within this scene. More privately, the scene may also reflect Shakespeare's personal irritation at being called to book by a silly parson, as he saw it, William Gilbard. From his dark madhouse cell in the inner stage Malvolio cries out desperately 'help me to a candle, and pen, ink, and paper: as I am a gentleman, I will live to be

Fig. 24 Cross-gartering, according to the late mediaeval fashion, worn by the Puritan satirist John Heywood, from Heywood, *Epigrams*, 1562.

thankful to thee for't' (*Twelfth Night*, 4.2.84–6). No-one in the play, not even Feste as Sir Topas, challenges Malvolio's assertion that he is a gentleman. Olivia, recalling him in the final scene, reflects, 'They say, poor gentleman, he's much distract' (5.1.278). Yet the bare title of 'gentleman', though socially affirmed, carried a man only so far and no further. In Malvolio's grotesquely inept attempt to advance himself into the favour of a wealthy noblewoman we may see Master William Shakespeare, Gent., making rich comic capital out of his own imagined or actual inability to cultivate the favour of high-born ladies. Soon, however, this was to be a far less grievous handicap, for the highest lady of all was near her end.

News of the old Queen's mortal illness was quick to reach the Middle Temple. After dining with the Queen's private chaplain Dr Parry in the Privy Chamber in Richmond Palace John Manningham wrote on 23 March 1603 of her three or four months of 'melancholy', her more recent refusal of both food and medicine, 'since Shrovetide sitting sometimes with her eye fixed upon one object many hours together', and of her silent affirmation of faith in salvation through Christ. On the following day, 24 March, Manningham wrote once more:

> This morning about 3 at clock her Majesty departed this life, mildly like a lamb, easily like a ripe apple from the tree, *cum leve quadam febre, absque gemitu.** Dr. Parry told me that he was present and sent his prayers before her soul; and I doubt not but she is amongst the royal saints in heaven in eternal joys.[42]

This account suggests appropriate shock and sadness at the ending of the long era of Elizabeth's life and forty-five-year reign. However, within a few days this mood has given way to signs of hopeful excitement about the newly proclaimed Stuart regime. Only a week later, the relief was palpable, and in that pre-feminist age was expressed without embarrassment. John Manningham and his Middle Temple room-mate speak on behalf of the rising generation:

> We worshipped no saints, but we prayed to ladies, in the Queen's time. (Mr Curle). This superstition shall be abolished, we hope, in our King's reign.[43]

Men of letters were bidding farewell to that whole age of courtly love and of lady-worship which had received elaborate expression in such works as Spenser's *The Faerie Queene* and Sidney's *Astrophil and Stella*. Shakespeare's evolving *Sonnets*, composed of a sophisticated male-on-male sequence and a misogynistic coda in which the speaker explicitly mocks all those courtly love poets who have belied their ugly mistresses 'with false compare', would be well-tuned to the coming times. In the famous 107, 'Not mine own fears', his speaker looks forward to an 'endless age' of male friendship presided over by a king.

*'With some light fever and without groaning'.

CHAPTER SEVEN

1603–07

The King's Man

Thus have I had thee as a dream doth flatter,
In sleep a king, but waking no such matter.

(Sonnet 87.13–14)

The oldest hath borne most; we that are young
Shall never see so much, nor live so long.

(*King Lear*, final lines)

Weep with joy

THE expected arrival from Scotland of James VI and his retinue provoked fevered excitement in the spring and early summer of 1603. Not only was he young, male, peace-loving and possessed of two sons – thus ensuring an end both to female rule and to the once seemingly endless 'succession question' – he was already an established poet, essayist and philosopher. As Richard Barnfield had put it, none too elegantly, in 1598:

> The King of Scots (now living) is a poet,
> As his *Lepanto*, and his *Furies*, show it.[1]

While James travelled South slowly, and to huge acclaim, London's printers worked at high speed and overtime. Well over fifty publications which survive from this period – others have probably vanished – reflect the determination of English individuals and institutions to get in quickly with their expressions of what some Cambridge poets called *Sorrowes joy*,[2] and Joseph Hall called *Weeping joy*.[3] One of many anonymous ballads bore the title *Weepe with joy*.[4] As these titles suggest, the vast majority of these writers, whether scholars, clergymen, poets or others, took on two apparently conflicting tasks. They lamented and memorialized Elizabeth, and they praised and welcomed the new King and his family. Some writers of modest talent handled the double genre surprisingly well. Robert Fletcher, who had been 'Yeoman Purveyor of Carriages for removes of our said late Sovereign Lady', composed a neat epitaph on the Queen in sixains, in which he praised her for keeping so long hidden the good news 'That we in her succession should be blessed'. He followed it with a poem on the expected arrival of James and concluded with an extended prayer, in prose, for the whole royal family. His book is dated 23 April 1603, St George's Day, and thus a bare month after the Queen's death. But many other songs, elegies and ballads had already appeared by this date, including, for instance, Robert Prickett's *A souldiers wish*,[5] to which the royal removal man Fletcher alludes. Though the balance, style and verse form varied, most writers adopted the same basic formula of lament and commemoration succeeded by happily expectant celebration. Janus-like, their compositions gazed backwards in grief and recollection and forwards in hopeful joy.

Though not all writers may fully have attained the rewards and preferments for which they hoped, many of them did well. Elizabethan office-holders, for instance, generally retained their offices. Because of the splendour with which he was entertained as he travelled south James formed the false impression that England was a wealthy country, and his own new coffers bottomless. As far as his new courtiers went, James was a true Lavish McTavish:

> The King responded lavishly in his own way, by making knights, hundreds of knights, too many knights, more in his first four months as King of England than had been created in the whole of Elizabeth's forty-five years on the throne.[6]

As early as 12 April John Chamberlain reported that because of the new King's immediately visible bounty 'the very poets with their idle pamphlets promise themselves great part in his favour'.[7] Yet some of these poets notoriously stumbled. One of the most comical casualties of the great change in the state was the ambitious Welsh Catholic Hugh Holland, who happened to be abroad tagging along with an embassy to Germany at the time of the Queen's death. Relying on the old Queen's continued survival, he had embarked on an ambitious poem, *Pancharis*, in celebration of Elizabeth's Welsh ancestor Owen Tudor. It is prefaced by a rather engaging verse autobiography recounting Holland's roots in Denbighshire, his education at Trinity College, Cambridge, and the pubertal sprouting of his black beard. When news of Elizabeth's death reached him in Amsterdam Holland made a swift about-turn, composing poems dedicating Book 1 of *Pancharis* to King James, to Queen Anne, and to Prince Henry, whom he hopes soon to see installed as Prince of Wales. Commendatory poems include one by Ben Jonson, who makes elaborate play with Holland's hirsute swarthiness by calling him a 'black Swan'.[8] More notable even than its many grand dedicatory and commendatory preliminaries, however, is the prose epistle at the end of *Pancharis* addressed to Holland's friend Sir Robert Cotton. Cotton allegedly pressed him to get *Pancharis* into print; Holland hopes that he will also testify to his long-standing loyalty to King James – Cotton himself being a direct descendant of Robert Bruce's brother. With wild implausibility, Holland claims that only the previous summer he had written out a fair copy of the poem which he was planning to take up in person to James in Scotland when he was suddenly called away by family troubles in Wales. An incomplete text, very neatly written apparently by Holland himself, survives among the Berkeley Castle muniments, but it is dated 1601, bears the title *Owen Tudyr*, and is firmly dedicated 'TO THE CONQUERING VIRGIN my most glorious & gracious soveraigne Queene ELIZABETH'.[9] Though Holland describes himself as incapable of flattery, he is, in fact, such a transparent name-dropper, wind-watcher and toady that even in this period in which the success-rate among aspirants to favour was unusually high he got nowhere. It was manifestly absurd to claim that an account of the sexual and social rise to favour of Owen Tudor would make a suitable gift for James, whose ancestry was distinctly different from Elizabeth's, even though he did also descend from Owen. In any case, the story was in itself grotesque. The handsomely swarthy Owen (a hopeful role model for Holland) has a lucky stumble while dancing a vigorous galliard before Queen Katherine, Henry V's widow, at Windsor:

> The Queen being very nigh,
> He fell, and, as he forward down declined,
> His knee did hit against her softer thigh.
> I hope he felt no great hurt by the fall,
> That happy fall, which mounted him so high.[10]

But Holland's own blundering attempt to dance, trip and 'mount' into royal favour was a disaster. The promised Books 2 and 3 of his poem, if they ever existed, remained unpublished, and according to Thomas Fuller the black Swan of Denbighshire 'grumbled out the remainder of his life in visible discontentment'. *Pancharis*, one of the most elaborate attempts to commemorate Elizabeth at the same time as cultivating James, was also one of the least successful.

Other poets, as we saw at the beginning of chapter 6, made grave errors of omission. The most notorious of these was Shakespeare's friend and Warwickshire neighbour Michael Drayton, who was among those who were extremely quick off the mark in their welcome to James. His *Gratulatorie Poem* to James was in print even before the old Queen had been buried, and his editors suggest that he may have 'joined the early northward riders and presented his poem in person'.[11] However, his attempt to claim special privilege from the King as an immortalizing poet is distinctly embarrassing in its crudely selfish thrusting aside of others:

> The praise I give thee shall thy welcome keep,
> When all the rude crowds in the dust shall sleep.[12]

Unlike Hugh Holland, Drayton takes pains to eulogize the specific branch of the royal tree that separates Stuarts from Tudors, laying great stress on James's descent from Margaret Douglas; a woodcut of James's family tree was appended to his poem. Yet we know for sure that Drayton's poem was a blunder. Chettle explicitly rebuked him for his failure to lament Elizabeth:

> Make some amends, I know thou loved'st her well,
> Think 'twas a fault to have thy verses seen
> Praising the King, ere they had mourned the Queen.

It was foolishly thoughtless of Drayton not to consider whether the King would be pleased by a tribute from a subject who had failed to shed even the most crocodilian of tears for his long-lived predecessor. As Shakespeare's Cleopatra was soon to say, in response to Antony's ungracious response to news of his wife Fulvia's death:

> O most false love!
> Where be the sacred vials thou shouldst fill
> With sorrowful water? Now I see, I see,
> In Fulvia's death how mine received shall be.
> (*Antony and Cleopatra*, 1.3.63–6)

It was essential that the rituals of mourning were fully solemnized before celebration of the new reign could begin. James himself had the tact to make his progress south a leisurely one, in order not to arrive in London before the Queen's funeral rites were fully completed.[13] Although Drayton was hired by the Goldsmiths' Company to praise James in 1604, this poem, too, seems to have been badly received, and his career never fully recovered from his initial gaffe. Twenty years later he still remembered it bitterly:

> It was my hap before all other men
> To suffer shipwreck by my forward pen:
> When King James entered; at which joyful time
> I taught his title to this isle in rhyme.[14]

Drayton had nourished golden dreams of success as a Jacobean court poet, but destroyed them through his precipitate and ill-judged eagerness.

A ballad not previously discussed in a Shakespeare biography includes an appeal for poetic memorials to Elizabeth:

> You poets all, brave Shakespeare,
> Jonson, Greene,
> Bestow your time to write
> for England's Queen.
> Lament, lament &c.[15]

It is striking that 'brave Shakespeare' is the foremost poet here, followed by Jonson. The allusion to 'Greene' is perplexing, since Robert Greene had been dead for a decade. Perhaps the ballad-writer was misled by the still continuing practice of attaching Greene's marketable name to pamphlets and satires,[16] or perhaps he just chose the name for its useful rhyme with 'Queen'. Like many printed ballads, this one gives the impression of having been tossed off by a hack poet in a matter of minutes. Yet there is an outside chance that the ballad-writer had some acquaintance with Shakespeare's cousin the lawyer Thomas Greene, who wrote a poem of welcome to King James strongly influenced by the poetry of his friend Michael Drayton, *A Poet's Vision, and a Prince's Glorie*. Like Drayton's *Gratulatorie Poem*, it is written in rhyming couplets, and also like Drayton's it incorporates no lament for Elizabeth. *A Poet's Vision* is cast in the form of a rather old-fashioned dream-vision, in which the solitary speaker sits on a hill at dusk. To his surprise,

> Soft drizzling drops upon my face did fall,
> Which sweeter were than that we nectar call.
> That tree that but one little drop receives,
> Though bare before, was spangled all with leaves.

These 'drizzling drops' allude both to the season when James arrived in London – high spring – and to that sacramental balm or chrism that was an even more potent symbol of kingship than the crown itself. Greene's speaker is visited by a fair Lady Muse who tells him about 'The virtuous North', where she and her sister Muses are still cherished. Not only does Greene fail to pay any tribute to Elizabeth, the account of the 'barbarism' of recent English poetry that he puts into the Muse's mouth is strongly critical of late Elizabethan culture and the fashion for satire:

> Others there are which with their railing Muse
> Offend grave ears, and do our names abuse
> In bringing forth such monsters to the light . . .

Under James, she prophesies, true poetry will once more be cherished, and England will acquire her own Mount Helicon. With suitable modesty, Greene speaks of himself as 'with skill unblessed' and is doubtful whether he can get far 'With childish issue of my fainter Muse'. However, he is warmly reassured by his Lady-friend:

> thy Muse may once* be blessed,
> And gently fostered in a kingly breast.
> What though the world saw never line of thine?
> Ne'er can thy Muse have a birth more divine.

Despite the hopeful conclusion of *A Poet's Vision*, however, only one further poem by Thomas Greene is known to have reached print, and this too belongs to 1603: a commendatory sonnet prefixed to his friend Drayton's revised version of *Mortimeriados, The Barons Warres*.[17] As mentioned in chapter 6, Shakespeare's cousin Thomas Greene achieved a highly respectable career as a lawyer and administrator, both in London and Stratford. But the flush of excitement that led him to believe that he could also gain preferment as a Jacobean poet was short-lived. He published no more poetry, and acquired no courtly patronage.

THE DROPS OF THIS MOST BALMY TIME

Meanwhile, what was 'brave Shakespeare' up to? He enjoyed immediate reward and preferment. Within ten days of his arrival in London, on 17 May, James instructed Robert Cecil to adopt as his own the company formerly known as the Lord Chamberlain's Men. Their patent is dated 19 May, and Shakespeare's name comes second, after that of Lawrence Fletcher – a newcomer, who had the advantage of being already known to the King, before whom he had twice performed in Scotland. Along with his 'fellows' Burbage, Augustine Phillips, Heminge, Condell, Sly, Armin and Cowley, Shakespeare now wore the red royal livery, and attended court junketings. Yet he appears to have written neither an elegy for Elizabeth nor a eulogy of King James. The disastrously impetuous attempt of his own muddy and sweaty Falstaff to gain favour from a newly crowned King (*2 Henry IV*, 5.5) may have taught him instinctive caution. Over-eagerness could easily backfire. Having been so quickly adopted as a King's Man, he may not have felt the need to draw further attention to himself. Also, if he was going to write something, it would have to be a splendid, complex and original piece that matched expectations aroused

*'once': eventually

by the still-popular *Venus and Adonis*, which had enjoyed at least three reprints in 1602. He had to live up to his own spectacular reputation. Possibly he embarked on such a poem, but failed to complete it; or perhaps he decided that his energies would be more rewardingly employed in writing fresh plays for performance by the King's Men. Or, having briefly considered a non-dramatic offering to James, he may soon have thought better of it, seeing the poor success of his fellow Midlanders Michael Drayton and Thomas Greene.

Instead, Shakespeare distilled his thoughts on the great changes in the state in a sonnet which was not to reach print until 1609. In sonnet 107, 'Not mine own fears', the speaker reflects on the unexpectedly happy and peaceful turn of events which has proved doomsters wrong. The allusion to the dead Queen in line 5, 'The mortal moon hath her eclipse endured', suggests no particular grief, merely an acknowledgement that a long-drawn-out cycle has been completed. Some literal-minded commentators have doubted whether Elizabeth's death could be called an 'eclipse', since eclipses are transient, yet the image seems perfectly applicable: the mortal moon Cynthia has become invisible on earth, though presumed to be shining in immortal glory in Heaven. The image was certainly applied to the Queen's death by other poets, such as 'I. L.':

> Lament the Lady of the Faery-land . . .
> For silver Cynthia has eclipsed her light,
> And with her absence makes eternal night.[18]

In the sestet Shakespeare's speaker rejoices in the great blessings brought both to himself and to his 'true love' by James's accession:

> Now with the drops of this most balmy time
> My love looks fresh, and death to me subscribes,
> Since 'spite of him I'll live in this poor rhyme,
> While he insults o'er dull and speechless tribes;
> And thou in this shalt find thy monument,
> When tyrants' crests and tombs of brass are spent.

Like Thomas Greene, Shakespeare makes play with sweetly beneficent 'drops' that allude both to the moistly flourishing season of May during which James arrived in London and to the precious sacramental balm with which he has been anointed. At least one of his courtly patrons participated in these holy 'drops' in a surprisingly physical sense. William Herbert, the twenty-two-year-old Earl of Pembroke (Fig. 25), stepped boldly out of line during the coronation ceremonies on 24 July. Whereas other earls came up and each in turn kissed the King's hand, the Venetian ambassador reported that 'The Earl of Pembroke, a handsome youth, who is always with the King, and always joking with him, actually kissed his Majesty's face, whereupon the King

Fig. 25 William Herbert, Earl of Pembroke, portrait by Daniel Mytens.

laughed and gave him a little cuff.'[19] Both Pembroke and his younger brother Philip Herbert knew just how to get on with James, and were quickly rewarded for their flirtatious boldness with signal favours. However, in lines 3–4, sonnet 107 seems also to allude to Shakespeare's earlier patron, the Earl of

Southampton, 'supposed as forfeit to a confined doom' for his complicity with the traitor Essex. Even before he reached London James had signed a warrant for Southampton's release from the Tower; Southampton immediately sped north and joined the court at Huntingdon where he was given the office of carrying the ceremonial sword of state.[20] In the final line of sonnet 107, the phrase 'tyrants' crests' primarily suggests the line of Tudor monarchs, now extinct, and safely labelled as 'tyrants'. Yet it could also contain an even bolder and rasher implication that the Stuarts, currently welcomed with such rapture, may one day also be remembered as tyrants.

Several careful studies of their diction and rhyme words suggest that the group of sonnets numbered 104–26 in the 1609 Quarto 'were composed significantly later than the rest'.[21] Whether or not Shakespeare attempted to write any other poem on the topic of James's accession, it seems that personal comments on the times, ranging from 1603 to 1606, are woven into these sonnets, and that a consistent picture emerges from them. The *Sonnets* speaker values private relationships infinitely more highly than public honour. His 'true love' – both the emotion he feels, and the person for whom he feels it – is all that matters to him, and he refuses to be either daunted or dazzled by great public events or spectacles. Yet a focus on private emotion is integral to the genre of sonnet-writing. It should not be assumed that, in his unpoetical daily life, Shakespeare was truly indifferent to the greatly changed environment in which he found himself. On a practical level, he could hardly be so, for in common with his 'fellows', he immediately encountered extreme difficulty because of the severe plague outbreak that began when Elizabeth was dying and continued with little intermission for a full year. Though the King's Men might now perform even more often at court, the Globe, with all the huge income that it represented, stood idle from 19 May 1603 to 9 April 1604.

Despite Shakespeare's and Greene's celebrations of the sweetly refreshing 'drops' that brought new life to the realm, the first year of James's reign was in truth one of fear and disappointment. Perhaps sacramental balm, combined with the privilege of living in strongly built rat-proof palaces, might offer the royal family and aristocracy some protection from infection. But for most of England's city-dwellers the very air they breathed carried the danger of sudden death. As Thomas Dekker put it theatrically in *The Wonderfull Yeare*:

> Imagine then that all this while Death (like a Spanish leaguer, or rather like stalking Tamburlaine) hath pitched his tents (being nothing but a heap of winding sheets tacked together) in the sinfully polluted suburbs: the plague is muster-master and marshal of the field.

In one of the first newly written plays that we know to have been performed for James and his court, *Measure for Measure*, Shakespeare demonstrated the hopelessness of any judicial attempts to cleanse the 'sinfully polluted suburbs'. Enforcement of Vienna's savage law that makes sex outside marriage a capital offence catches just the wrong people, and it is evident that it will never extirpate either prostitution or procurement, or the diseases associated therewith. In the scene immediately following the arrest of Pompey 'for being a bawd' the Duke himself functions as a 'bawd' in procuring Mariana as a substitute in bed for the sexually harassed Isabella. Starting, perhaps, as he hoped to go on, the King's Men's playwright wrote a comedy that bitterly subverted the conventions of his own earlier comedies, reducing love relationships to abusive or criminal transactions, and re-defining marriage, once the unquestioned happy end of romantic comedy, as a more severe form of punishment than death itself.

Measure for Measure was performed at court on 26 December 1604. This Christmas season opened with the recent 'Moor of Venis' (*Othello*), a play perhaps written while Shakespeare was still closely associated with Marston, for its Italian source in Cinthio's *Hecatommithi* had not been translated. Another recent piece was *The Merchant of Venice* – perhaps designed as a comic counterpart to the *Moor* – which was performed on 'Shrove Sunday', and then again, by the King's special command, on Shrove Tuesday. It has often been assumed that the repeat performance indicates that James particularly liked this play. However, Dudley Carleton had reported during the previous season that the King 'takes no extraordinary pleasure' in plays. An alternative possibility is that James, out on one of his almost daily hunting trips, had missed the Sunday performance, but heard such enthusiastic reports from the Queen and Prince Henry that he decided to give it a try, even though so many of his courtiers had already seen it only two days before. The new court also had a chance to catch up on Shakespeare's earlier work, going back as far as *The Comedy of Errors* and *Love's Labour's Lost*, and including also *Merry Wives* and *Henry V*.

Eighteen months into James's reign, it is evident that the King's own players were firmly established as the chief entertainers at court, to the chagrin of rival companies, and that Shakespeare was unchallenged as their leading 'poet'. While the 1604–5 Revels Accounts seem almost too good to be true, in the rich testimony they offer to the huge success of the work of 'Shaxberd', they have been subjected to rigorous tests which confirm their authenticity (Fig. 26).[22] These records also show Shakespeare in distinguished and congenial company. Sandwiched between *Measure for Measure* on 26 December and, on the 28th, *The Comedy of Errors*, was a masque with music presented by the Earl of Pembroke and Lord Willoughby celebrating the wedding of his younger brother Philip Herbert. Sadly, the text of this masque, *Juno and Hymenaeus*, does not survive. But its proximity to two King's Men's plays written by Shakespeare suggests that the company worked closely and co-operatively with

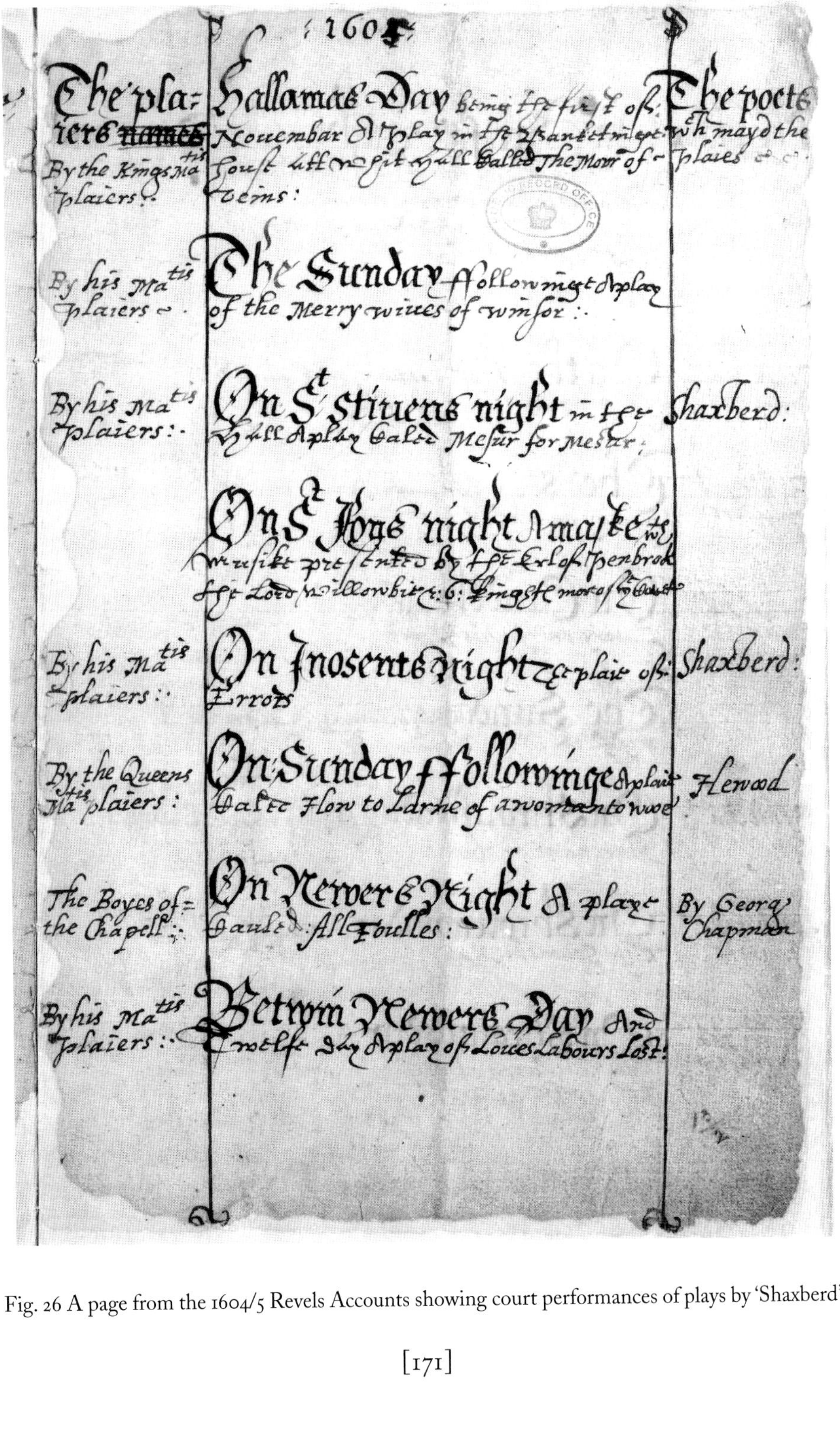

1604

The plaiers names		The poets wch mayd the plaies
By the Kings Matis plaiers:	Hallamas Day being the first of Nouembar A play in the Banketinge house att Whithall called The Moor of Venis:	
By his Matis plaiers	The Sunday ffollowinge A play of the Merry wiues of Winsor:	
By his Matis plaiers:	On St Stiuens night in the Hall A play called Mesur for Mesur:	Shaxberd:
	On St Jons night A maske wth musicke presented by the Erl of Penbrok the Lord Willowbie & 6 Knightes more of the Court	
By his Matis plaiers:	On Inosents Night the plaie of Errors	Shaxberd:
By the Queens Matis plaiers:	On Sunday ffollowinge A plaie Called How to Larne of a woman to wooe	Hewood
The Boyes of the Chapell:	On Newers Night A playe Called: All Foulles:	By Georg Chapman
By his Matis plaiers:	Betwin Newers Day And Twelfe day A play of Loues Labours Lost:	

Fig. 26 A page from the 1604/5 Revels Accounts showing court performances of plays by 'Shaxberd'.

Pembroke. By Christmas 1604 it is clear that both Shakespeare and Pembroke were richly sustained with the fertile 'drops' of princely favour. What is much less clear is what had been going on, for Shakespeare, during the first twelve months of James's reign, which requires some investigation.

The wonderful year 1603

In 1603–4 Shakespeare was in the intensely frustrating position of needing and wanting to provide new work for high-profile performance by his company while never knowing, from week to week, how soon any play(s) he had written could be publicly shown. A restraint on playing had already been in place at the time of the Queen's death, provoked at first by plague, and then renewed because of her mortal illness and the ensuing period of public mourning. All three of the documents relating to the new status of Shakespeare's company as King's servants license them to perform their plays publicly only 'when the infection of plague shall decrease'. Leeds Barroll has argued, I think persuasively, that the royal patronage so quickly accorded to the former Lord Chamberlain's Men did not derive from any special enthusiasm on James's part, but rather from the urging of a powerful young friend at court, James's new minion the Earl of Pembroke. However, James himself, unable to foresee the length and severity of the 'infection', may also initially have thought it desirable to secure players for days of rejoicing following his coronation, as well as for the delectation of visiting ambassadors.[23] In the event, the plague worsened during May and June, and entry to the coronation on 24 July was to be strictly controlled by the advance allocation of tickets. All gates into London were closely guarded, as were strategic river banks. There could clearly be no question of re-opening the public theatres at such a time. Indeed, given their own capacity to attract crowds, the King's Men may even have been sent away from London in advance of the coronation. Leeds Barroll poses the question:

> What was the situation for Shakespeare and his fellows, whose financial year certainly depended on the months when outdoor playhouses were at their most pleasant? June, July, August and September had come and gone with no profit to be had from the Globe playhouse.[24]

If Pembroke was the special friend to Shakespeare's company who ensured that they came under royal patronage, it would be nice to think that he was also able to protect them from the huge losses incurred during this summer. One much discussed allusion suggests that the King's Men's playwright, at least, did receive special protection from Pembroke's mother. It derives from an account of a document given by a nineteenth-century Countess of Pembroke to the Eton master W. J. Cory:

> we have a letter, never printed, from Lady Pembroke to her son, telling him to bring James I from Salisbury to see *As You Like It*; 'we have the man Shakespeare with us'. She wanted to cajole the King in Ralegh's behalf – he came.[25]

Unfortunately, for all sorts of reasons this is unlikely to have any foundation in fact. Shakespeare was the King's Man, not the Countess of Pembroke's. Despite the likelihood that he already enjoyed Pembroke's favour, he was hardly in a position, either socially or legally, to stay at Wilton House as an independent guest, as if for a country-house weekend. That much quoted phrase 'the man Shakespeare' is also suspect. It doesn't sound at all like the Countess's generally rather formal style, and, if he were to be precisely identified, 'player' or 'poet' would be a rather more effectively defining label than 'man'. Also, though it is probable that Pembroke accompanied James's West Country progress, he would scarcely need to be told by his mother (with whom he was on uneasy terms) that a royal visit to Wilton would be welcome. Cory himself was not shown the supposed letter, nor have any other letters written by the Elizabethan Countess survived at Wilton. Such documents, if they existed, are likely to have perished in the 1647 fire that destroyed most of the house. Documentary evidence supports a more stressful and far less glamorous scenario. The King's Men, unable to perform in the Globe because of the restraining order, took to the road. In the later part of the summer, while the King and his court travelled south, the King's players travelled north. Both groups were driven out of London by the increasingly severe and widespread infection. After an initial attempt, in August, to settle in Woodstock and Oxford, which turned out also to be infected, the court travelled south to Winchester, where the postponed Michaelmas Law Term was fixed for 12 November. The great business of this term was to be the trial of Lord Cobham and Sir Walter Ralegh, who had allegedly plotted with Spain to put Arabella Stuart on the throne. This savage proceeding, which culminated in mock-executions, brought out the compulsively sadistic side of King Lavish McTavish – that side which also required that the greater part of most days was spent in hunting.

The King's Men received 20 shillings for playing in Oxford town at some point this year.[26] It seems reasonable to conjecture that this payment was around the time of the brief stay in Oxford and Woodstock by James and his court, after which the King's Men seem to have parted company from their royal patron. In the course of the year – and most probably during September and October – they also received payments at Coventry, Bridgnorth and Bath, possibly in that order. At least the Midland tour gave Shakespeare an opportunity to see to his affairs in Stratford, and to gather in rents, debts and tithe income that offered some compensation for the disastrous playing season, which was almost as bad as that terrible summer of 1596 when the old Lord Hunsdon died. But by the end of November, if not before, both he and his company were back in the environs of London. One of their number, Augustine Phillips, had followed Shakespeare's prudent example in investing his Globe earnings in more secure real estate. He had acquired a large house and garden in Mortlake, on the south bank of the Thames – a place renowned for its tapestry works, and for being also the residence of the astrologer Dr Dee. It was adjacent to Richmond Palace, where the Queen had died.

As the 'wonderful', or terrible, year 1603 drew to its close things at last began to look up. It was from Mortlake that Shakespeare and his fellows were summoned to perform at court, requiring a speedy journey to Wiltshire, in late November or early December. The King's Men were at last re-united with the King's other servants. However, after only a couple of performances they may soon have embarked on the return journey, travelling to Hampton Court with Queen Anne and her retinue. The weather had turned cold and wintry, which was a cause for rejoicing, since it was believed – wrongly, as it turned out – that this finally spelt an end to the plague. The new Venetian ambassador, Nicholas Molin, reported in mid-December that 'no one ever mentions the plague any more', and that 'the City is so full of people that it is hard to believe that about sixty thousand deaths have taken place'.[27] The King's Men performed five times during Christmas festivities at Hampton Court. At least one of their plays, a comedy called *The Fair Maid of Bristow,* was not by Shakespeare, but there seems little doubt that two or three others were, probably including, as 'Robin Goodfellow', *A Midsummer Night's Dream.* Another likely candidate for performance in the 1603/4 Christmas season at court is Jonson's long-laboured Roman tragedy *Sejanus his Fall,* of which more below.

From being 'wonderful' in the sense of 'terrible', the year 1603 as it drew to a close became a time of blessings. The King's Men even received some compensation for their huge loss of earnings. In February 1604 'Richard Burbage, one of his Majesty's comedians' was given £30 to share among his fellows as a 'free gift' from the King to maintain them during the restraint on public playing, which had just been renewed yet again. No doubt this was too little and too late, but at least it showed recognition of their financial difficulties by their royal patron, who may again have been prompted by Pembroke. Finally, in the second week of April 1604, public playing was permitted once more.

Fig. 27 Arch erected in Gracechurch St, by Italian citizens of London, from Stephen Harrison, *The arch's of triumph erected in honour of the high and mighty Prince James* (1604).

Nothing novel, nothing strange

Since James's coronation had been solemnized privately in a London that was almost empty, an opportunity for public celebration of the new reign was eagerly awaited. It was arranged that on 15 March 1604 the King and Queen and Prince Henry should make a triumphant procession from the Tower of London through the City to Whitehall for the opening of Parliament. Seven hugely elaborate triumphal arches, partly prepared the previous year, were constructed under the direction of the superb master-carpenter Stephen Harrison (Fig. 28). These marked the stages of the royal progress, visibly expressing the loyalty to James of a wide range of his London subjects, such as the denizened Dutch and Italians, the public schools and above all the City Companies. Three of Shakespeare's fellow playwrights, Dekker, Jonson and Middleton composed 'devices' for the great day, and Edward Alleyn – now under the patronage of Prince Henry – performed the part of the Genius of the City.[28] His impressive physique and powerful voice equipped him well for this role. He was also a Londoner born, whose father had been one of the Queen's porters. However, James was not a patient listener, nor did he like crowded assemblies; only abbreviated versions of the entertainments as they reached print had actually been performed.

We may wonder why Shakespeare, the King's Men's leading playwright, did not compose anything for this great day. This leads also to a wider question: why, in this new reign that saw an efflorescence of royal and aristocratic masques and 'shows', was he never asked to write in this form, either in 1604 or later? As a notoriously rapid writer, he might seem a more obvious choice for such commissions than the slow and laboured Jonson. Part of the answer may be that Shakespeare was known to lack the ready access to classical literature and mythology that the genre required. Not only did masque-writers use or adapt classical deities as leading characters, they also made conspicuous use of Latin quotations, mottos and pseudo-inscriptions. The 'masques' in his late plays, such as Posthumus's vision in *Cymbeline*, or the cold and flat wedding masque in *The Tempest*, could be viewed as attempts by a chagrined Shakespeare, passed over as a writer of free-standing court masques, to show that he could handle this form quite as well as the next poet. Yet neither allegory nor panegyric seems to have come at all naturally to him, even when contained within the framework of a play. The sudden appearance of the god Hymen in the otherwise naturalistic final scene of *As You Like It* is a case in point, or the comical use of Mistress Quickly as Queen of Fairies in *Merry Wives* to invoke blessings on Windsor Castle. Shakespeare had far too strong a sense of humour to make a reliable court poet. Royal and noble persons might fear that they were being ridiculed rather than praised.

A further explanation for Shakespeare's non-contribution to the City entertainments for James in 1604 may be that he felt himself above such things. As a King's Man, he was himself part of the royal procession, and thus on the other side of the fence from Jonson, Dekker and the others, hired by the City committees. Who – in this period – would accept business sponsorship if he could enjoy royal patronage? What is almost certainly an allusion to the 1604 triumphal arches in sonnet 123 supports such a reading. Gazing at the vast and learnedly symbolic structures set up in the City, the speaker uses their very learnedness and pseudo-antiquity as ammunition against them:

> No! Time, thou shalt not boast that I do change;
> Thy pyramids, built up with newer might,
> To me are nothing novel, nothing strange;
> They are but dressings of a former sight . . .

Confronted by some of the most splendid displays the City of London had ever offered, the speaker – projected by the not-very-learned Shakespeare – adopts a blasé been-there, seen-that tone. True, the 'pyramids' are exotic and antique in style – 'pyramid', by the way, referred to any tall pointed structure, approximating to what we might now call an 'obelisk'. But as such, they are lacking in true life or originality. Though no classical scholar, Shakespeare was extremely well read in North's translation of Plutarch, and may have been already planning a tragedy on the subject of Cleopatra. In this, too, he conveyed contempt for Egypt's most celebrated architectural invention, by alluding to it in the the mouth of the feeble Lepidus: 'Nay, certainly, I have heard the Ptolemies' pyramises are very goodly things. Without contradiction I have heard that' (*Antony and Cleopatra*, 2.7.34–6). Since Lepidus is at this point in a state of drunken collapse, the effect, as in sonnet 123, is to suggest that only foolish people will allow themselves to be dazzled by the 'novelty' or 'strangeness' of pyramids. In any case, the sonnet-speaker's contention is with 'Time', and his claim is that temporal constructions, however elaborate, have no true weight or substance in comparison with personal devotion, to which Time can do no damage: 'I will be true despite thy scythe and thee'. Not only were those 1604 triumphal arches overloaded with antiquarian allusions, they were also transient structures, quickly removed, to be immortalized only in the fine engravings of them made by William Kip. It was the printed book, it seemed, not carpentry and painting, that promised true immortality.

In the course of 1604 Shakespeare acquired an additional motive for feeling smugly contemptuous of conspicuous parades of classical learning. He had played a leading role – probably that of the Emperor Tiberius – in Jonson's *Sejanus his Fall.* This Tacitean tragedy, which Jonson had flagged up at the end of *Poetaster* with his promise to 'sing high and aloof', was not only a spectacular failure with the public, it also got Jonson into serious trouble with the Privy Council. As Jonson reported to Drummond in 1618: 'Northampton was his mortal enemy for brawling on a St George's Day one of his attenders; he was called before the Council for his *Sejanus* and accused both of Popery and treason by him.' Jonson's quarrelsomeness, as well as his spell as a Catholic, were matters of which he was apt to boast. But the exact nature of the 'treason' attached to *Sejanus* is more debatable. It seems that Jonson, always a painfully slow writer, was unlucky enough to be overtaken by events. There is little doubt that he began work on his tragedy soon after finishing *Poetaster*, that is, early in 1602. But by the Christmas season of 1603/4, when it was probably performed at court, it seemed to offer unmistakable parallels to the monstrously unjust state trial of Sir Walter Ralegh in the trial in Act 3 of the military commander Silius. As Philip Ayres points out, the hot-headed Silius's defence of his actions 'owes nothing to Tacitus', but has much in common with Ralegh.[29] Performed at court only a month or so after Ralegh's conviction on 17 November, it must have seemed quite obvious that Jonson was stirring things up – and it is true that he was indeed a friend and supporter of Ralegh's. However, a reputation for topicality and contentiousness tends to be a popular selling point, and at some time after the playhouses re-opened in the summer of 1604 *Sejanus* was performed at the Globe. Here it fared even worse. Jonson himself, dedicating the learnedly annotated printed edition to his patron Esmé Stuart in 1605, acknowledged that 'It is a poem that, if I well remember, in your lordship's sight suffered no less violence from our people here than the subject of it did from the rage of the people of Rome.' Imperial minion Sejanus ended up being torn, limb from limb, finger from finger, by the Roman mob. Another witness, William Fennor, also testified to the play's resounding failure:

> With more than human art it was bedewed,
> Yet to the multitude it nothing showed;
> They screwed their scurvy jaws and looked awry,
> Like hissing snakes, adjudging it to die.[30]

Though Fennor claims, sympathetically, that 'wits of gentry' applauded the play, this can have been little consolation for Jonson. The reception of *Sejanus* nourished his already almost obsessive contempt for the unlettered majority on whose approval, and pennies, anyone writing for the larger playhouses relied. The artistic rift between Shakespeare and Jonson widened, and Jonson's envy of Shakespeare was severely exacerbated. He increasingly sought to establish his reputation through print-publication, with the visible endorsement of aristocratic patronage, while Shakespeare the King's Man could sit easy. Secure in the knowledge of his own ability to please everyone, both at court and in the public theatres, he could afford to dismiss the heroically learned labours of others as 'nothing novel, nothing strange'.

1604–5: friendly Shakespeare's tragedies

Jonson's grave error, in expecting audiences to appreciate a marmoreal Roman tragedy without any jokes in it, was not one that Shakespeare ever committed. He understood from within, having had to memorize and perform a major role in it, that *Sejanus* was virtually unplayable. It was a relief, at least, that Jonson's insistent cult of personality ensured that it was he, and not the players, who took the blame for its tediousness. His own fan club, meanwhile, continued to grow, and some of its members revealed a sophisticated understanding of what made his work so enjoyable. An obscure young gentleman called Antony Scoloker – perhaps the son or grandson of the mid-Tudor Protestant printer and translator of the same name – published a curious poem called *Daiphantus*.[31] This is most often cited because of its appended item, *The Passionate Mans Pilgrimage*, the poem beginning 'Give me my scallop shell of quiet' that was later attributed to Ralegh. Even the title of this poem has a pseudo-Shakespearean flavour, echoing the piratical *Passionate Pilgrim* of 1599. Elsewhere in the book Shakespearean reference is fully explicit. Adopting a motley, jesting style rather like that of the late Nashe,[32] Scoloker dedicates his poem to 'the Ancient Potentate *Quisquis*' (or 'anybody'). A good piece of writing should ideally, he claims, be

> like the never-too-well read *Arcadia*, where the Prose and Verse, (Matter and Words) are like his Mistress's eyes, one still excelling another and without corival: or to come home to the vulgar's element, like friendly Shakespeare's tragedies, where the comedian rides when the tragedian stands on tip-toe: faith, it should please all, like Prince *Hamlet*.

As the learned and aristocratic Sidney combined prose with verse, the popular and unlearned Shakespeare combined comedy with tragedy. These comments hit the mark very well, showing an early awareness of the qualities that have caused Shakespeare's work to endure. If they had been heeded by Heminge and Condell they would perhaps never have made that momentous division of Shakespeare's work into three genres. It has been suggested that in using the epithet 'friendly' Scoloker is claiming acquaintance with Shakespeare.[33] However, the epithet may, rather, be a literary judgement, approximating to what we might now call 'accessible', 'readable' or even 'reader-friendly'. Sidney's *Arcadia* is characterized as 'never-too-well read' – we can never read it too closely, or get to know it too well, for the task is a difficult one that few or none achieve. Shakespeare's writings, on the other hand, inhabit 'the vulgar's element', and can be enjoyed by everyone, including the uneducated. In particular, it is *Hamlet*, often regarded in modern times as a 'highbrow' work, that has the capacity to 'please all'. The truth of Scoloker's claim is borne out in the high incidence of boys given the name 'Hamlet' in the first decade of the seventeenth century.[34] In the body of *Daiphantus* Scoloker carries his enthusiasm for *Hamlet* further. The title-hero is a younger son, brought up in Venice (= London?), who first falls in love with two women at once, and then with two more women – number 3 unhappily married, and number 4, 'Vitullia fair, but brown', equipped with a brother. Confused by this concatenation of amorous experiences, Daiphantus runs mad. The manner of his madness may tell us something about how Burbage played Hamlet. Like Hamlet, Daiphantus is both a student and a second-rate versifier. He seizes his pen and sucks on it, grotesquely, as if it were a tobacco-pipe:

> His breath, he thinks the smoke, his tongue a coal,
> Then calls for bottle-ale, to quench his thirst:
> Runs to his ink-pot, drinks, then stops the hole,
> And thus grows madder, than he was at first.
> Tasso, he finds, by that of Hamlet, thinks
> Terms him a madman; then of his ink-horn drinks.

We should remember that ink, made of gall and copperas, was excessively bitter – one taste of it drives Daiphantus to call for bottle-ale – nevertheless, he then drinks deep from his ink-horn, while linking himself both with the mad love poet Tasso and the mad prince Hamlet. This suggests an allusion to memorable stage business, in which Burbage as Hamlet smoked his pen and drank from his ink-horn. Such stunts seem also to be indicated in Hamlet's defiant challenge to Laertes in the graveyard scene:

> Woo't weep, woo't fight, woo't fast, woo't tear thyself,
> Woo't drink up eisel, eat a crocodile?
> I'll do it.
>
> (*Hamlet*, 5.1.270–2)

In effect, Hamlet is telling Laertes that his grief for Ophelia is puny and inadequate, since it has not driven him frantic. He challenges him to display signs of mania as wildly florid as his own. 'Eisel' is vinegar, and the lines may be intended to remind the audience of earlier scenes in which Hamlet has wept, fought, torn his clothes and consumed strange substances, such as ink or vinegar. In the next stanza of *Daiphantus* the mad hero makes further allusions to *Hamlet* and staged madness:

> Calls players fools, the fool he judgeth wisest,
> Will learn them action out of Chaucer's Pander:
> Proves of their poets bawds even in the highest,
> Then drinks a health; and swears it is no slander.
> Puts off his clothes; his shirt he only wears,
> Much like mad Hamlet; thus as passion tears.

Inappropriately, Daiphantus then cries out repeatedly for 'Revenge', presumably alluding to the celebrated catchphrase 'Hamlet, revenge!' What made most impression on Scoloker, and presumably on many other playgoers, were the scenes in which Hamlet speaks 'wild and whirling words', and also – it seems – drinks strange substances and undresses down to his shirt. It was in such scenes above all that he found that 'the comedian rides, when the tragedian stands on tip-toe': tragic grandeur was leavened with comic entertainment value. One didn't know whether to laugh or cry, but above all one had to keep watching: such scenes had the power to 'please all'.

Knowing his market, Shakespeare in the early Jacobean period developed his skill in mixed genres yet further. He wrote comedies that were very nearly tragedies, like *All's Well* and *Measure for Measure*, and tragedies that were full of mad scenes and of comic or partly comic material, like *Lear* and *Macbeth*. His rate of production slowed down, partly because of the extended and recurrent periods of theatre closure, and partly because the King's Men had a large stock of his Elizabethan plays to draw on for court performance that were unfamiliar to the newly arrived Scottish courtiers.[35] Yet there was certainly no decline in the interest, diversity and originality of his writings, and at such times as the playhouses were open, 'friendly Shakespeare's tragedies' were what everyone wanted to see.

LIVE RICH AND HAPPY

The years discussed in this chapter used long ago to be labelled 'Shakespeare's Tragic Period', and it was claimed that some personal life crisis provoked him to write tragicomedies and tragedies. This scenario now seems far too simple, in separating Shakespeare from the complex social, economic and political environment in which he lived and worked. In part, at least, he wrote the historical tragedies *Lear* and *Macbeth*, with their early 'British' settings, because Britain was now a single kingdom, and furthermore the new monarch took a strong interest in British antiquity. Likewise, he wrote historical tragedies with Greek and Roman settings – *Timon*, *Coriolanus*, *Antony and Cleopatra* – in part because he had by no means exhausted the riches of Plutarch's *Lives*, and in part because audiences, both in the theatre and at court, included a growing number of individuals who were interested in such material.

Nevertheless, these years were undoubtedly also marked by a high incidence of risky and unpleasant 'life events'. The problems of the first great Jacobean plague have already been discussed. Just at the moment when he might have anticipated a life of prestige and privilege at court and elsewhere, Shakespeare in middle age was reduced once again to a stressful and uncertain period as a travelling player. He and his colleagues also experienced bereavement. Their patron, the affable and generous Sir George Carey, second Lord Hunsdon, died in September 1603, only six months after the death of his cousin and Queen. Closer to home, however, was the death in 1604 of the leading player Augustine Phillips, whose Mortlake house had offered shelter to the King's Men in the plague-ridden autumn of 1603. First mentioned among his colleagues, he left 'to my fellow William Shakespeare a thirty shillings piece in gold'. Phillips and Shakespeare were evidently close friends as well as close colleagues. Among many other plays, they had acted together in Jonson's festive *Every Man In* back in 1598, and in his grim *Sejanus* only a few weeks before Phillips's death. Unlike Shakespeare, he resided with his family, and was evidently on good terms with his 'loving wife' Anne and his four daughters.[36] This was a predominantly female family, with a mother, to whom Phillips left an annuity of £5, and two sisters to each of whom he left £10. His wife and executrix was to inherit a third share of his estate, while the three eldest daughters had a further share divided equally between them for their dowries. A different bequest is made to Phillips's youngest daughter, Elizabeth, who is to have immediate possession of his house and estate. In the year preceding that in which Shakespeare embarked on *King Lear*, the preference shown by Phillips for his youngest daughter over her elder sisters is eye-catching. Hers was surely the more solid and ample share, and unlike that of her sisters it could be enjoyed immediately – it was not contingent on her finding a husband. Presumably she was a favourite child, and perhaps her father hoped that she would grow up to be a comfort to her mother and grandmother.

Phillips's death must have come as a particular shock to Shakespeare, with whom he was closely matched both in seniority and experience. Just as the King's Men were emerging from the year-long plague epidemic that had so restricted their activities, here was a terrible reminder that wealth, talent and domestic happiness offered no protection against sudden death. Phillips's illness must have been of rapid onset, since he had so recently played a leading role in *Sejanus*; but it was probably not plague. Officially, at least, the infection was over by May 1604. But more significantly, plague generally left little time to the dying man for the drafting of a full and detailed will. In some cases, however, having apparently recovered, patients died three or four weeks after infection.[37] But whatever its cause, the death of his old friend and colleague must have left Shakespeare feeling older and more fragile. It perhaps played some part in prompting him to write tragedies in a very different vein from *Hamlet*. These could be called tragedies of survival, in which 'the oldest hath borne most', in contrast to those in which a young life of great promise – that of Juliet, or Hamlet – is cut short. In *Timon*, *Lear* and *Antony and Cleopatra* Shakespeare explores the miseries of living too long: Timon outlives his wealth and his friends, Lear outlives the daughter he loves, and Antony outlives his own dignity and greatness.

Of these three tragedies, *Timon* is by far the oddest. We have no record of early performance, and it has been plausibly suggested that the text is unfinished, never having undergone the theatrical leavening process that took place with such much performed and much revised, plays as *Hamlet* and *Lear*. Some of its most brilliant lines are almost tongue-twisters, to which Burbage, in the leading role, might have raised objection, such as Timon's response to Apemantus's question 'What wouldst thou have to Athens?' – 'Thee thither in a whirlwind' (*Timon*, 4.3.289–90). It seems also that the play was written in collaboration with young Thomas Middleton (born 1580), though Shakespeare's was by far the larger share.[38] We may see it as more a bitter dramatic meditation than a finished theatrical artefact: a meditation on financial and emotional bankruptcy. Paradoxically – and yet, perhaps, appropriately – the writing of *Timon* appears to belong to a period when Shakespeare, despite prolonged theatre closures, had become spectacularly wealthy. As Schoenbaum reports:

> On 24 July 1605 Shakespeare made his most ambitious investment. For £440 he procured a half-interest in a lease of 'Tythes of Corne grayne blade & heye' in three nearby hamlets – Old Stratford, Welcombe, and Bishopton – along with the small tithes of the whole of Stratford parish.[39]

This purchase, from an elderly Warwickshire gentleman called Ralph Hubaud, was overseen by the Stratford attorney Francis Collins, who presumably also acted as Shakespeare's 'assign' in ensuring that all this tithe income – which included profits from wool and mutton, as well as grain and grass – was duly paid. This was not a lease, like summer's in sonnet 18, that had 'all too short a date', for it still had thirty-one years to run. It appeared to secure a substantial income for Shakespeare and his descendants for a generation or more. Anticipation of his daughters' marriages probably lies in the background of the purchase, and Shakespeare may already have identified the successful and hard-working Stratford doctor, John Hall, as a desirable husband for Susanna. The scale of magnitude of this transaction, for a man whose 'gentle' status had been affirmed – and that questionably – less than a decade before, can hardly be exaggerated. Even if Shakespeare was not quite able to provide the whole sum of £440 'up front' – and a record of an outstanding debt to Ralph Hubaud's estate of £20 the following year suggests that he was not – it must at least have matched his 'credit level', being nearly half of that staggering debt of a thousand pounds that crushed Sir John Falstaff. It was the kind of sum that prodigal aristocrats squandered, or borrowed – not the sort of money naturally associated with a mere player and poet. When the daughter of Shakespeare's old patron Sir George Carey, Elizabeth Berkeley, was preparing to take part in Jonson's *Hymenaei* in 1606 she paid £100 to the goldsmith Sir William Herrick for a jewel for this splendid occasion; but meanwhile her husband Sir Thomas Berkeley, living a rustic life with his horses and hounds in Gloucestershire, was paid an allowance of £150 for his entire annual income.

Despite his evident prosperity, there continues to be no evidence that Shakespeare was engaged in any charitable activity, either on behalf of the poor of Stratford, or those of St Giles's, Cripplegate, the parish where he now lodged in London. An identification of Shakespeare's views with those of Timon would suggest – though this is no doubt far too simple – a belief that acts of munificence, or even of minor charity, were pointless, since the love or loyalty they procured would endure no longer than the wealth or credit of the patron. Even Timon's loving and faithful Steward – the forerunner of Kent in *King Lear* – gains small thanks from his former master, who advises him to be as misanthropic as himself:

> Go, live rich and happy,
> But thus condition'd: thou shalt build from men;
> Hate all, curse all, show charity to none,
> But let the famish'd flesh slide from the bone
> Ere thou relieve the beggar.
>
> (*Timon*, 4.3.529–33)

Much though we may hope to make a clear separation between Timon's savage misanthropy and Shakespeare's own mood in 1605, it is hard not to see in Timon's cursing epitaph on himself, derived from Plutarch, some anticipation of Shakespeare's own gravestone curse:

> *Here lie I, Timon, who, alive, all living men did hate.*
> *Pass by and curse thy fill, but pass and stay not here thy gait.*
>
> (5.4.72–3)

Nor can there be any doubt that Shakespeare's lease of tithes brought him major profit from the humble toil of the yeomen and labourers of Stratford. Some men might feel uncomfortable about acquiring such a source of income, especially given recent memories of bad harvests and episodes of starvation. However, it has to be acknowledged that the purchase of monopolies and taxes had become a perfectly normal way of raising income during the Elizabethan period. Shakespeare was only procuring for himself the kind of benefit that more socially elevated individuals were awarded by the crown, such as the late Essex's celebrated 'farm of sweet wines'.

The oldest hath borne most

While Shakespeare wrote no formal elegy on Queen Elizabeth, he showed a deep preoccupation, in the darkest of his tragedies, with the idea of a whole dynasty staggering towards a slow and desperately painful end. Some real-life events seem to have prompted both a revival of the old Queen's Men's tragicomedy *The True Chronicle Historie of King Leir* and Shakespeare's extraordinarily radical re-writing of it for the King's Men.

In the autumn following the Queen's death in 1603 one of her oldest court servants was fast becoming senile. Brian Annesley had probably begun to show signs of failing power a couple of years earlier, for he made his will on 1 April 1600, leaving the bulk of his estate to his youngest daughter. The Annesleys were a well-established gentry family associated with Kidbrooke and Lee, Kent, an area now assimilated into the London borough of Lewisham. His father had been officer of the royal cellars to Henry VIII, thus playing a vital supporting role in that bluff monarch's enjoyment of 'pastime with good company'. Brian Annesley was a Gentleman Pensioner from 1564, Master of Harriers from 1570 and Warden of the Fleet Prison – where he introduced the use of stocks – from 1574.[40] Annesley and his wife Audrey, née Tirrell (who died in 1591), showed strange prescience in their choice of names for their three daughters: Grace, Christian and Cordell. While the names of the elder daughters suggest Protestant piety, that of the youngest inevitably suggests an allusion to Geoffrey of Monmouth's narrative of the early British King Leir and his loving youngest daughter Cordill or Cordilla.[41] In the many accounts familiar to the Elizabethans it was Cordilla, not Leir, who was a tragic figure. After her father's death, despite her virtue and faithful love to her old father, Queen Cordilla was driven to suicide by the machinations of her evil nephews. As vividly described by John Higgins in the 1574 additions to *The Mirror for Magistrates* Cordilla's suicide in prison influenced Spenser's grim account of the Cave of Despair in *The Faerie Queene*, Book 1. Her story was already well known by the time of the old *Leir*, a text that Shakespeare knew extremely well, having acted in it during his period as a Queen's Man. The unknown author of this sentimental medley stopped well short of Cordilla's suicide, ending the play with a cheerfully penitent Leir going off to France for a recuperative stay with his youngest daughter and her husband. This Leir is often foolish, but never mad, and the murderous plots of his elder daughters are frustrated by convenient thunder claps that indicate the protective presence of Divine Providence. Anachronistically, since Leir supposedly reigned 800 years before the birth of Christ, the Queen's Men's poet locates the story in a vaguely medieval Christian world, in which the pious Cordilla is familiar with the Book of Common Prayer, and Leir and his jesting companion Mumford disguise themselves as pilgrims.

The widowed Brian Annesley was probably suffering from what is now called 'Alzheimer's disease'. While his elder daughters were married, Grace to Sir John Wildgoose, Christian to Baron Sandys, the unmarried Cordell still lived with her father. In October 1603 Sir John Wildgoose and his lawyers entered the Annesley house and attempted to make an inventory of his goods, 'finding him fallen into such imperfection and distemperature of mind and memory, as we thought him thereby become altogether unfit to govern himself or his estate'.[42] Cordell, however, prevented this attempt, and appealed to Robert Cecil for Sir James Croft to be permitted to take charge of her father's financial affairs for the remainder of his life. She thanks Cecil for his letters seeking alternative custody arrangements for 'my poor aged and daily dying father', but explains that

> that course so honourable and good for all parties . . . will by no means satisfy Sir John Wildgoose, nor can any course else, unless he may have him begged for* a lunatic, whose many years service to our late dread Sovereign Mistress and native country deserved a better agnomination,** than at his last gasp to be recorded and registered a lunatic.

Croft, she explains, is willing to take charge of her father's affairs out of pure altruism and concern for the family's honour, 'as also to prevent any record of lunacy that may be procured hereafter'. Cordell Annesley won her point. When her father died six months later her sister disputed his will, but its legitimacy was upheld by the Prerogative Court. In a brilliant essay Richard Wilson has discussed the way in which Annesley's will flouted the old Kentish custom of 'gavelkind', according to which property was equally divided between children regardless either of primogeniture or gender.[43] By giving the title 'Kent' to Lear's most faithful courtly follower (he had been Perillus in the old play) Shakespeare alerted his audience to the Kentish dimension of the opening scene, in which it appears at first that Britain has been divided into

* 'begged for': *OED beg v.* 5, 'to petition the Court of Wards . . . for custody of a minor, an heiress, or an idiot . . . hence also figurative, to beg for, take him for, set him down as, a fool'.
** 'agnomination': this very rare word, meaning 'the giving of an additional name', occurs also in Jonson's *Poetaster*, 3.1; Cordell Annesley's use of it may suggest that she was a playgoer.

three equal parts, but it then emerges that this is not so. Cordelia, had she been able to flatter her father as her sisters do, stood to gain 'A third more opulent' (*King Lear*, 1.1.86).

Most scholars have played down the relevance of the Annesley case to Shakespeare's play. The 1997 Arden editor, for instance, suggests only that 'it could well have had something to do with the revival and publication of the old play . . . and so, indirectly, with Shakespeare's'. However, the King's Men were surely better placed than most to hear about remarkable events concerning an old royal servant, and the extraordinary coincidence of Cordell Annesley's first name made it especially striking to those deeply familiar with the old play. There is also one feature of the Annesley case that connects it, not just with royal servants generally, but specifically with Shakespeare. One of the overseers of Annesley's will was another Gentleman Pensioner, the seafaring Sir William Harvey, who was from 1598 married, as her third husband, to the dowager Countess of Southampton. He was thus a youthful stepfather to Shakespeare's friend and patron Henry Wriothesley, Earl of Southampton. Even if relations between Shakespeare and Southampton were no longer very close, he could hardly have failed to keep himself fully apprised of his early patron's family connections. Harvey – who had been knighted for his part in Essex's Cádiz raid in 1596 – was a neighbour of the Annesleys, living at Kidbrooke. After the death of Southampton's mother he married Cordell Annesley, by whom he had seven children, though only one daughter survived to adulthood.[44] I believe that the Annesley case was the immediate trigger for both the revival of the old *Leir*, on stage and in print, and for Shakespeare's radical re-writing of it on behalf of the King's Men. The two plays complement and contrast with each other rather as did *Antonio's Revenge* and *Hamlet*. While the old play is a rambling, lightweight romance in an old-fashioned style, Shakespeare's play – labelled deceptively a *True Chronicle Historie*, not a Tragedy – is an entirely original and ground-breaking drama that must have terribly shocked early audiences who were expecting a happy ending. In particular, the alteration Shakespeare made to all the sources in having Cordelia pre-decease her father must have left audiences stunned: they must initially have been as reluctant as Lear is to believe that she really is dead.

Shakespeare made his play about Lear more 'true' than the old one by locating it authentically in a dark, pre-Christian world, as described by William Harrison in Holinshed's *Chronicle*, in which 'idolatry and superstition still increased more and more among us'. The virtuous characters search for evidence of divine providence or a moral order, but are perpetually frustrated. The clearest example of this comes in the final scene, when Albany cries out, 'The gods defend her', and immediately Lear enters carrying the dead Cordelia. That is what the gods have done for her. Shakespeare's most radical alteration of the plot is also his clearest location of the play in a darkly pagan prehistoric Britain, where there is cruel winter but no Christmas.

Other details in the play reflect the impact on it of the Annesley case. Most obviously, unlike the Lear of the sources, Shakespeare's King becomes a 'lunatic'. He moves in stages from rage, to wild, florid, madness, to pathetic confusion and forgetfulness, most evidently in the scene when he wakes up in Cordelia's tent. There are also a few verbal allusions. For instance, the Fool's bleak observation, 'Winter's not gone yet, if the wild geese fly that way', incorporates an 'in' reference to the greed and cruelty of Sir John Wildgoose and his wife. Lear's desire to give up kingship in favour of revelry and drinking with his retinue may allude to the Annesley family's association with the royal wine cellars. The placing of Kent in the stocks by Regan may be ironically connected with Annesley's introduction of the stocks to the Fleet Prison. There is also a whole area of imagery and allusion in Shakespeare's play that may have been set off by one aspect of the old Tudor servant. At the time of his death Annesley had for thirty-four years held the court office of Master of Harriers. Harriers were small hounds used chiefly for hunting hares (Fig. 28). It has often been noticed that *Lear* contains more dog imagery than any other of Shakespeare's plays. But it is not so often pointed out that the dogs referred to are for the most part small, humble, domestic dogs, not by any means the aristocrats of the canine kingdom. As Lear grows madder, he imagines himself besieged by small dogs: 'The little dogs and all, / Trey, Blanch and Sweetheart, see, they bark at me' (3.6.60–1). Edgar as Poor Tom tries to comfort his master by driving off this imaginary pack of dogs:

> avaunt, you curs! . . .
> Mastiff, greyhound, mongrel grim,
> Hound or spaniel, brach or him,
> Or bobtail tyke or trundle-tail,
> Tom will make him weep and wail . . .
>
> (3.6.62–8)

There are also pervasive allusions to hunting. When staying at Goneril's castle in 1.3 Lear and his retinue go out hunting. But as his reason disintegrates and his isolation increases the hunting becomes metaphorical, and Lear imagines himself as hunted, not hunter. When Cordelia's servant comes to rescue him he runs off stage as if pursued by beagles:

> Come, an you get it,
> You shall get it by running. Sa, sa, sa, sa.
>
> (4.6.198–9)

Though Foakes and others gloss 'Sa' as an ancient hunting cry, it seems also to

Fig. 28 A kennel for hunting dogs from George Gascoigne, *The Noble Art of Venerie* (1575).

be a cry addressed to dogs when they are being fed. Lear is both dog-owner and dog, harrier and hare. When despatched to prison with Cordelia, he sees himself first capturing her, like hunted prey, and then sharing with her the fate of small hunted animals:

> Have I caught thee?
> He that parts us shall bring a brand from heaven,
> And fire us hence like foxes.
>
> (5.3.21–3)

I would not wish to suggest that every time Shakespeare invokes small dogs in *Lear* he is making explicit allusion to Brian Annesley as Master of Harriers – still less that he expected everyone in his audience to make such a connection. Nevertheless, Annesley's long-standing association with one of the humbler species of hunting-dog may have set off a cluster of associations which, in Shakespeare's fertile brain, spawned yet more images of small dogs and country sports.

Cordell Annesley herself was probably among those who saw *Lear* at Whitehall Palace on 26 December 1607. As a favoured friend of the courtiers Robert Cecil and Sir William Harvey, as well as daughter and heir of an old court servant, she surely had access to court. Her presence is all the more likely if it was known that the King's Men's new play in some sense alluded to her father. In or soon after 1608, now married to Sir William Harvey, she caused a monument to her parents to be set up in St Margaret's Church, Lee, 'at her own proper cost and charges'. The wording is clearly her own. Her letter to Cecil, signed in a pretty italic hand, shows that she was fully literate. The inscription closes with a couple of lines of rather odd and erroneous Latin:

> Nec primus, nec ultimus; multi ante,
> Cesserunt, et omnes sequetitur [sic].

This can be construed as '[He is] not the first, nor the last; many have passed away before [him], and all will follow'. It may reflect an echo both of her namesake Cordelia's melancholy reflexion:

> We are not the first
> Who with best meaning have incurred the worst.
> (5.3.3–4)

and of the play's final couplet, which was originally spoken by Albany, figuring Scotland for a Jacobean audience:

> The oldest hath borne most; we that are young
> Shall never see so much, nor live so long.

Like his mistress the Queen, Brian Annesley had been unusually long-lived, but his longevity had not been a blessing. His long life, like Lear's, could be seen to symbolize the stretched-out misery of a regime that had gone on far too long. By 1606–7 it was safe to look back, albeit obliquely and symbolically, on the over-long, capricious and autocratic rule of the last of the Tudors.

CHAPTER EIGHT

1608–09

Painful adventures

WISHETH. THE. WELL-WISHING. ADVENTURER

(*Shakespeare's Sonnets*, Dedication)

In my school-days, when I had lost one shaft,
I shot his fellow of the self-same flight
The self-same way, with more advised watch
To find the other forth, and by adventuring both,
I oft found both . . .

(*The Merchant of Venice*, 1.1.140–4)

Adventures and adventurers

THE years to be discussed in this chapter were ones of major 'adventures', or undertakings. 'Adventurers' could be financial investors, like Bassanio's friend Antonio in *The Merchant of Venice*, who 'adventures' all his money on merchant ships that will, he hopes, return with valuable cargo. 'Adventurers', too, were the captains, sailors and colonizers who carried out such risky voyages – men like Henry Hudson, who in 1609 sailed two hundred miles from Manhattan Island up the river that still bears his name; or Sir Thomas Gates, who was shipwrecked on Bermuda in this same year, while trying to reach the distressed colony of Jamestown in Virginia. Many other individuals were 'adventurers' on dry land, such as the publishers who 'adventured' their financial support by 'setting forth', or making public in print books originally written by hand. Writing, too, was an extremely 'painful adventure' in the case of such dense, complex and insistently original writings as *Shakespeare's Sonnets*. In this period the word 'painful' suggested 'painstaking', as well as 'causing pain or suffering'; and as it does today, the word 'adventure' implied an element of exciting risk-taking, but not necessarily of a romantic or chivalric kind. An 'adventure' could be an extravagant gamble with money, talent or even life itself, that could bring great suffering and anxiety along the way, and yet always carried the hopeful possibility of material reward and great honour. Such 'adventurers' wished well both to themselves and to their enterprises. If they were travellers, they hoped not simply to return home alive, but to be handsomely rewarded for their great 'pains'. If they were investors, or 'merchant venturers', they hoped one day to learn, as Antonio does, that the ships on which they have spent so much 'Are richly come to harbour' (*The Merchant of Venice*, 5.1.277). On a smaller scale, too, craftsmen and tradesmen 'wished well' to their enterprises, hoping to gain the due reward of their labours.

These were years, too, of collective and institutionalized 'adventuring'. A new charter for the City of London in 1607 consolidated the City's control over its economic activities, centrally housed in Sir Thomas Gresham's Royal Exchange, and in the following year also in Robert Cecil's 'New Exchange', or 'Britain's Bourse', which was opened in the Strand on 11 April.[1] This has been described as a 'shopping centre', but it was also an opulent showcase for exotic and expensive goods, such as porcelain from China, which had been carried painfully to London by brave merchants and their hopeful sponsors.[2] The opening of the New Exchange was celebrated in the presence of the King and his family with a specially written playlet by Ben Jonson, the text of which has recently been discovered.[3] It seems likely that the King's Men, as well as the whole royal family, were in attendance on this occasion. 1609 was also the year of a new charter for the Virginia Company.

In Shakespeare's domestic sphere the period was punctuated by painful family events, such as the deaths of his favourite brother Edmund and of his mother, but also, more happily, by the birth of his first grandchild. The acquisition of Blackfriars Theatre by the King's Men altered the character of his professional life, and also that of his finances, for he immediately acquired a seventh-part share in its activities, which soon increased to a sixth-part share. *Pericles*, *Troilus and Cressida* and *Shakespeare's Sonnets* all saw print in 1609. All three texts reflect the 'painful adventures' of their creators, writers, publishers, compositors, and one of them, *Pericles*, had rather more exotic 'painful adventures' as its explicit theme. Behind these publishing ventures lay the return and continuance of severe plague, which led to yet another period of prolonged theatre closure with consequent loss of income for players, playwrights and 'sharers', all of them committed 'adventurers' in live performance.

PITY AND PIETY

Before looking in more detail at Shakespeare's external life in 1608–9 some scrutiny must be given to his inner beliefs. It is in this period especially that the question of his personal religion requires to be addressed, even if definite conclusions cannot be reached. In the aftermath both of the Gunpowder Plot and the 1607 'Midlands Rising' the need to affirm religious and national loyalty had become intense. Warwickshire was now far from being the easy-going backwater of Shakespeare's early childhood. The English reformation, largely untested and unenforced in the provincial England of the 1570s, had become a pressing reality. Many of those most closely associated with the Gunpowder Plot had been Midlanders, and families like the Shakespeares whose church-going practices had been lax were liable to fall under severe suspicion of Catholic allegiance, now viewed, even more than it had been during the later part of Elizabeth's reign, as tantamount to treason. Some Catholic gentry had hoped at the time of his accession that James would moderate the previous restrictions and financial penalties imposed on practising Catholics. Perhaps he might have done so, had not the 1605 Plot, which if successful would have blown up the King and Parliament in session, turned the tide entirely the other way, fuelling all James's worst fears of conspiracy. The Oath of Allegiance instituted in June 1606 required all English subjects to repudiate papal authority.[4] To what extent Shakespeare or his family had indeed been attached to the old religion is extremely hard to determine, since virtually all the evidence, including most of the literary evidence, can be read in contradictory ways. Shakespeare's avoidance of crude anti-Catholic satire in his plays, in the form of the hostile stereotypes of prelates and friars to be found in many other plays of the period,[5] can be read as reflecting either a cautious indifference or a principled determination not to endorse satire against religious structures that he himself held dear. Yet a third explanation, and perhaps the most plausible, is that, as a practised and popular playwright, Shakespeare was simply determined to please the widest possible audience, including upper-class Catholics.

A personal event that might appear to tell us something about where Shakespeare's own allegiance lay is the marriage of his elder daughter, Susanna, to the 'impeccably Protestant' Dr John Hall on 5 June 1607.[6] Yet this, too, can be construed in opposite ways, either as affirming the family's existing allegiance, or as providing it with the Protestant credentials that were now sorely needed. If Shakespeare's true personal devotion was or had been to the old religion, he could well have felt during the dangerous times that succeeded the trials and executions of the Gunpowder Plotters that such an alliance would effectively protect his family against suspicion in the future. He had seen his colleague Ben Jonson get into considerable danger and difficulty after the Plot. After

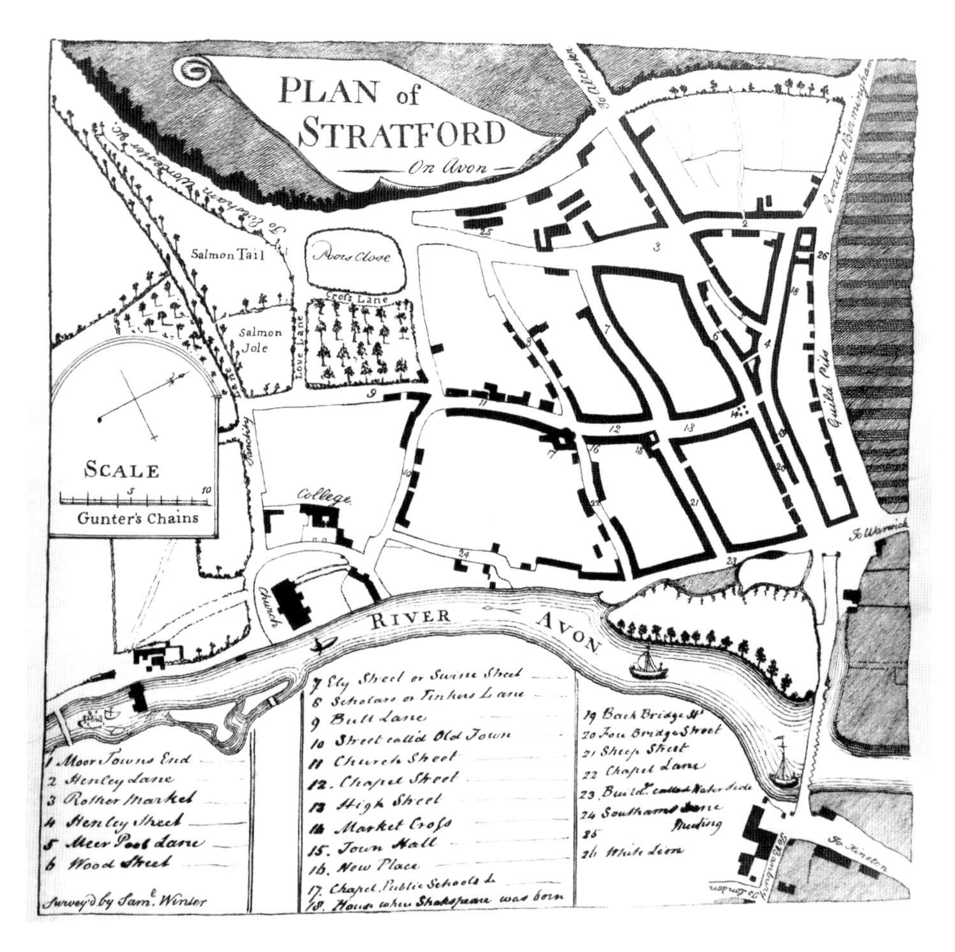

Fig. 29 Plan of Stratford made by Samuel Winter, *c.* 1768; Holy Trinity Church is on the river to the left, Henley St (numbered 4) upper right.

interrogation by the Privy Council Jonson quickly turned informer, having dined with Catesby and others a month before 5 November. Eventually he was to return flamboyantly to the Church of England, boasting of drinking up the whole chalice the first time he again took the Sacrament.[7] Shakespeare may have been determined not to jeopardize either his own position, or that of his family, and his daughter's marriage could reflect this determination. There might be an analogy here to the marriage of Philip Sidney in 1584 to Sir Francis Walsingham's only child. In the aftermath of the execution of his old friend, the Jesuit Edmund Campion, Sidney entered upon this alliance not so much because his natural sympathies were with his father-in-law's principled dedication to the reformed faith as because they were not. The Walsingham connection offered him excellent protection against the nagging suspicions of his loyalty by the Queen and senior courtiers that had been a major impediment to his advancement. By the same token, Shakespeare's acquisition of John Hall as a son-in-law could have provided a defence against questions by his masters about whether the leading King's Man was fully committed to the established form of religion.

Yet alternatively, Susanna Shakespeare's marriage to John Hall may simply reflect her father's own religious sympathies. Whatever the religious inclinations of his youth, perhaps slightly muddled and uninstructed ones, by this period Shakespeare may have become a committed and convinced Anglican. The day-to-day example of his King's Men colleagues John Heminge and Henry Condell, both of them excellent family men and faithful supporters of their parish church in London, might be among numerous influences bringing him to a greater respect for the formularies of the Church of England.[8] He may also have observed the social advantages of being a good churchgoing citizen. After long service to St Mary Aldermanbury Henry Condell eventually transcended the stigma of his profession of 'player' sufficiently to be appointed as Churchwarden.[9] But there is at least one further possibility, and it is one that I am inclined to favour. Repeated records of Shakespeare's non-payment of parish dues and of lapses in church attendance both by himself and by his close relations may point to a family who were, whether through conviction or temperament, habitually indifferent or resistant to public devotion. Even sheer indolence could have played some part. Because of the pattern of development of Stratford in the later middle ages Holy Trinity Church is surprisingly far away from many of its main streets, such as Henley Street (Fig. 29). The exertion of dressing up in one's best clothes and walking a mile or so through muddy streets on Easter Day only to rub shoulders with neighbours whom one disliked, or to whom money was owed, and to be bored stiff by a mediocre sermon or homily, may have seemed thoroughly irksome. The risk of having to pay a fine for non-attendance was preferable to the risk of being dunned by creditors.

In general Shakespeare's writings are notable for their adroit side-stepping of specific religious and ecclesiastical issues. Yet he is entirely conventional in showing prayer and churchgoing as vital props of a civilized and 'gentle' way of life. When Orlando in *As You Like It* seeks to ascertain the true 'gentility' of the banished Duke in the forest he does so with reference to their common culture, being reassured, antiphonally, in exactly the same formulas that he himself has used:

> True is it that we have seen better days,
> And have with holy bell been knoll'd to church,
> And sat at good men's feasts, and wip'd our eyes
> Of drops that sacred pity hath engender'd . . .
>
> (*As You Like It*, 2.7.120–3)

Fig. 30 Engraving by Hoogenborgh of the Gunpowder Plotters, above; their execution, below (1605).

From this point on, it is clear that Orlando and the Duke, despite the wildness of their present surroundings, recognize each other as 'gentle'. Both respect the rituals of a Christian culture, and both, above all, honour the needs of their common humanity, embodied in the frail and aged 'Adam'.

'Pity', in Shakespeare's poetic vocabulary, is close cousin to 'piety'. Whatever his own personal success may have been in the practice of either virtue, his plays repeatedly endorse moral and religious value in terms of compassion, whether as that 'quality of mercy' insisted on by Portia in *The Merchant of Venice*, or the 'pity, like a naked new-born babe' that Macbeth explicitly rejects in order to accomplish his sacrilegious murder of an anointed king and father-figure. In so far as any 'religious' view can be distilled from the plays – which is not at all far – we find a widespread endorsement of devotion, charity and kindness, and an equally widespread condemnation of impiety, selfishness and greed. The misanthropic passage from *Timon* quoted in the last chapter is a shocking exception. Painful though it is, King Henry V's command to his old companion Falstaff to 'fall to thy prayers' will be acknowledged by most audiences as manifestly just:

> Make less thy body hence, and more thy grace;
> Leave gormandizing; know the grave doth gape
> For thee thrice wider than for other men.
> (*2 Henry IV*, 5.5.52–4)

In the only poem Shakespeare wrote that can be claimed as in any sense devotional, sonnet 146, the speaker addresses his own 'Poor soul' in very much the same terms in which the newly crowned Henry addresses Falstaff, rebuking her for permitting the ageing body she inhabits to be grossly fed and excessively adorned:

> Why so large cost, having so short a lease,
> Dost thou upon thy fading mansion spend?
> Shall worms, inheritors of this excess,
> Eat up thy charge? Is this thy body's end?

There is every reason to suppose that the Jacobean Shakespeare did indeed eat heartily and dress expensively. Like Falstaff and the *Sonnets*-speaker, he was physically portly and conspicuously well clad, as befitted a leading King's Man. His appearance now approximated to that which would quite soon be represented in Gerard Johnson's Stratford Monument, described by J. Dover Wilson as having the expression of 'a self-satisfied pork butcher',[10] whose dull eyes and fat jowls seem to offer no clue as to what might be within, whether soul or imagination, telling us only that this man was a worldly success. Shakespeare's writings are comparably opaque to those who approach them hot for ideological certainties. In so far as the plays suggest moral lessons, they are wholly conventional ones, to which Catholics and Protestants alike would readily assent: pity and forgiveness, even if they do little good in worldly terms, are always to be preferred to cruelty and vindictiveness. The loving and compassionate Cordelia dies, and so does the unnamed Servant who, in the Quarto text of *Lear*, tries to save Gloucester from being blinded. Yet 'pity' is, again, closely akin to 'piety', and such tenderness is presented as an unchallenged good.

There are, however, a couple of passages in which Shakespeare appears to support a specific religious position, and both point to definite Protestant alignment in the Jacobean period. The celebrated Porter's speech in *Macbeth*, with its teasing play on 'equivocation', has been widely taken to allude to the unhappy Father Garnet, S. J., whose ingenious use of 'equivocation' in his own defence failed to save him from the scaffold in May 1606, or, in the eyes of rabidly Protestant observers, from consignment to 'the everlasting bonfire' of Hell:

> 'Faith, here's an equivocator, that could swear in both the scales against either scale; who committed treason enough for God's sake, yet could not equivocate to heaven . . . I had thought to have let in some of all professions, that go the primrose way to th'everlasting bonfire.
>
> (*Macbeth*, 2.3.8–11, 18–20)

Secondly, in sonnet 124 Shakespeare's speaker seems to comment on political and religious matters – again, most plausibly connected with the Gunpowder Plot and its consequences – yet does so in terms of such carefully poised ambivalence that the reflections have a quicksilver 'now you see it, now you don't' quality. In this sonnet, beginning 'If my dear love were but the child of state', the speaker glories in the safe remoteness of his own 'love' from the hazards of shifting power and 'policy', or political cunning. While others may enjoy brief and delusory favour before being subjected to 'time's hate', the speaker's private 'love' puts him far beyond and above such hazards as he invokes in the closing couplet:

> To this I witness call the fools of time
> Which die for goodness, who have lived for crime.

Readers in 1609 may well have construed these lines as alluding to the execution of the criminal Plotters, especially Father Garnet, who had been exalted by Catholics as martyrs dying 'for goodness' (Fig. 30). Read in this way, the couplet certainly suggests a smugly conformist, anti-Catholic Shakespeare, eager to ingratiate himself with the new monarch. Yet nothing, apart from their topicality as published in 1609, marks the lines as alluding definitely to the Gunpowder Plotters rather than to any of the many other pseudo-martyrs who could be said sardonically to have 'died for goodness' after committing the political 'crime' of inciting rebellion through their religious affiliation. And even if Shakespeare in the early Jacobean period was anxious to be seen as Protestant, we can still not conclude firmly, any more than we can about any other human being, that his own private devotion or belief was in truth of that nature.

YET EDMUND WAS BELOVED

The topic of 'pity and piety' leads naturally to a consideration of more intimate family pieties during Shakespeare's mature years. Four younger siblings survived to adulthood, three brothers and a sister, and it is rather striking that none of the young men ever married. Perhaps the spectacle of their talented older brother becoming reluctantly encumbered for life at the age of eighteen had acted as an awful warning to them. But probably above all it was financial constraints that made them not attractive as potential husbands. As we saw in chapters 1 and 2, there was precious little money around in the Henley Street household during the decade in which first Gilbert, then Richard reached marriageable age, 1585–94. Nor is there any evidence that the high-earning William chose to do anything much for these two, though Gilbert did occasionally stand proxy for him in his business affairs in Stratford. Their sister Joan, born in 1569, married some time in the late 1590s, her husband being a Stratford hatter called William Hart. Providing an adequate dowry even for this fairly modest union may have contributed to John Shakespeare's collapse into near bankruptcy at the end of his life, unless this was one family affair in which William did come to the rescue. His death-bed bequest of the Henley Street houses, his clothes and individual sums of money to Joan and her three sons indicates that he assumed substantial responsibility for this family, though the blank left in the will for the name of Joan Hart's middle son does not suggest that he took a particularly close interest in his nephews. It was presumably easier to recollect the name of William, his namesake and perhaps godson, born in August 1600, than that of his younger brother Thomas born five years later. The passages relating to them in the will suggest that Shakespeare's attitude to his Hart kinsfolk was one of distant affection, rather than of daily intimacy. He seems to have left it to his sister Joan to care for their mother in her widowhood, for when she died in early September 1608 it was the Harts who administered her estate.

The Shakespeare sibling closest to William's heart, as we have seen, appears to have been the youngest, Edmund. Only three years older than Shakespeare's own first-born child Susanna, his role may have been more like that of an adopted son than a brother to him, especially after the death of little Hamnet in 1596. It may have been in him that he invested, or adventured, his deepest hopes for posterity. Edmund alone seems to have joined William in London, and to have entered his profession of 'player'. The three poignant records of his adult life that survive link him with his elder brother's two chief stamping grounds in London – the parish of St Giles's, Cripplegate, where he lodged with the Huguenot Mountjoys in Silver Street, and that of St Saviour's, Southwark, where he worked by day at the Globe Theatre. It seems reasonable to presume that Edmund also lodged in the Mountjoys' large residence, and that like his celebrated elder brother he performed at the Globe Theatre, though in a rank well below that of 'sharer' either in the King's Men or in the Globe syndicate, as an apprentice eventually becoming a 'hired man'. As we shall see later in this chapter, some of the Mountjoys' associates were a somewhat louche and bohemian lot, and their lodgers may at times have included unmarried couples and bastard children.

All of the records found for Edmund Shakespeare relate to burials, the first being that of his infant son: '1607, Aug, 12. B[urial]. Edward son of Edward Shackspeere, Player: base-born' – that is, born out of wedlock. This notoriously inaccurate parish clerk's resolution of the less common name 'Edmund' to the more common 'Edward' is probably not significant, except in suggesting that father and son held the same name, Edmund's son being also an 'Edmund'. Whether Edmund junior was a new-born infant or a child of a few years old we can only speculate; if the latter, then it would certainly seem likely that Shakespeare's brother had been resident in London for some years, which is in any case quite probable. He could have been brought to London by William at the end of one of his regular summer visits to Stratford, perhaps even as early as August 1596, immediately after the death of young Hamnet. As a youth of sixteen Edmund would be just ready to begin to make his way in the world, with the patronage and financial support of his distinguished elder brother. William may have decided, after Hamnet's death, to groom Edmund to become his heir and executor, at least with reference to his property and professional life in London.

But if so, the two further records, from the parish register of St Saviour's, Southwark, show that these hopes were cruelly dashed, for they report the burial on 31 December 1607 of 'Edmond Shakespeare, a player: in the Church', and also the payment of 20 shillings for 'a forenoon knell of the great bell'.[11] Burial in the church, rather than in the churchyard, was an expensive privilege, and would not normally have been permitted for someone of less than gentry status, such as a common 'player'. We may reasonably assume that the eminent King's Man paid for a splendid interment for his favourite brother, as well as for an unusually prolonged tolling of St Saviour's Church's 'surly sullen bell' (sonnet 71) on the day of his funeral, as a signal to the whole neighbourhood of how deeply 'Edmund was beloved' (*King Lear*, 5.3.238). As the son and brother of gentlemen, Edmund was probably interred under a flat stone tablet in the church floor: 'Persons of the meaner sort of gentry, were interred with a flat gravestone comprehending the name of the defunct, the year and day of his decease, with other particulars, which was engraven on the said stone, or upon some plate.'[12] Though honourable, this form of memorial was a degree below that already envisaged by his elder brother, surely keenly aware, during the arctic winter of 1607–8, of his own mortality: 'Gentlemen which were of more eminency had their effigies or representation cut or carved upon a term or pedestal, as it were of a pillar, raised somewhat above the ground, *umbelico tenus*.'[13]

The capacious church of St Saviour's[14] – still often referred to by its previous dedication, as St Mary Overy – was physically close both to the Globe and Rose theatres (Fig. 31). It was also a church strongly associated with secular revelry. While the great Cathedral of St Paul's, with its dozens of abutting

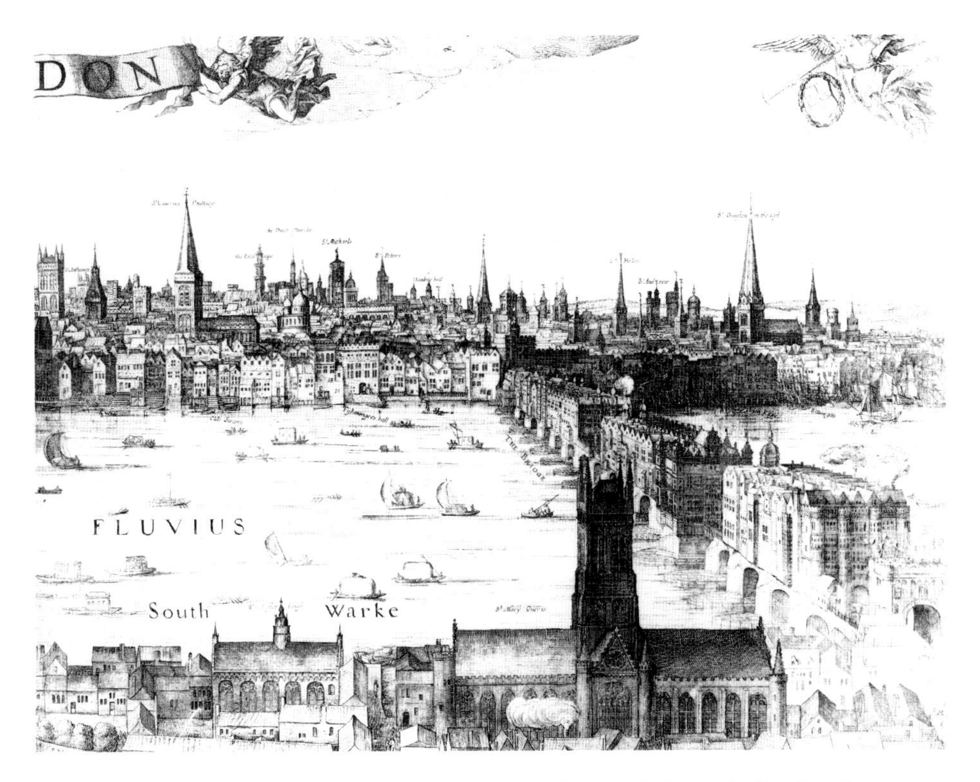

Fig. 31 Detail from Visscher's *View of London*, showing St Saviour's, Southwark and London Bridge (1616).

bookshops and its wide aisle where young men paraded and gossiped, was the hub of London's book trade, law and business, St Saviour's, in the Liberty of the Clink, was connected with many kinds of recreation. Soon after Elizabeth's accession the Lady Chapel had been walled off and leased out for use as a bakehouse, and at some time there were also pigsties within the church walls. It may have been felt to be important to secularize and in effect deconsecrate the Lady Chapel, which had been used as a Spiritual Court during the reign of Mary Tudor for the show trials of Protestant martyrs such as John Rogers and John Hooper. That great theatrical adventurer Philip Henslowe was one of the leading 'ancients of the vestry' of St Saviour's – a privileged club of thirty men who controlled the church's government[15] – and it was no doubt under Henslowe's affable influence that the vestrymen took to 'wasting the parochial funds in feasts and banquets, and involving the church in dangerous lawsuits'.[16] Though Edmund Shakespeare's death was a deeply melancholy event, at least his mortal remains rested in a place appropriate to his profession of 'player', an environment that was part church, part food outlet, part banqueting house. It was there, I believe, that his elder brother hoped to be buried one day, and he may already have been making plans for his own monument.

It is curious that in a play written a couple of years before the deaths both of his brother Edmund's bastard and namesake and of Edmund himself Shakespeare should have included a character called Edmund who is characterized as being both a bastard and a younger brother. Perhaps it is just one of those strange half-correspondences between art and life that crop up so often. Yet Shakespeare must have made a deliberate and considered decision to call the Duke of Gloucester's younger, bastard, son 'Edmund', the equivalent character in his source, Sidney's *Arcadia*, being 'Plexirtus'. True, he was systematically replacing Sidney's Greek names with appropriately British ones, and Edgar and Edmund are both names borne by early Saxon kings. But Edmund, the name of the celebrated ninth-century martyred king from whom Bury St Edmunds takes its name, seems to offer surprisingly noble and pious resonances for a character so conspicuously godless and self-serving as the Edmund of the play. It would seem much more natural to have applied that name to the virtuous and unselfish elder brother, rather than to the villainous, though attractive, young bastard. But as R. A. Foakes points out,[17] Edmund is an engaging and lively character whose three soliloquies in Act 1 give him opportunities to establish a strong rapport with the audience. If the twenty-three-year-old Edmund Shakespeare was by 1604–5 a fast maturing 'hired man' in Shakespeare's company, it seems not impossible that the role was created for him, in this sprawling tragedy whose unusually large cast of complex characters stretched the personnel of the King's Men beyond its normal limits. The role of Edgar requires a virtuoso performer, a quick-change artist who can transform himself swiftly from a bland young nobleman into Poor Tom, a half-crazed Bedlam beggar, and then into two different rustics in quick succession in the 'Dover Cliff' scene. The part of his brother Edmund is much less demanding, requiring mainly strong presence and some skill in commanding audience attention, but no exceptional subtlety or finesse. The character's determination to make his way in the world through willpower and sexual charisma, pursuing adulterous affairs with both Goneril and Regan, seems perfectly consonant with what we know of Edmund Shakespeare, firmly labelled both as a 'Player' by profession and as the acknowledged father of a child born outside wedlock.

FROM ASHES ANCIENT GOWER IS COME

Shakespeare could not summon his beloved brother back from beneath his stone slab in St Saviour's. But it may have been gloomy meditation on that sad memorial that led him to summon up the spirit of a more celebrated figure from his visible interment in that same church, the fourteenth-century poet John Gower (Plate 8). Gower's effigy, though moved from its original position, is still one of the most striking sights in what is now Southwark Cathedral. As Chorus, perhaps acted by Shakespeare himself, Gower frames *Pericles*, introducing adapted episodes from Book 8 of his *Confessio Amantis* retailing the adventures of Apollonius of Tyre and illustrating his encounters with 'Unlawful Love'.[18] The change of name, to 'Pericles' or 'Pirocles', conflates Apollonius with one of the heroes of Sidney's *Arcadia*, while suggesting the 'perils' he endures. There are also many verbal links with the *Arcadia*.[19] Though the latest editors of *Pericles* put the writing of the play in 1607,[20] it could equally well have been written in the early months of 1608, and in the immediate aftermath of Edmund Shakespeare's death.[21] Its publication in the summer of that year substituted for further performance, as plague yet again closed the theatres – an outbreak that may also have been the cause of young Edmund's death. *Pericles* had been performed 'divers and sundry times' at the Globe, being enjoyed on one occasion by an audience that included both French and Venetian ambassadors and a Florentine dignitary.[22] The theatre trip cost the Venetian Giustinian 'more than twenty crowns'. The success of this prestige performance, so quickly followed by closure orders, may have created a particularly strong demand for versions of this play, which appears, rather extraordinarily, to have been Shakespeare's most sought-after work since *Hamlet*. Popular demand was met both by the publishers of the 1609 quarto text of the play and, even more speedily, by a new associate and collaborator of Shakespeare's, the poet, vintner and brothel-keeper George Wilkins, who rapidly wrote up a prose romance partly based on it.[23]

It was such polyglot audiences as that party of French and Venetian ambassadors that Shakespeare now had chiefly in mind. The requirement to entertain foreign diplomats had been clearly established soon after the accession of James, when the newly accredited King's Men spent eighteen days in attendance on the Spanish delegation lodged at Somerset House in August 1604.[24] It was evident that a major part of their remit would be to offer the kind of plays that could be enjoyed by such high-profile visitors, whether in royal palaces or the public theatres. But Shakespeare and his company had even more recent and pressing reasons for thinking very carefully about the tastes and prejudices of such audiences. The learned but often unfortunate George Chapman had courted serious trouble with his two-part tragedy, the *Conspiracy* and *Tragedy of Charles Duke of Byron*. Its performance at the Blackfriars Theatre early in 1608 came to the notice of the very same French ambassador, De la Boderie, who had enjoyed *Pericles*. He objected vehemently to the plays' representation of recent troubles at the French court, and above all to an undignified scene in which Henri IV's Queen verbally abused the King's mistress and gave her a slap (*soufflet*). After the French ambassador's angry complaint to Robert Cecil further performance of the *Byron* plays was forbidden, though Chapman soon procured a licence for their publication, with the offending scene removed. The company that had performed it, the Children of the Revels, were banished from their small but attractive premises, and some of the players endured a spell in prison.[25] For a few days all London theatres were closed down as a punishment. It was after this debacle that the King's Men were at last able to take possession of the Blackfriars Theatre, a property which had been acquired by Richard Burbage's father James as long ago as 1596. Because of the circumstances in which they moved in, the company were intensely aware of the need to choose their repertoire with great care, both for the 'private', upmarket Blackfriars, and, when summer weather allowed, for the still flourishing and lucrative Globe. Recent European history was evidently taboo, and so were strong political themes that could be taken amiss by viewers with less than perfect mastery of the nuances of contemporary English. This precluded performance of such dark, difficult and satiric works as *Troilus and Cressida* and *Timon*. One of Shakespeare's most recently written plays, *Coriolanus*, with its treatment of food riots, civil rebellion and a war hero turned invader was also now far too explosive for performance, despite its ancient Roman setting. From now on Shakespeare was to write plays that were generically ambiguous – not quite tragedies, yet certainly not rumbustuous comedies, either. Their settings were vaguely 'antique' in time and exotic in location, their structures episodic, and their narrative well leavened with scenes of pageantry, music and dance. Much of their effect depended not upon verbal nuance or narrative complexity but on striking costumes, scenic display and music. Audience members who had poor English and a strong desire to break off for a drink or two were not going to miss too much of the essentials.

From this point of view *Pericles*, the earliest of Shakespeare's four 'late romances', was also the most successful. Its absence from the First Folio, combined with a widespread and growing belief that it is partly the work of Wilkins,[26] has led to a poor reputation in modern times. Yet the evidence that it was hugely and immediately successful, both with gentry and with groundlings, is overwhelming. The author of a curious Skeltonic satire on the popularity of ale-drinking compares the huge crowds rushing to buy newly brewed liquor in Hoxton to those flocking to see *Pericles*:

> Amazed I stood to see a crowd
> Of civil throats stretched out so loud:
> As at a new play, all the rooms
> Did swarm with gentles mixed with grooms,
> So that I truly thought, all these
> Came to see *Shore*, or *Pericles*.[27]

For the remaining years of Shakespeare's life, and many years beyond, this play was notoriously and continuously popular. As soon as it reached print in 1609 it was eagerly read and quoted. For instance, one seventeenth-century admirer inscribed a couple of misquoted lines from it at the end of his copy of Chapman's *An Humorous dayes mirth*: 'Thomas Bentley owes this booke / he is a foole that scann / the Inward habitts by the outward man / Shackesphere'.[28] Robert Tailor, author of a satirical play that got its young performers thrown into gaol early in 1613, expressed a vain hope in the Prologue that it would be 'fortunate like *Pericles*'.[29] It was the play's enduring popularity – wholly undeserved, as he saw it – that led Jonson to dismiss *Pericles* as a 'mouldy tale', his key example of why, as a sophisticated poet, he had finally decided to cancel his membership of 'the Play Club' after the failure of *The New Inn* in 1629.[30] For Jonson, the writer of so many learned court masques, the bad taste of upper-class audiences was particularly galling. *Pericles* had enjoyed at least one performance at a great house in Yorkshire in 1610, and was probably taken on tour. It is rather striking that Cholmeley's Men, who performed *Pericles* at Gowthwaite Hall in Nidderdale at Candlemas, 1610, also included a play partly by George Wilkins in their repertoire, *The Travailes of the Three English Brothers*, along with *King Lear*.[31] Much though Shakespeareans may wish to dissociate the greater man from the second-rate Wilkins, the evidence that for a few years both the men and their work were connected is abundant.

Pericles continued to be staple fare for ambassadors. The Duke of Lennox arranged for it to be performed for a French delegation at Whitehall Palace on 20 May 1619, with an interval after the first two acts for the consumption of wine and sweetmeats. However, one member of the party, Shakespeare's old patron the Earl of Pembroke, withdrew from the spectacle because 'I being tender hearted could not endure to see [it] so soon after the loss of my old acquaintance Burbage.'[32] No doubt the play set off double recollections of its chief player and of its author, both now dead. Extraordinary though this may appear, *Pericles* seems to have made Shakespeare as famous and popular with courtiers as *Hamlet* had made him with students. Mr Do-it-all had done it again.

SHAKESPEARE IN BAD COMPANY: GEORGE WILKINS

Little attention has been given to the abundant evidence of connections between Shakespeare and George Wilkins during the years 1604–8 – connections that were both professional and personal. Shakespeareans have been reluctant to confront the existence of a close association, especially at this late stage of his career, with a distinctly second-rate, though by no means talentless, writer. But still more, following the discoveries about Wilkins's scandalous life made by Roger Prior in the early 1970s, biographers have understandably held back from sustained contemplation of Shakespeare's possible friendship with a man who was clearly what the Book of Common Prayer would call 'a notorious evil liver'.[33] Park Honan is candid, but cursory, saying defensively that 'Shakespeare is not to be blamed for the company he kept.'[34] Like Mistress Quickly's house in Eastcheap, George Wilkins's house at the corner of Turnmill Street and Cow Cross was part tavern, part brothel, and Wilkins and his guests were frequently in trouble with the authorities. As well as engaging in the unlicensed sale of food and drink, Wilkins had a persistent habit of violence, presumably when drunk. On one occasion he kicked a pregnant woman in the belly, on another stamped on a woman he had already beaten up so severely that she had to be carried home in a chair. In both cases the women appear to have been prostitutes, widely regarded as 'fair game'. Going to Turnmill Street to beat up whores was a traditional pastime for high-spirited young men throughout the Tudor period. But what could 'gentle Shakespeare' possibly have been doing in the company of such a man?

There are two answers, one general, one particular. As we saw in chapter 4, Shakespeare had already had important professional dealings – in his purchase of a grant of arms – with another man, of much higher rank, who had a nasty habit of making vicious physical attacks on women, Sir William Dethick, Garter King of Arms. In a society whose dominant members below the rank of nobility were exclusively male, there were probably few men who chose their colleagues or drinking companions on the basis of their treatment of women. Manningham's 'William the Conqueror' anecdote, discussed in chapter 6, gives Shakespeare himself a reputation as quite a 'lad' – not, perhaps, violent towards women, but more than happy to view a woman opportunistically as 'fair game'. For the young men of the Middle Temple such laddish exploits were both comic and enviable – there was no question of considering the sensitivities of the woman who had fancied Burbage but ended up in bed with Shakespeare. But the more particular answer to the question of what could have brought Shakespeare into the bad company of Wilkins is practical and domestic. Both men were summoned to give evidence in the Belott–Mountjoy suit at the court of Requests in 1612, in which the wig-maker Stephen Belott sued his father-in-law Christopher Mountjoy for non-payment of the promised dowry of £60.[35] Shakespeare's part in this affair was a crucial one. He had lodged in the Mountjoys' house, and acted as an intermediary in the apprentice Stephen Belott's courtship of his master's daughter – or rather, in Marie Mountjoy's scheme to get her daughter married to the 'very honest', but reluctant, Belott. It was he who witnessed their troth-plight. However, Shakespeare claimed to remember little about the amount of any promised dowry. Wilkins's role was that of landlord to the young couple, who 'came to dwell in [his] house in one of his chambers, and brought with them a few goods or household stuff'. It should not be imagined that the young people were moving from a pious and well-regulated French Protestant household to a loose and disorderly English one, for the Mountjoys, too, were of dubious reputation. Mme Mountjoy had consulted the self-taught magus Simon Forman in November 1597 to discover whether she was pregnant, and in March 1598 her adulterous lover, a mercer of Swan Alley called Henry Wood, consulted Forman about the continuance of their affair.[36] Her husband was eventually excommunicated from the French Church because of 'sa vie desreglée et desbordée' ('his unruly and unregulated life').

It is possible to reconstruct the likely connections that led Shakespeare first to the Mountjoys, and then to George Wilkins. Several routes could have led him to the Mountjoys. One is through the French Protestant community, with which his printer and schoolfellow the stationer Richard Field was connected both professionally and through marriage. However, skilled artisans tended to be grouped together, physically and socially, according to their 'mystery', or particular craft. Field was more likely to introduce Shakespeare to other stationers than to members of a very different group of artisans, the tire- and wig-makers who clustered in and around Silver Street. As we saw in chapter 2, players were distinguished from non-players above all by their sporting of elaborate head-dresses – a 'forest of feathers', as Hamlet put it – which made them look tall and conspicuous on stage. The playing companies must constantly have called on the skills of tire- and wig-makers. For instance, as Shakespeare suggested metaphorically in sonnet 53, such artifice could transform a good-looking boy into a dangerously beautiful woman:

> On Helen's cheek all art of beauty set
> And you in Grecian tires are painted new . . .

Such artifice could also metamorphose a humble, and perhaps also bald, player into a King, a Queen or a Knight, a noble Moor or a swaggering Frenchman. When Shakespeare came to lodge with the Mountjoys in or about 1603 he had probably already got to know his landlord Christopher Mountjoy because of his highly skilled creation of headwear for the Chamberlain's / King's Men. He may himself have worn some of Mountjoy's handiwork on the stage of the Globe. His baldness, one of the few features of his physical appearance of which we can be confident, may often have required him to wear a wig or head-dress. Scholars and professional writers are known to have found it convenient to lodge with the stationers whose craft turned their work from manuscript to print. Nashe, for instance, lodged with John Danter, and may occasionally have made money as a jobbing press-corrector; his enemy Gabriel Harvey lodged with the much more upmarket John Wolfe. Players, by the same token, may have found it natural to take lodgings with skilled craftsmen who assisted them in their manufacture of theatrical illusion.

As for the route to George Wilkins: we can work backwards from the attested fact that Stephen Belott and his bride moved to his house from that of the Mountjoys. Presumably the young Belotts went to live there because they already knew the Wilkinses – George Wilkins had married one Katherine Fowler in 1601 – and much the likeliest reason why they knew them is that Belott was accustomed to take meals at the house of the 'yeoman victualler'. Shakespeare was evidently on terms of friendly intimacy with the young man and had influence over him, since Mme Mountjoy looked to him to persuade Stephen Belott to marry her daughter. Mountjoy was a tire-maker, not a victualler, and there were probably no cooked meals available on the premises for their lodgers, and perhaps not always for their apprentices. Most likely, then, both men often dined or supped in Turnmill Street, where Shakespeare customarily stopped on his way back from the Globe Theatre, at least on days when he had not been invited to dine more splendidly with aristocratic patrons or with his fellow King's Men. A barge across the Thames from Paris Garden to Queenhithe would carry him to a point from which a walk due north would lead to Turnmill Street, in its 'suburb without the walls'. From here, after dinner or supper, it would be a short stroll south-east to sleep at Silver Street, back within the City walls and under the City's jurisdiction.

In 1600, as we have seen (in chapter 6), Shakespeare had worked in friendly collusion and competition with a talented younger man, John Marston. He encountered Marston through his cousin Thomas Greene, and in the richly stimulating environment of the Middle Temple. As a university graduate and a fluent reader and speaker of Italian, it is evident that Marston had had much to offer, despite his youth.[37] Analogously, during the years 1604–8, Shakespeare seems once again to have worked in collusion and friendly competition with a younger man, the victualler George Wilkins, born about 1576. But it is much less obvious this time what it was that the younger man had to offer to the older, and the environment of Turnmill Street and Cow Cross was, to put it mildly, less intellectually sophisticated than that of the Middle Temple. Indeed, Turnmill or 'Turnbull' Street was virtually synonymous with brothels and roistering, as in Falstaff's bantering allusion to the wild days of Justice Shallow's youth 'and the feats he hath done about Turnbull Street' (*2 Henry IV*, 3.2.299–300). A collection of epigrams published in 1610, Roger Sharpe's *More Fooles yet,* includes several vignettes of Turnbull Street characters, such as the epigram on 'Captaine Ninny', a Pistol-like swaggerer:

> Brave Magnaninny sways in Turnbull Street,
> Commands the whores be prostrate at his feet:

'Fetch me some wine, you bawd, and shut the door,
Come hither varlet, where's the other whore?'[38]

However, the swaggering captain soon gets his come-uppance from the whores, who shave him and fire him off the premises. Wilkins's house was a place of much resort and merriment, a good place to swap bawdy jokes and theatrical anecdotes over dinner. Some of these found their way into *Jests to make you Merie*, a compilation by Dekker and Wilkins published in 1607, and give us some of the flavour of Shakespeare's hours of relaxation. Misogyny and playgoing figure in many of them, such as number 6:

> 'Do you see yonder bawd?' says one to his companion (sitting in a play-house together), 'she should have been burnt once in Paris for a martyr': 'A Martyr?' quoth the other – 'why she has suffered for the truth here in London, for she was carted* but last week.'

Or number 31:

> A lady that by sitting to see a play at court, came home late, called for victuals, and swore she was as hungry as a dog: 'It may be as a bitch, Madam,' said her page, standing by, 'else the comparison will not hold'.

Perhaps it is a reflection of the coarsening influence both of Wilkins and of his open house in Turnmill Street that *Pericles* contains Shakespeare's only sustained scene located in a brothel, where the man destined to marry the virginal heroine appears to be a regular customer. We are required to accept Lysimachus as her Prince Charming even after his vile opening comment on Marina – 'Faith, she would serve after a long voyage at sea' (*Pericles*, 4.6.42). The works produced by Shakespeare and Wilkins during their period of association were popular successes, and *Pericles*, as we have seen, was often presented to ambassadors. However, the fact that neither the playlet *A Yorkshire Tragedy* nor the collaborative romance *Pericles* was included in the First Folio may reflect the wider King's Men's view of this episode, and possibly also that of their generous patron, the Earl of Pembroke. Though both plays had been performed by the company, as had Wilkins's best single-authored play, *The Miseries of Inforst Mariage*,[39] the period of Shakespeare's association with Wilkins was a distressing deviation from his commanding role as the King's Men's leading playwright.

All of Wilkins's published works are contained within the years 1604–8. The earliest appears to have been the prose narrative *Three Miseries of Barbarie*, a

**OED* cart *v.* 2: 'To carry in a cart through the streets, by way of punishment or public exposure (esp. as the punishment of a bawd)'.

xenophobic account of plague and famine striking Muslims far more severely than Christians. This was presumably intended to offer some comfort to Londoners during the first great Jacobean plague.[40] Works based on 'reportage', rather than poetic fictions, were Wilkins's speciality. The plays written in parallel or collusion by Wilkins and Shakespeare show the latter, for the only time in his career, so far as we know, venturing into the genre of documentary drama, depicting recent 'news'. A young gentleman of Yorkshire called Walter Calverley had drunk and gambled away both his own fortune and that of his wife, and had sunk into a deep depression. On 23rd April 1605 – a date striking to Shakespeare, if this was his birthday – he killed his two older children, and then tried to kill his wife and a baby at nurse. Shakespeare may have written his short, raw, powerful *A Yorkshire Tragedy* within days of the appearance of a pamphlet describing Calverley's murders, in the summer of 1605.[41] However, I do not accept the argument that the play was necessarily written 'before the news of Calverley's trial and execution had yet reached London',[42] for its final line alluding to the Husband as lying on 'a deadlier execution' indicates clearly that he is bound for trial and death. The playlet is designedly brief, having been performed by the King's Men as part of a medley of 'Four Plays in One'. Once the Husband has repented and the Wife's extraordinary loyalty has been celebrated its brief action is done.

As the play's most recent editors acknowledge, 'there is very strong evidence for Shakespeare's authorship of *A Yorkshire Tragedy* – stronger than for his authorship of any of the other plays added to the third and fourth Shakespeare folios'.[43] Many contemporary scholars attribute the play to Middleton on stylistic grounds, and it is to be included in the Oxford edition of Middleton being prepared under the general editorship of Gary Taylor. Yet there is really not much evidence against Shakespeare's authorship except for 'the dubious reputation of Pavier', publisher of the 1608 Quarto that attributes the play to Shakespeare (Fig. 32). But few publishers in this period – including those of the First Folio – were not at times 'guilty of sharp practice', as Pavier was to be a decade later. Though unique in its small-scale genre, *A Yorkshire Tragedy* fits thematically into the preoccupations of Shakespeare's Jacobean work. One can see just why he would have been drawn to the grim story of Walter Calverley. Other men in his Jacobean plays – Lear, Posthumus, Leontes – get carried away with psychopathic rage against women, being eventually 'redeemed' from their fury by the devotion and forgiveness of the women they have wronged. The scene of the murder of Lady Macduff and her children strongly parallels the scene in which the Husband kills his eldest son on stage, a scene which also fits in with the larger picture of Shakespeare throughout his career as the supreme master of 'calf-killing' scenes. Like other children who get killed in Shakespeare, this little boy, though still in long skirts, is precocious and

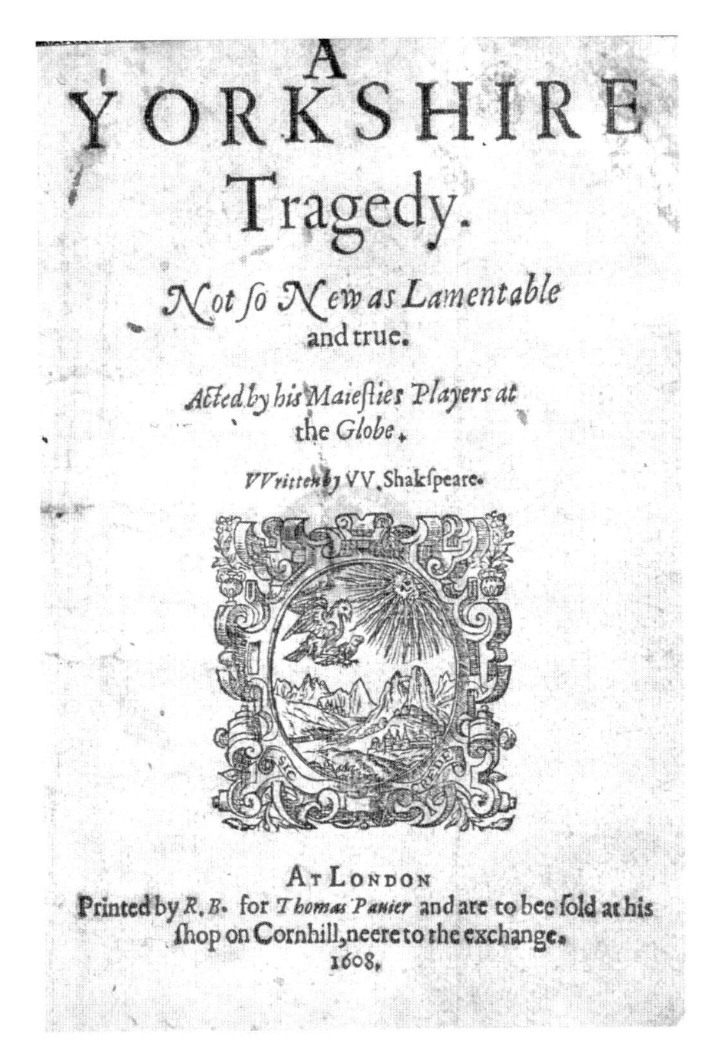

A
YORKSHIRE
Tragedy.

Not ſo New as Lamentable
and true.

Acted by his Maieſties Players at
the *Globe*.

VVritten by VV. Shakſpeare.

At London
Printed by *R. B.* for *Thomas Pauier* and are to bee ſold at his
ſhop on Cornhill, neere to the exchange.
1608.

Fig. 32 Title-page of *A Yorkshire Tragedy* (1608).

bookish, with his heart-rending dying question, 'How shall I learn now my head's broke?' Stylistically, the play appears to me overwhelmingly Shakespearean in its metaphoric strength, as when the Husband, in prose, laments his diminished fortunes:

> My lands showed like a full moon about me. But now the moon's i'th'last quarter, waning, waning, and I am mad to think that moon was mine. Mine and my forefathers', generations, generations. Down goes the house of us; down, down it sinks.

It also shares images with other plays, especially *Lear*:

> The Scythians in their marble-hearted feats
> Could not have acted more remorseless deeds
> In their relentless natures than these of thine.

Compare *Lear*, 1.1.117–18: 'The barbarous Scythian, / Or he that makes his generation messes', and 1.4.251: 'Ingratitude, thou marble-hearted fiend'. No writer other than Shakespeare appears to have used the epithet 'marble-hearted', according to a search of the Chadwyck Healey database of English Poetry and English Drama (LION). The parts both of Husband and Wife are richly realized, with the Wife near the end responding to her husband's repentance in lines that are virtually a quotation from *Lear*:

> It makes me e'en forget all other sorrows
> And have part with this.

Compare:

> if it be so,
> It is a chance which does redeem all sorrows
> That ever I have felt.
>
> (*King Lear*, 5.3.263–5)

However, if *A Yorkshire Tragedy* was written as early as its editors suggest – in the summer of 1605 – these phrases would have to be, not echoes of *Lear*, but anticipations of it. The positive evidence for Shakespeare's authorship of the piece has been seriously understated by twentieth-century scholars.

In 1600 it was Shakespeare who wrote the big tragedy, Marston who wrote the miniature one. In 1606–7, however, Shakespeare's role was reversed. He wrote a playlet that was unsparingly nasty, brutish and short, perhaps at high speed to meet an urgent demand for a contribution to the King's Men's 'Four Plays in One'. At more leisure, but also for the King's Men, George Wilkins elaborated and expanded the Calverley story into a full-length, and often poignant, tragicomedy. *The Miseries of Inforst Mariage* was performed about six months before *Pericles*, if we are to trust the word 'now' on the title-page of the 1607 quarto. It had been entered in the Stationers' Register on 31 July 1607. This single-authored play represents Wilkins's greatest literary achievement. It has attracted some admiration in modern times, especially for the moving portrait of the young hero's previous fiancée, the Yorkshire heiress Clare Harcop, who counters her lover's letter reading brutally 'Forgive me, I am married' with the even more unsparing 'Forgive me, I am dead'. Both its prose dialogue and some of its verse speeches can be distinctly powerful, in a slightly moralistic and tear-jerking style; and it is perhaps not surprising that Wilkins, the victualler of Turnmill Street, should also be particularly good at realistic tavern scenes.

Given the evidence of Shakespeare's previous association with Wilkins, I suggest that *Pericles* was written by the two men in co-ordinated collaboration, with Wilkins writing the first two acts, Shakespeare the rest. Wilkins's agreed share in the play's design and authorship may have made him feel entitled to raise cash, after the closure orders, with his prose version *The painfull Adventures* in the summer of 1608. However, Shakespeare and his colleagues may have been much annoyed by Wilkins's over-adventurous opportunism. There is no reason to think that Wilkins ever again worked for the King's Men, or that he had any further connection with Shakespeare. His career as a published writer ended as abruptly as it began. Perhaps he collapsed into the prodigality and drunkenness that figures in several of his writings. As Roger Prior has shown, between April 1610 and October 1618 he was connected with at least eighteen cases heard by the Middlesex Sessions of the Peace, many of them involving violence against the person.

W.H. and T.T.

Shakespeare entered the year 1609 with one auspicious and one dropping eye. His first grandchild, Elizabeth Hall, baptized on 21 February 1608, had been conceived within days of her parents' marriage the previous June. Despite her disappointing gender, her birth and survival can be assumed to have caused great delight. We might imagine that in selecting the name 'Elizabeth' the family were making reparation for their failure to mourn the old Queen, but it seems more likely that the leading King's Man was honouring the King's elder daughter. Shakespeare's mother enjoyed a single summer as a great-grandmother before dying at the beginning of September 1608. This might have been the natural moment for her son William to commission a monument to his parents in Holy Trinity, but he did not do so. Instead, he adopted a different and far more adventurous route towards the conquest of oblivion.

The plague that closed the London theatres from July 1608, coming so soon after major expenditure on Susanna's marriage settlement, had left him feeling distinctly straitened. What Schoenbaum called 'a trail of records more numerous than interesting'[44] bears witness to this. Seven documents ranging in time from 17 August 1608 to 7 June 1609 record the struggles in Stratford's Court of Record of 'Shakespeare *generosus*', or rather of his attorney on his behalf, to recover a sum of £6, with 24*s*. damages, from a minor tradesman called John Addenbrooke. This is not a unique case – back in 1604, for instance, Shakespeare had sued a Stratford apothecary called Philip Rogers for a debt of

35*s.* 10*d.* with 10*s.* damages.[45] The records of such cases that survive are probably only a small proportion of what once existed. We may reasonably assume that transactions like these were among Shakespeare's regular day-to-day 'adventures', or investments. They are all of a piece with Richard Quiney's hope in 1598 that Shakespeare would lend him £30 for the benefit of the Corporation of Stratford, and with Shakespeare's recent major investment in tithe income from neighbouring villages. As head of a family that was rising in the world, he needed to maintain both income and land befitting his gentle status, and could not afford to be too tender-hearted with his economic and social inferiors, especially during periods when income from the theatre had dried up.

The continuance of plague from 1608 into 1609 prolonged and exacerbated Shakespeare's financial difficulties, and drove him, as the severe plagues of 1593 and 1594 had done, to prepare and publish non-dramatic poetry, and to seek aristocratic patronage for it. He may have written some sonnets, or at least one sonnet, as early as 1582 (see above, pp. 18–19), and by 1598 he had acquired a reputation for his 'sugared sonnets among his private friends'.[46] From the time of the adventurous pirate William Jaggard's publication of *The Passionate Pilgrim* in 1599 Shakespeare had been well aware that a full and authentic collection of his sonnets would be highly marketable, and he may deliberately have held in reserve the possibility of one day raising a substantial sum of money by publishing such a collection. Writing, revising and re-ordering sonnets was probably a regular activity throughout his adult life, though one that he was careful to share only with those 'private friends' whom he could trust. It was in 1609, that great year for new adventures, that exceptional pressures and a new cultural climate finally provoked him to shape sonnets written over a long period of time into a new and ambitious structure, and to sell them to a publisher.

With the public theatres still closed by plague – they were to remain closed throughout 1609 – those who normally lived by them had to look elsewhere for income. Some other members of the King's Men turned to print publication: Robert Armin, for instance, published a jest book, and John Lowin published a treatise on the wholesome use of dancing.[47] Better-established writers turned also to the court and courtiers. To such writers, it seemed that the time was now ripe for works that combined misogyny with elements of homoeroticism or what might now be called 'camp' – works that would surely not have flourished in the ambience of the old Queen. It was in 1609, for instance, that Jonson's *Epicoene, or the Silent Woman* was performed by the Children of the Queen's Revels, presumably at court. Despite its sponsorship by Queen Anne, this play made cruel game of the idea of female learning, in its grotesque depiction of the 'Ladies Collegiates'. Its central conceit, the trick played on the noise-hating Morose in marrying him off to a 'silent woman' who is really a

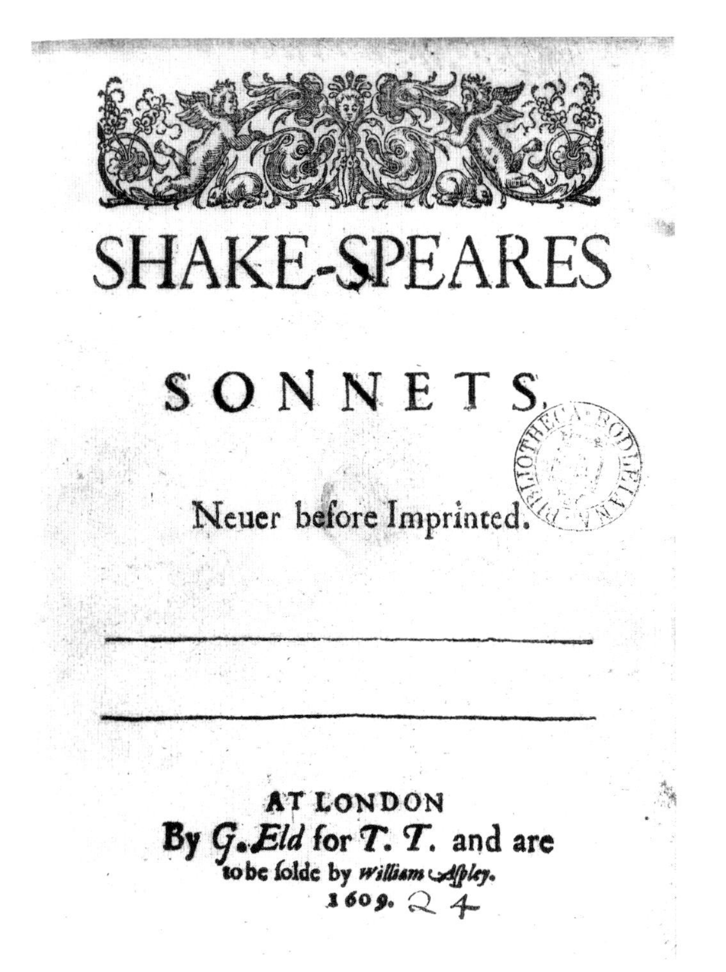

SHAKE-SPEARES

SONNETS.

Neuer before Imprinted.

AT LONDON
By G. Eld for T. T. and are
to be solde by William Aspley.
1609.

Fig. 33 Title-page of *SHAKE-SPEARES SONNETS* (1609).

boy, combines a rather knowing sexual tease with the implication that no anatomically female person could ever in truth be 'silent'.[48] To Shakespeare, well aware of the King's open fondling of his aristocratic minions, such as William Herbert and his brother Philip, the moment may have seemed propitious for bringing to light a sonnet sequence that flouted existing traditions of sonnet-writing in idealizing a well-born male love object, while, as an apparent afterthought, also satirizing a sexually available woman. The so-called 'dark lady' sonnets constitute a poetic equivalent of the beating up of whores that was such a popular holiday pastime for young men of high status.

Shakespeare's Sonnets – the title both proclaims the genuine authorship of the poems and suggests Shakespeare's authentic 'presence' in them (Fig. 33) – is one of the longest sonnet sequences of the English Renaissance. Its length reflects the long period of time during which it was composed, while also marking the sequence as unusually weighty and ground-breaking. Some of the first seventeen, in which the speaker tries to persuade a young male addressee to marry in order to reproduce his worth and beauty, may have been originally written for Southampton during his period as a reluctant bridegroom in the early 1590s, though echoes of Sidney's *Arcadia* were more apt for William Herbert, Sidney's nephew. Modern readers have often complained that the young man whose beauty is so triumphantly affirmed in sonnets 1–126 is never explicitly described, only labelled as pre-eminently 'fair'. There may be two reasons for this. First, Shakespeare, well practised in writing scripts that could be performed by different players and for different occasions, may have deliberately avoided furnishing the male love object with any very strong distinguishing characteristics. Like the young man complained of in the closing poem of the volume, *A Lover's Complaint*, he was a practised re-cycler of love tokens. Expressions of devotion written for one young nobleman were skilfully re-deployed for another. But another good reason why the young man is not described may be that some of the poems addressed to him (whoever 'he' was at the time) were presented to him in manuscript, like verse letters. There would be no need to tell the recipient what he looked like, only to praise his looks.

This is not the place for full commentary on the whole sequence. I have gone into some detail elsewhere about the vexed question of dating.[49] However, while some sonnets may have been written up to twenty years before the book's publication, there are others that seem definitely to belong to the early Jacobean period, and are therefore relevant to this chapter. In particular, the group of topical-seeming sonnets 123–5 which closes the sequence proper may be read as the clearest statement Shakespeare ever made of his political and religious position. What they appear to tell us is that he has decided to make a virtue of necessity. Excluded from major office in the state or at court by his lowly origins and stigmatized profession of 'player', the speaker creates a space for himself in poetry that is even more lofty than that of a courtier, and far more secure. Shakespeare's kings, almost to a man, envy those of low rank who can sleep well at night and need not fear usurpation or assassination. Sonnets 123–5 explore the opposite position, articulating the contentment of one who is 'poor, but free'. The speaker defines a private space for himself, raised by loving friendship far beyond and above the vagaries of the 'suborned informer' Time. He refuses either to be dazzled by court pageantry ('thy pyramids, built up with newer might'), or to envy those who hold conspicuous court office ('Were't ought to me I bore the canopy'). He is safely remote from the force of 'accident' to which eminent courtiers and statesmen are subject, and is determined to risk his position neither through religious affiliations which have caused some

(Catholics?) to 'die for goodness', nor political ambitions which have led others, like Essex, to 'Lose all, and more, by paying too much rent'. Despite what was said above about Shakespeare's identification of 'piety' with 'pity', the position defined in these sonnets seems rather smug and unfeeling. Nevertheless, as an affirmation of the value of personal friendship or 'love' as infinitely preferable to political or institutional allegiance, they will strike an echo in many bosoms.

Sonnet 125, 'Were't ought to me I bore the canopy', appears more particular in its eyewitness testimony to the falls of court favourites:

> Have I not seen dwellers on form and favour
> Lose all, and more, by paying too much rent,
> For compound sweet forgoing simple savour,
> Pitiful thrivers, in their gazing spent?

This would allude most naturally to the spectacular fall of the Earl of Essex, who had for so long been assiduous in his cultivation of the 'form and favour' of Elizabeth. As Earl Marshal, he had been the ultimate arbiter of all heraldic tokens of honour, or 'form', including the questionable grant of arms awarded to Shakespeare himself in 1596. Shakespeare's company had been closely connected with Essex and his confederates, with their specially commissioned performance of *Richard II*, and were well aware of how close they had come to being pulled down with him. Essex's sharp decline began with his 'gazing' on the Queen undressed (see above, pp. 126–7), and was also marked by the non-renewal of his monopoly on the tax on sweet wines, alluded to in the phrase 'compound sweet'. As an eminent nobleman, the speaker's friend has more in common with Essex than is altogether comfortable. The closing 'fair youth' poem, 126, warns him of the hazards of cosmic and political minionhood. The poet has done his utmost to preserve the young man against the savage depredations of Time, but one day, inevitably, Time will win, at least in taking possession of the youth's physical body. Nevertheless, as proclaimed in many sonnets earlier in the sequence, the poems themselves will stand 'So long as men can breathe or eyes can see' (18), and 'My love shall in my verse ever live young' (19).

The ephemeral and the permanent exist in a close and paradoxical relationship in *Shakespeare's Sonnets*. The valuable and much laboured-over text was sold in May 1609, surely for a good sum, to the publisher Thomas Thorpe, who had recently published works by Jonson, Chapman and Marston.[50] The capitalized dedication, signed by Thorpe, but authorized by Shakespeare, took a fashionable quasi-lapidary form. Jonson's *Volpone*, which like the *Sonnets* was published by Thorpe and printed by George Eld, had carried a similar capitalized dedication to 'THE TWO FAMOUS UNIVERSITIES', and in the same year Barnabe Barnes's *The Divels Charter*, also printed by Eld, and published by

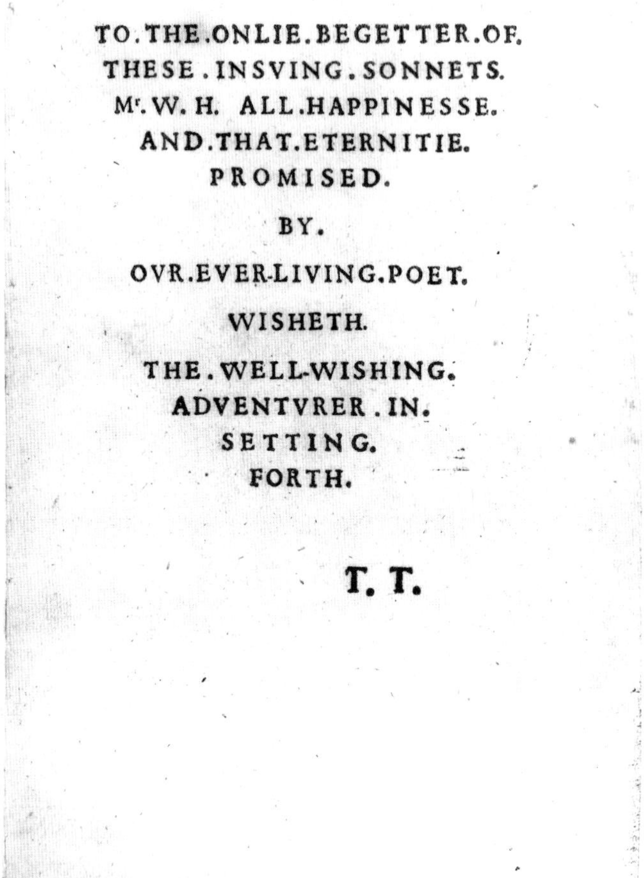

TO.THE.ONLIE.BEGETTER.OF.
THESE.INSVING.SONNETS.
Mr.W.H. ALL.HAPPINESSE.
AND.THAT.ETERNITIE.
PROMISED.

BY.

OVR.EVER-LIVING.POET.

WISHETH.

THE.WELL-WISHING.
ADVENTVRER.IN.
SETTING.
FORTH.

T. T.

Fig. 34 Dedication leaf of the *Sonnets.*

John Wright, one of the booksellers of *Shakespeare's Sonnets,* also had a capitalized and centred dedication leaf.[51] In this lean year both Shakespeare and Thorpe hoped for a substantial reward from the volume's dedicatee and 'ONLY. BEGETTER', William Herbert, Earl of Pembroke (Fig. 34). T. T. wishes that 'Mr. W. H.' may enjoy 'THAT. ETERNITY. / PROMISED. / BY. / OUR. EVER-LIVING. POET'. Shakespeare's now celebrated greatness – he is 'EVER-LIVING' because his writings are deathless – appears to guarantee the efficacy of his poetic immortalizations of his 'fair friend'. Yet later generations have not agreed even on the identity of 'Mr. W. H.', and anyone who reads through *Shakespeare's Sonnets* as a continuum – a demanding, perplexing, painful experience – will come away with a powerful sense of mortality. The speaker's 'lovely Boy' must be yielded up to old age and death (126); and the last two 'dark lady' sonnets (153–4) equate desire for the female body with infectious disease and its 'cure' which is almost worse, the mercury-infused sweating tub.

WHEN HE IS GONE

Although it was published some months earlier than *Sonnets* – probably in January 1609 – I have deferred discussion of the Quarto *Troilus and Cressida*. Like the *Sonnets*, this was printed by Eld, though published by R. Bonian and H. Walley. Like the *Sonnets*, too, the text is almost certainly the product of revision. When originally entered for publication, on 7 February 1603, it had been described as 'acted by my Lord Chamberlain's Men'. Thoroughgoing authorial revision of the play, deliberately transformed from an acting text to one designed above all to be read, would explain the discrepancy of the earlier description of the play as 'acted' with the claim made in the epistle to the reader in the 'second state' 1609 printing that this is 'a new play, never staled with the stage, never clapper-clawed with the palms of the vulgar' (Fig. 35). Rather as the *Sonnets* needed to be 'packaged' in a way that underlined their difference, both in substance and authenticity, from the piratical *Passionate Pilgrim*, *Troilus* needed to be 'packaged' in a manner that drew attention both to the popularity of the play's theme – a *Famous Historie*, as the revised title-page calls it – and to its 'elite' status as a clever and difficult work that will, paradoxically, achieve great popularity. The epistle itself invites comparison with the celebrated dedication of *Sonnets*. This, too, I see as a collaboration between Shakespeare and the publishers – or possibly even an insertion written by Shakespeare himself, designed to sell the work by drawing attention to its upmarket status. Despite the modest headline description of the epistle's author as 'A Never Writer', he is a master of supple, slippery punning language, full of alliteration and assonance. This seems like Shakespeare parodying his own most insistently playful manner. He also reminds readers of the continuity of his witty comedies with his earliest work, recently printed probably for the ninth time in 1608,[52] *Venus and Adonis*: 'they seem, for their height of pleasure, to be born in that sea that brought forth Venus'. In miniature, the epistle is a defence of the value of play-texts against 'all those grand censors, that now style them such vanities', as well as a wider puff for Shakespeare as above all a writer of witty, crowd-pleasing comedies that make audiences come away cleverer than when they went in, 'feeling an edge of wit set upon them more than ever they dreamed'.

The parallels between *Troilus* and *Sonnets* run wider still. While the *Sonnets* offer a defamiliarizing re-fashioning of the Petrarchan tradition of courtly love poetry, *Troilus* is a darkly cynical re-write of Chaucer. Where Chaucer writes

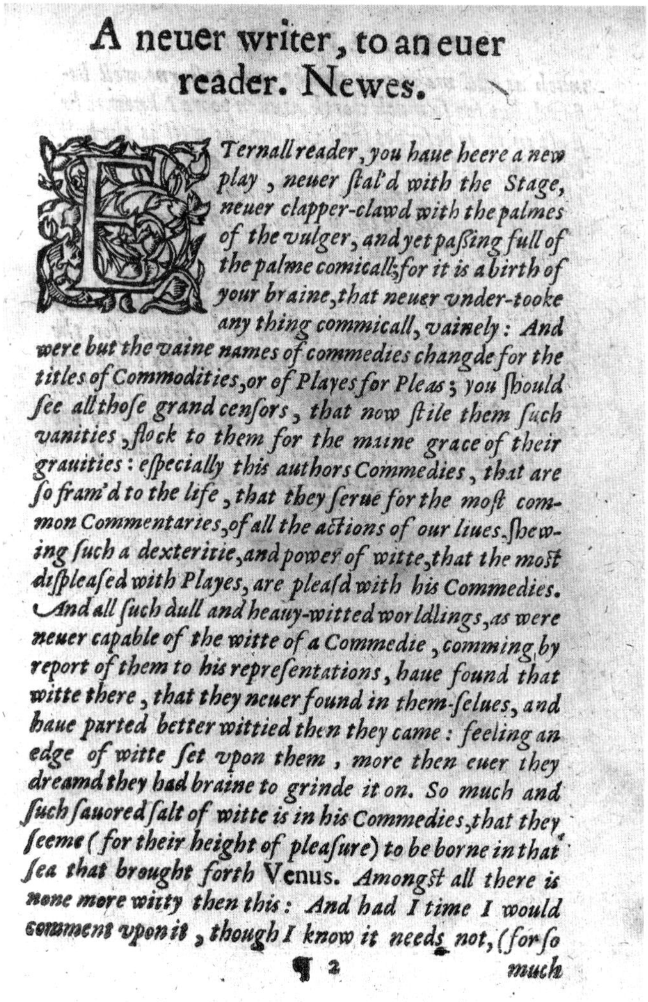

A neuer writer, to an euer reader. Newes.

Eternall reader, you haue heere a new play, neuer ſtal'd with the Stage, neuer clapper-clawd with the palmes of the vulger, and yet paſsing full of the palme comicall; for it is a birth of your braine, that neuer vnder-tooke any thing commicall, vainely: And were but the vaine names of commedies changde for the titles of Commodities, or of Playes for Pleas; you ſhould ſee all thoſe grand cenſors, that now ſtile them ſuch vanities, flock to them for the maine grace of their grauities: eſpecially this authors Commedies, that are ſo fram'd to the life, that they ſerue for the moſt common Commentaries, of all the actions of our liues, ſhewing ſuch a dexteritie, and power of witte, that the moſt diſpleaſed with Playes, are pleaſd with his Commedies. And all ſuch dull and heauy-witted worldlings, as were neuer capable of the witte of a Commedie, comming by report of them to his repreſentations, haue found that witte there, that they neuer found in them-ſelues, and haue parted better wittied then they came: feeling an edge of witte ſet vpon them, more then euer they dreamd they had braine to grinde it on. So much and ſuch ſauored ſalt of witte is in his Commedies, that they ſeeme (for their height of pleaſure) to be borne in that ſea that brought forth Venus. *Amongſt all there is none more witty then this: And had I time I would comment vpon it, though I know it needs not, (for ſo*

¶ 2 *much*

Fig. 35 Epistle from 'A Never Writer', prefixed to *Troilus and Cressida* (1609).

with tender subtlety of the central characters, drawing us deep within their consciousness, Shakespeare pushes them almost to the edge of their own story. Where Chaucer's Troilus is deeply touching, Shakespeare's is merely weak and silly. Neither romantic love nor chivalric heroism can withstand the relentless satiric onslaughts that they receive. Patroclus, the young 'masculine whore' of the languid Achilles, spends his days 'like a strutting player', wittily mocking the heroic pretensions of the ageing Greek generals, while Thersites outdoes even Patroclus in savagely ingenious railing. The play is profoundly misogynistic, or at least, delivers a resoundingly misogynistic challenge to the old courtly love ideal of lives well lost in the service of a fair lady. No woman, it seems here, is worth fighting or suffering for, not even Helen of Troy. As Hector, the wisest voice in the play, tersely remarks, 'she is not worth what she doth cost / The holding' (2.2.51–2). And Pandarus and Thersites between them ensure that we can never forget the association of heterosexual love with disease. It seems that this, rather than the slaughter of war, is the inevitable doom that hangs over the Greek army: 'the vengeance on the whole camp! Or rather, the Neapolitan bone-ache! For that, methinks, is the curse dependent on those that war for a placket' (2.3.16–19). By the time we reach the play's extraordinarily dark close – the darker in lacking any sense of tragic release or access to a higher wisdom – Pandarus himself has become sick with 'A whoreson phthisic', or wasting sickness. He suffers from the aching bones that were the stereotypical symptom of venereal disease, or *morbus gallicus*, and delivers a uniquely disturbing Epilogue in which he threatens the audience that at the time of his death 'Some two months hence' he will ensure that they suffer the same fate:

> Till then I'll sweat and seek about for eases,
> And at that time bequeath you my diseases.
>
> (5.11.55–6)

For readers in the severe plague year 1609 this was uncomfortably apt. Though the playhouses continued to stand empty to inhibit the spread of infection, London book-buyers who had gained access to a play-text by an apparently cleaner, safer route still found themselves savagely reminded of the association between close encounters with drama and the risk of infection. With the playhouses shut down, many young men may have gone more frequently to those other houses of live entertainment, brothels, where they risked contracting not just swift-acting bubonic plague, but the slow and humiliating 'French pox', 'Neapolitan bone-ache', or syphilis.

Not only does the shrunken Pandarus at the end of the play threaten to infect the audience, there is a strong hint in the prefatory epistle that the author, too, is understood to be terminally ill. Given that Shakespeare was only forty-five, we may be struck by A Never Writer's urgent preoccupation with mortality and posterity: 'believe this, that when he is gone and his comedies out of sale, you will scramble for them and set up a new English Inquisition'. Like the *Sonnets*, the 1609 *Troilus* is deeply rooted in an awareness of death, and of the desperate struggle to make one's voice heard before disease destroys both pen and phallus:

> Full merrily the humble-bee doth sing,
> Till he hath lost his honey and his sting;

> And being once subdued in armed tail,
> Sweet honey and sweet notes together fail.

As Nashe had shown so brilliantly in his 'Choice of valentines' (see above, pp. 57–8) a visit to a brothel could be one of the most 'painful adventures' of all. Though Shakespeare was to survive for nearly seven years more, his visits to Turnmill Street may have left him with an unwanted legacy of chronic and humiliating sickness. As Peter Pan was to say three centuries later, 'To die will be an awfully big adventure'. This was the adventure on which Shakespeare was preparing to embark.

CHAPTER NINE

1610–13

Our revels now are ended

> Our revels now are ended. These our actors,
> As I foretold you, were all spirits and
> Are melted into air, into thin air . . .
> Bear with my weakness; my old brain is troubled.
>
> (*The Tempest*, 4.1.148–59)

A sad distempered guest

FROM *Pericles* onwards, all of Shakespeare's surviving work can be described as retrospective. This applies equally to single-authored and collaborative texts. *Pericles*, the earliest 'late play', looks back explicitly to Gower and his *Confessio Amantis*, while *The Two Noble Kinsmen*, the last, looks back to Chaucer and his *Canterbury Tales*. Chaucer's *Troilus and Criseide* had already been given a savagely satiric makeover. In *The Winter's Tale* Shakespeare recalls a more recent writer, Robert Greene, whose much chronicled death and 'repentance' had been closely associated with Shakespeare's own literary debut (see above, chapter 2). In *Cymbeline* Shakespeare returned to the part of Holinshed's *Chronicle* on which he had drawn for *Lear*, looking back once again to a pre-Christian Britain, while also echoing some of his own earliest work, most conspicuously *Lucrece*. Though different from the other late plays in being ostensibly historical rather than romance-like, *Henry VIII* also looks back, staging a period that had been taboo during Elizabeth's reign and, now that the Tudor line was safely extinct could be given a softened, even sentimentalized treatment. His most strikingly original work of retrospection, *The Tempest*, has seemed to many readers and audiences inescapably personal and valedictory – the artistic equivalent of the cliché of the drowning man's whole life passing before his eyes. Modern treatments of it as a 'psychodrama', such as Peter Greenaway's film *Prospero's Books* (1991), reflect a sense that this play comes nearest of any that Shakespeare wrote to being a one-man show, with its central controlling consciousness a transparent image of that of the artist–magician William Shakespeare. It has sometimes been pedantically objected to the view of *The Tempest* as a 'farewell to his art' that Shakespeare was to live on for about five more years, and continued to have some involvement in writing for the King's Men, even if only as a secondary collaborator.[1] However, the Psalmist's plea, 'Lord, make me to know mine end: and the measure of my days' (Psalms, 39.4), is one that is rarely answered. Even today, medical estimates of the proximity of death are rarely precise. The question is not so much whether Shakespeare was in truth near death at the time when he wrote *The Tempest* as whether he felt that he was. Intimations of impending mortality appear to colour all of the late plays' retrospections, although in the event Shakespeare turned out to be considerably longer-lived than most males in his family. His younger brother Gilbert died at the beginning of February 1612, Richard just a year later.[2]

As we saw in chapter 8, disturbingly graphic images of sweating tubs and venereal infection close both *Troilus and Cressida* and *Shakespeare's Sonnets*. Taken in conjunction with repeated gestures of retrospection and valediction in the late work, these images seem to me to support a supposition that Shakespeare's visits to Turnmill Street had left him with an unwanted legacy of infection, or at the very least, that he may have believed that they had done so. Again, it makes little difference whether, from about 1608, he was indeed venereally infected, or whether he merely thought he was. Syphilis, which Sir William Osler was to label the 'Great Imitator', continues to be notorious for its capacity to manifest itself in a wide variety of symptoms.[3] In Shakespeare's period it was not at all well differentiated from many other conditions, both sexually transmitted and otherwise. Anyone who had had unwise sexual congress and who found himself suffering thereafter from severe headache, bone-ache, skin lesions, fever, burning urine or virtually any other disagreeable symptom might naturally suspect himself to be syphilitic. Stress-induced migraine, age-induced arthritis, or even rapidly advancing baldness, might all equally, if mistakenly, be construed as tokens of an unwelcome visitation by the 'sinister shepherd' of Fracastoro's poem *Syphilis* (1530).[4] The treatment for syphilis was as much to be feared as the disease itself. In the chivalric burlesque *The Knight of the Burning Pestle*, hastily written by Francis Beaumont for the Children of the Queen's Revels about 1607, the monster 'Barbaroso' (a

Fig. 36 Title-page of Thomas Randolph's Latin play *Cornelianum Dolium* (1638), showing a man being treated for syphilis in a sweating-tub.

barber–surgeon) imprisons gentle knights and ladies in his cave and tortures them with mercury and sweating tubs. An 'errant knight' tells of finding his lady love among 'her friends in Turnbull Street' and living happily with her until

> at this unhappy town
> We did arrive, and coming to this cave
> This beast us caught and put us in a tub
> Where we this two months sweat.[5]

In the final image we have of him, the speaker of the *Sonnets* presents himself as 'a sad distempered guest' who seeks relief from the burning agony of love in 'a seething bath' (sonnet 153) (Fig. 36). Another distinctive feature of syphilis is its undulant nature. The sufferer may enjoy remission for some months or even years, before relapsing with fresh symptoms. A period of relative health denoted only a suspended sentence, not a full reprieve from the sinister shepherd's visitations. If Shakespeare believed himself to be syphilitic, therefore, he would derive only limited comfort from periods of remission.

As viewed by most English Renaissance commentators, syphilis was a disease that women gave to men. One of the more enlightened writers on the subject, Peter Lowe, whose treatise on it was dedicated to the Earl of Essex in 1596 (one wonders why), remarked that 'this malady proceedeth chiefly from the act of Venus, when men have to do with women polluted with that infection'.[6] He also attributes it to lower-class women rather than gentry, seeing the infection of genteel infants as transmitted by their midwives or wet-nurses, rather than by their mothers. For the infected women themselves there was little sympathy or concern, either from the medical profession or from the world in general. Even a woman who looked young, beautiful and innocent might harbour in the hidden parts of her body the power to infect a man with a painful, humiliating and ultimately fatal disease. This mode of thinking both reflected and reinforced existing patterns of misogynist imagery. The jealous husband feared openly for his own and his family's honour; but also, more covertly, for his own health and survival. The misogynist rage that seizes men such as Leontes and Posthumus in the late plays should be viewed against this background.

Greene's ghost

If good married men had some cause for anxiety about the 'French pox' or 'Neapolitan bone-ache', bad ones had even more. Persisting almost like a mental infection in Shakespeare's imagination was the memory of Robert Greene, whose status as a gentleman and a Master of Arts had not protected him from an early and shameful death, drunk, deep in debt and bearing the 'ulcerous sores' of syphilis. According to *Mamillia: Greenes Vision* (1592) he was visited in the last summer of his life by the spirits of Chaucer and Gower; the name Mamillius in *The Winter's Tale* derives from this romance medley. In his own more thoroughgoing adaptations of works by Gower and Chaucer Shakespeare may have been deliberately re-enacting a more leisurely equivalent of Greene's last days.

Like the haunted man who 'dwelt by a churchyard' in the child Mamillius's ghost story (*The Winter's Tale*, 2.1.24–31) Greene allegedly played out the last act

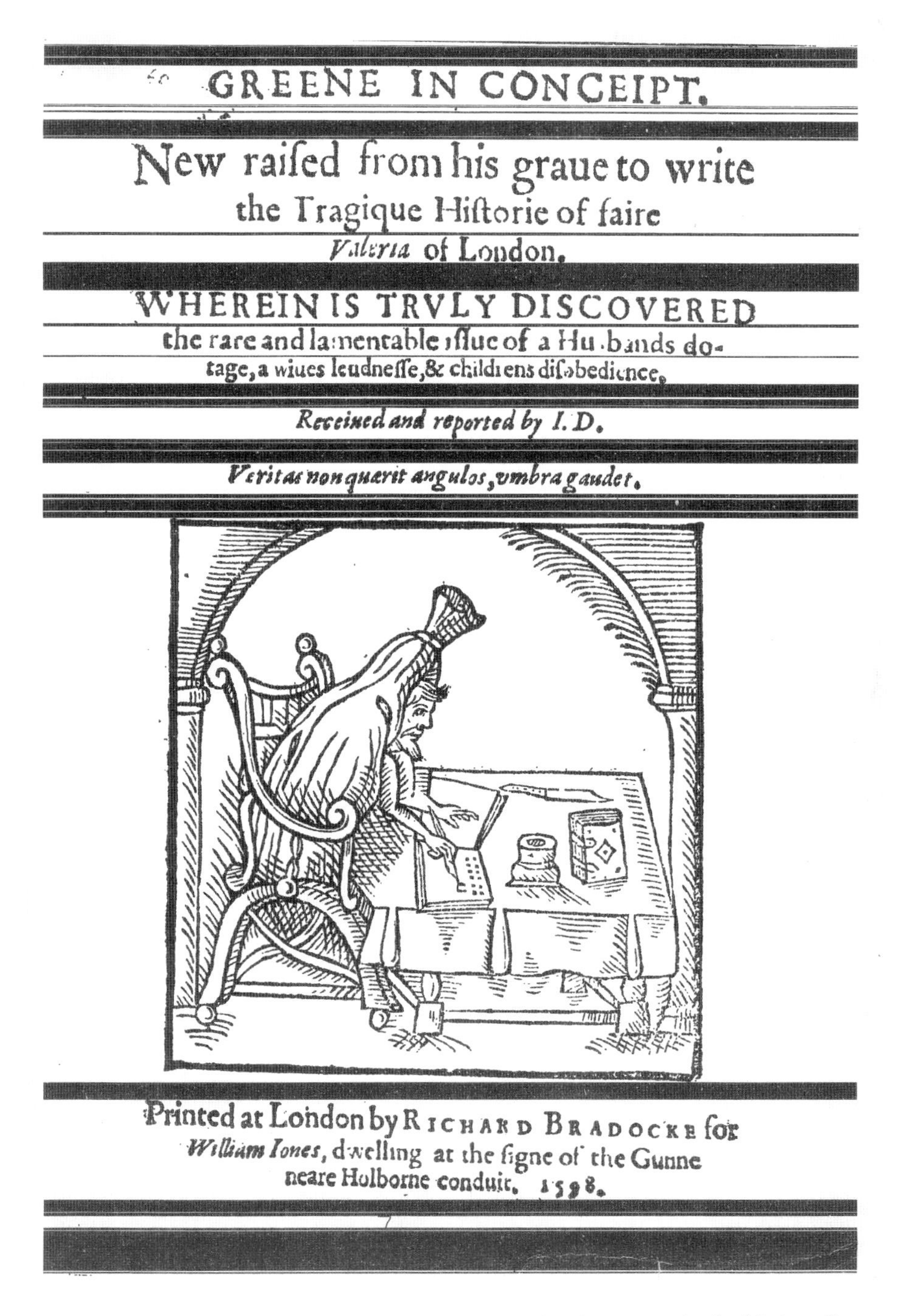

GREENE IN CONCEIPT.

New raiſed from his graue to write the Tragique Hiſtorie of faire *Valeria* of London.

WHEREIN IS TRVLY DISCOVERED the rare and lamentable iſſue of a Huſbands dotage, a wiues leudneſſe, & childrens diſobedience.

Receiued and reported by I. D.

Veritas non quærit angulos, vmbra gaudet.

Printed at London by RICHARD BRADOCKE for *William Iones*, dwelling at the ſigne of the Gunne neare Holborne conduit. 1598.

Fig. 37 Title-page of John Dickenson's *Greene in Conceipt* (1598), showing the dead Robert Greene still busily writing.

of his life not far from the 'New churchyard near Bedlam' where he was buried, his corpse being crowned with bays by his kind landlady the shoemaker's wife Mistress Isham.[7] The swelling tide of apocryphal writings by and about Greene kept his image and mythos alive well into the early 1600s, ensuring that in his literary afterlife he continued to 'dwell by a churchyard', that of St Paul's, with its dozens of bookshops.[8] He was apparently as prolific a writer in death as he had been in life. John Dickenson described him as 'a well-proportioned man, suited in death's livery, who seemed to write as fast as I could read', and the title-page of *Greene in Conceipt* showed Greene tied up in his shroud but still busy at his writing desk (Fig. 37).[9] Shakespeare's most explicit re-animation of Greene, *The Winter's Tale*, is closely based on Greene's *Pandosto, The Triumph of Time* (1588). Since the wording of the Oracle shows that he drew on one of the earlier printings,[10] he may have kept a copy by him for many years. Perhaps his friend Richard Field, who printed the second edition of *Pandosto* in 1592, sold or gave him a copy in the year of Greene's death, and quite soon after Shakespeare's own arrival in London. As a narrative of a cruel husband repudiating an innocent wife *Pandosto* furnished parallels to Greene's own life story. He had for some years lived apart from his wife, 'a gentleman's daughter of good account',[11] supposedly writing her a penitent letter the day before he died. Both stories, too, include the pathetic death of a little boy: Greene's bastard child 'Infortunatus', who died soon after his father, and King Pandosto's son Garinter, the equivalent of Shakespeare's Mamillius, who dies soon after his mother is defamed. But while *Pandosto*, like Greene's much told life story, is a tragedy, Shakespeare's play is a somewhat strained and sensational tragicomedy. Rather as the earliest audiences of *King Lear* must have been astonished to encounter its grimly tragic final scene, with Cordelia pre-deceasing her father, early audiences familiar with Greene's still-popular romance must have been amazed to find the King and Queen of Bohemia alive and reconciled at the end – all the more so, perhaps, since Mamillius's assertion that 'a sad tale's best for winter' seemed to sound a clear signal that a play so entitled would also be 'sad'. *Pandosto* ends with the Queen long dead, and the King, ashamed of having lusted after his own daughter, killing himself. Shakespeare's version, instead, in the last of several startling changes of generic register, moves into masque-like mode in the final scene, appropriating the device of a statue in a gallery coming to life that had recently been used by Ben Jonson in his 'Britain's Burse' entertainment at Robert Cecil's New Exchange in April 1609. There the statue had been one of Apollo; the important part played by Apollo's oracle in the *Pandosto* story made this a ready association. Perhaps the boy singer who had achieved statuesque stillness at the opening of the New Exchange[12] was also the first to perform Hermione. Another device apparently borrowed from a Jonson masque, perhaps for a later and revised version of *The Winter's Tale*, was the 'dance of twelve satyrs' at the sheep-shearing feast (*Winter's Tale*, 4.4.336), in imitation of Jonson's *Oberon: The Faery Prince*, performed by Prince Henry and others on 1 January 1611.[13] However, it's just possible that this time the influence went the other way. My own guess is that Shakespeare's play could have been written during the summer or autumn of 1610, in anticipation that the cold winter season to which its title alludes might bring an abatement of plague and the possibility of performance being resumed at least in the indoor Blackfriars. In the event, the closure orders seem to have been suspended only for December and January, and it is not clear whether any public playing took place then.[14] This play, whose effect depended so much on surprise, may have been held in reserve by the King's Men before being eventually performed at court in the Banqueting House at Whitehall on 11 November 1611, this being its premiere.[15] Whether Shakespeare had included the satyrs' dance in his text before or after Jonson's *Oberon*, its re-enactment would be immediately recognized and enjoyed by the court audience.

Like Shakespeare, Greene had been an exceptionally versatile writer. He was celebrated as much for his 'rogue' pamphlets as for his romantic plays and prose romances. That Shakespeare in *The Winter's Tale* was consciously revisiting the life and works of Robert Greene, not merely appropriating some of the useful plot material of *Pandosto*, is confirmed by the fact that he also drew on one of his 'cony-catching' pamphlets, *The Second Part of Conny-Catching* (1592) for the Autolycus scenes in Act 4. The trick played by Autolycus on the Clown, in which he pretends to be in a faint after being robbed and injured, and, while the Clown tries to revive him, picks his pocket, is directly based on Greene's 'A kind conceit of a foist performed in Paul's'. Some other details and phrases are drawn from the same work. For instance, Autolycus's stealing of sheets derives from Greene's account of the 'Curber' who removes sheets hung out to dry by means of a long hook; the roguish phrase 'a snapper-up of unconsidered trifles' also comes from Greene.

Shakespeare's decision to contribute to the substantial body of literature derived from Greene's writings can be viewed in one way as a settling of scores. Greene had been identified in *Groats-worth* as Shakespeare's earliest and most savage rival, who had cursed the non-graduate 'upstart Crow' with his dying breath. The long theatre closures of 1608–10 must have carried with them vivid recollections of those of 1592–4, and of the literary squabbles that broke out then among out-of-work playwrights. *The Winter's Tale* can be seen as Shakespeare's long-delayed revenge on Greene, written from his now securely established position as the King's Men's leading playwright and a celebrated writer who had triumphantly overcome the disadvantages of his birth and lack of education. Yet given the lapse of nearly eighteen years since this memorable episode, the calling up of Greene's ghost could equally well be read as Shakespeare's belated acknowledgement that they were in many ways kindred spirits: prolific, popular, prodigal talents doomed to die, and destined inevitably to be misunderstood and mythologized by posterity. A severe disappointment for Shakespeare in 1609–10 was the failure of his *Sonnets* to win esteem or popularity. Whereas both *Venus and Adonis* and *Lucrece* had been immediately quoted, imitated and reprinted, *Shakespeare's Sonnets* was neither quoted, imitated nor reprinted. If, in addition, he was now suffering from one of Greene's shaming 'life-style' diseases, it would not be surprising if he felt dispirited and demoralized, even to the extent of inviting an identification of his own writing with that of a ridiculous hack, a recycler of trite and sensational romance narrative – while also no doubt hoping to achieve further popular success by doing so.

SHAKESPEARE IN GOOD COMPANY: FLETCHER AND BEAUMONT

The King's Men emerged from the plague-ridden period 1608–10 impoverished and unfocused. The thirteen sharers and part-sharers in the company[16] were determined to find compensation for this long period of economic hardship. During the brief intervals when the public theatres were open, Shakespeare's existing work continued to furnish much of their repertoire. On 30 April 1610, for instance, a performance of *Othello* was seen at the Globe by Prince Lewis Frederick of Würtemberg.[17] But as scholars have often observed, Shakespeare's rate of production appears to have declined from two or even three plays a year to barely one or two, after which a new pattern of collaboration and collusion with other writers set in. I have already suggested that, in spite of the courtly and popular success of *Pericles*, Shakespeare's professional 'fellows' may not have relished his association with George Wilkins. This could be among the reasons why the play was to be excluded from the First Folio, which did include some other products of collaboration, notably *Henry VIII*. Shakespeare, they knew, often worked at his best with the stimulus and friendly competition of a younger man. A deliberate policy designed to create such conditions may lie behind the recruitment of John Fletcher, who was eventually to succeed Shakespeare as the company's 'ordinary' playwright. As Richard Proudfoot has suggested, 'It is likely that in Fletcher Shakespeare recognized his natural successor and that their collaboration represents his gradual withdrawal in favour of the younger dramatist.'[18]

By the time he wrote *Philaster*, his first play for the King's Men, in collaboration with his friend and room-mate Francis Beaumont, Fletcher had already established his writerly credentials through collusion, collaboration and independent authorship. As a son of a Bishop of London, and a Cambridge alumnus, Fletcher was both a 'gentleman born' and a young man of some learning. If we can believe Aubrey's account, he maintained a relaxed existence with his friend Francis Beaumont in the neighbourhood of the Globe Theatre:

> They lived together on the Bankside not far from the playhouse, both bachelors, lay together, had one wench in the house between them, which they did so admire, the same clothes and cloak etc, between them.[19]

But it was his fluency and originality as a poet[20] and playwright that was his chief recommendation to Shakespeare's company. Like Shakespeare himself, he wrote both fast and well, chiefly in verse, and established early on distinctive gifts for dramatizing pastoral romance and for sustaining long-drawn-out emotional cliff-hangers with an off-beat sexual dimension (Fig. 38).[21] According to Aubrey, again, Beaumont's 'main business was to correct the superflowings of Mr Fletcher's wit'. Though there is no reason to think that Shakespeare collaborated with Beaumont, he must have been well acquainted with both young men. Beaumont, too, was a gentleman born. An alumnus of Oxford and the Inner Temple, he had also spent some time in Cambridge, where he got into trouble for semi-criminal gambling.[22]

Whether *Cymbeline* was written before or after *The Winter's Tale* – or even, as J. M. Nosworthy has suggested,[23] at the same time – there is little doubt that it both followed Fletcher and Beaumont's *Philaster*, written in the summer of 1609, and is strongly influenced by it.[24] Though there are only three closely connected passages, the genre of the play, a tragicomic pastoral romance, and one of its most distinctive strands, the travels and sufferings of the disguised and defamed Innogen, closely resemble *Philaster*. In *Philaster* the disguised page Bellario – whose name prompted Shakespeare's Belarius – endures great suffering, both emotional and physical, analogous to that undergone by Innogen. In both cases there seems no adequate reason for the protracted deferral of the revelation of the page's true (female) gender except to maximize the theatrical effects of pathos, suspense and surprise. Behind both narratives lies the reported episode of the lovesick princess Zelmane in Sidney's *Arcadia,* who cuts her golden hair short and dresses like a boy in order to serve her cousin the young prince Pyrocles, with whom she is in love. Sidney's girl–boy page reveals her true identity and gender, 'with pale and yet even-in-paleness-lovely lips', only when she is on the point of death, imploring Pyrocles to 'think of me after my death with kindness, though you cannot with love'.[25] Audiences of both *Philaster* and *Cymbeline* surely relished the plays' echoes of this episode. They must have been relieved to find, in *Philaster*, that though cruelly wounded while asleep (three instances of gratuitous wounding support the play's subtitle, *Love Lies a-Bleeding*) the page Bellario survives, and is still alive – though unmarried – at the end of the play. Shakespeare makes the parallel to Sidney closer, in having Innogen / Fidele fall sick and (apparently) die, her

Fig. 38 Portrait of John Fletcher, engraved by William Marshall, from the 1679 folio edition of the plays of Beaumont and Fletcher.

funeral rites being performed with a scattering of flowers and a choric recitation of the song 'Fear no more the heat o'th' sun' by the young men who are – though they do not know it – her brothers (4.2). But in having Innogen wake up next to a fresh corpse Shakespeare was inviting recollections of one of his own earliest plays, *Romeo and Juliet*, in which Juliet is terrified of waking up in the Capulet vault close to the fresh corpse of her cousin Tybalt. Behind Fletcher's and Shakespeare's interest in dramatizing tear-jerking material taken from Sidney – which Fletcher and Beaumont had already done explicitly in *Cupid's Revenge* (1608) – may have lain a desire to please that 'incomparable pair of brethren', William Herbert, Earl of Pembroke, and his brother Philip, who were Sidney's nephews. Sidney had written the first version of the *Arcadia* to amuse his sister the Countess while she was pregnant with her first son, William; and his younger brother was Sidney's godson and namesake. From the earliest weeks of James's English reign these handsome young noblemen had played a leading part in fostering a wide range of theatrical activity at court. Heminge and Condell would hardly have dared to remind the brothers in the First Folio in 1623 that 'your Lordships have been pleased to think these trifles something, heretofore; and have prosecuted both them, and their author living, with so much favour' had this not indeed been true. Few members of a court audience in this period would have been unfamiliar with Sidney's *Arcadia* as printed, but the Herbert brothers, most famously, had drunk it in with their mother's milk in an almost literal sense. They had grown up with it, probably having passages read aloud to them by their mother, its dedicatee, in their earliest years. They may have explicitly invited the King's Men's playwrights to dramatize 'Arcadian' material. As we have seen in previous chapters, it was during plague outbreaks that aristocratic patronage was most needed by professional playwrights. In an earlier procedure some plays which had already established popular success in the public playhouses were selected, months or even years later, for performance at court, but the long lean years 1608–10 seem to have provoked a reverse pattern. Plays were now being written with private performance primarily in view, since this was the only form of performance that could continue during epidemics – but always with the hope that they could be played in public in due course. The strangely long-drawn-out and miscellaneous action of *Cymbeline* may be the outcome of a period when Shakespeare had too much time on his hands. But the play's amplitude may be also a deliberate strategy to enable Sir George Buc, the Master of the Revels since 20 August 1610,[26] to select from this long text the scenes and episodes he thought best for the occasion, while pruning or omitting others.

In addition to their 'Arcadian' dimension, most visible in the 'princess-as-page' motif, *Philaster* and *Cymbeline* share a preoccupation with royal lineage and genealogy which fitted them very well for court performance. In both plays this is expressed through the image of a great cedar tree – the cedar being symbolically associated both with royalty and with peace – whose branches represent children, first lost and apparently lopped, then eventually found (Fig. 39). In a strange semi-masque scene in the last act of *Philaster* Bellario enters 'in a robe and garland', presenting the tyrannical King with his daughter and son-in-law:

> These two fair cedar branches,
> The noblest of the mountain where they grew,
> Straightest and tallest, under whose still shades
> The worthier beasts have made their lairs, and slept . . .
>
> (5.3.25–8)

Shakespeare, too, makes formal and symbolic use of the cedar image, in the scroll containing Jupiter's prophecy:

> *when from a stately cedar shall be lopp'd branches, which, being dead many years, shall after revive, be jointed to the old stock, and freshly grow, then shall Posthumus end his miseries, Britain be fortunate, and flourish in peace and plenty.*
>
> (*Cymbeline*, 5.5.438–43)

However, Shakespeare elsewhere adds shades of tragic melancholy to the pervasive image of the 'family tree'. The banished lord Belarius, foster-father to the lost princes, in one of several passages in *Cymbeline* that echo the recently published *Sonnets*, connects his sudden fall from Cymbeline's favour with the cruel stripping of a tree:

> then was I as a tree
> Whose boughs did bend with fruit. But in one night,
> A storm, or robbery (call it what you will)
> Shook down my mellow hangings, nay, my leaves,
> And left me bare to weather.
>
> (3.3.60–4)

This closely parallels the opening of sonnet 73, in which the speaker identifies his own physical ageing (and perhaps baldness) with the sight of a great tree being stripped of leaves at the approach of winter:

> That time of year thou mayst in me behold,
> When yellow leaves, or none, or few do hang
> Upon those boughs which shake against the cold,
> Bare ruined choirs where late the sweet birds sang . . .

Cymbeline was to be placed among the Tragedies in the First Folio, and there are several ways in which, although it is technically a tragicomedy, its ending

Fig. 39 The Stuart family tree accompanying Drayton's *Gratulatorie Epistle* (1603).

feels very much more sombre than that of *Philaster*. In what Tennyson identified as 'among the tenderest lines in Shakespeare' the penitent Posthumus is re-united with his wife Innogen: 'Hang there like fruit, my soul, / Till the tree die' (5.5.264–5). Shakespeare's play, unlike Fletcher's, leaves us with a spine-tingling sense that in the midst of love we are in death.

THESE OUR ACTORS

The Tempest is a uniquely original work of synthesis. In it Shakespeare foregrounds two topics of immediate interest to his contemporaries in 1611–12: the discovery and plantation of new territories, and the prospect of exotic royal marriages as an appeasement of ancient enmities. Marriage prospects for the King's eldest children, Prince Henry and Princess Elizabeth, were the subject of increasingly excited rumour. Yet *The Tempest* seems also to be the most revealingly personal of all Shakespeare's plays – the one in which commentary on his lifelong craft is most deeply woven into the text. It is the final demonstration of that gift as a 'factotum' that was noticed so early on in his career. Awareness of the play's multi-faceted character may be among the reasons why Heminge and Condell placed it at the forefront of the First Folio. It is their colleague's last and most self-revealing work, and yet also a highly performable piece whose themes were still topical in 1623. Their injunction 'To the great Variety of Readers' to 'read him' is followed by *The Tempest*, rather as if it is here, *par excellence*, that he can be 'read'.

Most of Shakespeare's courtly patrons were active in developing the 'plantation' of Virginia. In particular, the Earl of Pembroke, who became a member of the King's Virginia Company in May 1609, just as the *Sonnets* were reaching print, was an outstandingly enthusiastic and generous 'adventurer'. By 1618 he was to become its largest single investor. If any subject matter was calculated to please him even more than material drawn from his uncle's *Arcadia*, it was surely New World adventure (in every sense of that word). Pembroke, the *Sonnets* and *The Tempest* are linked together in a threefold nexus. In addition to that conspicuous word 'ADVENTURER.' in the dedication, there are bibliographical links between *Shakespeare's Sonnets* and the swelling tide of books about Virginia in 1608–12, for George Eld, who had printed the *Sonnets* in 1609, was also the printer of *A True and Sincere declaration of the purpose and ends of the Plantation begun in Virginia* (1610), one of many semi-official works on the subject. However, a book with a more immediate bearing on *The Tempest* is Silvester Jourdain's *A Discovery of the Barmudas, otherwise called the Ile of Divels*, also published in 1610, an eyewitness account of Sir Thomas Gates's unlucky-lucky shipwreck en route for the colony at Jamestown. The book's subtitle may have helped to set Shakespeare off towards reflections on an island inhabited by 'spirits' – the more neutral word he uses in preference to 'devils' – rather than human beings. The fishiness of Caliban may owe something to Jourdain's praise of Bermuda's fish:

> fish there is so abundant, that if a man step into the water, they will come round about him; so that men were fain to get out for fear of biting . . . and infinite store

> of pilchards, with divers kindes of great fishes, the names of them unknown to me; of crayfishes very great ones . . .[27]

Although strictly speaking Prospero's island should be in the southern Mediterranean, it is generally agreed that Shakespeare drew on several recent sources that related to Atlantic islands, especially Bermuda; and also that Caliban owes something to Montaigne's account of the 'Cannibals' of Brazil. Such artistic licence is normal in romance; in *The Winter's Tale* the landlocked Bohemia acquires a sea-coast, and in *Cymbeline* Roman Britain seems to be connected with Renaissance Italy and its crafty Machiavels. One topical parallel to Prospero's banishment from Milan may be coincidental, though rumours of it could have been current in London. The navigator Henry Hudson, leading an expedition in search of the North-West Passage into that vast Bay that bears his name, provoked a mutiny. On 23 June 1611 his crew sent him off into the ice floes in a small boat, together with his son and seven others. Nothing more was ever heard of them.

But *The Tempest* also has deep theatrical roots. The name Prospero, suggesting (in Italian) 'one who is lucky, prosperous', was one that Shakespeare knew well from Jonson's *Every Man In his Humour*, in which he had acted in 1598. But in applying it to a bookish magus he was looking back to one of the plays most celebrated in his own earliest years in London: Marlowe's *Doctor Faustus*, for the name Faustus, too, signifies (in Latin) – 'lucky, prosperous'. In both plays considerable irony attaches to the idea that a man who can command spirits has been designated 'lucky', and in both a strict time limit is set to this apparent 'luck'. After twenty-four years the necromancer Faustus is dragged off to hell and everlasting damnation; Prospero, ostensibly a practitioner of 'white magic', enjoys only twelve years of power. It may be significant that this is exactly half the time allotted to Faustus. While Faustus promises only when it is too late – indeed, in the terrifying final line of the play – that 'I'll burn my books', Prospero, in a supreme act of self-mastery, voluntarily renounces his power:

> I'll break my staff,
> Bury it certain fathoms in the earth,
> And deeper than did ever plummet sound
> I'll drown my book.
>
> (*The Tempest*, 5.1.54–7)

Marlowe's play, in what is now known as the 'A-text', had been reprinted in 1609, which recalled it to the memory of older readers, while also making the text available to a generation too young to remember the glory days of Edward Alleyn's performances at the Rose. Since the printer was, once again, George

Eld, printer of the *Sonnets*, and the publisher was John Wright, one of the two booksellers advertised as selling the *Sonnets*, Shakespeare must have been well aware of this latest edition of *Doctor Faustus*, on display in Wright's shop by Christ Church, Newgate, alongside his own latest work, and probably commanding noticeably better sales.

While we are never left in much doubt that Faustus's pact with Lucifer is both foolish and damnable, Prospero's role is more ambiguous. But analogies to Marlowe's play become insistent in the final act, especially in Prospero's great summary of his past achievements (5.1.33–50), which draws on a celebrated and sinister speech by the witch Medea in Ovid's *Metamorphoses*. We discover with some shock that the magus Prospero, like Faustus in his summoning up of Helen and Alexander, has brought back the dead to life. But it seems that Shakespeare deliberately substitutes water for fire, suggesting that Prospero's ultimate destination is a redemptive 'sea change', rather than the flames of hell. His magic book is consigned to drowning rather than burning,[28] and in the Epilogue he pleads for the wind of applause to waft him safely back across the sea to Milan – or, more literally, back north across the Thames to the City of London. For Shakespeare's play, more explicitly even than Marlowe's, uses magic as a metaphor for theatrical spectacle.

Prospero's island, on which he has a store of '*glistering apparel*' (4.1.193 stage direction), many 'twangling instruments' (3.2.137), and such elaborate props as animal heads, artificial wings and a fake banquet, is obviously an image of the playhouse and its backstage equipment. More valuable even than these props and costumes are the island's resident personnel, led by the 'tricksy Ariel', who can flame, fly, swim and dance at his master's command, at various points representing an avenging angel, a harpy, a musician, an invisible trickster and finally 'a nymph of the sea'. Though modern productions can rarely suggest this, *The Tempest* is the nearest Shakespeare ever came to framing a play for boys rather than men. It is this unusually large and technically accomplished troupe of boy players whose combined activities express the magicality of the island. While accounts of Sir Thomas Gates's shipwreck on Bermuda indicate that there were women and children on board,[29] the shipwrecked wedding guests in Shakespeare's play are all adult males. It is only on the island that a single girl (Miranda), and many 'spirits', all roles to be presented by boys, are to be encountered. In theatrical terms, it is rather as if the King's Men have arrived at the Blackfriars playhouse (or the Banqueting House at Whitehall, where the play was performed on 1 November 1611) to find it already in the possession of a children's company – perhaps the Children of the Queen's Revels, who had received a new patent in January 1610.[30] Though Prospero explains to Ferdinand and Miranda that 'These our actors . . . were all spirits' (4.1.148–9), on a literal level it would be more accurate to say that 'these our so-called "spirits" were all boy actors'. In such scenes as that of the masque followed by a dance of reapers and nymphs as many as a dozen or more boys would be desirable. As Prospero says to Ariel, 'bring a corollary* / Rather than want a spirit' (4.1.57–8). In a wish-fulfilment dream of absolute control, it seems that Shakespeare / Prospero attempts to sustain, during the three hours of 'actual time' that the play enacts, a total mastery of theatrical illusion, which can only be achieved through the use of highly trained boys who are too young to challenge his authority. Even so, Prospero fears the slightest sign of resistance. Rather as children in this period were kept under control with constant chiding and threats of worse punishment, Prospero keeps exhorting Miranda to listen to his tale – 'I pray thee mark me' – 'Dost thou attend me?' – 'Thou attend'st not' – 'Dost thou hear?' (1.2). Most of all, Prospero fears desertion by the spirit Ariel, bonded to him, like a boy apprentice, for an agreed period of twelve years' service, and keeps him in order with violent threats. His schemes are vitally dependent on his slave's dazzling array of skills, and he is obsessed with the possibility that Ariel may abandon him before his projects are complete. The line between black magic and white is by no means clearly drawn here. Ariel's prolonged bondage to Prospero is not founded on any promise of reward or payment, but simply on his gratitude for being liberated from the pine-tree in which Prospero found him imprisoned by the witch Sycorax; nor is there any suggestion that Ariel can ever become a master magician.[31] And Prospero, supposedly the more civilized employer, threatens Ariel with exactly the same torment that he received from Sycorax:

> If thou more murmur'st, I will rend an oak,
> And peg thee in his knotty entrails till
> Thou hast howled away twelve winters.
>
> (1.2.294–6)

In practice, however, the serious threats to Prospero's power come from clod-hopping men, not dainty boys. Like Faustus, he is plotted against by a servant, the 'demi-devil' Caliban. Caliban's 'foul conspiracy' with Stephano and Trinculo, combined with the growing weakness of his master's 'old brain', nearly spoils everything. Many of the shipwrecked noblemen, likewise, are strongly resistant to Prospero's attempts at control, most notably his usurper brother Antonio, who fails to express penitence, thus rendering the whole scheme of punishment and forgiveness rather pointless.

The Tempest offers the spectacle of an old man of huge but failing power – 'Bear with my weakness; my old brain is troubled' (4.1.159)[32] – manipulating the skills of boys, or 'spirits'. For a while it seems that these highly trained children,

* 'corollary': surplus.

rather like outstanding young gymnasts, musicians or dancers today, can do almost anything. Yet the brilliance of their displays is suffused with a sense of its innate fragility. At the very point when a boy performer came to his peak he also approached the onset of puberty, from which there could be no turning back. These 'spirits', or boy players, present a constant reminder of mutability. Though they may appear to triumph over both temporal and physical constraints, through their beauty, suppleness and performative energy, a non-negotiable time limit is set both to their contractual obligation to their adult masters, and to their own capacity to transcend the ageing process. That strange poem numbered 126, perhaps written shortly before the publication of the *Sonnets*, explores this same paradox, and the way in which a beautiful boy may appear – yet delusively – to extend both his own life and that of the older man who loves him:

> O thou my lovely Boy, who in thy power
> Dost hold time's fickle glass, his sickle hour,
> Who hast by waning grown, and therein show'st
> Thy lover's withering, as thy sweet self grow'st . . .

In the play, Prospero appears to love his 'delicate Ariel' (4.1.49) far more tenderly than he does his daughter, or his old friends or his dull son-in-law. Having bid farewell to Ariel in the final line of the play, he stands front stage in the Epilogue as a vulnerable and dying old man in ordinary clothes: 'Now I want, / Spirits to enforce, arts to enchant'. Whatever the actual nature of Shakespeare's position among the King's Men in 1611 – whether his poetic throne was indeed being usurped, or legitimately assumed, by younger dramatists – *The Tempest* certainly seems like a farewell to power. And as in the closing 'fair youth' poem of the *Sonnets*, loss of power is expressed in terms of the ending of a relationship with a 'lovely Boy'. As Shakespeare's public literary career had opened with an exploration of doomed love for a 'tender boy' (Adonis), so it closed.[33]

O HOW FULL OF BRIERS IS THIS WORKING-DAY WORLD![34]

There is no doubt that Shakespeare was now a leading court playwright. *The Tempest* and *The Winter's Tale*, both performed at Whitehall at Hallowmas (early November) 1611, were to be called for once again at the splendid celebrations surrounding the marriage of Princess Elizabeth to the Elector Palatine in February 1613. *Othello* and *Much Ado about Nothing* were also among the fourteen plays performed by the King's Men at this time. The reward of £153 6*s.* 8*d.* given to the company was the best they had ever received. Though never invited to write a court masque, Shakespeare could nevertheless view himself as the poet whose work was most sought after and admired by courtiers. Yet there was still much of his life – the greater part, indeed – that was led away from court, and there was, as always, much wearisome business to tax his failing spirits. His pursuit of the obscure John Addenbrooke for a debt of £6 plus 24*s.* in 1609 has already been mentioned. In the seventh and last surviving document relating to this case Shakespeare is described as '*generosus, nuper in curia domini Jacobi, nunc regis Angliae*' – 'a gentleman, lately in the court of the lord James, now King of England'. This pompous phrase suggests an attempt by Shakespeare's attorney, perhaps at the prompting of Thomas Greene, who at that time lodged in New Place, to 'pull rank' on his client's behalf, in order to secure the sum owed. Legally, this was effective; the jury found for Shakespeare. But Addenbrooke himself had fled the borough, and it is unlikely that the money was ever recovered. Such surviving records as those of the 'Addenbrooke case' – we can assume that records of many similar legal and financial negotiations have disappeared – chronicle vexations from which Shakespeare was never to be free. His status as a King's Man could not insulate him against difficulties with money, property and family. Like most men of property in this period he was frequently involved in litigation, and like others he often experienced both 'the law's delay' and the law's frequent incapacity to deliver a clear or just outcome. Uncertainty about the wealthy landowner William Combe's threat to 'enclose' large parts of farmland in and around Stratford, possibly jeopardizing Shakespeare's major investment in tithe income, was to persist to his dying day. Some affairs at least offered the promise of personal advantage. For instance, in September 1611 he contributed, along with seventy other citizens of Stratford, to the legal expenses of a proposed Highways Bill.[34] Had this been successful, the state would have become responsible for the maintenance of major highways, an obvious benefit to regular commuters between Stratford and London.

Of Shakespeare's non-courtly activities in this period, by far the best-documented is the 'Belott–Mountjoy suit' of 1612. In this affair, Shakespeare stood to gain nothing personally. Indeed, he must have resented the time taken up by his enforced appearance at the Court of Requests on 11 May 1612, as well as the reminders the case offered of his period as an associate of George Wilkins (see above, chapter 8). Shakespeare was the key witness – the initial summons was to 'William Shakespeare gentleman and others' – for it was both in his presence and as a result of his friendly intervention in 'many conferences' that Stephen Belott and the younger Marie Mountjoy plighted their troth in the autumn of 1604, marrying on 19 November. From the outset, this marriage had much to do with money and property, little with romantic love or attraction. The depositions make it plain that Christopher Mountjoy had always been a grudging master to his 'good and industrious servant' Stephen. Shakespeare was among several witnesses who remembered Stephen Belott saying that he had not obtained 'any great profit and commodity by the service'. I wonder whether he saw any parallels here to the unpaid service exacted from Ariel over many years by the autocratic Prospero. The marriage seems to have been a contrivance of Mme Mountjoy's both to secure a reliable husband for Marie, and to ensure that some of her husband's considerable wealth and property came into the hands of his former apprentice, who had clearly earned it. With the death of Mme Mountjoy in October 1606, the young people lost their champion. For a while they moved back into the house in Silver Street, becoming partners to the widower; but things didn't work out, either financially or professionally, and Mountjoy 'sank into dissipation'.[36] The object of the 1612 suit was for Stephen Belott to secure from his now alienated father-in-law the substantial sum of money that he believed had long been due to his wife and himself. The most depressing aspect of the case is the picture it presents of a father who had no affection for his only legitimate child, and no concern for her material welfare. Perhaps Christopher Mountjoy cared more for his two children born out of wedlock than he did for Marie,[37] or perhaps he simply was a mean, overbearing and self-willed man. At one point he had been heard to exclaim that 'he would rather rot in prison than give them any thing more than he had given them before'.[38] His nature may have been soured by his early experiences as a refugee from the massacres of Protestants in France in 1572, followed by a long struggle to establish himself legally as a 'denizen', or naturalized alien, in London.

All that he had given the young Belotts, it was claimed, was a pitifully threadbare collection of 'household stuff'. Even allowing for some exaggeration on the part of the plaintiff, it is clear that Mountjoy was not lavish with his daughter's marriage portion. Certainly he had not gone out shopping for wedding presents. She embarked on married life with an old feather bed and old feather bolster, together with 'a thin green rug, two ordinary blankets woven, two pair of sheets'; her sticks of furniture and useful articles included 'an old drawing table, two old joint stools . . . two pair of little scissors . . . one bobbin box'. As a master tire-maker of considerable wealth Mountjoy surely possessed a great deal of sewing equipment; those two small pairs of scissors sound like a couple of workshop tools that he would hardly miss. Like several other witnesses, Shakespeare had no comment to make either on the composition or on the overall value of these gifts in kind, which were all the dowry that had ever been delivered. Like other witnesses, too, he could not recall what specific sum of money – if any – his landlord had promised to his daughter by way of dowry, 'nor knoweth that the defendant promised the plaintiff £200 with his daughter Mary at the time of his decease'. Though

Schoenbaum says that on this crucial point 'Shakespeare's memory faltered', it could be that he was fairly certain that no specific sums of money ever had been promised, but did not wish to compromise his young friend Belott's prospects of winning the case by saying so. George Wilkins, who gave testimony at the second hearing, on 19 June, was at least rather more forthcoming on the matter of the 'household stuff'. When they came to lodge with him they brought 'a few goods' with them for which he 'would not have given above five pounds if he had been to have bought the same'.

By the time of this second hearing Shakespeare may have been away in Stratford, seeing to his family and financial affairs in the aftermath of the sad death of his brother Gilbert in February. A marginal note 'William Shakespeare' beside the fourth set of questions to be put to witnesses on 19 June associates him with the 'motion of marriage', but this time he was evidently not present. At a third hearing on 23 June witnesses testified for Mountjoy. No-one on either side supported Belott's claim that a dowry as large as £60 had ever been promised, and most witnesses were, like Shakespeare, quite vague on the whole matter. The Court of Requests referred the case on to the Elders of the French Church, who ordered Mountjoy to pay his son-in-law the relatively modest sum of twenty nobles – £6 13*s.* 4*d.* – which, however, he failed to do.[39] Whether Shakespeare took any further interest in the welfare of the young Belotts, whose marriage he had brokered on the strength of what was evidently an unreliable promise of a good financial settlement, we don't know.

The chief interest of the Belott–Mountjoy suit lies in the picture it presents of Shakespeare in a humdrum setting, among men and women of middling rank. On 11 May he probably sat through the deposition of Joan Johnson, the forty-year-old wife of a basket-maker, who signed her deposition with a mark, as well as that of Daniel Nicholas, an old friend of Belott's stepfather, who signed in a neat italic script. Joan Johnson had been a servant in the Mountjoys' house, and may often have waited on their lodger Shakespeare. She recalled that there had been a 'show of good will' between the young people, and that 'one Master Shakespeare that lay in the house' had been drawn into the affair by Mountjoy. She also remembered talk 'in the house' of a sum of £50, but didn't know whether this was to take the form of a dowry or a legacy. The value she set on the couple's 'household stuff' was £8. Daniel Nicholas, a gentleman of the parish of St Alphage, whose father had been Lord Mayor of London and a benefactor to the neighbourhood, was not dependent on servants' hall gossip. He had talked with Shakespeare in person about Belott's good work for Mountjoy, and about the marriage plans. He had been closely implicated in the affair, having gone to see Shakespeare on Belott's behalf to ask about the likely size of the marriage portion – 'about the sum of fifty pounds', he thought – on the strength of which the marriage took place. One odd discrepancy suggests the general fallibility of written records of oral depositions. On 11 May Daniel Nicholas was described as aged fifty-two, while on 19 June he was sixty-two. At the second hearing Nicholas testified that it was in Shakespeare's presence that the young couple were 'made sure', or bindingly betrothed. He also reported a conversation with 'one George Wilkins' about 'some implements' of little worth that Wilkins had housed after the marriage.

The Belott–Mountjoy depositions map out a social network that connects two playwrights, Shakespeare and Wilkins, both with the highly respectable citizen Daniel Nicholas and with the bloody-minded but prosperous tire-maker Christopher Mountjoy. Another major person of the drama was Humphrey Fludd, a King's trumpeter, who was Belott's stepfather, and had often bought clothes for him. He was probably known to Shakespeare professionally as one of the large number of musicians required in the performance of his own late plays.[40] Indeed, it may have been Fludd who first brought Shakespeare into the Silver Street household as a lodger, as he had brought his stepson Stephen. Yet it is difficult to know what larger conclusions to draw from the whole affair. As we might well have guessed, Shakespeare proves to have had a wide and varied acquaintance in London, some of whom had direct or peripheral connections with the King's Men, and some not. What he really felt about any of these individuals, except that he was on terms of some intimacy with young Stephen Belott, we cannot tell. Still less can we tell what any of them felt about him, except that they regarded him as reliable and approachable. In the end, perhaps, all the case does is add contemporary reinforcement to Jonson's much later description of 'our fellow countryman Shakespeare': 'He was (indeed) honest, and of an open and free nature'.[41] In echoing Iago's comments on *Othello* – 'The Moor is of a free and open nature / That thinks men honest that but seem to be so' (1.3.398–9) – Jonson hinted that Shakespeare, like Othello, was gullible, and could be taken in by appearance. He had perhaps been taken in by Mountjoy, whom he trusted to treat young Stephen as generously as he deserved, promoting the marriage to Mountjoy's daughter on this false assumption. Likewise, he had trusted his collaborator George Wilkins, who had also turned out to be a self-interested opportunist of no integrity. While Jonson in his plays presents men who are too open and trusting as 'gulls', Shakespeare's treatment is far more sympathetic. The 'free and open' Othello is not entirely to blame for trusting the seemingly honest Iago, and King Duncan is positively saintly in his belief that he will be kindly entertained in Macbeth's castle. A late example of a too trusting man who lives to reflect on his mistake is Cymbeline, who admits that he was deceived by his wife's beauty and flattery, and justifies himself nevertheless: 'It had been vicious / To have mistrusted her' (*Cymbeline*, 5.5.65–6).

Whether Shakespeare, likewise, felt justified in having at one time put faith in his landlord Christopher Mountjoy the documents do not tell us. Still less can we judge whether he felt foolish for having often lent money to unreliable borrowers. Reminders of his own mistaken judgements of the past may have blighted his final years. Yet it continued to be the case that all major business agreements had to be founded to some extent on trust. It's possible, however, that after many 'working-day' disappointments and frustrations, the older Shakespeare became increasingly cautious, and reliant on his attorneys to stop all possible loop-holes. We may find indications of this in both of the last two major enterprises of his life, his purchase of the Blackfriars gatehouse, to be discussed shortly, and his will, to be discussed in the final chapter. Sweet Master Shakespeare was deteriorating into a bitter, wary, 'ungentle' man, no longer the 'open' and 'free' character praised by Jonson.

Candle-rents

Among men of property in this period the prevailing view was that the most reliable form of investment was the purchase of land. On balance, despite the variability of harvests, productive farmland offered a good yearly return. Possession of it also enhanced an individual's status. If a man's country estates dwindled, like those of the prodigal Husband in *A Yorkshire Tragedy*, so proportionately did his standing. In the course of fifteen years or so Shakespeare's estates, conversely, had greatly expanded. As we have seen, he made substantial investments in land from 1602 onwards, and also purchased a large holding in tithe income from land owned by others. To his substantial gentleman's residence, New Place, the good-sized Henley Street house had been added by inheritance on his father's death, and he had also acquired, by purchase, a cottage on the south side of Chapel Lane. His daughter's marriage had added to the family's empire John Hall's houses and lands both in Stratford and in Acton, the latter a convenient stopping point on the journey between Stratford and London. Such property both provided seemly residences for Shakespeare and his family and kept their collective profile high in Warwickshire.

For men of lesser status than court magnates, London property was much less desirable. While a man like Robert Cecil might adorn and furnish his great house in the Strand, as well as rebuilding Hatfield in Hertfordshire, lesser gentry generally chose, as Shakespeare did until 1613, to build up estates in the country. The poet and antiquary Hugh Holland, discussed in chapter 7, offers a counter-example. He had hoped for appointment to a major court office, such as that of Clerk to the Privy Council, or else a lucrative and high-profile post as a Herald. Failing in these ambitions, according to Thomas Fuller, he was compelled to subsist on 'a competent estate in good candle-rents in

London'. 'Candle-rent', according to the *OED*, was 'rent or revenue derived from house-property (which is continually undergoing deterioration or waste)'. While the value of farmland kept up with the current prices of grain and livestock, house property in London was a notoriously fragile investment. This is illustrated in Chapman's comedy *May-Day* (printed 1611). The foolish youth Innocentio is easily persuaded by the worldly-wise Quintiliano to sell off his 'row of houses':

> QUINTILIANO Let 'em walk, let 'em walk; candle-rents: if the wars hold, or a plague come to town, they'll be worth nothing.
>
> INNOCENTIO True, or while I am beyond sea, some sleepy wench may set fire i'th'bed-straw.

Like a candle burning down to its stump, a London house could diminish in value almost moment by moment; and a literally burning candle could destroy it entirely. Fire insurance had yet to be invented.

Nevertheless, on 10 March 1613 Shakespeare made his own major investment in 'candle-rents'. Along with three co-purchasers, who were in practice trustees, he acquired the substantial property known as the Blackfriars gatehouse. Built above the strongly built eastern gate of the thick-stone-walled Dominican priory, it was not at so much risk of destruction as Innocentio's rows of modern townhouses. This great gate had originally led to the Prior's lodging, surely the grandest part of this extremely grand monastic complex. A good-sized plot of land called Ireland's Yard came with it, named after a haberdasher called William Ireland who had rented it from the previous owner of the gatehouse, Henry Walker, 'citizen and minstrel of London'. Though Schoenbaum and others have doubted whether Shakespeare ever intended to live in the property, its location strongly suggests that he must have done. It was opposite the King's Wardrobe, and within yards of the wharf called Puddle Dock, from which a barge would take him almost in a straight line across the Thames to the Globe Theatre. Other features were even more attractive. It was only 'a couple of hundred yards from the winter playhouse of the King's Men'[42] – and perhaps Shakespeare saw the upmarket Blackfriars Theatre as his chief source of theatrical income from now on, plague permitting. Even better, if possible, was the gatehouse's proximity to Baynard's Castle, the palatial London residence of the Earls of Pembroke (Fig. 40). On the western side stood the Temple and Inns of Court, which continued to furnish an excellent supply of young theatregoers.

Two points have persuaded previous biographers that Shakespeare neither lived there nor intended to live there. The first is that by the time of his death it was occupied by 'one John Robinson'. Yet the deed of purchase makes it clear that the property was quite big enough to allow Shakespeare to retain or rent back several rooms for his own use, if Robinson was a tenant, and I find it

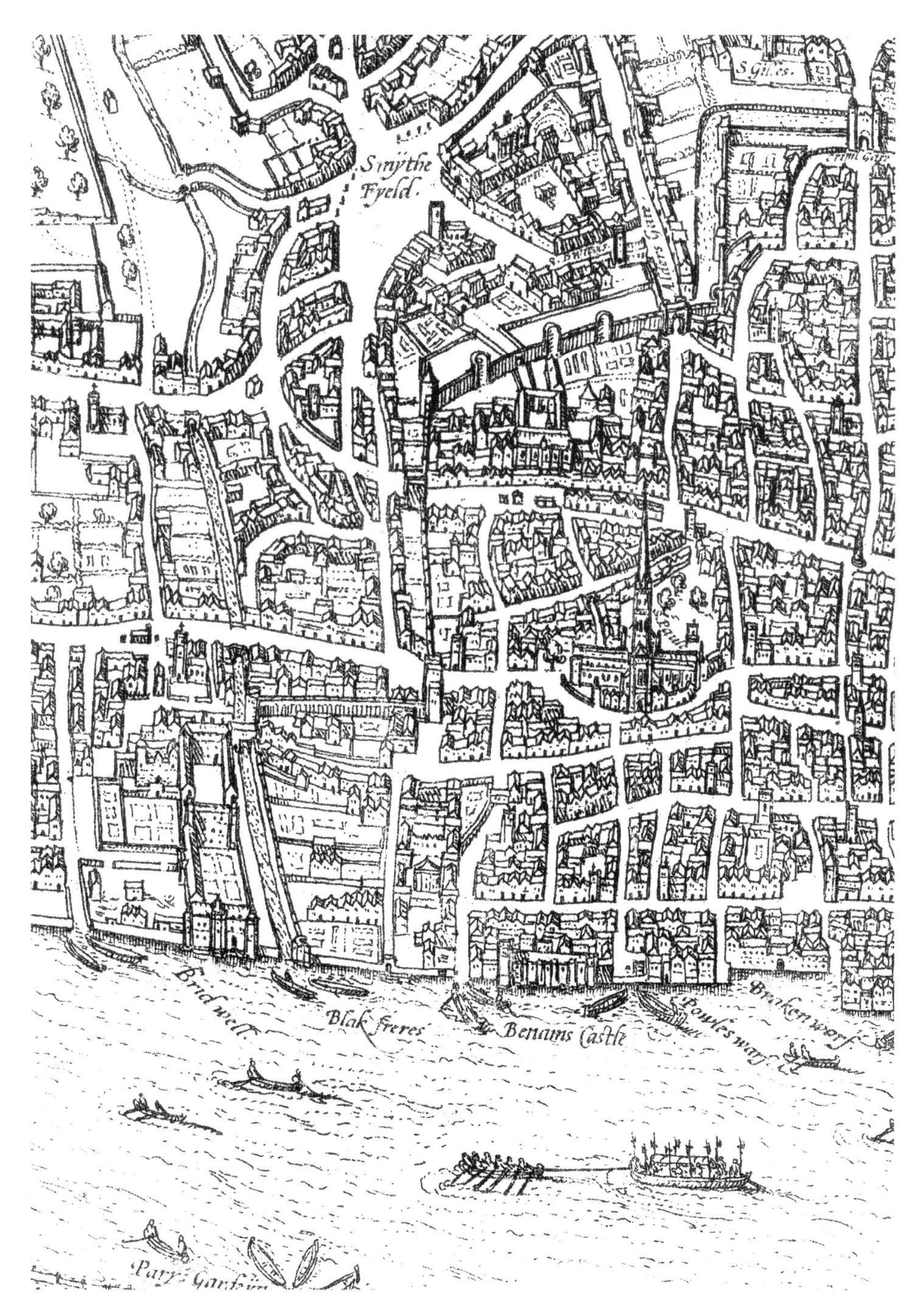

Fig. 40 Part of the City of London, showing the Blackfriars complex and Baynards Castle on the bank of the Thames, from Braun and Hoogenborg map (*c.* 1575).

unlikely that he would not have done so. But in any case, as Park Honan suggests,[43] John Robinson was probably Shakespeare's servant or steward, rather than his tenant. The second is the description of Shakespeare as 'of Stratford-upon-Avon in the County of Warwick gentleman', which has been read as implying that Stratford, not London, was where he now resided. But this formula simply identifies an individual through his place of origin. John of Gaunt, for instance, was 'of Gaunt' only in the sense that he was born there. In Shakespeare's case, as we have seen, there was a good deal more to it than this; property in his native Stratford underpinned his now established status as a 'gentleman'. This status, in turn, validated his credit-worthiness, which was important, since £60 of the purchase price of £140 was on mortgage, and remained so at the time of his death. But the phrase 'of Stratford' does not necessarily tell us anything about where he planned to spend his remaining years. It is unlikely that he did not hope to spend at least part of each year at this excellent address in London. Drawing attention to his newly elevated status, Ben Jonson proudly signed the Epistle to *Volpone* in 1607 'From my house in Blackfriars'; he was still living there in 1616. The Burbage family had been acquiring major parts of the former conventual buildings ever since 1576. By 1614, when the brothers Cuthbert and Richard Burbage purchased a tenement formerly occupied by Christopher Fenton, 'the Burbages had practically the whole of the ground lying west of the theatre to Water Lane'.[44] This was the best possible area in London for a King's Man, and I cannot doubt that some of the time in 1613–15 Shakespeare did live there.

I have suggested in earlier chapters that for most of his professional life in London Shakespeare led a peripatetic life in bachelor lodgings, sometimes south of the Thames, sometimes north. Though he might get caught up in other people's family lives in London, as he did in brokering Stephen Belott's marriage, he put down no family roots of his own. There is no reason to think that Anne or the children visited him in London, though Susanna may have done so after she became Mrs Hall. It was the Halls who were to inherit the gatehouse. However, there is a sense in which the gatehouse, too, was not domestic. Its curiously complex purchase, by a panel of four trustees, had the effect of excluding Shakespeare's wife from any claim on it should she outlive him. Although Schoenbaum questions it, I am inclined to endorse Sidney Lee's comment that 'Such procedure is pretty conclusive proof that he had the intention of excluding her from the enjoyment of his possessions after his death'.[45] It may have been to the gatehouse that a servant of the new Earl of Rutland came with a request to Shakespeare to devise an *impresa* for the Accession Day tilt of 24 March 1613. Shakespeare was paid 44 shillings 'in gold' for the design, Burbage the same amount 'for painting and making it'.[46] Unfortunately we do not know the details of the Shakespeare-Burbage *impresa*, though it may later have been publicly displayed, as many others were, in the Shield Gallery at Whitehall.[47] Francis Manners, sixth Earl of Rutland, succeeded his brother Roger, who died, possibly of venereal disease, in June 1612. Francis was a lively young man and an enthusiastic courtier, who first entertained the King at Belvoir Castle in August 1612, as an eyewitness reported:

> His Majesty is at Belvoir Castle, where the Prince meets him before he come to Sherwood Forest. It is thought that the new Earl of Rutland shall entertain his Majesty, for my Lord that last was is lately dead at Cambridge. This young gentleman is very well liked by the greatest number and best sort of people here.[48]

Young Rutland's employment of Burbage and Shakespeare to further his own budding career as a courtier is a clear indication of the high profile of these two leading King's Men, both now possessed of substantial Blackfriars property. He was clearly satisfied with their work, for Burbage was paid handsomely for painting another *impresa* in the year of Shakespeare's death.

Everything connects the gatehouse purchase with Shakespeare's social and professional life in London. The first-named of his three co-purchasers, William Johnson, was the affable host of the Mermaid Tavern in Bread Street. Though gatherings of 'wits' at the Mermaid may have been over-mythologized, there is plenty of contemporary evidence that such meetings really happened. The best evidence is to be found in Francis Beaumont's epistle to Ben Jonson from the country, which may belong to the very year, 1613, in which Shakespeare purchased the gatehouse:

> What things have we seen
> Done at the Mermaid! heard words that have been
> So nimble, and so full of subtle flame,
> As if that every one from whom they came
> Had meant to put his whole wit in a jest . . .[49]

It was also from the Mermaid that Jonson promised to procure 'a pure cup of rich Canary wine' in his poem 'Inviting a friend to supper',[50] and it was after dining too well 'At Bread Street's Mermaid' that two knights decide to take a boat up the running sewer that was the Fleet Ditch in Jonson's mock-heroic poem 'The Famous Voyage'.[51] In 1616 the comic traveller Thomas Coryate addressed a letter from India to the 'Worshipful Fraternity of Sirenaical' gentlemen, otherwise 'Mermaid-ical', who meet at the tavern on the first Friday of every month. Whether or not meetings of writers there were quite so regular as Coryate's address to them suggests, there is no reason to doubt that they did happen, nor that Shakespeare was sometimes present. Not only did Shakespeare involve the Mermaid's host closely in his last and most ambitious investment, the second of his co-purchasers, John Jackson, was also one of

Thomas Coryate's 'Sirenaical' brothers, and also associated with the wine trade. Leslie Hotson identified him as a freeman of the East India Company, and lessee of 'all the duties on wines from Spain, Portugal, Candia, and parts of Levant' brought into eastern ports, including Jackson's native Hull.[52] Jackson contributed a poem arranged in the shape of an egg to *Coryat's Crudities* (1611), in which he thoroughly entered into Coryate's conceit of his travel book as a mess (or meal) of undigested food:

> Thy hungry praises in this Egg I sing
> At thy request, else in another fashion
> I would have pointed at thy commendation:
> Thy other Heliconian friends bring store
> Of salt, of pepper, and vinegar sour
> To furnish thy Italian banquet forth ...

I have suggested earlier that some of Shakespeare's associates were competent versifiers rather than major poets – men like Richard Barnfield, or Shakespeare's cousin Thomas Greene or Sir John Salusbury. John Jackson, investor in wine imports, can be added to the list. The third and last of Shakespeare's co-purchasers is a more familiar figure: the actor and theatrical share-holder John Heminge, who had been his friend and colleague for at least a quarter of a century. Heminge was a particularly practical, level-headed and loyal man, who was prepared to devote a great deal of energy to safeguarding the property of his colleagues.[53]

We may assume that the purchase of the gatehouse was celebrated with a festive 'drinking' by the four co-purchasers, either at the gatehouse itself, or round the corner in a private room at the Mermaid. These four middle-aged men of property were far too prudent to include fireworks in their party. Nevertheless, it was fire that dealt a terrible blow to Shakespeare and his colleagues. As Globe sharers, they were soon to discover that the investment they had made in 1599 was indeed a 'candle-rent'.

PLAYING WITH FIRE

It may have been at the Blackfriars gatehouse, in the high spring of 1613, that Shakespeare and Fletcher wrote *Henry VIII*, as it is called in the First Folio. Contemporary allusions show that it was performed at the Globe that June under the title *All is True*. In many respects the play is old-fashioned and backward-looking, as suited events now nearly a century old. It presents a sequence of medieval-seeming rise-and-fall tragedies of great persons: first Buckingham, then Katherine of Aragon and finally Wolsey fall from royal favour – showing, as the Prologue puts it, 'How soon this mightiness meets misery'. Only Archbishop Cranmer is rescued from imprisonment by the King, and is confidently in the ascendant at the end of the play. But the audience were well aware that he, too, was to suffer a spectacular fall from glory, being burnt at the stake by Mary Tudor in 1556. The ecclesiastical theme of this play – its enactment of England's break from papal authority as a defining stage in her history – was particularly well suited to the instincts and knowledge of Fletcher, son of a senior Anglican bishop.

Shakespeare's contribution was to give emotional and dramatic complexity to what could easily have been a predictable pageant of Protestant triumphalism.[54] Rather as, in *Macbeth*, he had explored the consciousness of an evil usurper with such depth as to risk diverting sympathy from the King's own forebears, so, here, in a play whose climax is the birth of Anne Boleyn's child, the 'maiden phoenix' Elizabeth, he nevertheless gave extraordinary depth and strength to the rejected Katherine of Aragon. The scene of Katherine's trial seems to have been strongly influenced by that of the arraignment of Vittoria in John Webster's *The White Devil*, performed at the Red Bull in 1612. In both scenes a vulnerable woman boldly confronts hostile prelates and lawyers, challenges their use of Latin and of arcane legal terms, and wins her case, theatrically if not legally. Katherine's gentle but stubborn defiance of the grossly overweening Cardinal Wolsey was bound to win her much audience sympathy, as did Vittoria's of Cardinal Monticelso. Her plight is explored further in the next scene (3.1), which echoes the 'moated grange' scene in Shakespeare's own *Measure for Measure* in showing a forsaken woman, all but wife, trying to snatch comfort from music. Katherine's repudiation, not just of the corrupt Wolsey, but of England itself, is both defamiliarizing and heartbreaking:

> Would I had never trod the English earth . . .
> Shipwrecked upon a kingdom where no pity,
> No friends, no hope, no kindred weep for me,
> Almost no grave allowed me, like the lily
> That once was mistress of the field and flourished,
> I'll hang my head and perish.
>
> (3.1.143–53)

It is a reflection of Shakespeare's myriad-minded artistic brilliance that he could give such dignity and eloquence to a neglected wife, given that he seems for many years to have neglected his own wife. However, if he had a real-life analogy in mind – and he need not have – it is more likely that he was thinking, not of his own wife, but of his former landlady Marie Mountjoy, who had been brought, like Katherine, from a foreign country to live in England, only to endure unhappy marriage to a man who valued neither her nor their daughter.

In a third major scene (4.2) Katherine, shortly before her death, hears news of the fall and death of her enemy Wolsey, which she receives with generous sympathy. As she listens to funereal music, she is blessed with a 'Vision' in which six white-robed 'Spirits of peace' dance for her and hold a garland above her head. As in *The Tempest*, a symbolic dance of 'spirits', performed by boy actors, is used to herald the close approach of someone's demise. But while the 'spirits' of Prospero's island partake of the moral ambivalence of Prospero himself, there is no doubt that this 'blessed troop' is composed of angels who summon the dying Queen to a celestial banquet. In an astonishing balancing act, Shakespeare and Fletcher had constructed a play about Henry VIII's divorce and break with Rome that could to some extent be enjoyed even by Catholics.

On the afternoon of 29 June 1613, however, the Globe's large audience had no opportunity to see the three fine scenes focused on Queen Katherine. A further feature of the play is its use of lavish, loud and dazzling spectacle, which gave the playhouse audience an 'authentic' taste of court ceremonial. Had the play been performed to the end they could have enjoyed such visually striking entrances as that of the 'KING *and others as masquers, habited like shepherds*' (1.4), or '. . . BUCKINGHAM *from his arraignment . . . the axe with the edge towards him*' (2.1), as well as the full ceremonial of Anne's coronation (4.1), and, at the end (5.4), that of the infant Elizabeth's christening. There was much work here for Humphrey Fludd and other royal trumpeters and musicians, players of cornets, hautboys and drums. But one witness, the former Venetian ambassador Henry Wotton, suggested that on this occasion the King's Men were carrying their mimicry of courtly splendour too far:

> The King's players had a new play, called *All is True* . . . which was set forth with many extraordinary circumstances of pomp and majesty, even to the matting of the stage; the Knights of the Order with their Georges and garters, the Guards with their embroidered coats, and the like; sufficient in truth within a while to make greatness very familiar, if not ridiculous.[55]

In the light of what followed, Wotton may have felt that this opulent display was the product of tragic hubris on the part of the King's servants, conducting themselves as if they were in truth the King's courtiers. The play's title, *All is True*, implied that their performance of the ceremonial of the Henrician court was not a fiction, but an authentic enactment.

The climax of Act 1 is the scene in which, at a revel at Cardinal Wolsey's house, Anne Boleyn is introduced to the King. The King's arrival at York Place was heralded not merely by '*Drum and trumpet*', but by '*chambers discharg'd*' –

Fig. 41 Small cannon of early seventeenth century (1630).

small cannons or cannon-like chambers stuffed with tinder and gunpowder (Fig. 41). The gunners stationed behind the theatre had presumably been instructed to fire upwards to avoid damage to life or property, and since the play had already been performed a couple of times without mishap they were skilled in doing so. But playing with fire is notoriously unwise, and this, in a literal sense, is what the King's Men were doing. As Wotton describes it:

> King Henry making a masque at the Cardinal Wolsey's house, and certain chambers being shot off at his entry, some of the paper, or other stuff, wherewith one of them was stuffed, did light on the thatch, where being thought at first but an idle smoke, and their eyes more attentive to the show, it kindled inwardly, and ran round like a train, consuming within less than an hour the whole house to the very grounds.

The unusual addition of matting to the stage ensured that the stage platform itself had no chance of surviving the conflagration. Miraculously, however, the theatre was evacuated with only a minor casualty – 'one man had his breeches set on fire, that would perhaps have broiled him, if he had not by the benefit of a provident wit put it out with bottle ale'.[56] This incident may have been more heroic than it sounds, for another reporter describes a man getting scorched while saving a child.[57] Otherwise, apart from the building itself, the only loss, according to Wotton, was 'a few forsaken cloaks' left behind by fleeing audience members. However, Wotton may not have known, any more than we do, quite what was lost from the tiring-house in the way of documents, including play-texts, prompt-books and actors' 'parts'. Andrew Gurr has suggested that the fact that the fire at least happened in broad daylight, unlike that at the Fortune in 1621, was providential, and that we owe the survival of eighteen Folio-only plays to the efficient salvage of King's Men play-books.[58] Yet equally, for all we know, others may have been lost.[59] Almost certainly, as the fire took hold, a certain number of trunks of costumes and deed-boxes of documents had to be abandoned. Even if we have lost none of Shakespeare's plays in that fire, we may well have lost John Heminge's account books and day-books, which, had they survived, would have been even more valuable than those of Philip Henslowe.

Shakespeare's Prospero had foreseen that in the course of time

> The cloud-capped towers, the gorgeous palaces,
> The solemn temples, the great globe itself,
> Yea, all which it inherit, shall dissolve . . .
>
> (*The Tempest*, 4.1.152–4)

On 29 June 1613 these words written only a couple of years earlier seemed eerily prophetic. Whereas Prospero had resolved to drown his book, Shakespeare now saw some of his books, or at least those of his colleagues, go up in flames. The fact that the fire broke out during a performance of one of his own plays would be enough to make even the least superstitious man tremble. Had he over-reached himself by practising the wrong kind of magic, aiming at a level of illusion that was permitted only to God? Certainly the play's title had been changed by 1623 to the more neutral *Henry VIII*. On a more mundane level, there was a huge financial loss to be met. Although a new Globe was built on the site almost at once, being finished in less than a year, each of the Globe sharers had to put up a substantial contribution of £50 or £60, which may eventually have risen to £100, towards the cost of this. Rather than commit himself to yet another risky investment in candle-rents, Shakespeare may at this point have sold off his Globe share. After making his positively last contribution as a King's Men playwright, to Fletcher's *The Two Noble Kinsmen*, a play perhaps written for performance at the Blackfriars playhouse in the winter of 1613/14, he may also have sold his Blackfriars share.[60] Certainly neither share was to figure in his will. While younger King's Men playwrights picked themselves up and started again, Shakespeare, increasingly tired and unwell, opted out. His theatrical revels were ended.

CHAPTER TEN

1614–16

His line of life

though his line of life went soon about,
The life yet of his lines shall never out.

(Hugh Holland, 'Upon the lines and life of the famous scenic poet Master William Shakespeare', First Folio, sig. A5^{r})

Cares and business

FROM Nicholas Rowe in 1709 to Samuel Schoenbaum in 1975, biographers have liked to imagine that at the end of his life Shakespeare enjoyed a period of bucolic retirement to Stratford. Now at last, they suggest, came his long-deferred opportunity to immerse himself in domesticity, gardening and playing with his grand-daughter. Schoenbaum both quotes and endorses Nicholas Rowe's claim:

> The latter part of his life was spent, as all men of good sense will wish theirs may be, in ease, retirement and the conversation of his friends . . . [he] is said to have spent some years before his death at his native Stratford.[1]

This myth, with William and Anne Shakespeare sentimentalized into a mellow Darby and Joan couple, has found expression more recently in Peter Whelan's play *The Herbal Bed*.[2] Yet the records of Shakespeare's final years, as E. A. J. Honigmann has pointed out, hardly support such a relaxed scenario. Nor does Gerard Johnson's Stratford monument, with its two naked boys up aloft representing 'Labour' and 'Rest'. Only death could bring true repose, and the right-hand boy rests his right hand on a skull (Fig. 43).

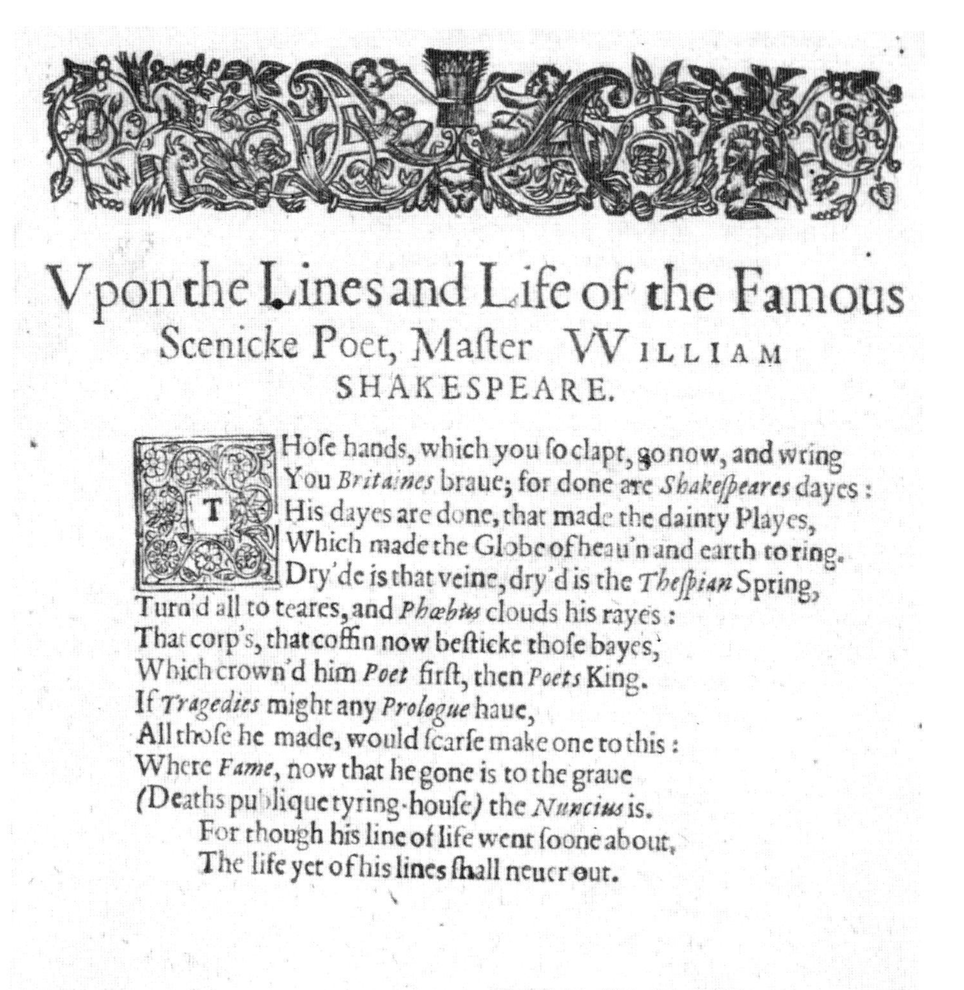

Vpon the Lines and Life of the Famous
Scenicke Poet, Maſter WILLIAM
SHAKESPEARE.

THoſe hands, which you ſo clapt, go now, and wring
You *Britaines* braue; for done are *Shakeſpeares* dayes:
His dayes are done, that made the dainty Playes,
Which made the Globe of heau'n and earth to ring.
Dry'de is that veine, dry'd is the *Theſpian* Spring,
Turn'd all to teares, and *Phœbus* clouds his rayes:
That corp's, that coffin now beſticke thoſe bayes,
Which crown'd him *Poet* firſt, then *Poets* King.
If *Tragedies* might any *Prologue* haue,
All thoſe he made, would ſcarſe make one to this:
Where *Fame*, now that he gone is to the graue
(Deaths publique tyring-houſe) the *Nuncius* is.
For though his line of life went ſoone about,
The life yet of his lines ſhall neuer out.

HVGH HOLLAND.

Fig. 42 Sonnet by Hugh Holland in the First Folio edition of Shakespeare's plays (1623).

Even if it was not quite 'business as usual' – for he had stopped writing plays, and was in process of selling his company and playhouse shares – Shakespeare's life continued to be moderately active, and continued also to be beset by the 'cares and business' of which the ageing King Lear had so unwisely tried to divest himself (*King Lear*, 1.1.38). As a man of considerable property and fame, he enjoyed a status which inevitably carried with it some 'cares'. He also regularly spent time in London. For instance, on Wednesday, 17 November 1614

Fig. 43 The top of the Shakespeare monument in Holy Trinity Stratford, showing two boys representing 'Labour', on the left, and 'Rest', on the right.

Thomas Greene, now solicitor for the Stratford Corporation, went to see his cousin Shakespeare, presumably at the Blackfriars gatehouse: 'my cousin Shakespeare . . . coming yesterday to town I went to see him how he did'.[3] The larger purpose of Greene's visit will be discussed shortly. But the immediate point suggested by Shakespeare's arrival in mid-November is that, like most men of substance, he needed to be in London during part of the law term, when litigation and other business could be dealt with. Michaelmas Term ended on 25 November, so arrival on the 16th gave him just over a week in which to attend to such matters. It should also be noted in passing that Greene's 1614–17 'diary' includes very few expressions of emotion. The remark that 'I went to see him how he did' suggests both that he felt particularly close to Shakespeare, and that there may have been some especial cause for concern about 'how he did'.

As Keith Thomas has shown, a period of unproductive retirement at the end of an individual's life was seldom viewed positively in the early modern period, even though certain civic duties could be declined by those over sixty.[4] Whether lowly artisans or eminent statesmen, old people were most admired when they continued to exercise their particular skill or office until close to death. This judgement can be seen broadly reflected in Shakespeare's own plays. King Lear makes a terrible blunder in seeking leisure and pleasure at the end of his life, while Prospero, though old and weary, rightly returns to Milan to die fully possessed of the dukedom from which he had been unjustly banished. Shakespeare's most explicit, even didactic, model of active old age is offered by Adam in *As You Like It*, who has worked hard and lived temperately all his life, and has saved the greater part of his wages against the infirmity of age. However, he is luckily not infirm:

> Though I look old, yet I am strong and lusty . . .
> Therefore my age is as a lusty winter,
> Frosty, but kindly.
>
> (2.3.47–53)

Though near eighty, he is determined to continue in his lifelong service to the De Boys family, putting both his money and bodily strength at the service of young Orlando.

Clearly, the exemplary model of old Adam was one that could scarcely ever be realized, especially in a period in which few individuals lived even beyond sixty, and those few who did, as we saw in the case of Brian Annesley (chapter 7), were often by no means 'strong and lusty'. Some seventeenth-century writers estimated that barely one in 500, or even one in 1,000, lived to be sixty.[5] In 1614 Shakespeare was only fifty, but had already outlived three younger brothers, one, Edmund, very much younger. Whatever genetic weaknesses predisposed male Shakespeares to die rather young were presumably shared by William. They may have been exacerbated rather than mitigated by his material success. As a man of considerable wealth he is likely to have indulged in the heavy diet of fat meat and sweet, or sweetened, wines habitual in his class. And if he was now spending longer periods in Stratford, he enjoyed greater access to the excellent veal and beef produced in the Forest of Arden.[6] His 'mountain belly' may by now have rivalled Ben Jonson's, making the three-day ride from Stratford to London increasingly uncomfortable.

Nevertheless, the rewards of winter residence in London were considerable. Not only could he see to his many business affairs; he could also look forward to witnessing new plays, both at the Blackfriars, and, from Christmas onwards, at court. At the Blackfriars he may have watched his good friend Burbage play the sinister psychopath Ferdinand in John Webster's *Duchess of Malfi*, a play riddled with echoes both of Sidney's *Arcadia* and of his own plays. The winter of 1614–15 was marked by a dozen or more performances by the King's Men at court, some for Prince Charles, some for the King.[7] Unfortunately their titles are not known, but it seems unlikely that the programme did not, as usual, include several of Shakespeare's own plays, and perhaps especially the still-new *Henry VIII*. This may have been an instance of all publicity being good publicity, the conflagration at the Globe making court audiences all the more eager for a chance to see the play 'through'. A tradition deriving from the Restoration theatre of William Davenant, who masterminded a revival of the play, suggests that Shakespeare may once have been closely involved in its performance:

> The part of the King was so right and justly done by Mr Betterton, he being instructed in it by Sir William [Davenant], who had it from old Mr Lowin, that had his instructions from Master Shakespeare himself, that I dare and will aver none can or will come near him in this age in the performance of that part.[8]

The exceptionally long-lived player John Lowin[9] should have been a reliable witness to Shakespeare's later activities among the King's Men. His reported testimony suggests that right up to the end of his career as a playwright, or even beyond, Shakespeare continued to be concerned with the performance of his plays as what would now be called a 'director'. Given his unique skill and experience, he may also have continued to 'instruct' leading actors in plays by other King's Men poets, such as Webster, Fletcher and Beaumont. Such 'business' was surely the kind of activity that came easily to him, even when ill and weary.

LOCAL DIFFICULTIES

Life in Stratford, though comfortable, was much less inspiriting. The visible prosperity of the Shakespeares – their extensive property holdings, their fine clothes, their altogether well-fed air – made them the mark of envy. Older inhabitants who remembered the former bailiff John Shakespeare's collapse into near bankruptcy may have viewed his son William as a mushroom gentleman. He had risen too far, too fast, and through a lightweight and morally dubious profession. While similar charges could be brought, analogously, against the actor and entrepreneur Edward Alleyn, his generosity in setting up charitable foundations in his chosen neighbourhood of Dulwich ensured that he was held in high regard there. In May 1613, for instance, he signed a contract for the erection of a school, a chapel and twelve alms-houses.[10] Citizens of Stratford, conversely, may have felt that the wealthy Shakespeares were doing far too little for the poor and homeless. The heads of the family also resolutely evaded civic responsibilities, although ownership of a house as large as New Place occasionally brought with it obligations that could not be dodged – at some time in 1614 a visiting preacher was entertained there with 20 pence worth of 'claret wines' paid for by the Corporation.[11] However, Shakespeare's son-in-law John Hall repeatedly refused to serve on the Corporation, and when eventually elected, paid fines rather than attend meetings. While we may admire his decision to give priority to attending his patients among the county gentry, at this time it was regarded as morally incumbent on men of education and standing to play their part in local government. A dislike of such time-consuming business may have formed one of the strongest bonds between son-in-law and father-in-law.

Shakespeare's witty elder daughter, Susanna, was also independent-minded. In May 1606 she was cited among twenty-two citizens of Stratford who had failed, in the dangerous aftermath of the Gunpowder Plot, to take Communion on Easter Day. Others included the Shakespeares' old friends and neighbours Hamnet and Judith Sadler. Whether Catholic sympathy or some other cause underlay Susanna's negligence we don't know. Her failure to appear to answer the charge in the vicar's court may indicate stubbornness, courage, indifference, or a mixture of all three. Rather than become subject to swingeing fines, she appears to have stepped in line. Marriage to the devoutly Protestant (though tolerant) John Hall a year later ensured that she never again neglected the required religious observance.[12] However, resplendent in her status as John Hall's wife and William Shakespeare's daughter, Susanna seems to have comported herself with considerable confidence and social freedom, refusing to play the part of a demure and silent matron. In mid-July 1613 – just at the time when her father was suffering the immediate trauma of the burning of the Globe – Susanna brought a case to the Bishop's Consistory Court in Worcester Cathedral. A wild and drunken young man called John Lane had slandered her 'about 5 weeks past' – that is, in early June – claiming that she 'had the running of the reins [kidneys] and had been naught with Rafe Smith at John Palmer' – that is, that she had conducted an adulterous affair, and was suffering from gonorrhoea. Susanna was represented in court by Robert Whatcott, who was to be one of the witnesses of her father's will; she won her case. Young Lane made a habit of speaking freely against authority figures, such as the Vicar and Aldermen. His onslaught on Susanna Hall suggests that she too was a figure of some standing in Stratford, and that she bore herself with a self-assurance that excited disapproval.

If the 'running of the reins' allegation is more than wild abuse – for it was standard practice to insult women in these terms – it may reflect misunderstanding of some gynaecological disorder. Susanna's daughter had been born in February 1608, and there seem to have been no further pregnancies. Gossip emanating from servants in the Halls' house could suggest that she was undergoing treatment for infertility that was misconstrued as treatment for venereal disease, especially since John Hall often made use of the New World bark called 'guiacum' originally imported as a treatment for syphilis.[13] In 1615, for instance, Hall treated a young woman in Shipston-on-Stour for 'uterine flux' with a pill containing guiacum resin.[14] If such treatment led to small-town abuse rather than sympathy, the Halls had every reason to feel indignant. For Susanna Hall's father, the lack of further grandchildren, and in particular of a son who could have become his chief heir, must have been a severe disappointment. Though he made formulaic provision in his will for a succession of up to seven 'heirs male . . . lawfully issuing' from Susanna, he was probably sadly aware that this was an unlikely prospect. The best that could be hoped for in the remote future was that his grand-daughter Elizabeth might turn out to be more fertile.[15]

The best documented affair impingeing on Shakespeare's life in Stratford in 1614–16 is the controversy concerning the 'Welcombe enclosures'.[16] Thomas Greene's visit to him in London on 17 November 1614, already mentioned, had to do with this. The major Stratford landowner William Combe, whose father and namesake had died in 1610, was proposing to 'enclose' parts of his lands in Old Stratford and Welcombe – that is, to surround them with ditches and hedges, turning them over to sheep, increasingly profitable because of the great demand for English wool. As Joan Thirsk explains, 'To enclose land was to extinguish common rights over it, thus putting an end to all common grazing.'[17] The process of enclosure had been going on piecemeal all over England since the late middle ages. It was discussed satirically by Thomas More in *Utopia*, where Raphael Hythloday reports on it as one of the abuses of England's government:

> Your sheep . . . that commonly are so meek, and eat so little; now, as I hear, they have become so greedy and fierce that they devour men themselves. They devastate and depopulate fields, houses and towns. For in whatever parts of the land sheep yield the finest and the noblest wool, there the nobility and gentry, yes, and even some abbots though otherwise holy men, are not content with the old rents that the land yielded to their predecessors.[18]

If there was insufficient common land remaining, enclosure led inevitably to poverty and depopulation. But while the passage in *Utopia* presents enclosure as an unmitigated evil, not everyone saw it that way. Landowners, of course, enjoyed much higher profits, and some would argue that in the long term these benefited the whole community. John Norden estimated that an enclosed acre was worth half as much again as one of land held in common; others put the difference even higher.[19] Both Shakespeare and Greene were potentially affected by Combe's plans, for both had substantial investments in tithe income. However, they seem to have held opposing positions. While Greene devoted a huge amount of energy and legal expertise to opposing Combe's plans to enclose, his repeated attempts to secure support from his eminent cousin failed. On 17 November Shakespeare tried to reassure him:

> he told me that they assured him they meant to enclose no further than to Gospel bush and so up straight (leaving out part of the dingles to the field) to the gate in Clopton hedge and take in Salisbury's piece; and that they mean in April to survey

> the land and then to give satisfaction and not before; and he and Master Hall say they think there will be nothing done at all.

As well as revealing Shakespeare's close familiarity with the fields around Stratford, this passage shows him determined not to enter into Thomas Greene's passionate resistance to Combe's plans. Unlike Greene, he is on very friendly terms with the Combe family, alluded to as 'they'. According to Shakespeare, not much land is under discussion; the plans will not be drawn up until a proper survey has been made; and his son-in-law – who, as a physician, was closely acquainted with many local families, including the Combes[20] – shares his belief that in practice 'there will be nothing done at all'. There may have been an element of hypocrisy here. Shakespeare must have realized that in the longer term, once enclosure and pasture had been successfully established, he and his heirs could enjoy better tithe income from pasture than from arable. Yet he may also have genuinely believed that Greene was getting worked up about nothing. If so, he was posthumously vindicated, for the enclosures were indeed not implemented.

On 23 December 1614 two letters were written to Shakespeare, one on behalf of the Corporation, the other a personal plea from Greene himself with 'a note of the inconveniences [which] would grow by the enclosure'. Meanwhile, the affair was becoming heated, and Stratford's Aldermen were smarting under insults from William Combe and his nephew Thomas, who had reportedly called them 'dogs and curs' and 'Puritan knaves'. But still Greene got no support from Shakespeare. A note dated September 1615, 'W. Shakespeare's telling J. Greene that I was not able to bear the enclosing of Welcombe', has often been discussed. Schoenbaum finds it strange that Shakespeare 'should have found it necessary to tell Greene's brother [John Greene] what he must have already known'. However, the reason may be that Shakespeare and Thomas Greene were no longer on speaking terms, and that he had heard with dismay from his brother John that Shakespeare felt that he was over-reacting. Thomas Greene could not 'bear', or endure, the proposed enclosure: in Shakespeare's eyes, this was a foolish over-reaction. Thomas Greene should try to 'bear it like a man', and remember the profit that would eventually accrue to him if the enclosures took place. While Greene was admirably public-spirited, concerning himself with the well-being of Stratford as a whole, including its poorest inhabitants, Shakespeare's was the selfish landowner's view. Such a position was all of a piece with his minimal bequest to the poor of Stratford in his will – £10, considerably less than the sum of £13 6*s*. and 8*d*. that he left to his attorney Francis Collins – and with his failure to set up any kind of local charity.

Nor was Thomas Greene to be remembered in Shakespeare's will, whereas William Combe's nephew young Thomas Combe received the symbolic bequest of Shakespeare's sword. The omission of Greene from the will offers the clearest evidence that they had fallen out over the enclosure controversy. Greene had once been a particularly intimate friend of his famous 'cousin',[21] and he and his family had even lodged in New Place for a couple of years. It was almost certainly Shakespeare who first encouraged him to settle in Stratford. By the same token, it may have been not just the stressful enclosure controversy, but the painful cessation of this major friendship with Shakespeare, now dead, that provoked Greene's decision to leave Stratford, lamenting the fact that he had not received 'recompense to a greater value for my golden days and spirits spent in Stratford's service'.[22] John Hall treated Greene's eldest daughter Anne successfully for a skin rash in 1616,[23] but in the following year the family moved to Bristol, and Greene began to build up the successful career in London that culminated in his appointment as Treasurer of the Middle Temple in 1629.

Contrary to Rowe's picture of Shakespeare peacefully enjoying 'the conversation of his friends', Shakespeare seems, at the end, to have fallen out with several of them. The Greenes' eldest children, William and Anne, were probably godchildren of Shakespeare and his wife; but, again, they were not to be remembered in his will.[24]

A merry meeting?

John Ward, a doctor and clergyman who settled in Stratford in 1662, recorded what he had heard from local tradition about the circumstances of Shakespeare's death: 'Shakespeare, Drayton and Ben Jonson had a merry meeting, and it seems drank too hard, for Shakespeare died of a fever there contracted.'[25] Most biographers make little of this account. Its picture of a convivial, even Falstaffian, Shakespeare who died after surfeiting in male company does not fit in with Nicholas Rowe's picture of the poet's retirement to quiet and provincial domesticity. Still less, perhaps more importantly, does it fit in with the sour and angry tone of the will. Yet in its broad outlines, as Schoenbaum acknowledges, it 'does not strain credulity'. If John Aubrey's account that Shakespeare 'was not a company keeper', and habitually refused invitations to heavy drinking sessions, is to be believed,[26] his health may indeed not have stood up well to an unwonted bout of alcoholic consumption, let alone to many such bouts. There are several reasons why, in the years 1615–16, he may indeed have been drinking more than was his wont, and sometimes doing so in the company of his close friends, whether Stratford landowners or London poets. The first and most compelling reason was that he was already ill. He did not become ill because he had been drinking, as Ward's account suggests, but took to drinking because he was ill.

If he 'drank too hard' towards the end, it was most probably in an attempt to palliate pain or distress. Secondly, he was stuck in Stratford for the whole winter, perhaps for the first time for many years, with occasions for drinking provided first by a provincial Christmas and then by a family wedding.

The illness that led eventually to Shakespeare's death on 23 April 1616 seems to have developed gradually, or in fits and starts. He had new and substantial projects in hand, which at some points it seemed he could complete, but worsening illness cut them short. This is implied by Heminge and Condell's remark in their First Folio epistle 'To the great Variety of Readers':

> It had been a thing, we confess, worthy to have been wished, that the author himself had lived to have set forth and overseen his own writings; but . . . it hath been ordained otherwise, and he by death departed from that right.

Hugh Holland also hinted that his death left some of his current projects uncompleted – 'his line of life went soon about'. Indeed, it could be that Heminge and Condell were aware that Shakespeare planned to emulate Jonson's example in gathering up and editing ('overseeing') the best of his own works for publication ('setting forth'). To do so would be to make war on time 'a mightier way' than by investing in the fragile rewards of theatrical performance. From 1614 onwards, the editing of his own plays, rather than provincial domesticity, may have been his overriding goal and preoccupation. Erecting such a printed monument, analogous to the 'eternal lines' of the *Sonnets*, but far more substantial, would make very good sense after the two traumatic conflagrations of 1613 and 1614, first the burning of the Globe, and then, on 9 July 1614, the burning of nearly half of the domestic buildings of Stratford. To see the two places in which he had invested so much creative energy and money (respectively) damaged in successive years was a crushing experience. The first disaster would account for a decision to write no more plays, even in collaboration, but instead to gather up his works and prepare them for durable folio publication.[27] Interestingly, both the other writers mentioned by John Ward were comparably employed at this time. The first volume of Michael Drayton's great topographical poem about Britain, *Polyolbion* had been published in 1612 (Plate 12), and he was hard at work on its continuation; and Ben Jonson was busily assembling and punctiliously editing poems, plays and masques for his folio *Workes* (Fig. 46). When Shakespeare returned to Stratford early in 1614 he was also setting out to strengthen his economic base there, one supposedly less fragile than a wooden playhouse. When that, too, was severely threatened he may indeed have felt singled out as 'fortune's fool'. Though none of the fifty-four houses burnt in Stratford happened to be his property, it fell to the prosperous gentry of Stratford to contribute substantially to their repair and re-building, just as it had fallen to the wealthy Globe shareholders to bear the

Fig. 44 Title-page of the *Workes* of Ben Jonson (1616).

cost of replacing their playhouse. Shakespeare may have resented this obligation. Also, in so far as the Stratford fire impoverished the town as a whole, it reduced the capacity of tenants and labourers to pay rents and tithes, thus jeopardizing Shakespeare's income from this source.

Whatever the precise nature of Shakespeare's final illness – my own guess is that heart and circulatory trouble were now added to latent syphilitic infection – there seems little doubt that as it tightened its grip he must also have been battling with severe 'reactive' depression in the aftermath of the Globe fire. If Drayton and Jonson really did join Shakespeare for a 'merry meeting' in Stratford early in 1616, they must have had much to talk about, and to compare notes about, concerning their respective literary projects. Jonson, in particular, is likely to have boasted about the cash and prestige he hoped to gain by his self-editing venture, as well as about his remarkable triumph in being awarded a pension of a hundred marks by the King. However, his Stratford friend and colleague may already have been too unwell and too preoccupied with family worries to take the kind of detailed interest in these matters that he might have done some months earlier. Jonson's vigour, tenacity and fresh enjoyment of royal favour served only to underline to Shakespeare the imminent death of all his hopes.

IS THERE A DOCTOR IN THE HOUSE?

Alcohol is one of the oldest palliatives known to humanity, and if Shakespeare was both depressed and in physical pain during the Christmas season of 1615–16 he may well have resorted to its liberal use. He presumably also received medical treatment from his son-in-law, especially since no other physician or surgeon is mentioned in the will. No record of any treatment of his famous father-in-law appears in Hall's surviving case-books, although he does record treatments given to his wife and daughter, as well as to the poet Drayton, whom he treated with syrup of violets. But doctors are naturally more interested in recording success than failure; and there may be an additional reason for the omission. There are few allusions to venereal infection in Hall's case-books as gathered up and published by Dr James Cooke. Indeed, there are only two. One, that of William Clavel, concerns a man not of gentle status; the other, that of Sir Francis Harvey, has been 'cryptically edited' by Cooke to obscure the cause of his condition.[28] If, as I have conjectured, syphilis was one of Shakespeare's suspected or actual disorders, this might account for the absence or excision of Hall's notes on the case. As a doctor who ministered to the aristocracy and landed gentry, Hall may have been habitually careful to avoid explicit mention of this shaming condition, even when he observed it.

We can only guess at the treatments Shakespeare may have undergone. Like other doctors of the period, Hall was keen on applying extraordinary substances to the feet, head or trunk, such as sliced radishes, freshly killed hens, spiders' webs or extremely alcoholic poultices, all with the object of drawing out excessive 'humours'.[29] When his wife Susanna was ill with colic he treated her with an enema of 'a pint of sack made hot'.[30] He also prescribed cordials based on spirits of wine or *aqua vitae*, the equivalents of brandy or whisky, which were taken by mouth. It can be surmised that Shakespeare was distinctly corpulent, since both the Stratford bust (Fig. 45) and the Martin Droeshout engraving (Fig. 48) show him as plump-faced. Given that most portraits aim to flatter, he was probably in truth plumper still. If his father-in-law was fat and florid, and thus classified as sanguine and phlegmatic, according to Galen's system of humours, Hall may have subjected him to violent purges over a period of many days, followed by blood-letting. Mercifully, however, he was unusually 'moderate' in his use of the latter.[31]

Concrete evidence for Shakespeare's worsening physical condition is offered by the fact that some time in January 1616 he summoned his Stratford lawyer Francis Collins to draw up his will, a draft which was to be partially re-written on 25 March. For most people, making a will is bound to be a melancholy business, even at the best of times. Despite the disclaimers routinely offered – like most testators, Shakespeare claims to be 'in perfect health and memory, God be praised' – most men in this period did not make their wills until they had become sufficiently ill for death to be clearly in view. Among the large collection of 'playhouse wills' assembled by E. A. J. Honigmann and Susan Brock it is estimated that 'The average time elapsing between the making of a will and the day of burial . . . is two weeks'.[32] Seen in this context, Shakespeare was unusually provident – or else whatever condition killed him took a good deal longer to do so than he and his advisers anticipated, since he did not die until three months after the first draft of the will, one month after the second. Perhaps, after all, Hall did succeed in keeping his father-in-law alive for a little longer than was at first anticipated, though this case could hardly be chronicled as one of his therapeutic triumphs.[33]

Yet have I left a daughter[34]

In addition to poor health, probably accompanied by severe pain, Shakespeare had an even more pressing and urgent reason for setting his affairs in order in January 1616. He needed both to provide for and to control his younger daughter Judith, who was about to marry Thomas Quiney, an undistinguished younger son of Shakespeare's old friend the Stratford bailiff Richard Quiney, now long dead.[35] Unlike his younger brother George, who went to Balliol College, Oxford, and was described by John Hall after his death in 1624 as 'a man of a good wit, expert in the tongues, and very learned',[36] Thomas Quiney had very little talent even as a minor tradesman. Most probably it was the fact of her rich father's worsening health that made the thirty-one-year-old Judith suddenly so attractive to the twenty-six-year-old Quiney, especially since they must have known each other all their lives. She was practically the girl, or the woman, next door. In this period older women were generally attractive as marriage partners for younger men either because, as widows or orphans, they had recently inherited substantial money or property, or because they looked as if they were about to do so. Shakespeare's own courtship of the orphaned yeoman's daughter Anne Hathaway in 1582 was an unusual exception. Nevertheless, as Honigmann has plausibly suggested, Thomas Quiney's courtship of Judith may have reminded Shakespeare unpleasantly of his own marriage thirty-four years before – and all the more so if Judith's mother had colluded with her younger daughter in promoting this match. There was clearly an element of rush about the proceedings, although the bride in this case does not seem to have been pregnant, for the Quineys's first child, Shakespeare, was born in early November 1616, just over nine months after the wedding. The marriage of Judith Shakespeare to Thomas Quiney took place on 10 February 1616, which was within the period of pre-Lent prohibition. It had not been legitimated, as it ought to have been, by the purchase of a special licence. The couple were summoned to appear before the Consistory Court, and Thomas Quiney was excommunicated. Presumably banns had been called in Holy Trinity Church on the three preceding Sundays. The forthcoming nuptials would therefore have been well known to the people of Stratford from mid-January, and it may have been during the period when banns were being read that Shakespeare drew up the first draft of his will.

There is every reason to think that Shakespeare was unenthusiastic about his younger daughter's marriage, and that he was determined to frustrate Thomas Quiney's designs on his wealth. As Honigmann, again, has pointed out, in the surviving, revised, version of the will he 'carefully avoids naming Thomas Quiney'.[37] The curious allusion to 'such husband' as Judith may have 'at the end of three years' suggests a strong desire for the young man to drop down dead, combined with a suspicion that Judith would be quite capable of contracting another equally unsuitable marriage. Judith, it seems, was not a favourite daughter. She may have suffered, in her father's eyes, from having had the insensitivity to stay alive so many years after the death of her much loved twin brother Hamnet at the age of eleven. Though Susanna, 'Witty above her sex', commanded some degree of literacy, Judith seems to have had none. She signed documents only with the crudest of marks.[38] She may well have been intelligent, but no time or money had been devoted to her early education, nor was she to enjoy the later advantage that Susanna did of marriage to a highly educated husband. That she was fully aware of her inferior status, and keenly resented it, may be suggested by the gravestone of her brother-in-law John Hall, who died in 1635. Between the lines recording that 'HEE MARRIED SUSANNA THE DAUGHTER OF WILLIAM SHAKESPEARE, GENT' the words '& coheire' have been inserted in very much smaller letters. It seems that the widowed Susanna Hall may have intended to present herself visibly as Shakespeare's one and only daughter. But someone, probably Thomas Quiney, had intervened to insist on the addition. It was a neat insertion, for while it avoided mentioning Judith Quiney by name, it managed to imply that she had been comparable to her sister Susanna in esteem and in inheritance from the now celebrated poet Shakespeare.

But this, as we shall see, was very far from being the case. While Susanna, with her husband and daughter, were left all of Shakespeare's Stratford property as well as the Blackfriars leasehold, together with virtually all of his 'plate, jewels and household stuff', and were residuary legatees, Judith was to receive only £100 (in addition to her marriage portion), with a further £50 on condition that her husband could offer £100 worth of security. The discrepancy between the bequests to the two daughters is even greater than can be accounted for in terms of the advantage conferred by primogeniture. It is also noticeable that John Hall's will contains no bequest to his sister-in-law. Though this is only a 'nuncupative' (summary and dictated) will, if his sister-in-law Judith had been on close or warm terms with her sister he would surely have remembered to mention her.

Although what survives is only the revised, 25 March, version of Shakespeare's will, it indicates that the 'portion', or dowry, assigned to Judith in January had been a fairly minimal £100. This was about the least that a man as wealthy as Shakespeare could get away with, and clearly very much less than had been bestowed on Susanna when she made her excellent marriage to John Hall in 1607. Though the original marriage agreement does not survive, Mairi Macdonald has recently discovered that Shakespeare settled 105 acres of land in Old Stratford on her at the time of her marriage.[39] She has suggested convincingly that this valuable property was provided by Shakespeare to match an equivalent amount of money to be brought to the match by John Hall. It is very striking that in the document, of the 1620s, in which Shakespeare's settlement of this large parcel of land is recorded, it is also stated, wrongly, that he 'had one daughter'. By this period, apparently, the gulf between the sisters was so wide that many people were unaware that Judith Quiney the obscure wine-seller's wife, as well as Susanna Hall the distinguished doctor's wife, was a daughter of the celebrated Stratford playwright. The elder sister was a prosperous, self-assured and conspicuous lady; the younger so ungenteel as to be socially invisible.

From the outset Susanna's husband had been manifestly eligible. John Hall was a gentleman and a Cambridge graduate. He had travelled in France, where he probably received his medical training, perhaps at Montpellier. At the time of his marriage he was beginning to build up a distinguished network of patients among the nobility and gentry of Warwickshire. He was already possessed of a good house and some wealth. Thomas Quiney, on the other hand, did not go to university, and had rarely, if ever, left his native Stratford. He ran a small wine shop, Atwood's, in Stratford High Street. Perhaps he hoped that his prospective father-in-law would help him financially in his pre-marital transfer to larger premises, 'The Cage', at the corner of High Street and Bridge Street. But if so, he hoped in vain. As Shakespeare no doubt realized, Thomas Quiney was not a good bet. In later life, he failed to become an alderman, and at different times was charged with swearing, with allowing townsmen to tipple in his house, and with selling bad-quality wine.[40] In 1633 his lease of The Cage was taken over by John Hall and his son-in-law Thomas Nash. Presumably Quiney's business had by then declined to such an extent that he could no longer keep up payments on the lease.[41] Shakespeare evidently had no objection in principle to the friendship of inn-keepers and wine merchants. As we have seen, he had been closely associated with the unlicensed victualler and brothel-keeper George Wilkins. He had also chosen William Johnson, landlord of the Mermaid Tavern, as the first of the three co-purchasers of his Blackfriars gatehouse. An epitaph on the wealthy brewer Elias James is attributed to him.[42] But all of these, even the unsavoury Wilkins, were what Shylock would call 'good men' – men of credit and substance, who commanded both a wide range of business interests and some ready cash. Thomas Quiney's business was barely more than a provincial corner shop, and he lacked ready money. He failed to provide, as he had been required to do, property to the value of £100 to match Judith Shakespeare's portion, and thus showed himself unequal even to the moderate support of her asked of him by his father-in-law.

But this was not the worst of his misdemeanours. Just over a month after his marriage to Judith Shakespeare another young Stratford woman, Margaret Wheeler, died in childbirth, and Thomas Quiney was named as the father of her child. He was required to perform public penance, wearing a white sheet, in Holy Trinity Church on three successive Sundays. Though payment of a fine of 5 shillings – this, at least, he could come up with – exempted him from the penance, this was an extremely painful and embarrassing episode for all three families involved, the Wheelers, the Quineys and the Shakespeares. Most probably Shakespeare had not been aware, until the grim news of her death broke, either of Margaret Wheeler's pregnancy, or of its cause. If his wife and daughters, or Judith, at least, had known about it, but kept it from him for fear of jeopardizing Judith's nuptials, that may well have contributed to the sour and mistrustful tone of the will, as well as to the omission from its main text of any allusion whatsoever to his wife Anne. Indeed, there may have been a whole confederacy of family members and friends who had known very much more than Shakespeare had about the deeply undesirable exploits of his son-in-law Thomas Quiney, or so at least it may have seemed to him in his wretchedly enfeebled state.

Two of the distinctively disagreeable features of Shakespeare's will to which Honigmann draws attention are the large number of 'names omitted' and of names struck out, which offer 'many signs . . . of anger or disappointment'.[43] It has been suggested that the striking out of the name of Richard Tyler the elder, originally left 26*s.* 8*d.* for a ring, relates to Tyler's failure to contribute to the re-building of Stratford after the 1614 fire. But this was no longer such a live issue in January–March 1616, and in any case, as we have seen, Shakespeare himself could not be relied on to concern himself with matters of local government. It seems equally possible that the deletion has something to do with Tyler's involvement, supposed or actual, in the Quiney–Wheeler affair. When news of Margaret Wheeler's condition broke, Shakespeare must have felt humiliated and duped. He had been coerced into accepting as a son-in-law a young man who had neither profession, talent, nor, as this latest scandal showed, personal integrity. If the young man was going to get married in a hurry, Margaret Wheeler was clearly the girl who ought to have been his bride. After all, he himself had spent his whole adult life encumbered with a marriage honourably if reluctantly made in such circumstances. But though the Wheelers leased four houses in Henley Street,[44] they were nothing like so wealthy as the King's Man and master of New Place. Thomas Quiney's abandonment of the pregnant Margaret Wheeler was the final proof of his mercenary motives in wooing Judith Shakespeare. The surviving, later, draft of the will was composed just a day before Thomas Quiney was due to answer charges in Stratford's Bawdy Court. It was drawn up in such a way as to discourage fortune-hunting aspirations not merely on the part of Thomas Quiney, but also on the part of any other suitor whom Judith might be foolish enough to acquire in the future. Though she is promised a further £150 three years after her father's death – adding to the amount of her marriage portion – that, too, is to be paid to her only on condition that 'such husband as she shall at the end of . . . three years be married unto' can match the sum with property of equal value. The executors, Susanna and John Hall, were to make absolutely sure that this condition was met. There is no suggestion that Shakespeare's wealthy heirs might themselves offer any support to the Quineys.

My second best bed

Scholars have made many ingenious excuses for the late interlinear insertion into the will of the celebrated clause 'Item, I give unto my wife my second best bed with the furniture'.* A. L. Rowse even went so far as to claim that the bequest 'showed exceptional care for the comfort of his widow'.[45] Yet it surely is indeed the disagreeable and reluctant afterthought that Edmond Malone called it:

> His wife had not wholly escaped his memory; he had forgot her, – he had recollected her, – but so recollected her, as more strongly to mark how little he esteemed her; he had already (as is vulgarly expressed) cut her off, not indeed with a shilling, but with an old bed.[46]

But one point about that 'second best bed' has not been much stressed. Shakespeare, master of the five-gabled New Place, of the Blackfriars gatehouse, the Chapel Lane cottage, and much land and property besides, was surely at that moment being nursed in the best, or 'master', bed. He was determined that Anne should never occupy it, even after his death.

His firm exclusion of her from this domestic and intimate space is entirely consistent with the format of the monument in Holy Trinity, presumably commissioned by John Hall from the Southwark sculptor Gerard Johnson according to what he knew to be his father-in-law's wishes, as a 'scholar's type' half-length front-facing effigy (Fig. 45).[47] Hall himself may have composed the inscription, with its slightly lumbering pun on all future writings as the 'page' to dead Shakespeare's:

IUDICIO PYLIUM, GENIO SOCRATEM, ARTE MARONEM:
TERRA TEGIT, POPULUS MAERET, OLYMPUS HABET.**

> Stay Passenger, why goest thou by so fast?
> Read if thou canst, whom envious Death hath plast
> Within this monument Shakspeare: with whom
> Quick nature died: whose name doth deck this tomb
> Far more than cost: sith all that he hath writ
> Leaves living art, but page to serve his wit.

This type of monument was designed to commemorate a talented individual, not the head of a family.[48] No space was left even for a mention of the great man's obscure wife, let alone for the incorporation of any supplementary

* 'Furniture' here refers to the mattress, hangings, coverlets and such like that went with the bed.
** 'The earth covers, the people mourn, Olympus holds [a man who was] a Pylius [= Nestor] in judgement, a Socrates in wisdom, a Virgil in literary skill.'

Fig. 45 Monument to Shakespeare in Holy Trinity Church, Stratford.

memorial concerning her once she, too, was dead. She had played no part in the fashioning of his art or ensuing fame, and could not expect to share in his posthumous glory. Still less, evidently, could she hope that her dead bones might one day be laid quietly beside his. Shakespeare guessed that Anne, though seven years older than himself, would be long-lived, and devised that famously savage gravestone curse to ensure that, however many years hence her death might be, the sexton of the day could not possibly be induced to open up her husband's grave:

GOOD FRIEND FOR JESUS SAKE FORBEARE
TO DIGG THE DUST ENCLOASED HEARE.
BLESTE BE THE MAN THAT SPARES THES STONES
AND CURST BE HE THAT MOVES MY BONES.

Part of the object of this inscription was to ensure that the poet's bones were never transferred to the charnel house, the door to which was only a few feet away from the monument. But clearly it also ensured that neither his wife's remains nor those of any other family member could ever be inserted in the deeply dug grave.

The exclusion of certain close relations from epitaphs or memorials seems to have become a family habit. When Anne Hathaway died in 1623, aged sixty-seven, someone – probably, once again, John Hall – wrote a six-line Latin epigram praising her for having given life and milk to the speaker, but making no allusion either to her later life or to her younger children, let alone to her husband. She is not, for instance, praised as a faithful or loving wife. The poem is spoken as if by her first-born Susanna – note the singular '*vae mihi*' ('woe is me'), not '*vae nobis*' ('alas for us'), and '*dabo*', not '*damus*' ('I give', not 'we give'). The speaker offers, in exchange for the breasts, milk and life that she has received, nothing but stones and a prayer for her mother's soul to ascend to heaven. It appears that Anne's only memorable achievement during her long life had been to give life and nourishment to a single child. And, as already mentioned, when John Hall died in 1635 Susanna tried to exclude her sister from the epitaph inscribed on his gravestone. The late insertion of the squeezed-in words '& coheire' is strangely analogous to the squeezed-in insertion of the 'unto my wife' clause in Shakespeare's will.

We may wonder, indeed, why such a late insertion into the will was ever made. Why was Anne not, rather, excluded altogether? Perhaps one of the daughters – my guess would be the despised and newly wed Judith – on hearing the whole draft will read through before her father signed it, noticed the absence from it of any allusion to her mother, and implored her father to leave her at least some token of affection. It is noticeable that the insertion occurs just above the line bequeathing Judith 'my broad silver gilt bowl', a bequest which itself, though part of the main revised draft, appears from its location to be an afterthought. That the bequest of the bowl to Judith was an afterthought is also suggested by the interlinear insertion on the previous sheet of this single exception to his bequest of all his plate to his grand-daughter Elizabeth. In response to what may have been a tearful appeal from Judith, perhaps even seconded by the unloved Anne herself, Shakespeare, gravely ill, angry and utterly exhausted by the whole wearisome business of dictating the will, consented only to the most minimal bequest, a bequest which was more a put-down than a sign of love. He made no specific provision for his wife to be allowed to continue to live at New Place, though it has always been assumed that she did so, or for her to be allowed to continue to enjoy such clothes, chattels and furniture as she had done hitherto. In contrast to a small number of male friends to whom he left money for mourning rings,[49] he left her no jewel, portrait or token of remembrance. He used no formulaic term of endearment or affection, nor even her Christian name. All that she was to have was a bed that was not the one in which he himself was accustomed to lie, and in which he was most probably lying while the will was being drawn up.

It has often been claimed that the 'second best bed' was a particularly handsome one, reserved for distinguished visitors. But even if this is true, it by no means mitigates the brutal quality of the bequest, for it relegates Anne to the status of guest in what she may have hoped still to think of as her own home. Although widows normally inherited a third of their husband's goods, she would in practice have been dependent for this on the good will of the Halls, to whom New Place and all the rest of its furniture had been left, and who were executors. It is not inconceivable that it was understood that she was to have that 'second best bed' carted off to some more modest dwelling, as the solitary trophy from her marriage. Perhaps she was handed over to the mercies of her Hathaway kin, none of whom rates a mention in the will.

A less than merry meeting

And as for that 'merry meeting': it is probable that a week or two of revelry, as was customary, accompanied Judith Shakespeare's marriage. For her depressed and ailing father, a period of carousing with his London and Stratford friends[50] may have been the only thing that could make the event half-way tolerable. Michael Drayton, a Warwickshire neighbour, and a friend and patient of John Hall's, was very likely to have been of the party. Shakespeare's long-standing friend and colleague John Heminge, also a Warwickshire man in origin, could have been there too, though unmentioned by John Ward. Ben Jonson, a notoriously energetic traveller, may have leapt at the opportunity for a winter journey to Stratford. After the double triumphs of seeing work on his great Folio set in train and, on 1 February, being awarded his lifelong royal pension,[51] he was surely in holiday mood. The pre-Lent season was a traditional time both for travelling and for revelry. Jonson may have been all too eager both to gloat over the provincial and ailing Shakespeare, and to drink deep at his expense. But if he came for a wedding, he must also have witnessed the beginnings of a death bed, being much struck by the bitter anger and disharmony prevailing in New Place.

Though Jonson's presence in Stratford in February 1616 cannot be definitely established, there are some thought-provoking details in the very next play he wrote, *The Devil is an Ass*, performed by the King's Men at the Blackfriars Theatre in October or November 1616, which may reflect either eyewitness impressions or hearsay about Shakespeare's end. In the closing scene the protagonist, Fabian Fitzdottrell, is 'discovered in bed'. He is apparently mad and apparently dying (Fig. 46). He laughs crazily, abuses his wife as a whore, foams at the mouth, uses foul language to an eminent lawyer, and comes out with childishly obscene fragments of English doggerel and bad Greek, Spanish and French. But as so often in Jonson's comedies, the purpose behind all this is nothing like so foolish as it seems. Fitzdottrell, a passionate playgoer, has picked up some remarkable acting skills. By feigning madness he hopes to invalidate the deed of 'enfeoffment' with which he has signed away all his property to a lightweight young man.

Whether or not the Blackfriars audience picked up any parallels to Shakespeare's death here, his former colleagues the King's Men surely did. In the autumn of 1616 memories of their great fellow, dead in Warwickshire only a few months before, were still green. Jonson was not to write a formal tribute to Shakespeare for another seven years, when he provided Heminge and Condell with two rather double-edged commendatory poems for the First Folio. Meanwhile, in characteristically callous fashion, he seems to have incorporated a reductive reflection of some of his friend's traits into this darkly disturbing comedy. Jonson's later application to Shakespeare of the epithet 'gentle' may carry with it yet another dig at Shakespeare's questionable purchase of a grant of arms and of back-dated 'gentle' status for his father in 1596. But *The Devil is an Ass* offers a much cruder picture of a man who is willing to sign away all his property for the sake of the absurd and valueless title 'The Duke of Drown'd-Land'. There are some explicit Shakespearean allusions elsewhere in the play. For instance, Fitzdottrell's asinine belief that 'the play books' offer the most 'authentic' account of Thomas of Woodstock, Duke Humphrey and Richard the Third (2.4) is evidently a side-swipe at Shakespeare's still popular English history plays and the many liberties he took with the chronicles. Though the character of Fitzdottrell can hardly be claimed as a portrait of Shakespeare, any

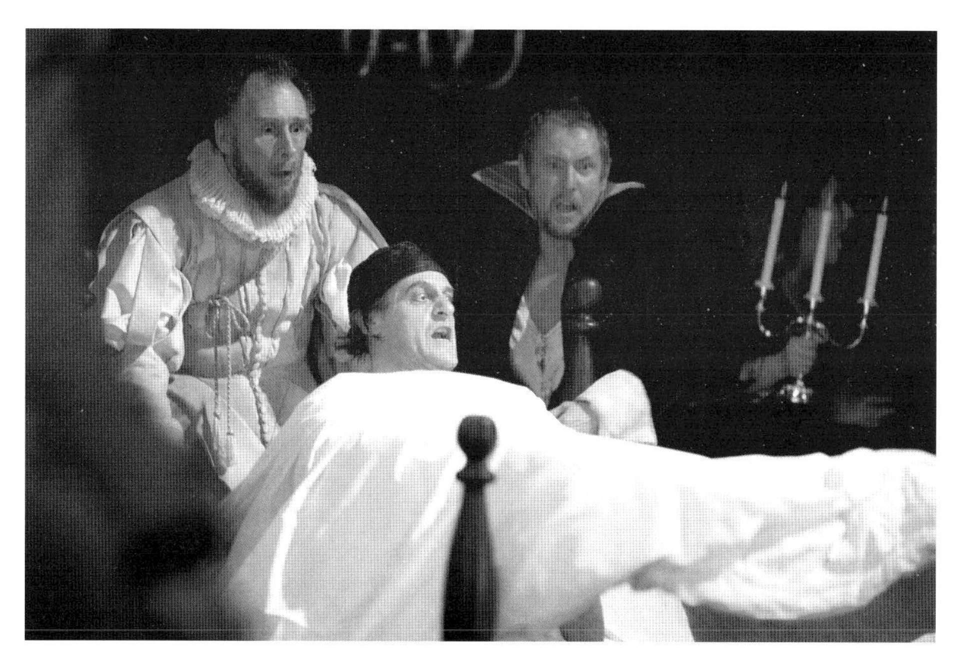

Fig. 46 David Troughton as Fitzdottrell (with Christopher Godwin as Everill and John Nettles as Meerecraft) in the final scene of Jonson's *The Devil is an Ass* (Royal Shakespeare Company, 1995).

more than can that of Sogliardo in *Every Man Out of his Humour*, distinct parallels between the play's final scene and Shakespeare's protracted will-making and death bed may have impressed themselves on those of the King's Men who were his close friends, and had heard the details of his death (Fig. 48). Even when recovered from his feigned madness, Fitzdottrell has an acute sense of alienation from all those around him, his wife most of all:

> these are cozeners still,
> And have my land, as plotters, with my wife,
> Who, though she be not a witch, is worse, a whore.
>
> (5.8.147–50)

If Jonson did join the wedding party in Stratford, we can be pretty sure that this meeting was very far from merry. The will shows that Shakespeare was ill and furiously angry with many of those around him, his 'nearest and dearest' – perhaps almost mad with anger. Or even, great old player that he still was, he may have over-acted his anger and madness the better to discomfit and gain mastery over those around him.

In his First Folio tribute Jonson's portrait of the 'sweet swan of Avon' is by no means 'gentle' in the modern sense of that word. He describes Shakespeare

Fig. 47 Signature 'By me William Shakspeare' from Shakespeare's will.

as living up to the flamboyant aggression suggested by his surname in writing lines of verse

> In each of which he seems to shake a lance
> As brandished at the eyes of ignorance.
>
> (5.8.390–2)

And though he is finally deified as a 'star of poets', it is 'with rage', rather than with gentleness, that he is implored to admonish the theatre of latter days.

The unhappy circumstances of Shakespeare's death may have been widely known among his London friends. We know nothing of what ceremonies attached to his funeral in Stratford on 25 April. They perhaps accorded with instructions given orally or in writing to John Hall, or else may have conformed to Hall's own austerely Protestant inclinations. There is no reason to think that patrons or fellow poets assembled to attach their tributes to his hearse. It is striking that there was no immediate rush of elegies or epitaphs from his friends, colleagues or admirers.[52] Even what may be the earliest poetical tribute, a sonnet by William Basse, seems to have been written some time later, to judge by its retrospective subtitle 'he died in April 1616'. It may have taken several years for recollections and rumours of the unpleasant details of Shakespeare's end to fade, to be replaced by a return to what, after all, was the best of him: his writings.

Perhaps it was precisely because his death-bed demeanour had been, notoriously, so very far from 'gentle' that this epithet was to play such a major part in the fashioning of his literary reputation. By the 1660s, when John Ward was making his enquiries, Stratford gossip retained a memory that drink had played a part in Shakespeare's end, and that some of his London friends had come up to see him. But his angry alienation from his wife and younger daughter, and fury with his new son-in-law, had dropped out of oral tradition. It may have been Judith Quiney herself, who had died only a few weeks before Ward's arrival, who promoted the affably 'merry' version of her father's last days. As a bibulous wine-seller's wife, she may have derived some comfort from the 'Falstaffian' myth, with its exclusion of any account of the shabby treatment

Fig. 48 Title-page of the First Folio and the portrait of Shakespeare by Martin Droeshout.

meted out both to herself and to her mother. Yet Shakespeare's gravestone curse, and Anne's separate interment, survive in Holy Trinity Church as stony testimony to his angry and unshared death bed.

More cheeringly, however, once the short line of Shakespeare's life was fully spun, the long life of his lines could begin.

Epilogue
Read him

JOHN Heminge and Henry Condell were in no doubt that the true quintessence of their friend and colleague was to be found in his writings. Untroubled by post-modern anxieties about either the existence or the death of 'the author', they exhorted readers of the 1623 Folio not to 'read his plays', but to 'read him', reporting in their epistle *To the great Variety of Readers* that

> His mind and hand went together, and what he thought, he uttered with that easiness that we have scarce received from him a blot in his papers. But it is not our province, who only gather his works and give them you, to praise him. It is yours that read him. And there we hope, to your divers capacities, you will find enough, both to draw, and hold you: for his wit can no more lie hid, than it could be lost. Read him, therefore; and again, and again.

The authentic Shakespeare, for those who had known him well, was to be found in his writings. Though the man himself was dead, these transmitted a faithful image of his 'mind'. Ben Jonson, likewise, closed his epigram on Martin Droeshout's portrait engraving on the title-page with a brisk exhortation to the reader to 'look / Not on his picture, but his book'. Given the childish clumsiness of this portrait – not much improved, in the 'second state' version, by the addition of some extra shading to Shakespeare's left cheek and collar – Jonson may have been suggesting that readers should not allow young Droeshout's inept and witless-looking image of his friend 'gentle Shakespeare' to prejudice them against the plays they are about to read.

Book-buyers had been alerted to the forthcoming Folio a year earlier, when it was included in John Bill's catalogue of English books prepared for the Frankfurt Book Fair in October 1622. By the time it at last appeared for sale in late November 1623 it was fallen upon eagerly, despite a high price ranging from 15 shillings to a pound.[1] Appropriately for a book dedicated to two eminent

Earls, that 'incomparable pair of brethren' William and Philip Herbert, it seems to have been speedily acquired by noblemen, such as John Milton's future patron John Egerton, first Earl of Bridgewater, and Thomas Arundell, Baron Wardour. One early owner, perhaps one of the Johnstones of Dumfries, annotated the whole volume with great care, underlining passages and scenes and drawing attention to notable points, including some of special interest to a Scot, such as, in *1 Henry IV*, 'Douglas his valour highly honoured by the prince, who gives him life and liberty'.[2] Copies were also bought by the play-loving Sir Edward Dering, of Kent, and by at least two bishops. But the luckiest readers of all got their Folios free. No doubt the two earls were presented with particularly high-quality copies inscribed by Heminge and Condell, and no doubt they gave the player editors the lavish rewards for which they were celebrated. Sadly, neither of these copies appear to be extant. But a copy that does survive shows that at least one further individual received a free one. This copy was given by the printers to Augustine Vincent,[3] a close friend and ally of the Clarencieux Herald William Camden. During the very period in which the great Shakespeare Folio was in preparation Vincent had composed a defence of Camden against the severe criticisms of his fellow herald Ralph Brooke, a book which was published by the Jaggards, father and son, in 1622.[4] Implicit in this connection is a linkage of Shakespeare, and his dear-bought 'gentle' status, fully endorsed by Camden but fiercely challenged by Brooke, with a powerful network of antiquaries including Camden himself, his former pupil Jonson and the would-be herald Hugh Holland, whose sonnet 'Upon the lines and life of the famous scenic poet Master William Shakespeare' occupies a whole page of the Folio's preliminaries (Fig. 44). Heminge and Condell were themselves in search of 'gentle' status, and may have cultivated friends and patrons in and around the College of Arms partly in order to further their own ambitions. Augustine Vincent, currently Rouge Croix Pursuivant, was to be appointed Windsor Herald in 1624. Though the Folio's editors were not so bold as to include Shakespeare's disputed coat of arms in their instructions to young Droeshout for the portrait, they may have taken some pains to ensure that all the writers of commendatory verses remembered to call Shakespeare 'Master', and if possible to draw attention to his status. Hugh Holland awarded him a metaphorical crown of bay,[5] calling him the 'poets' King'. Jonson, characteristically, drew attention to his 'beloved' Shakespeare's 'gentle' status so persistently and knowingly as in effect to mock it.

But the issue of the social status that could be achieved by a talented player–poet, though of pressing interest to Heminge and Condell and their fellow King's Men, was of course peripheral to the book's main purpose. The commendatory verses were urgent signposts, whose function was to persuade readers first to 'buy' the handsome volume, and then, with all possible speed, to 'read' it. They are not meant to be lingered over. We know that at least one body of young men who were lucky enough to enjoy free access to a fine copy of the Folio availed themselves liberally of this opportunity. These were Oxford undergraduates who had achieved the privilege of reading in the Bodleian Library. A ground-breaking agreement between the Bodleian and the Stationers' Company in 1611 ensured that 'one perfect copy' of every book published under their jurisdiction should be given to the Bodleian. Even though neither the library's founder, Sir Thomas Bodley, nor its first Librarian, Thomas James, were at all well disposed towards such light literature as 'play-books', the agreement ensured that a mint copy of the 1623 Folio[6] was promptly delivered, being sent by the Librarian to an Oxford book-binder, William Wildgoose, in February 1624. Once returned, the book was chained to a shelf in the part of Duke Humfrey's Library known as Arts End by means of a clip through its front cover. Young men at Oxford during the reign of Charles I perused the volume with such enthusiasm that parts of some pages were entirely worn away by the friction of their hands and elbows, despite the unusually high quality of the Crown paper, normally reserved for Bibles, on which it was printed. This provides a unique early record of the relative popularity of Shakespeare's plays among exactly the kind of young men who had been his greatest fans at the turn of the sixteenth century. Just like those Elizabethan students, these Caroline ones most admired Shakespeare as a poet of love. They voted with their elbows for *Romeo and Juliet* as far and away their favourite play, and the 'balcony scene' as far and away their favourite passage. Parts of the facing leaf, where many arms rested, have vanished altogether. Oxford in the 1630s and 1640s was a hive of poetic activity, with young men at Christ Church and elsewhere assembling substantial manuscript collections of the poems of Jonson, Donne, Carew, Herrick and other witty love poets. Though few extracts from Shakespeare appear in these poetical commonplace books, the wear and tear inflicted on the Bodleian Folio suggests that he was an equally powerful presence among these literary coteries. The second most popular play was not *Hamlet*, which one might have imagined would appeal to university students, but *Julius Caesar*. This play's depiction of an overweening ruler who is assassinated by his own friends and advisers probably seemed grippingly topical in the years leading up to the execution of Charles I. Overall, it seems, 'the Tragedies were most read, and the Histories least'.[7] Least popular of all was *King John*.

But the whirligig of time brought in its revenges. Soon after the publication of the Third Folio in 1663–4 the Curators of the Bodleian voted unanimously to sell the library's much read First Folio, presumably because they regarded it as now superseded. No record of a Bodleian copy of the Second Folio (1632) has ever been found, so that edition may have been immediately sold by order

Fig. 49 James I gives his works to Fame, on the left, and the University of Oxford, on the right; sculpture by John Clark in the Schools Quadrangle, Bodleian Library, Oxford.

of the then Curators in order to discourage further time-wasting on what Sir Thomas Bodley had called 'baggage books' by Oxford undergraduates during that excessively poetical period. However, in 1905 a gentleman from Derbyshire, Mr G. M. R. Turbutt, brought a badly damaged copy of the First Folio along to the library for an expert opinion. It was quickly recognized 'that the binding was an Oxford one, and that the wanderer from the shelves had re-visited its old home'.[8] A major fund-raising campaign was launched among Oxford alumni to buy the volume back for £3,000, matching the amount being eagerly offered by a rival purchaser[9] in America. The appeal was successful, and the Bodleian Folio was at last brought back to the Bodleian Library. But its physical state, because of the damage done to it during the middle decades of the seventeenth century, is so fragile that it is not now available for inspection by scholars. Though the University of Oxford made belated reparation for what now looks like extraordinary folly on the part of the Bodleian's Curators in the Restoration period, she purchased her honour at a very high price.

Despite many cultural changes, there is some surprising continuity in Shakespeare's reputation. School teachers, not editors, now urge young people to 'read him', and the play that they most often encourage their pupils to read first is *Romeo and Juliet*, closely followed by *Julius Caesar* and, another favourite with undergraduates in the seventeenth century, *Macbeth*. Students are no longer, perhaps, encouraged to believe that in reading these plays they are gaining direct access to the author's mind and personality. Yet it is here, without doubt, that the best of him is to be found. It is entirely because of what we have encountered in Shakespeare's plays, poems and sonnets that we are curious to know something also about his life. But this will inevitably disappoint. It's far better not to read yet another biography, but to 'read him'.

Selective Chronolgy

This lists only documented events, and does not attempt to cover the dates of composition of Shakespeare's writings.

1558 17 November: death of Mary Tudor; accession of Queen Elizabeth I (born 1533), daughter of Henry VIII and Anne Boleyn.

1559 Reformed religion, independent of the Pope, re-established in the Act of Uniformity.

1564 26 April: William Shakespeare, eldest son of John Shakespeare and his wife Mary, née Arden, christened in Holy Trinity Church, Stratford-upon-Avon.

1566 13 October: Gilbert, second son of John Shakespeare, christened.

1568–9 John Shakespeare serves as Bailiff of Stratford.

1569 15 April: Joan, daughter of John Shakespeare, christened.

1571 28 September: Anne, daughter of John Shakespeare, christened.

1572 Leicester's Men play at Stratford.

1574 11 March: Richard, third son of John Shakespeare, christened.
Warwick's and Worcester's Men play at Stratford.

1575 July–August: the Queen goes on progress to the Midlands, spending two weeks as the guest of the Earl of Leicester at Kenilworth Castle, Warwickshire.

1578 Strange's and Essex's Men play at Stratford.

1579 4 April: Anne Shakespeare buried.

1580 3 May: Edmund, fourth son of John Shakespeare, christened.
Berkeley's Men play at Stratford.

1581 Worcester's Men play at Stratford.

1582 27 November: Bishop's licence issued for the marriage of William Shakespeare to Anne Hathaway.
Berkeley's Men play at Stratford.

1583 26 May: Susanna, daughter of William and Anne Shakespeare, christened in Holy Trinity Church, Stratford-upon-Avon.
Formation of new playing company, the Queen's Men.

1585 2 February: Hamnet and Judith, twin son and daughter of William and Anne Shakespeare, christened.

1587 John Shakespeare expelled from Corporation of Stratford for persistent failure to attend meetings.

1588 Arrival and dispersal ('defeat') of the Spanish Armada in the English Channel.

1592 Attack on Shakespeare, as 'the only Shake-scene in a country' and an 'upstart Crow', in the printed book *Greene's Groats-worth of Wit.*

1592
1593 Plague twice closes public theatres.

1593 Publication of *Venus and Adonis*, dedicated to Henry Wrothesley, Earl of Southampton.

1594 Publication of *Lucrece*, also dedicated to Southampton.
Publication of *Titus Andronicus.*
Publication of the 'bad Quarto' *Taming of a Shrew.*
28 December: performance of *The Comedy of Errors* at Gray's Inn.

1595 Shakespeare a member of the Lord Chamberlain's Men, who perform at court.

1596 11 August: burial of Shakespeare's son Hamnet.
20 October: Shakespeare applies to the College of Arms for a patent of gentility on behalf of his father.

1597 Shakespeare purchases New Place, a large mansion in Chapel Street, Stratford.
Shakespeare listed as a tax defaulter in the parish of St Helen's, Bishopsgate, London.

1598 Francis Meres praises Shakespeare in his book *Palladis Tamia*, listing twelve plays by him and alluding to his 'sugared sonnets among his private friends'.
25 October: Stratford neighbour Richard Quiney writes to Shakespeare in London asking for a loan of £30.

1599 Shakespeare listed as holding ten quarters of corn and malt during period of grain shortage in Stratford.
Shakespeare applies unsuccessfully to the College of Arms to quarter the Shakespeare arms with those of a branch of the Arden family.
New Globe Theatre built in Southwark, constructed partly from the timbers of the 'Theatre' in Shoreditch.
21 September: Swiss traveller Thomas Platter sees a performance of *Julius Caesar.*

1601 7 February: *Richard II* performed at the Globe by the Lord Chamberlain's Men at the special request of friends of the Earl of Essex.
8 February: Earl of Essex leads rebellion in the City of London.
25 February: Earl of Essex executed; Shakespeare's patron the Earl of Southampton imprisoned in the Tower.

1601 Poem by Shakespeare, 'The Phoenix and the Turtle', appended to Robert Chester's poem *Loves Martyr* in *Poeticall Essaies*.
8 September: John Shakespeare buried.

1602 2 February (Candlemas): *Twelfth Night* performed at the Middle Temple.

1603 24 March: Queen Elizabeth dies at Richmond Palace.
First mourning, then plague, closes public theatres.
Former Lord Chamberlain's Men, led by Shakespeare and Burbage, licensed by James I as King's Men.
August: King's Men attend the Spanish ambassadors for eighteen days at Somerset House.
Trial and condemnation for treason of Sir Walter Ralegh.

1603–4 Shakespeare plays a leading role at court in Ben Jonson's Roman tragedy *Sejanus his Fall.*

1604 Spring: plague continues.
May: Shakespeare is bequeathed 30 shillings in gold by his fellow actor Augustine Phillips.
24 July: Progress of King James through the City of London, greeted with speeches and triumphal arches; King's Men presumably in attendance.
November–December: five or more of Shakespeare's plays performed at court.

1605 24 July: Shakespeare purchases substantial portion of tithes in and near Stratford.
5 November: discovery of the 'Gunpowder Plot', intended to blow up Parliament.

1606 6 May: Shakespeare's daughter Susanna is among twenty-two citizens of Stratford fined for failing to receive Communion on Easter Day.

1607 5 June: marriage of Susanna Shakespeare to John Hall.
31 December: burial of Shakespeare's brother Edmund, 'Player', in St Saviour's, Southwark.

1608 21 February: Shakespeare's grand-daughter Elizabeth Hall christened at Holy Trinity, Stratford.
9 September: Shakespeare's mother Mary buried.
Publication of *A Yorkshire Tragedy* and of *The History of King Lear*.

1609 Severe plague closes theatres.
Publication of Shakespeare's Sonnets, dedicated by 'T.T.' to 'Mr. W.H.'

1610 2 February: *Pericles* and *King Lear* performed by Cholmeley's Men at Gowthwaite Hall, Yorkshire.
1 November: *The Tempest* performed at court (Whitehall Palace).

1611 September: Shakespeare is among seventy citizens of Stratford who contribute to the legal expenses of a proposed Highways Bill.

1612 3 February: Shakespeare's brother Gilbert is buried.

1612 11 May: Shakespeare gives evidence at the Court of Requests in suit of Stephen Belott against his father-in-law Christopher Mountjoy.

6 November: death of King's elder son Henry, Prince of Wales.

1613 4 February: Shakespeare's brother Richard is buried.

1613 14 February: King's daughter Elizabeth married to Frederick, Elector Palatine.

10 March: Shakespeare buys substantial property above the eastern gate of the former Dominican Priory at Blackfriars; method of purchase, with three co-purchasers, excludes his wife from inheritance of this property.

31 March: Shakespeare and Burbage each paid 44 shillings by Francis Manners, sixth Earl of Rutland, for designing and painting an *impresa* for him for the Accession Day tilt.

29 June: Globe Theatre burnt to the ground during a performance of Shakespeare's *All is True* (later entitled *Henry VIII*).

9 July: Fire in Stratford destroys fifty-four houses, none of them owned by Shakespeare.

1614 10 July: Shakespeare is bequeathed £5 by the wealthy Stratford landowner John Combe.

Opening of the rebuilt Globe Theatre.

1616 January: Shakespeare dictates his first draft of his will.

10 February: Shakespeare's younger daughter, Judith, marries Stratford tradesman Thomas Quiney (born 1589).

25 March: Shakespeare dictates revised version of his will.

25 April: Shakespeare buried in Holy Trinity, Stratford.

23 November: 'Shakespeare', first son of Judith and Thomas Quiney, christened.

1619 9 March: death of Richard Burbage.

1623 6 August: death of Shakespeare's widow Anne.

November: Publication of *Mr William Shakespeare's Comedies, Histories & Tragedies* (the 'First Folio'), edited by Shakespeare's fellow actors John Heminge and Henry Condell.

Notes

PREFACE

1 For the text of the curse, see chapter 10, p. 274.
2 For a charming taste of his method, see 'Cleaning one's teeth at Henley St', Honan, xi–xii.
3 I hope myself to develop further the work I have done on Shakespeare's dealings with the College of Arms.
4 Sir Hugh Clopton founded six scholarships for poor boys from Stratford to go to Oxford and Cambridge; see *DNB*.
5 But for a powerful account of the 'Lancashire connection', see E. A. J. Honigmann, *Shakespeare: The 'Lost Years'* (Manchester, 1985, revised 1999).
6 *DL*, 43.
7 See S. A. Tannenbaum, *Shakesperian Scraps and Other Elizabethan Fragments* (New York, 1933), 1–35.

ONE 1564–88 ANOTHER EDEN, ANOTHER ARDEN

1 R. W. Ingram, ed., *Records of Early English Drama: Coventry* (Manchester, 1981), xix–xx.
2 *Minutes*, 2.3–8.
3 Ibid., 2. xxxiii.
4 See the quotation at the head of this chapter.
5 Thomas Churchyard, *The Worthines of Wales* (1587), sig. 21^{r}. Thomas Ashton was schoolmaster of Shrewsbury School, where his pupils included Philip Sidney and Fulke Greville; he made major use of dramatic declamation and performance as a teaching aid.
6 H. R. Woudhuysen, *Sir Philip Sidney and the Circulation of Manuscripts, 1558–1640* (Oxford, 1996), 10.
7 Eccles, 60.
8 I call him 'Heminge' not 'Heminges' because this is the form in which his name appears in the First Folio.

9 That is, the journeyman playwrights who wrote plays for the theatrical entrepreneur Philip Henslowe (d.1616) for performance at the Swan, the Rose and elsewhere.
10 Chambers, *Shakespeare*, 2.247.
11 *Minutes*, 2.35.
12 Ibid., 2. xxxv.
13 *DL*, 89.
14 Ian Dunlop, *Palaces and Progresses of Queen Elizabeth*, vol. 1 (London, 1962), 143.
15 R. J. P. Kuin, ed., *Robert Langham: A Letter* (Leiden, 1983), 7.
16 Ibid., 9.
17 William Dugdale, *The Antiquities of Warwickshire* (1656), 160.
18 Modernized from Kuin, ed., *A Letter*, 56.
19 Although this passage does not tally exactly with Laneham's account, after twenty-one years a conflation of Arion with the Lady of the Lake is unsurprising – and in any case, the passage may be intended as a prompt to audience memory rather than an accurate chronicle.
20 Nicholas Rowe, ed., *The Works of Mr William Shakespeare*, 6 vols (1709), vol.1.
21 See *DL*, 36–8 for a full account.
22 *DL*, 60.
23 As Schoenbaum claimed.
24 Douglas Hamer, review of Schoenbaum, *Shakespeare's Lives*, *RES*, 85 (1971), 484.
25 Paul West, *I, Said the Sparrow* (London, 1963).
26 Warm thanks to Andrew Gurr for drawing my attention to this point.
27 E. I. Fripp, *Shakespeare's Haunts Near Stratford* (Oxford and London, 1929), 19–20.
28 Richard Rastall, 'Female roles in all-male casts', *Medieval English Theatre*, 7.1 (1985), 25–51. Grateful thanks to Professor Gordon Kipling for drawing my attention to this important article.
29 Thomas Tusser, *A Hundreth Good Pointes of Husbandrie* (1577), sig. $A4^{r-v}$.
30 Andrew Gurr, 'Shakespeare's first poem: sonnet 145', *Essays in Criticism*, 21 (1971), 221–6.
31 William Dugdale, *The Antiquities of Warwickshire* (1656), 487.
32 Nikolaus Pevsner, *Warwickshire* (London, 1966), 433.
33 Thirsk, 94.
34 *DL*, 88.
35 *DL*, 87–8; *Minutes*, 3. xliii–xlviii.
36 *Minutes*, 3. xlviii.
37 *DL*, 87.
38 It was entered in the Stationers' Register as 'to be staied', 4 August 1600.

NOTES

TWO 1589–92 THE QUEEN'S MAN

1 Eccles, 82.
2 E. I. Fripp, *Shakespeare's Stratford* (London, 1928), 9–10. This site is now occupied by a Beefeater Steakhouse.
3 *Queen's Men*, 42; cf.196, on Robert Moon, a player, probably a Queen's Man, slain in Bridgwater in December 1597.
4 Both the cities of Cambridge and Oxford paid them on occasion 'not to play'; see *Queen's Men*, 175, 182, 185.
5 Chambers, *Elizabethan Stage*, 2.105; *Queen's Men*, 42–3.
6 Nashe, 1.215; Thomas Heywood, *Apology for Actors* (1612), 40.
7 Public Record Office, Patent Roll 29 Eliz., part 16 (c66/1301, m.20).
8 *Queen's Men*, 124–7 and *passim*.
9 A. Feuillerat, ed., *The Prose Works of Sir Philip Sidney* (repr.1962), 3.167; the original letter is in British Library Harley MS 285, item 1.
10 Ibid., 124.
11 Uncharacteristically, the authors of *The Queen's Men*, 22–3, misquote and misdescribe this passage.
12 William Kempe, *Kemps nine daies wonder. Performed in a daunce from London to Norwich* (1600).
13 Chambers, *Elizabethan Stage*, 2.90.
14 Henry Chettle, *Kind hart's Dream* (1592), 6.
15 Letter of Rowland Whyte to Robert Sidney, 6 October 1595: 'It was told me that some lady of the Privy Chamber demanded of John Symons what Madam did; he answered she was well when he saw her and delivered unto her certain perfumed skins from Sir Robert Sidney: and this hath been told the Queen'; HMC, *De L'Isle and Dudley*, 2.131.
16 *CSP Domestic 1581–90*, 541–2.
17 Eccles, 76.
18 This man's son and namesake was, with Henry Goodere, one of the witnesses of Sidney's will in Arnhem in 1586.
19 Eccles, 80.
20 Katherine Duncan-Jones, *Sir Philip Sidney: Courtier Poet* (London, 1991), 31.
21 Fripp, *Shakespeare's Stratford*, 30–1.
22 R. A. Rebholz, *The Life of Fulke Greville* (Oxford, 1971), 5.
23 Nashe, 3.323–4.
24 I think that McMillin and Maclean (*Queen's Men*, 168) overstate the oppositional status of Marlowe, claiming that the Queen's Men plays 'called Marlowe the enemy'. Though his surviving plays were written for rival companies, he was probably willing, like his friend and collaborator Nashe, to write for any company that would pay him. He was perhaps more rival than enemy, with the Queen's Men's *Selimus* a clear attempt to ape the success of the Lord Admiral's Men's *Tamburlaine*.

25 *Queen's Men*, 44–6, 52–3 and *passim*.
26 Nashe, 1.188.
27 Nashe, 3.244. For obvious reasons this passage has not been modernized.
28 Dutton, *Revels*, 74–6.
29 However, Richard Proudfoot tells me that some scholars believe that this is an error for 'hearty knee'.
30 See G. M. Pinciss, 'Thomas Creede and the repertory of the Queen's Men 1583–92', *Modern Philology*, 67 (1969–70), 321–30.
31 Lost play, based on an episode in Jorge de Montemayor's *Diana*, which is a likely source for *The Two Gentlemen of Verona*. The scenes between Launce and his dog point to the Queen's Men origins of *Two Gentlemen*, for one of Tarlton's most celebrated turns was a scene in which, armed with a longstaff ('launce') and dagger, he pretended to fight with one of the Queen's small dogs.
32 *DL*, 115.
33 Nashe, 1.287–8.
34 Ibid., 1.287.
35 Cf. Warren B. Austin, *A Computer-aided Technique for Stylistic Discrimination: The Authorship of 'Greenes Groatsworth of Wit'* (Washington, D. C., 1969).
36 Nashe, 1.287–8. For the possible identity of 'Will Monox, see Benjamin Griffin, 'Nashe's dedicatees: William Beeston and Richard Lichfield', *N&Q*, 242 (1997), 47–9.
37 Timothy Kendall, *Flowers of Epigrammes, out of sundrie most singuler authors selected, as well auncient as late writers* (1577), fol. 26^{v}.
38 Ben Jonson, *The New Inn*, 2.5., in Jonson, 6.432.
39 Nashe, 2.318.
40 Nashe, 3.174.
41 Nashe, 2.326.
42 Ibid., 327.
43 '[H]ow unsearchable are [God's] judgments, and his ways past finding out', Romans, 11.33.
44 *Groats-worth*, 84.
45 Nashe, 1.35, 168, 173.
46 Nashe, 3.315.
47 H. J. Oliver, ed., *Dido Queen of Carthage and The Massacre at Paris* (London, 1968), xxiii.
48 See Jonathan Bate's discussion in the Arden 3 *Titus Andronicus* (1995).
49 Gustav Ungerer, 'An unrecorded Elizabethan performance of *Titus Andronicus*', *Shakespeare Survey*, 14 (1961), 102–9.

Notes

three 1592–4 Plague and poetry

1 The exact figure varied, as did the number of parishes included in the computation: see Gurr, *Playing Companies*, 89–90.
2 It is much more often encountered as a metaphor for the 'infection' of love, as in 'Write "Lord have mercy on us" on those three. / They are infected' (*Love's Labour's Lost*, 5.2.419–20); grateful thanks to Henry Woudhuysen for this reference.
3 F. P. Wilson, *The Plague in Shakespeare's London* (Oxford, 1927), 55–6.
4 Modernized from British Library Lansdowne MS 99, fol. 87^{v}, letter to Lord Burghley and the citizens of London, 21 September 1593.
5 Wilson, *Plague*, 61.
6 Cf. also *Timon of Athens*, 4.1.21–3, 'Plagues incident to men, / Your potent and infectious fevers heap / On Athens ripe for stroke!'
7 Nashe, 1.212.
8 Michael Hattaway, ed., *The First Part of King Henry VI* (Cambridge, 1990), 34–5.
9 R. A. Foakes and R. T. Rickert, eds, *Henslowe's Diary* (Cambridge, 1961), 16.
10 Nashe, 1.155.
11 Nashe, 3.412. Cf. also the explicit dedication 'To the right Honourable the Lord Strainge' in MS Folger V.a.399, fol. 53^{v}.
12 For texts of his four surviving poems, see S. W. May, *The Elizabethan Courtier Poets* (Columbia, Missouri, 1991), 369–76.
13 British Library Lansdowne MS 99, fols. 81^{r}–87^{v}; cf. also K. Duncan-Jones, 'Much Ado with Red and White: the earliest readers of Shakespeare's *Venus and Adonis* (1593)', *RES*, 176 (1993), 479–501.
14 MS Folger V.a.460, fol. 3^{r}.
15 Ibid., fols. 43^{r},61^{v},61^{r}.
16 Ibid., fol. 8^{v}.
17 '*Ora licet tenera vix dum lanugine vernent*': from John Sandford, *Apollinis et Musarum Euktika Eidyllia* (Oxford, 1592).
18 G. P. V. Akrigg, *Shakespeare and the Earl of Southampton* (London, 1968), 33. See also Charles Martindale and Colin Burrow, 'Clapham's Narcissus: A Pre-Text for Shakespeare's *Venus and Adonis* ?', *English Literary Renaissance*, 22 (1992), 147–76, which provides a useful text and translation of *Narcissus*, to which should be added the details of the poem's title-page, and the fact that a copy of *Narcissus* survives at Hatfield, the Cecil mansion.
19 Phyllis Grosskurth, ed., *The Memoirs of John Addington Symonds* (London, 1984), 62–3. Symonds was born in 1840, so he is recalling a time that happens to coincide with publication of the Victorian poem most shaped by *Shakespeare's Sonnets*, Tennyson's *In Memoriam* (1850).
20 Victor A. Doyno, ed., *Barnabe Barnes: Parthenophil and Parthenope* (London and Amsterdam, 1971), lxxii, 132.

21 Akrigg, *Shakespeare and Southampton*, 33.
22 Nashe, 2.229. I have quoted the last clause because it may have influenced Shakespeare's presentation of Henry V's banishing from court of the 'fat gross' Falstaff in *2 Henry IV*.
23 Nashe, 2.286–7.
24 Nashe, 2.271–9; and see Katherine Duncan-Jones, 'Nashe and Sidney: the tournament in *The Unfortunate Traveller*', *Modern Language Review*, 63 (1968), 3–6.
25 Sandford, *Apollinis et Musarum Euktika Eidyllia*.
26 David H. Horne, *The Life and Minor Works of George Peele* (New Haven, 1952), 271.
27 Nashe, 2.292.
28 Needless to say, I do not support Jonathan Bate's late dating of the play to 1593–4 in his otherwise excellent Arden 3 edition (1995).
29 Nashe, 2.295.
30 See Gurr, *Playing Companies*, 91.
31 After barely six months as Earl of Derby, Ferdinando Stanley died at Knowsley on 16 April 1594. It was widely alleged that he had been poisoned. Strange's Men appear to have dispersed, some of its sharers being adopted by other companies; Gurr, *Playing Companies*, 264–5.
32 Sidney, 218. Although the *Defence* was not published until 1595, this is one of several links with it that suggest that Shakespeare may have read it in manuscript: see Katherine Duncan-Jones, 'Rose-water doubly distilled: Shakespeare's re-writings of Sidney', *Sidney Journal and Newsletter*, 15.4 (Fall 1997), 3–20.
33 The conceit of this stanza, showing a woman reversing her utterance by means of the single word 'not', recalls sonnet 145, discussed and quoted in chapter 1, and may confirm Gurr's hypothesis that this sonnet was written very early.
34 Nashe, 3.92.
35 Jonson, 4.209.
36 A 'Captain Edmonds's' company of soldiers is referred to as being at Carrickfergus: cf. *CSP Ireland*, 507.
37 Modernized extract from Cecil Papers, Hatfield House, M/485/41. vol. 83, fol. 62.

four 1595–8 Spear-shaking Shakespeare

1 Cf. Kate Bennett, 'Baldock's "Gentrie": social climbing in *Edward II*', *N&Q*, 242 (1997), 483–4.
2 John Ferne, *The Blazon of Gentrie* (1586), 91.
3 Ibid., 75.
4 See chapter 3, pp. 56–7.
5 *Venus and Adonis* was printed at least twice in 1594, and again in ?1595 and 1596.
6 In the five years 1595–1600 he seems to have got through more than £30,000; see

Lawrence Stone, *Family and Fortune* (Oxford, 1973), 217–18. According to Stone, his imprisonment in the Tower after Essex's rebellion was a blessing, in so far as it inhibited further spending.

7 According to *DNB*; and see Anthony Wagner, *Heralds of England* (London, 1967), 147.

8 Nicholas Rowe, ed., *The Works of Mr William Shakespeare* (1709), 1.2.

9 Personal communication.

10 MS Folger V. a.156, fols. 2v–3r.

11 Ibid., fol. 12v.

12 Ibid., fols. 14v–15r.

13 *Every Man out of his Humour*, 3.4.47, in Jonson, 3.502–6.

14 The draft patent, College of Arms Shakespeare Drafts 2, refers to the 'achevement' as available to be borne on 'seales, ringes, edefices, Buildinges, utensiles, lyverees, Tombes, or monuments'.

15 Ferne, *The Blazon of Gentrie*, 77.

16 *DL*, 136.

17 Cf. David Wiles, *Shakespeare's Almanac* (London, 1993), 162.

18 For a text of this letter, see Katherine Duncan-Jones, '*Christs Teares*, Nashe's "forsaken extremities" ', *RES*, 194 (1998), 167–80.

19 Francis Bamford, ed., *A Royalist's Notebook: The Commonplace Book of Sir John Oglander Kt. of Nunwell* (London, 1936), 88–91.

20 Nashe, 5.194.

21 Dutton, *Revels*, 106.

22 Jonson, 1.139–40.

23 Ibid., 8.41.

24 William Smith, Rouge Dragon, 'A breeff Discourse of the causes of Discord amongst the offices of Armes', MS Folger V. a.157, an autograph draft dedicated to the Earl of Northampton; cf. also MS Folger V. a.199, a scribal copy dedicated to Lord Burghley.

25 College of Arms, Shakespeare Drafts 1, 2.

26 'X', *The Right to Bear Arms* (London, 1900), 22.

27 Nashe, 1.35.

28 C. W. Scott-Giles, *Shakespeare's Heraldry* (London, 1950), 33.

29 Gerard Legh, *The Accedence of Armorie* (1591 edn), fol. 3v.

30 G. R. French, *Shakespeareana Genealogica* (1869).

31 Scott-Giles, *Shakespeare's Heraldry*, frontispiece; see Plate 4.

32 H. R. Woudhuysen, *Sir Philip Sidney and the Circulation of Manuscripts, 1558–1640* (Oxford, 1996), 34; cf. also 21n., 29, 47.

33 P. Hanks and F. Hodges, *A Dictionary of Surnames* (Oxford, 1988), 487.

34 Nashe, 1.179.

35 Scott-Giles, *Shakespeare's Heraldry*, 200–1.

36 B. H. Newdigate, *Michael Drayton and his Circle* (Oxford, 1941), 150–1.
37 *OED sv.* feather 8b, first example 1581.
38 Grateful thanks to Dr Martin Wiggins for this suggestion.
39 T. W. Craik, ed., *Merry Wives of Windsor* (Oxford, 1989), 3.
40 Rowe, ed., *Works*, 1.viii–ix.
41 *Astrophil and Stella*, Song 2, in Sidney, 182.
42 *Merry Wives*, 1.1.14ff.; and cf. Leslie Hotson, *Shakespeare versus Shallow* (Boston, 1931).
43 Modernized extract from British Library Lansdowne MS 18, fols. 9^{v}–8^{r}.
44 *DNB*; and for a full account of 'Dethickes abuses' see Bodleian MS Ashmole 857, fols. 493–7.
45 MS Folger V.b.7, Henry Howard, Earl of Northampton, 'A briefe discourse of the right use of gevinge armes, with the late abuses about that matter, and the beste meane by which they may be reformed orderly', circa 1600.
46 Ralph Brooke, *A Discoverie of Certaine Errours, published in print in the much commended Britannia in 1594. Very prejudiciall to the discentes and successions of the auncient Nobilitie of this Realme* (1596).
47 Ibid., sig. $A3^{r-v}$.
48 Ibid., p. 17.
49 Ibid., p. 79.
50 MS Folger V.a.156; see also MS Folger V.a.350.7.
51 *OED sv.* ability 4; and note the quotation from Baret's *Alvearie* (1580): 'To be of ability; to live like a gentleman'.
52 Ferne, *The Blazon of Gentrie*, 62.
53 John Davies of Hereford, *Microcosmos* (Oxford, 1603), 215.

FIVE 1599 OUR BENDING AUTHOR

1 *1 Henry IV* was printed in quarto this year, 1599, as was *Romeo and Juliet*.
2 Could it have been awareness of this that made Shakespeare put the passage 'I saw young Harry with his beaver on' in *1 Henry IV*, 4.1 into the mouth of her forebear Sir Richard Vernon?
3 Letter of Rowland Whyte to Sir Robert Sidney, 19 January 1598. HMC, *De L'Isle and Dudley*, 2.312.
4 Gervase Markham, *The Most Honourable Tragedie of Sir Richard Grinvile, Knight* (1595), sig. $A4^{r}$, sonnet to Southampton beginning:

   Thou glorious laurel of the Muses' hill,
   Whose eyes doth crown the most victorious pen.

5 Some of his friends and associates backed off from him during this period: for instance his kinsman Thomas Arundell claimed in a letter to Robert Cecil of

18 February 1601 that 'I saw him but once this two year', alarmed by his extravagance and lack of self-control (Bodleian MS Ashmole 1729, fols. 189–90).

6 Francis Meres, *Palladis Tamia. Wits Treasury* (1598), fols. 281^{v}–2^{r}.

7 Thomas Dekker, *The pleasant Comedie of Old Fortunatus* (1600).

8 HMC, *De L'Isle and Dudley*, 2.401.

9 Thomas Dekker, *Satiro-mastix. Or the untrussing of the Humorous Poet. As it hath bin presented publikely, by the Right Honorable the Lord Chamberlaine his Servants; and privately, by the Children of Paules* (printed 1602).

10 Bearman, 31–6.

11 In which, as Anne Barton has cogently suggested, Shakespeare himself may have been Jonson's collaborator: *Ben Jonson, Dramatist* (Cambridge, 1984), 93–4.

12 Bodleian MS Top. Oxon. e.5, fol. 359.

13 Andrew Gurr, ed., *King Henry V* (Cambridge, 1992), 27–8.

14 *DL*, 162–3.

15 According to Schoenbaum, *DL*, 163, 'At that time Surrey and Sussex managed with one sheriff between them.'

16 J. G. Nichols, *Progresses of Queen Elizabeth*, 3 vols (1823), 3.438–41

17 Quoted in *DL*, 106.

18 See Matthew Steggle, *Wars of the Theatres: The Poetics of Personation in the Age of Jonson* (Toronto, 1998), 27–9.

19 *Parnassus Plays*, 337–8.

20 However, if my suggestion in the next chapter that Shakespeare worked closely with Marston is correct, Jonson's attack on Marston might carry with it a sidelong glance at his more senior friend.

21 Jonson, 9.410. Asper, the 'ingenious and free spirit' who is the hero of *Every Man Out* is of course Jonson's flattering self-portrait.

22 Jonson, 1.141.

23 Ibid., 188.

24 Alan Brissenden, ed., *As You Like It* (Oxford, 1993), 2–3.

25 HMC, *De L'Isle and Dudley*, 2.395–6.

26 Ibid., 397.

27 Chambers, *Elizabethan Stage*, 2.204–5.

six 1600–3 Sweet Master Shakespeare!

1 In Ovid's *Metamorphoses*, 4, Melicert is the baby son of Ino, who falls into the sea with her and is metamorphosed into the sea god Palaemon; however, Chettle probably chose the name because of 'mel', meaning 'honey, and is echoing Francis Meres's phrase 'mellifluous and honey-tongued *Shakespeare*'.

2 Henry Chettle, *Englands Mourning Garment* (1603).

3 Perhaps the paramount reason for this failure was that Shakespeare viewed the Queen, after the execution of Essex and condemnation of Southampton to life imprisonment, as a cruel tyrant who had lived too long.
4 British Library Harley MS 5353, fol. 29[v]; and *Manningham's Diary*, 75, 319.
5 J. Dover Wilson, ed., *The Sonnets* (Cambridge, 1967), xcix–ci.
6 It is possible that *Othello* belongs here, too; in the Arden 3 edition E. A. J. Honigmann argues that it was performed in 1602. However, I am more inclined to see it as written in the following year.
7 E. A. J. Honigmann, ed., *John Weever: A Biography of a Literary Associate of Shakespeare and Jonson, together with a photographic facsimile of Weever's Epigrammes (1599)* (Manchester, 1987).
8 Hotson, *Sonnets Dated*, 45; see also E. I. Fripp, *Master Richard Quyny* (Oxford, 1924), 154–7.
9 For a detailed study of many of the Middle Templars who came from the Midlands, and especially from south of Stratford, see Christopher Whitfield, 'Some of Shakespeare's contemporaries at the Middle Temple', *N&Q*, 211 (1966), 122–5; 283–7; 363–9; 443–8. For Thomas Russell, see Eccles, 116–18.
10 *Manningham's Diary*, 172, 374.
11 Philip Finkelpearl, *John Marston of the Middle Temple* (Cambridge, Mass., 1969), 11.
12 Quoted ibid., 20.
13 One of his own direct descendants was Dr Johnson's friend Hester Thrale, née Salusbury.
14 Carleton Brown, ed., *Poems by Sir John Salusbury and Robert Chester* (Early English Text Society, Extra Series, 113 [1914]), xvi.
15 George Puttenham, *The Arte of English Poesie* (1589), 186.
16 For this reason, I cannot accept the suggestion of Anthea Hume that *Loves Martyr* and its coda 'is concerned with . . . the relationship between Queen and people in the aftermath of the Essex Rebellion, and the solution to the succession problem through the person of James Stuart, the New Phoenix' (see Anthea Hume, '*Loves Martyr*, The Phoenix and the Turtle' and the aftermath of the Essex Rebellion', *RES*, n.s. 40 [1989], 48–7). Nevertheless, her very full and lucid account of the poem and of the various theories about it can be recommended.
17 The evidence that Catherine's grandfather Sir Roland Veleville was the acknowledged son of Henry VII is set out by W. R. B. Robinson, 'Sir Roland Veleville and the Tudor dynasty: a reassessment', *Welsh History Review*, 15 (1991), 351–67.
18 See John Ballinger, *Katheryn of Berain: A Study in North Wales Family History* (London, 1929; reprinted from *Y Cymmrodor*, 60).
19 Carleton Brown, ed., *Poems by Sir John Salusbury*, 38–40.
20 Ibid., 20–1.
21 The fact that Jonson, a notoriously slow writer, seems to have re-cycled a poem he

had written earlier (his 'Epode'), points to haste in the compilation of the *Poeticall Essaies*.

22 *DL*, 188.

23 Ibid., 188–9.

24 Katherine Duncan-Jones, *Sir Philip Sidney: Courtier Poet* (London, 1991), 11–13.

25 W. Reavley Gair, ed., *Antonio's Revenge: John Marston* (Manchester and Baltimore, 1978), 12–14.

26 See also Marston's allusions to the popularity of *Romeo and Juliet* in Satyre 11 in *The Scourge of Villanie*, and to *Richard III* in the opening line of Satyre 7.

27 *Antonio's Revenge*, 30.

28 *DL*, 155–6. Early estimates of his annual income range from £200 (Malone) to £1,000 (John Ward); Schoenbaum settles cautiously for about £250.

29 Cerasano, 'Alleyn', 20–3.

30 Eccles, 52–3; Fripp, *Shakespeare's Stratford*, 51.

31 Fripp, *Shakespeare's Stratford*, 51; see also the same author's *Master Richard Quyny* (Oxford, 1924), 60.

32 Harold Jenkins, ed., *Hamlet* (Arden Shakespeare, Second Series, 1982), 7–13.

33 The flower alluded to is probably the early purple orchid whose Latin name is *orchis mascula*.

34 In the source, Bandello / Belleforest, Hamlet returns to Denmark on the day when his own funeral is being celebrated.

35 Translated from a report on the inquest held on 11 February 1580, Public Record Office, Ancient Indictments, 652; *Minutes*, 3.50–1.

36 *Manningham's Diary*, 48.

37 See, for instance, the Arden Second Series *Twelfth Night*, ed. J. M. Lothian and T. W. Craik, xli.

38 *Antonio's Revenge*, 30.

39 The momentousness of this year is suggested by Milton's sonnet beginning 'How soon hath time the subtle thief of youth / Stol'n on his wing my three and twentieth year'. Marston, unlike Milton, did eventually take orders, and may already have had it in mind to do so.

40 Philip Finkelpearl, *John Marston of the Middle Temple* (Cambridge, Mass., 1969), 167ff.; for counter-arguments, see Matthew Steggle, *Wars of the Theatres: The Poetics of Personation in the Age of Jonson* (Victoria, B. C., 1998), 40ff.

41 M. Channing Linthicum, *Costume in the Drama of Shakespeare and his Contemporaries* (Oxford, 1936), 264.

42 *Manningham's Diary*, 207–8.

43 Ibid., 221, entry dated 1 April.

seven 1603–7 The King's Man

1 Barnfield, 182. Most of James's works were printed in London in the spring of 1603.
2 *STC*, 7598.
3 *STC*, 12678.
4 *STC*, 7605.3.
5 *STC*, 20341.
6 Maurice Lee Jr., *Great Britain's Solomon: James VI and I in his Three Kingdoms* (Urbana, Illinois, 1990), 107.
7 N. E. McClure, ed., *The Letters of John Chamberlain*, 2 vols (Philadelphia, 1939), 1.192.
8 Jonson's poem may also allude obliquely to the bird allegory of another poem linked with Denbighshire, Chester's *Loves Martyr*.
9 Berkeley Castle Select Book (unbound) No. 81.
10 Drayton had described Owen Tudor's legendary stumble rather more delicately in *Englands Heroicall Epistles*, in Drayton, 2.209, 212.
11 Drayton, 5.54.
12 Drayton, 1.471.
13 Lee, *Great Britain's Solomon*, 106.
14 Epistle 'To Master George Sandys', in Drayton, 3.206.
15 Anon, *A mournefull Dittie entituled Elizabeths losse, together with a Welcome for King James.*
16 A work probably by Samuel Rowlands, *Greenes ghost haunting cony-catchers*, had been printed in 1602.
17 Drayton, 2.6.
18 I. L., *An Elegie upon the death of the high and renowned Princesse, our late Soveraigne ELIZABETH* (1603), sig. A3^{v}.
19 *CSP Venetian 1603–7*, 77.
20 T. M., *True Narration of the Entertainment of his Royall Majestie* (1603).
21 MacD. P. Jackson, 'Rhymes in Shakespeare's *Sonnets*: evidence of date of composition', *N&Q*, 244 (1999), 213–19; see also A. K. Hieatt, C. Hieatt and A. Lake Prescott, 'When did Shakespeare write *Sonnets* 1609?', *Studies in Philology*, 88 (1991), 69–109.
22 See W. R. Streitberger, ed., *Jacobean and Caroline Revels Accounts, 1603–1642* (Malone Society Collections XIII, Oxford, 1986), 7–15.
23 For a discussion of the King's Men's entertainment of the Spanish ambassadors, see chapter 8, p. 203.
24 Barroll, *Plague*, 106.
25 Chambers, *Shakespeare*, 2.329.
26 Gurr, *Playing Companies*, 304.
27 This figure is of course far too high.
28 For a full account, see Richard Dutton, ed., *Jacobean City Pageants* (Keele, Staffordshire, 1995).
29 Philip J. Ayres, ed., *Sejanus his Fall* (Manchester and New York, 1990), 20.

30 Quoted ibid., 38.
31 An. Sc., *Daiphantus, Or the Passions of Love. Comicall to Reade, but Tragicall to Acte ... Whereunto is added, The passionate mans Pilgrimage* (1604).
32 Nashe seems to have died early in 1601. An epitaph on him by Ben Jonson has lately come to light; see Katherine Duncan-Jones, '"They say a made a good end": Ben Jonson's Epitaph on Thomas Nashe', *Ben Jonson Journal*, 3 (1996), 1–19.
33 *DL*, 205.
34 For instance, two daughters of Queen Elizabeth's former Latin tutor John Baptist Castillion had sons called 'Hamlett'; cf. Bodleian MS Ashmole 852, fol. 43^r.
35 See Barroll, *Plague*, 123–6 and *passim*; Gurr, *Playing Companies*, 298–9.
36 See *Playhouse Wills*, 72–5.
37 Barroll, *Plague*, 78.
38 See Honan, 347.
39 *DL*, 192; and see plate 155 for a reproduction of the indenture. After the dissolution of the monasteries tithes that had been paid to the clergy passed into the hands of secular landowners.
40 For a biography, see P. W. Hasler, *The House of Commons 1558–1603*, 3 vols (London, 1981) 1.346.
41 This may have been a coincidence: it has been plausibly suggested that she was named after Queen Elizabeth's Master Cook, William Cordell of Fulham; see Gyles Isham, 'The prototypes of King Lear and his daughters', *N&Q*, 199 (1954), 150–1; however, she was sometimes referred to as 'Cordella' or 'Cordelia'.
42 HMC, *Salisbury*, 15.262, 265–6.
43 Richard Wilson, 'A constant will to publish: Shakespeare's dead hand', in *Will Power: Essays on Shakespearean authority* (New York and London, 1993), 215–29.
44 See Hasler, *The House of Commons*, 2.267.

EIGHT 1608–9 PAINFUL ADVENTURES

1 For a detailed discussion of the impact of these developments on the theatres, see Janette Dillon, *Theatre, Court and City, 1595–1610: Drama and Social Space in London* (Cambridge, 2000), chapter 6 and *passim*.
2 James Knowles, 'Cecil's shopping centre', *TLS* (7 February 1997), 14–15.
3 By James Knowles (ibid.).
4 Barroll, *Plague*, 142.
5 An example from this period is Barnabe Barnes's *The Divels Charter*, printed 1607, concerning the spectacularly evil machinations of the Borgia Pope Alexander VI (see below, n. 51).
6 *DL*, 235.
7 Jonson, 1.141.

8 Yet another business associate of Shakespeare's, the goldsmith Thomas Savage, has recently been shown by Professor Alan Nelson to have been a dedicated and generous member of his parish church (paper delivered at the 'Lancastrian Shakespeare' Conference, University of Lancaster, July 1999).
9 Grateful thanks to Dr Arnold Hunt for drawing this to my attention.
10 Quoted in *DL*, 26.
11 The later winter months were generally 'the period of highest seasonal mortality'; see Jeremy Boulton's study of Southwark, *Neighbourhood and Society: A London Suburb in the Seventeenth Century* (Cambridge, 1987), 49.
12 John Weever, *Ancient Funerall Monuments* (1631), chapter 3, 'Of Sepulchres answerable to the degree of the person deceased', 10.
13 Ibid.
14 Now Southwark Cathedral.
15 See Boulton, *Neighbourhood*, 150.
16 *Victoria County History of Surrey*, 4.154.
17 *King Lear*, ed. R. A. Foakes (Arden Shakespeare, Third Series, 1997), 44.
18 There was a current fashion for the use of a Chorus: cf. Barnes's *The Divels Charter*, George Wilkins's *The Travailes of the Three English Brothers*, Heywood's *The Golden Age* (1611).
19 For an account of echoes of Sidney in *Pericles*, see Katherine Duncan-Jones, 'Rose-water doubly distilled: Shakespeare's re-writings of Sidney', *Sidney Journal and Newsletter*, 15.4 (Fall 1997), 3–20.
20 Doreen DelVecchio and Antony Hammond, eds, *Pericles* (Cambridge, 1998), 1.
21 This date is favoured also, for different reasons, by Barroll, *Plague*, 193–6.
22 Chambers, *Shakespeare*, 2.335.
23 George Wilkins, *The painfull Adventures of Pericles Prince of Tyre. Being The true History of the Play of Pericles, as it was lately presented by the worthy and ancient Poet John Gower* (1608); see also the edition by Kenneth Muir (Liverpool, 1953). The connection of Wilkins's text with the play is convincingly reaffirmed by Roger Warren, 'Theatrical use and editorial abuse: more painful adventures for Pericles', *RES*, 196 (1998), 478–86.
24 For a very full discussion of this episode, see Ernest Law, *Shakespeare as a Groom of the Chamber* (London, 1910).
25 Chambers, *Elizabethan Stage*, 2.53–4; Allan Holaday, ed., *The Plays of George Chapman: The Tragedies* (Urbana, 1987), 266–9.
26 Linguistic and stylistic study in recent years has corroborated the traditional view that Wilkins is the author of Acts 1 and 2: see for instance MacD. P. Jackson, 'The authorship of *Pericles*: the evidence of infinitives', *N&Q*, 238 (1993), 197–200; see 199n. for a useful list of other studies confirming the role of Wilkins.
27 Anon, *Pimlyco. Or, Runne Red-Cap. 'Tis a mad world at Hogsdon* (1609), sig. C1^r.
28 Copy of Chapman, *An Humorous dayes mirth* (1599), in the Folger Shakespeare Library (*STC*, 4987, Copy 1); the lines are adapted from *Pericles*, 2.2.55–6, 'Opinion's

but a fool, that makes us scan / The outward habit by the inward man'. Bentley's garbled version suggests recollection of a performance.

29 See Katherine Duncan-Jones, 'Prentices and prodigals: a new allusion to *The Hogge hath lost his Pearl*', *N&Q*, 241 (1997), 88–90.

30 Jonson, 6.492.

31 See C. J. Sisson, 'Shakespeare's Quartos as prompt-copies, with some account of Cholmeley's Players and a new Shakespeare allusion', *RES*, 18 (1942), 129–43.

32 British Library Egerton MS 2592, fols. 81–2.

33 Roger Prior, 'The life of George Wilkins', *SS*, 25 (1972), 137–52; 'George Wilkins and the young heir', *SS*, 29 (1976), 33–9.

34 Honan, 329.

35 *RI*, 20–39.

36 Bodleian MSS Ashmole 226, fols. 263^{v}, 316^{v}; Ashmole 195, fol. 15^{v}; cf. also A. L. Rowse, *Simon Forman: Sex and Society in Shakespeare's Age* (London, 1974), 96–9.

37 Marston had now abandoned the theatre for the church, possibly because he got into trouble through association with Chapman's *Byron* plays; he was imprisoned in Newgate for a while in June 1608. In December 1609 he applied for permission to read in the Bodleian Library, and on Christmas Eve he was ordained priest by the Bishop of Oxford.

38 Roger Sharpe, *More Fooles yet* (1610), sigs. B4^{v}–C1^{r}. For many more literary allusions to Turnmill or Turnbull Street see E. H. Sugden, *A Topographical Dictionary to the Works of Shakespeare and his Fellow Dramatists* (Manchester, 1925), 533–4.

39 George Wilkins, *The Miseries of Inforst Mariage. As it is now playd by his Majesties Servants* (1607).

40 However, one early reader, who made detailed notes on the book, appended the comment: 'Add on to these the Plague at the entrance of King James, not yet ended. 1607'; see Bodleian MS Add. B.97, fols.2^{v}ff.

41 Anon, *Two most unnatural and bloodie Murthers* (1605).

42 A. C. Cawley and Barry Gaines, eds, *A Yorkshire Tragedy* (Manchester, 1988), 2.

43 Ibid.: note also strong arguments for the text's punctuation as distinctively Shakespearean: Glenn H. Blayney, 'Dramatic pointing in the 'Yorkshire Tragedy', *N&Q*, 220 (1957), 191–2.

44 *DL*, 184.

45 Ibid.

46 Francis Meres, *Palladis Tamia. Wits Treasury* (1598), fols. 281^{v}–2^{r}.

47 Robert Armin, *A nest of ninnies* (1608); John Lowin, *Brief conclusions of dancers and dancing* (1609).

48 Many of the satires and epigrams published in 1609 also combine misogyny with some 'knowingness' about same-sex relationships.

49 *Shakespeare's Sonnets*, ed. Katherine Duncan-Jones (Arden Shakespeare, Third Series, 1997), 1–28.

50 For a full account of Thorpe's publishing career, see Katherine Duncan-Jones, 'Was the 1609 *Shakespeares Sonnets* really unauthorized?', *RES*, 34 (1983), 151–71.

51 Barnes's play is notable both for its mimicry of Shakespeare's *Antony and Cleopatra*, in the scene in which the Pope murders two young boys with 'aspics', and for its strong and ambivalent treatment of homoeroticism. Though Pope Alexander's passionate attempt to woo the boy Astor is shown as evil, the scene may nevertheless have been calculated to please the King, before whom the play was performed at Candlemas 1607. The very same boys who had played Cleopatra and Charmian may have played Astor and his brother.

52 *STC*, 22360a, misdated 1602.

NINE 1610–13 OUR REVELS NOW ARE ENDED

1 Schoenbaum, for instance, argues in a somewhat circular manner that in 'a speech of such evident dramatic propriety' we need not hear 'autobiographical reverberations', *DL*, 228.

2 Ibid., 230.

3 See Johannes Fabricius, *Syphilis in Shakespeare's England* (London and Bristol, Pennsylvania, 1994), 270.

4 Chapter 2; and see Geoffrey Eatough, ed., *Fracastoro's Syphilis* (Liverpool, 1984). In the poem the diseased shepherd Syphilus is cured by the New World tree 'guaiacum'; however, this had not in practice displaced treatment with mercury.

5 See S. P. Zitner, ed., Francis Beaumont, *The Knight of the Burning Pestle* (Manchester, 1984), 121 and *passim*.

6 Peter Lowe, *An easie, certaine, and perfect method, to cure and prevent the Spanish sicknes* (1596), sig. B6^{r}.

7 Gabriel Harvey, *Foure Letters, and certaine Sonnets* (1592), 22; the churchyard was created by Sir Thomas Roe in 1569, 'for burial and ease of such parishes in London as wanted ground convenient within their parishes' (C. L. Kingsford, ed., *John Stow: A Survey of London* [Oxford, 1908], 1.165).

8 See, for instance, Samuel Rowlands, *Greenes ghost haunting cony-catchers* (1602).

9 John Dickenson, *Greene in Conceipt. New raised from his grave to write the Tragique Historie of faire Valeria of London* (1598).

10 See Bullough, 8.118; the wording of the Oracle used in *The Winter's Tale* is that of the 1588, 1592 and 1595 editions, not that of 1607 onwards.

11 Robert Greene, *The Repentance. Robert Greene, Maister of Artes* (1592), sig. C3.

12 See James Knowles, 'Jonson's *Entertainment at Britain's Burse*', in Martin Butler, ed., *Re-Presenting Ben Jonson* (London, 1999), 139–40.

13 Among the participants was Shakespeare's former patron the Earl of Southampton, who danced with Princess Elizabeth; see Jonson, 10.522–3.

14 Barroll, *Plague*, 186.
15 *Tx C*, 131. As explained in the Preface, I am not convinced that the supposed testimony of Simon Forman to have seen it at the Globe in April 1611 is authentic.
16 See Gurr, *Playing Companies*, 387–8: in 1610 they were Robert Armin, Richard Burbage, Henry Condell, Alexander Cook, Richard Cowley, John Duke, Lawrence Fletcher, John Heminge, John Lowin, William Ostler, William Shakespeare, Nicholas Tooley and John Underwood.
17 Barroll, *Plague*, 184.
18 Richard Proudfoot, 'Shakespeare and the new dramatists of the King's Men 1606–1613', *Stratford-upon-Avon Studies 8: Later Shakespeare* (1966), 235–61.
19 Bodleian MS Aubrey, fol. 116^v^; edited in Andrew Clark, *'Brief Lives' by John Aubrey*, 2 vols (Oxford, 1898), 1.96.
20 A neat epigram addressed 'To the true Master in his Art, B. Jonson' prefaced to *Volpone* (1607) seems to have been Fletcher's first published work.
21 See Sandra Clark, *The Plays of Beaumont and Fletcher: Sexual Themes and Dramatic Representation* (London, 1994).
22 See Hilton Kelliher, 'Francis Beaumont and Nathan Field: new records of their early years', *English Manuscript Studies 1100–1700*, 8 (2000), 1–42.
23 J. M. Nosworthy, ed., *Cymbeline* (Arden Shakespeare, Second Series, 1995), xvi.
24 See Andrew Gurr, ed., Beaumont and Fletcher, *Philaster, or Love Lies a-Bleeding* (London, 1969), xxviii.
25 V. J. Skretkowicz, ed., *Sidney, The Countess of Pembroke's Arcadia (The New Arcadia)* (Oxford, 1987), 266–7.
26 Dutton, *Revels*, 194ff.
27 Silvester Jourdain, *A Discovery of the Barmudas, otherwise called the Ile of Divels* (1610), 11–12.
28 There were precedents for both: 'Roger Bacon burned his books and John Dee claimed to have done so; Albertus Magnus drowned his' – David Bevington and Eric Rasmussen, eds, *Doctor Faustus* (Manchester and New York, 1993), 197.
29 See, for instance, William Strachey's narrative, Bullough, 8.276.
30 Chambers, *Elizabethan Stage*, 2.56.
31 See Andrew Gurr, 'Industrious Ariel and idle Caliban', in J.-P. Maquerlot and M. Willems, eds, *Travel and Drama in Shakespeare's Time* (Cambridge, 1996), 193–208.
32 Indications that the author's 'old brain' was also troubled are presented in the unusually large number of 'mistakes' and loose ends in this play; see the Arden 3 edition (ed. Virginia Mason Vaughan and Alden T. Vaughan, 1999), 16, to which I would add the major 'mistake' that the benevolent Gonzalo is punished rather than rewarded.
33 A strangely close parallel to Shakespeare's play is offered by Thomas Mann's novella *Death in Venice* (1912), in which the writer von Aschenbach gazes in his dying moments at the boy Tadzio wading out to sea. For an account of the context of

Mann's composition of the story – in which Shakespeare seems not to have figured – see David Luke, trans., *Death in Venice and Other Stories,* (London, 1990), xxxiv–xlvii.

34 *As You Like It*, 1.3.11–12.

35 *DL*, 229.

36 Ibid., 211.

37 *RI*, 39.

38 Ibid., 24.

39 Remarried, he died in 1620 after having devised a will 'in which he endeavoured to defraud his only legitimate offspring of her share in his estate'; *RI,* 39.

40 For the career of Humphrey Fludd, or Lloyd, see Andrew Ashbee and David Lasocki, *A Biographical Dictionary of English Court Musicians* (Aldershot, 1998), 1.433–4. Between 1609 and 1618 he was frequently employed to carry letters from the English court to Paris.

41 Jonson, 8.584.

42 *RI*, 47.

43 Honan, 379.

44 W. W. Greg, ed., *Malone Society Collections,* 2.1: *The Blackfriars Records,* 84. Since 1940 Water Lane has been called Blackfriars Lane.

45 Quoted in *DL*, 223.

46 Ibid., 220.

47 See Alan R. Young, 'A note on the tournament impresas in *Pericles*', *SQ*, 36 (1985), 453–7.

48 Modernized from letter of Thomas, Viscount Fenton, to John, Earl of Mar, 14 July 1612; see HMC, *Mar & Kellie: Supplementary Report*, 42. James was to make five further visits to Belvoir.

49 Jonson, 11.374–7.

50 Jonson, 8.64–5.

51 Ibid., 85.

52 'John Jackson and Thomas Savage', in Hotson, *Sonnets Dated,* 125–40. See also Michael Strachan, *The Life and Adventures of Thomas Coryate* (London and New York, 1962), 281.

53 See C. B. Wallace, 'Shakespeare and his London associates', *University Studies of University of Nebraska*, 10 (1910), 305ff., for documents in the Witter–Heminge case, in which John Heminge protected the interests both of the Globe sharers and of Augustine Phillips's widow against her fortune-seeking second husband, John Witter; Witter's case grumbled on from 1606 to 1620, but was eventually dismissed.

54 I do not mean by this that he is sole author of the scenes I discuss; I believe that the jury is still out on the question of the exact distribution of work between Shakespeare and Fletcher, and I shall not attempt to settle the matter.

55 Logan Pearsall Smith, ed., *The Life and Letters of Sir Henry Wotton*, 2 vols (Oxford, 1907), 2.32–3, letter to Edmund Bacon dated 2 July 1613.

56 Ibid.
57 See M. J. Cole, 'A new account of the burning of the Globe', *SQ*, 32 (1981), 352; see also H. R. Woudhuysen, '*King Henry VIII* and "All is True"', *N&Q*, 229 (1984), 217–18.
58 Personal communication.
59 An obvious candidate is the master-copy of Shakespeare and Fletcher's *Cardenio*, performed at court in May 1613, but not included in either the Shakespeare Folio or the Beaumont and Fletcher one.
60 For the play's likely date, see Lois Potter, ed., *The Two Noble Kinsmen* (Arden Shakespeare, Third Series, 1997), 34–5. The lack of any printing until 1634 and of any early allusions suggests that it was not a popular success.

TEN 1614–16 HIS LINE OF LIFE

1 *DL*, 228.
2 Peter Whelan, *The Herbal Bed* (London, 1996).
3 *RI*, 77.
4 Keith Thomas, 'Age and authority in early modern England', *Proceedings of the British Academy*, 62 (1976), 205–48.
5 Ibid., 233.
6 See Thirsk, 94: 'the Arden country was concerned first and foremost with meat production, particularly veal and beef'.
7 Gurr, *Playing Companies*, 389.
8 John Munro et al., eds, *Shakespeare Allusion-Book*, 2 vols (London, 1932), 2.437–8.
9 See Chambers, *Elizabethan Stage*, 2.328–9.
10 Cerasano, 'Alleyn', 23.
11 *DL*, 230.
12 Ibid., 234–5.
13 Lane, *Hall*, *passim*.
14 Ibid., 61.
15 In the event, both of Elizabeth Hall's marriages were childless, though her second, to the widower Sir John Barnard, was socially advantageous.
16 Most of what follows is based on *RI*, 72–92.
17 Thirsk, 200.
18 G. M. Logan and R. M. Adams, ed. and trans., *Thomas More: Utopia* (Cambridge, 1989), 18–20.
19 Thirsk, 207.
20 Lane, *Hall*, 239, 263.
21 The Greenes and the Shakespeares may have been connected by marriage rather than blood, though possibly by both; see Anthony Arlidge, *Shakespeare and the Prince of Love* (London, 2000), 40–2 for a useful discussion and family tree.

22 *RI*, 72.
23 Lane, *Hall*, 127–8.
24 Another godchild, William Walker, was remembered, being left 20 shillings in gold.
25 *DL*, 242.
26 Quoted in Samuel Schoenbaum, *Shakespeare's Lives*, rev. edn (Oxford, 1991), 66.
27 Work in progress by A. K. Hieatt and others may furnish linguistic evidence to support the hypothesis that some Folio texts have been authorially revised.
28 Lane, *Hall*, 145, 261–3.
29 Ibid., 21, 38–9, 56, 245, 271, 285.
30 Ibid., 345.
31 Ibid., xxxiv.
32 *Playhouse Wills*, 17.
33 For some supplementary information about Hall's medical practice, see Nicholas Barton, 'Physician of Stratford. Dr John Hall: his life, times and patients', *Journal of Medical Biography*, 8 (2000), 8–15. I am grateful to Dr Trevor Hughes for drawing this to my attention.
34 *King Lear*, 1.4.246.
35 Richard Quiney had died in May 1602 after being attacked and wounded by some drunken servants of Sir Edward Greville's; for a full account, see Eccles, 98–9.
36 Lane, *Hall*, 33–4.
37 E. A. J. Honigmann, 'The second-best bed', *New York Review of Books*, 38.18 (7 November 1991), 30.
38 *DL*, 241.
39 Mairi Macdonald, 'A new discovery about Shakespeare's estate in Old Stratford', *SQ*, 45 (1994), 87–93.
40 *DL*, 241.
41 Edgar I. Fripp, *Master Richard Quyny* (Oxford, 1924), 207.
42 *DL*, 223.
43 Honigmann, 'The second-best bed', 30.
44 Eccles, 42.
45 A. L. Rowse, letter to the *TLS*, 25 November 1994.
46 Quoted in *DL*, 248.
47 For an account both of this type of monument, and of the work of the Johnsons, see Margaret Whinney, *Sculpture in Britain 1530 to 1830* (revised by John Physick, London, 1988), 47–9, 431.
48 See Diana Price, 'Reconsidering Shakespeare's monument', *RES*, 48 (1997), 168–82, for a suggestion that details of Shakespeare's family were planned for inclusion on a tomb below the monument: personally I am not convinced.
49 These included his 'fellows' Heminge, Burbage and Condell. However, the sum he bequeathed for the purpose, 26*s.* 8*d.*, was less generous than the 30*s.* bequeathed

to Shakespeare and two other King's Men by Augustine Phillips in 1605; see *Playhouse Wills*, 73.

50 Thomas Russell and Francis Collins, who were to be appointed overseers of his will, were probably among Stratford guests, as well as Thomas Combe.

51 Jonson, 1.232.

52 This contrasts with the death of Ben Jonson, who had lived to become a legend in his own lifetime: his funeral procession in London included 'all or the greatest part of the nobility and gentry then in the town', and a volume of memorial poems, *Jonsonus Virbius*, was published the following year; Jonson 1.115–16.

Epilogue Read him

1 For what follows, see Peter Blayney, *The First Folio of Shakespeare* (Washington, D.C., Folger Library Publications, 1991).

2 Akihiro Yamada, *The First Folio of Shakespeare: A Transcript of Contemporary Marginalia in a Copy of the Kodama Memorial Library of Meisei University* (Tokyo, 1998), 117.

3 Although Vincent described the copy (now in the Folger) as a gift from William Jaggard, it was presumably presented by his son Isaac, since William Jaggard had died in October 1623.

4 Augustine Vincent, *A Discoverie of Errours in the first Edition of the Catalogue of Nobility Published by Raphe Brooke, York Herald, 1619* (1622).

5 Whereas Jonson, Drayton and Fletcher are all shown in early portrait-engravings wearing a crown of bay, it is odd that Shakespeare, whose baldness might most seem to require such flattery, is not.

6 The presence of the Droeshout engraving in its 'first state' shows that this is a copy produced during the earliest print-run.

7 F. W. Madan et al., *The Original Bodleian Copy of the First Folio of Shakespeare (The Turbutt Shakespeare)* (Oxford, 1905), 7 and *passim*.

8 Ibid., 14.

9 Henry Clay Folger.

Abbreviations

Barnfield	George Klawitter, ed., *Richard Barnfield: The Complete Poems* (London and Toronto, 1990)
Barroll, *Plague*	J. Leeds Barroll, *Politics, Plague, and Shakespeare's Theatre* (Ithaca and London, 1991)
Bearman	Robert Bearman, *Shakespeare in the Stratford Records* (Stratford-upon-Avon, 1994)
Bullough	Geoffrey Bullough, *Narrative and Dramatic Sources of Shakespeare*, 8 vols (London, 1957–75)
Cerasano, 'Alleyn'	S. P. Cerasano, 'Edward Alleyn: 1566–1626', in Aileen Reid and Robert Maniura, eds, *Edward Alleyn: Elizabethan Actor, Jacobean Gentleman* (Dulwich Picture Gallery, 1994)
Chambers, *Elizabethan Stage*	E. K. Chambers, *The Elizabethan Stage*, 4 vols (Oxford, 1923)
Chambers, *Shakespeare*	E. K. Chambers, *William Shakespeare: A Study of Facts and Problems*, 2 vols (Oxford, 1930)
CSP	*Calendars of State Papers*
DNB	*Dictionary of National Biography*
DL	Samuel Schoenbaum, *William Shakespeare: A Documentary Life* (Oxford, 1975)
Drayton	J. W. Hebel, Kathleen Tillotson, Bernard Newdigate et al., eds, *The Works of Michael Drayton*, 5 vols (London, 1961)
Dutton, *Revels*	Richard Dutton, *Mastering the Revels* (Iowa, 1991)
Eccles	Mark Eccles, *Shakespeare in Warwickshire* (Madison, Wisconsin, 1961)
Groats-worth	D. Allen Carroll, ed., *Greene's Groats-worth of Wit . . . attributed to Henry Chettle and Robert Greene* (Binghamton, N.Y., 1994)
Gurr, *Playing Companies*	Andrew Gurr, *The Shakespearian Playing Companies* (Oxford, 1996)
HMC	Historical Manuscripts Commission, *Reports on Manuscripts*

Honan	Park Honan, *Shakespeare: A Life* (Oxford, 1998)
Hotson, *Sonnets Dated*	Leslie Hotson, *Shakespeare's Sonnets Dated and Other Essays* (London, 1949)
Jonson	C. H. Herford and Percy and Evelyn Simpson, eds, *Ben Jonson*, 11 vols (Oxford, 1925–52)
Lane, *Hall*	Joan Lane, *John Hall and his Patients: The Medical Practice of Shakespeare's Son-in-Law* (Stratford, 1996)
Manningham's *Diary*	R. P. Sorlien, ed., *The Diary of John Manningham of the Middle Temple* (Hanover, New Hampshire, 1976)
Minutes	*Minutes and Accounts of the Corporation of Stratford-upon-Avon 1553–1620*, vols 1–4 ed. R. Savage and E. I. Fripp, vol. 5 ed. Levi Fox
MS	Manuscript
Nashe	R. B. McKerrow, ed., *The Works of Thomas Nashe*, 5 vols, 2nd edn, ed. F. P. Wilson (Oxford, 1958)
N&Q	*Notes and Queries*
OED	*Oxford English Dictionary*
Parnassus Plays	J. B. Leishman, ed., *The Three Parnassus Plays (1598–1601)* (London, 1949)
Playhouse Wills	E. A. J. Honigmann and Susan Brock, eds, *Playhouse Wills 1558–1642* (Manchester and New York, 1993)
Queen's Men	Scott McMillin and Sally-Beth Maclean, *The Queen's Men and their Plays* (Cambridge, 1998)
RES	*The Review of English Studies* (referred to by through-number not volume)
RI	Samuel Schoenbaum, *William Shakespeare: Records and Images* (London, 1981)
Sidney	Katherine Duncan-Jones, ed., *The Oxford Authors: Sir Philip Sidney* (Oxford, 1989)
SQ	*Shakespeare Quarterly*
SS	*Shakespeare Survey*
STC	A. W. Pollard and G. R. Redgrave, eds, *A Short-title Catalogue of Books printed in England, Scotland and Ireland 1475–1640*, rev. W. A. Jackson and F. S. Ferguson, completed by Katharine F. Pantzer, 3 vols (London, 1976–91)
Thirsk	Joan Thirsk, ed., *The Agrarian History of England and Wales IV: 1500–1640* (Cambridge, 1974)
TLS	*The Times Literary Supplement*
TxC	Stanley Wells and Gary Taylor, with John Jowett and William Montgomery, *William Shakespeare: A Textual Companion* (Oxford, 1987)

Index

CONCORDIA UNIVERSITY LIBRARY
3 9371 00052 7572

